BRAHMS AND HIS WORLD

REVISED EDITION

BRAHMS
AND HIS WORLD

REVISED EDITION

EDITED BY WALTER FRISCH AND KEVIN C. KARNES

PRINCETON UNIVERSITY PRESS

PRINCETON AND OXFORD

Copyright © 2009 by Princeton University Press

Published by Princeton University Press, 41 William Street,
Princeton, New Jersey 08540
In the United Kingdom: Princeton University Press,
6 Oxford Street, Woodstock, Oxfordshire OX20 1TW

For permissions information, see page xiii.

Library of Congress Control Number 2009922539

ISBN: 978-0-691-14343-9 (cloth)
ISBN: 978-0-691-14344-6 (paperback)

British Library Cataloging-in-Publication Data is available

This publication has been produced by the Bard College Publications Office:
Ginger Shore, Director
Michelle Eddison, Cover design
Natalie Kelly, Design
Text edited by Paul De Angelis and Erin Clermont
Music typeset by Don Giller

Printed on acid-free paper. ∞

press.princeton.edu

Printed in the United States of America

1 3 5 7 9 10 8 6 4 2

Contents

PART I
ESSAYS

PART II
RECEPTION AND ANALYSIS

Preface and Acknowledgments

The original edition of *Brahms and His World* was prepared in conjunction with the first Bard Rediscoveries Festival in 1990. Both the book and the festival aimed to present an in-depth exploration of the life, music, and cultural-historical milieu of the composer. At the time, no one involved in this enterprise could have foreseen what have since become a long-running, prestigious series of books and an internationally renowned annual program of concerts, lectures, and symposia. When Walter Frisch conceived the 1990 volume at the invitation of Leon Botstein, the goal was a new kind of publication that would appeal both to scholars and a general public. Its contents comprised essays by respected experts alongside carefully selected and edited historical documents, including program notes, memoirs, and reviews. That general plan (like the volume's title) became the model for subsequent books in the Bard Music Festival Series, which has continued to be published by Princeton University Press and, in 2006, won a Deems Taylor Special Recognition Award from the American Society of Composers, Authors, and Publishers.

In preparing this revised version of *Brahms and His World*, the editors have sought to remain close to the vision behind the 1990 edition, while also making the volume congruent in appearance and scope with more recent books in the series. To this end, we have retained most of contents of the original but have removed two items that were specific to the 1990 festival: Donald Tovey's program note about Joseph Joachim's *Hungarian* Concerto, and Eduard Hanslick's 1889 review of some recent compositions by Brahms.

In the "Essays" section, all of the original contributions have been retained and, in most cases, updated. We deeply regret that the death of Peter Ostwald in 1996 prevented him from being part of the revision process. To the original essays we have added three new ones, by Styra Avins, Kevin Karnes, and Roger Moseley. The "Reception and Analysis" section has been reshaped and augmented to present a double historical trajectory, extending across both Brahms's oeuvre and critical responses to it. This latter section begins with Adolf Schubring's account of Brahms's early works from 1862 and extends to Max Kalbeck's discussion of the *Four Serious Songs*, op. 121, originally published in 1914. In between, we have added new selections by Hanslick and Heinrich Schenker, and we have reprinted Hermann Kretzschmar's analyses of

Brahms's four symphonies. We have also included a new section on the reception of Brahms's First Symphony on the other side of the Atlantic—in New York and Boston in the later 1870s. All of these selections are newly introduced and annotated.

Among the richest sources of information on Brahms are the many memoirs—large and small—written by those who knew him. With this in mind, we have expanded the original "Memoirs" section in several ways. We have added a moving account by Hanslick of Brahms's final months. We have provided a complete translation of a unique document that was only partially translated in the original *Brahms and His World*: the 1905 memoir of Brahms's only regular pupil in composition, Gustav Jenner. And we have included two additional, vivid accounts of Brahms, recorded by his friends Richard Heuberger and Heinz von Beckerath. Recollections by two representatives of a younger generation of composers, Alexander von Zemlinsky and Karl Weigl, round out the section. The volume concludes with Walter Frisch's catalog of books, compositions, and artworks dedicated to the composer through the turn of the twentieth century.

In any undertaking of this nature and scope, the editors must rely upon the help of others. With respect to the latter, we wish to thank Irene Zedlacher for editorial assistance and troubleshooting, Don Giller for resetting the musical examples he first prepared in 1990, Paul De Angelis for line-editing and Erin Clermont for copyediting the manuscript, Natalie Kelly for composition and design, and Ginger Shore for overseeing the series.

Walter Frisch
Kevin C. Karnes
New York and Atlanta, July 2008

Preface and Acknowledgments

from the First Edition

This volume was conceived as a companion to a music festival entitled "Rediscovering Brahms," held at Bard College in Annandale-on-Hudson, New York, in August 1990. The festival placed Brahms in the context of his own time by programming his works alongside those of such figures as Joseph Joachim, Karl Goldmark, Clara Schumann, Johann Strauss, Alexander Zemlinsky, Eugen d'Albert, and Robert Fuchs.

The book seeks a complementary contextualization by means of a three-part design. In Part I, six scholars probe aspects of Brahms's relationship to his world. The kinds of relationship treated might be categorized roughly as personal (Ostwald, Reich), cultural-aesthetic (Botstein), compositional (Brodbeck, Frisch), and piano-technical (Bozarth and Brady).

Part 2 comprises substantial selections from contemporary or near-contemporary analyses and reviews. The commentaries by Schubring, Kretzschmar, Hanslick, and Tovey all form part of a characteristic nineteenth-century tradition whose verbal language and imagery reveal much about the way Brahms's music (and that of other composers) was understood in its day. The excerpts by German commentators appear here in English for the first time.

In Part 3, important memoirs of Brahms are presented in translation, also for the first time. The excerpt from Gustav Jenner contains invaluable testimony from Brahms's only private pupil in composition. The Hanslick segment is notable for its avoidance of sentimentality (unlike many Brahms memoirs) and for its wealth of information about Brahms's views on such topics as Beethoven's compositional development and contemporary art and politics. The brief memoirs by Zemlinsky and Weigl suggest how much Brahms was revered by a younger generation of Viennese composers that had only a brief opportunity to know him as a living figure.

Many dexterous hands and sharp minds helped bring this book into being in a remarkably short time. Elizabeth Powers of Princeton University Press displayed quiet and firm faith in the project when it was only fractionally baked. Dan Schillaci and Cynthia Saniewski have guided the book smoothly through the production process. Leon Botstein generously and enthusiastically shared his encyclopedic knowledge of Viennese culture; he contributed the introductions to the Kretschmar and Hanslick selections and provided many helpful annotations for parts 2 and 3. Susan Gillespie deserves mountains of gratitude for translating large chunks of difficult German prose with extraordinary speed and elegance. I am grateful to the Wiener Stadtbibliothek for permission to make use of Brahms's handwritten list of dedications, which forms the basis of the Appendix [Part IV]. Virginia Hancock kindly provided me with a photocopy of this document and also helped transcribe the composer's occasionally problematic handwriting. Gregory Leet diligently tracked down vital information about many of those obscure composers who appear in the Appendix and who formed the interstellar dust in the nineteenth-century musical galaxy where Brahms shone brightly. The handsome musical examples for this book were prepared by Don Giller. Karen Painter prepared the index. The editor of this volume and the organizers of "Rediscovering Brahms" also acknowledge the generous assistance of the Andrew W. Mellon Foundation.

Earlier, briefer versions of the articles by Nancy Reich, George Bozarth and Stephen Brady, and Walter Frisch appeared in the *American Brahms Society Newsletter,* respectively in issues 3/2 (Autumn 1985), 6/2 (Autumn 1988), and 7/1 (Spring 1989). The article by Peter Ostwald appeared in a previous form in German as "Johannes Brahms: 'Frei aber (nicht immer) froh,'" in *Johannes Brahms: Leben, Werk, Interpretation, Rezeption. Kongreßbericht zum III. Gewandhaus Symposium* (Leipzig, 1983), pp. 52-55. A more expanded version will appear as "Johannes Brahms—Music, Loneliness, and Altruism," in *Psychoanalytic Explorations in Music*, ed. Stuart Feder, Richard Karmel, and George Pollock (Madison CT, forthcoming). The editor gratefully acknowledges the permission of Oxford University Press to reprint Donald F. Tovey's essay on the Joachim Hungarian Violin Concerto.

Walter Frisch
New York, May 1990

Permissions and Credits

The "Brahms Fog," by Walter Frisch: Examples 4, 5, and 6 of excerpts from Arnold Schoenberg's Piano Piece, *Mädchenlied,* and String Quartet in D Major, are reproduced by permission of Belmont Music Publishers; the portrait of Max Reger was taken in 1902 by the Gebrüder Lutzel, kgl. bayrische Hofphotographen (Royal Bavarian Court Photographers), Munich. Private collection, used with permission.

"Between Work and Play: Brahms as Performer of His Own Music," by Roger Moseley: Figure 1, the photograph of Robert Hausmann, Johannes Brahms, and Maria Fellinger, taken by Maria Fellinger in 1896, is reproduced with the permission of the Austrian Johannes-Brahms Society and the Brahms-Museum, Mürzzuschlag; Figure 2, page 5 of Brahms's autograph score of the first movement of op. 99, is reproduced by permission of the Gesellschaft der Musikfreunde, Vienna; Figure 3, the photograph of Brahms and friends taken by Eugen von Miller zu Aichholz in 1894, is reproduced from Robert Haven Schauffler, *The Unknown Brahms* (New York, 1933), 134.

"Brahms, Max Klinger, and the Promise of the *Gesamtkunstwerk,*" by Kevin C. Karnes: Figures 2, 3, 4, and 6, from Klinger's *Brahms-Phantasie,* are reproduced by permission of the Staatsbibliothek zu Berlin–Preußischer Kulturbesitz, Musikabteilung mit Mendelssohn-Archiv; Figure 7, the illustration by Johann Ulrich Krauß, is reproduced by permission of the Pitts Theology Library, Emory University.

"Johannes Brahms: The Last Days" and "Memories and Letters," by Eduard Hanslick: the portrait of Hanslick is reproduced with permission of the Bildarchiv, Austrian National Library.

"My Early Acquaintance with Brahms," by Richard Heuberger: the portrait of Heuberger is reproduced with permission of the Bildarchiv, Austrian National Library.

"Remembering Johannes Brahms: Brahms and His Krefeld Friends," by Heinz von Beckerath: the photograph of Brahms and the Hagerhof circle comes courtesy Eugene Drucker, in memory of Ernest Drucker.

"Johannes Brahms as Man, Teacher, and Artist," by Gustav Jenner: the portrait of Jenner was taken by Maria Fellinger and is reproduced from Gustav Jenner, *Johannes Brahms als Mensch, Lehrer und Kunstler. Studien und Erlebnisse* (repr. Munich: Wollenweber, 1989; repr. of 2nd ed., Marburg, Elwert, 1930).

"Brahms and the Newer Generation: Personal Reminiscences by Alexander von Zemlinsky and Karl Weigl": the portrait of Alexander von Zemlinsky is reproduced with permission of the Bildarchiv, Austrian National Library; the portrait of Karl Weigl was taken by C. Pietzner Studio, Austria, and is reproduced with permission of the Gilmore Music Library, Yale University (photo no. 6, Box 28, Folder 903, MSS 73, Karl Weigl Papers).

PART I

ESSAYS

Time and Memory: Concert Life, Science, and Music in Brahms's Vienna

LEON BOTSTEIN

How can one grasp the nature and impact of Brahms's musical language and communication in his own time? In the first instance one has to guard against an uncritical sense of the stability of musical texts, their meaning, and how they can be read and heard. The acoustic, cultural, and temporal habits of life of the late nineteenth century in which Brahms's music functioned demand reconsideration if the listener in the early twenty-first century wishes to gain a historical perspective on Brahms's music and its significance. A biographical strategy and the history of critical reception themselves are insufficient.

Brahms's considerable success and notoriety, in Vienna and in German-speaking Europe as a whole, can be approached by a speculative effort to understand better the making of music, the thinking about music, and the listening to music during the latter half of the nineteenth century. In reconstructing the world in which Brahms worked and trying to reimagine the exchange between Brahms the composer and the various publics to which his music was directed—the meaning of musical discourse in Brahms's era—one aspect of nineteenth-century life and culture on the periphery of musical life can be useful: science and the philosophical and psychological speculation related to it.[1]

Understanding Brahms, his ambitions as an artist, and his impact on his contemporaries requires a grasp of the centrality of science and technology in Brahms's world. His friend the Swiss writer J. V. Widmann described Brahms's own perspective: "Even the smallest discovery, every improvement in any sort of gadget for domestic use; in short, every sign of human reflection, if it was accompanied by practical success, delighted him thoroughly. Nothing escaped his notice . . . if it was something new, in which progress could be discerned." Except for the bicycle, Brahms "felt himself lucky that he lived in the age of great discoveries, and could not praise enough the electric light, Edison's phonograph, and the like."[2] For example, Brahms welcomed innovations in the design and manufacture of pianos.[3]

This widespread late nineteenth-century fascination with scientific progress was sufficiently pervasive to influence the conception of music and the musical experience. The enormous body of writing about the physics of sound, the psychology of hearing, the design of sound-producing instruments, and the aesthetics of music from the latter half of the nineteenth century mirrors the intersection of the intense enthusiasms for both music and science. The application of varied scientific and philosophic methods to the nagging questions of beauty, memory, time perception, the nature and meaning of music, consonance, and the historical evolution of musical communication illuminates habits of musical expectation, listening, and judgment. Systematic thinking, talking, and writing about the lure and consequence of music in themselves were important aspects of the musical experience, particularly in Brahms's Vienna. The writings of such diverse individuals as Hermann Helmholtz, H. A. Koestlin, Heinrich Ehrlich (Brahms's colleague in the 1850s), Theodor Billroth, and other members of the university faculties of Vienna and Prague (e.g., L. A. Zellner, Richard Wallaschek, and the great Ernst Mach) provide evidence of conceptions of music that both mirrored and influenced the contemporary evaluation of the experience of music. In order to make this connection, however, dimensions of the musical world Brahms inhabited require clarification.

I. The Character of Viennese Musical Culture

The salient dimensions of Viennese musical life during Brahms's years were (1) the existence of an active amateur choral tradition; (2) the broadening, redefinition, and domination of music education (as well as the transformation of the ideal of musical sound) by the modern piano in the form it took after the late 1860s; (3) the evolution of musical connoisseurship through reading about music in newspapers, journals, and books; (4) the slow extension of concert life until the 1890s and the gradual formation of a canon in the repertoire; and (5) the professionalization of music history as an aspect of historicism in musical taste.[4]

When one thinks of Brahms's public, particularly in Vienna between 1862 and 1897, one can distinguish among three discrete generations. The first was composed of those who had come of age before 1848: a cohort that included individuals of the ages of Franz Grillparzer (1791–1872), Felix Mendelssohn (1809–47), and Robert Schumann (1810–56). The second was made up of Brahms's exact contemporaries, those born between 1825 and 1848: individuals who had reached full maturity during Brahms's lifetime. The third and last group included those who were young in comparison to Brahms: the generation around Gustav Mahler, individuals born in the 1850s, '60s, and early '70s.

The first group witnessed the great expansion of musical culture. The piano, although the subject of steady technological change between 1820 and 1860, became the leading instrument of musical communication. The first great period of virtuosity and concert life occurred between the years 1815 and 1848. Central to this first generation, however, was the voice and singing. The piano still played a secondary role in music education, in the cultivation of a mode of musical expression that linked words and music. Furthermore, amateur proficiency on string instruments competed and held its own against keyboard amateurism. This was the generation for whom Beethoven remained the towering presence. The rediscovery of the musical past, beyond the occasional Handel oratorio, was begun by Mendelssohn and his contemporaries. This generation fought the first - battle for the attention of a wider public on behalf of serious music, past and present, and for music as a Romantic art expressive of the poetic and the spiritual. The fight was against the philistine tendencies of theatricality evident in virtuosity and the puerile sentimentality of efforts to entertain a rapidly growing public for music.

It is instructive to speculate about the impression the Viennese from this first musically informed generation might have had when Brahms arrived in Vienna in 1862. Apart from the legendary article Robert Schumann wrote about Brahms in 1853, an article on Brahms published in 1856, in perhaps the leading encyclopedic musical lexicon of the era, revealed the extent to which Brahms was regarded as unformed and a radical new spirit, possibly and ironically at odds with a Classical aesthetic. The author, Julius Schladebach (1810–72), a trained physician who composed church music but worked primarily as a journalist, wrote that apart from the enthusiasts who agreed with Schumann's assessment, there were those

> moderates who found certainly talent and much courage, but also much rawness, lack of skill, and complete immaturity. The courage was not attributed by them as deriving from Brahms's uncanny artistic powers but, to the contrary, from a lack of skill in formulation, and therefore courage appeared to them rather as presumption, one that overrides arrogantly the laws of beauty and perpetrates lawlessness, without having sufficiently understood and recognized rules and laws; in other words, without having climbed to that level of artistic

training from which one can distinguish freedom from licentious-
ness. Which of the two camps is right cannot yet be decided today.[5]

This judgment possesses a dimension of irony, considering Brahms's
later reputation as a conservative and a Classical master, a reputation best
demonstrated by the ceiling painting of the Zurich Tonhalle, which opened
in 1895. Brahms was placed next to Beethoven and on a par with Gluck,
Haydn, Bach, Handel, and Mozart. Wagner was also depicted, but in profile and slightly obscured.[6]

This early criticism is also significant in view of Brahms's severe self-
criticism regarding his command of musical form and materials. Brahms's
drive to conquer and extend Classical procedures in his work may have
been spurred by the awareness of such criticism from an older established
generation. Those contemporaries of Schumann who did not share
Schumann's enthusiasm did so not because they followed the path set by
Liszt but because they maintained a sensibility far more traditional than
Schumann's. Historians have a tendency to overlook dominant tastes and
aesthetics that seem not to play themselves out through some progressive
and teleological historical narrative. Schumann, after all, generally was not
viewed by his contemporaries as a conservative.

It was in the second generation, however—Brahms's exact contemporaries—that the piano advanced substantially over all other mediums of
musical activity. Among amateurs, solo singing was overshadowed by the
intense interest in choral singing. In this generation the professional musician came to dominate musical life. In Vienna, for example, only in the
later 1850s did the Gesellschaft der Musikfreunde place all activities under
the direction of professionals and systematically begin to eliminate all amateur instrumentalists from official concerts open to the public at large.

In the midcentury, between 1860 and 1880, music education experienced an explosive growth, fueled by the piano, a stable, cheaply produced
item of modern engineering and industry. The piano's growing emi-
nence began to direct the mode of musical education away from techniques
of ear-training and pitch recognition to rote methods for training dexterity so that individuals could play finished works. But in this generation
amateur musical literacy remained high by today's standards. Billroth,
for example, possessed exemplary skills and was able to play several
instruments and read scores.[7] Brahms valued his judgment. Amateur
composers existed. But during the midcentury musical education increasingly depended on reading about music and the teaching of repertoire
and an historical canon, usually beginning with Bach and ending with
contemporary composers.

Nevertheless, the overwhelming character of musical culture was one that underscored musical communication as a mode of contemporary expression. New works by living composers took central stage, making music publishing a thriving business, fueled by new works for home and concert hall. The skills of professional and amateur were directed at a vital art form. Perhaps the most important aspect of these years was the phenomenal growth in numbers of individuals engaged in music. This engagement, however, was still tied to the conceit of active playing and singing; and to the conception of hearing, as it related to one's capacity to anticipate, follow, recall, and reproduce what one heard. But it was also in this generation that a tension was felt between the widening of the audience and future standards of taste. Musicality and the appreciation of music were clearly understood to be matters of education and training and superior discernment; emphasis was placed on a high order of cultural development.

The last generation to encounter Brahms as a living composer experienced the gradual decline of the choral tradition, the almost total domination of musical culture by the piano, the erosion of amateur singing and instrumental playing as an alternative, and the centrality of music journalism. Coincidentally, the change in the mode of musical education away from the active command of musical skills toward the training of mechanical facility to reproduce existing works strengthened a perceptible shift in taste. The historical became defined through familiarity, through the repetition of selected repertoire.

Concert life achieved some greater frequency. In 1890 in Vienna, for example, there were roughly 240 concerts among the Bösendorfer, Ehrbar, and Musikverein halls. This number included amateur choral groups and group recitals of students. There were only seventeen professional concerts using large orchestral and choral forces.[8] And tickets for these were spoken for by an elite. The access to live professional concerts was limited to a mere fraction of the public.

In the decade of the 1880s, a resident of Vienna lucky enough to possess a subscription to the Vienna Philharmonic (which began its tradition of a limited series of regular concerts only in the 1860s) had to wait for nearly a decade to hear all Beethoven symphonies performed by a professional orchestra. The Vienna Philharmonic gave only eight concerts a year, and the tradition of traveling orchestras began in earnest only in the 1890s.[9] Brahms was in his twenties when he first heard Beethoven's Ninth Symphony in Cologne.[10] It was performed in Vienna only thirteen times in the thirty-four years between 1863 and 1897. In the five seasons from 1890 to 1895, the great Classical composers, from Haydn to Schumann, occupied 35 percent of the repertoire; Brahms, Wagner, and Bruckner accounted for 12 percent.[11] Musical literacy, therefore, depended on active skills, not merely the capacity for listening. When Brahms continually emphasized the need for "proper" learning, the value of hard work, and the essentials of the craft and technique of musical composition, in the sense of historical models as well as normative aesthetic imperatives; and when later in life he complained bitterly about the level of contemporary musical education and training, he was expressing more than his legendary habits of being critical and self-critical. He was articulating a form of generational and cultural criticism.

The transition from the first generation in the musical public to the third generation included a weakening of the skills of literacy, the kind that made Elisabeth von Herzogenberg so alluring. These included the capacity to read a score and hear music, to write down what one heard as well as to play and sing new and old printed music. The shift to piano-based music education and the increasing opportunity, however limited, to be a mere listener only served to weaken the level of active literacy, much less thorough training.

Brahms articulated a widespread concern for the decline in standards that accompanied the extension of the audience during his lifetime. The newer generation became the consumers of lexica, concert guides, and journalistic accounts—genres that experienced enormous success in the 1880s and 1890s. Hermann Kretzschmar's famous concert guide, which first appeared in 1887—an excerpt appears elsewhere in this volume— gives a glimpse of the standard of education in the late nineteenth century. Kretzschmar assumed sufficient training to hear key changes, melodic lines, and orchestral timbres. The Vienna Philharmonic first felt the need in the 1890s to introduce written descriptive program notes. In both these notes and Kretzschmar's guide, narrative description functioned as a translating mechanism, designed to enable the hearer to follow and remember by offering a descriptive narration akin to prose fiction, travel guides, or journalistic reportage.

Part of the impetus behind the criticism of Wagner and Bruckner that came from Brahms's amateur partisans in Vienna (Theodor Billroth, for example) was the recognition that Wagner, through the use of leitmotivs and thematic repetition, and Bruckner, through his own reliance on repetitions and extended moments of exposition, pandered to the new habits of hearing. Their popularity, Billroth suspected, was the result of the public's ignorance and insufficient musical education.[12] Brahms demanded the true connoisseur: the musical cognoscenti of his and Hanslick's generation who understood the communicatory power and logic of music alone and could hear a dense, purely musical discourse. As a result of the shift in music education, the superficial, foreground habit of hearing, recognizable in program notes and guides, became the norm. It was against this norm that both Heinrich Schenker and Arnold Schoenberg—following explicitly a concept of form and technique derived from their understanding of Brahms, and mirroring Brahms's own critique of composition, his own and others'—would expend their unforgettable vitriol.

Despite Brahms's suspicion that a decline in musical standards was occurring during his lifetime, the modern reader should not underestimate the extraordinary aura carried by live performances, the premium on memory, and the level of musical literacy the late nineteenth-century audience possessed. Arthur Schnitzler provides a reasonable example. The passion of his youth (his father Johann Schnitzler was a laryngologist who treated many singers) had been the theater. Although Schnitzler was trained as a physician, he played the piano well, using the instrument in quite typical middle-class fashion, playing four-hand repertoire—with his mother and later with the music critic and theorist Viktor Zuckerkandl—often reading through orchestral music.[13] Schnitzler was literate enough to write a light waltz or two.

Likewise, the type of amateur choral singers with whom Brahms had worked in Hamburg and Vienna in the 1860s and '70s still existed at the turn of the century. But that tradition was under siege within the amateur world with the dramatic success of the operetta and the resultant popular song. In short, a dimension of Brahms's self-image as the last of a tradition, and the view of him as conservative and poised toward the past and not the future, was the consequence of his sense that a tradition within the musical public was dying: the mode of musical communication he sought depended on a literacy in increasingly short supply. As he often commented, his critique of Wagner was hardly musical in the narrow sense, but was directed against his influence. Those who attacked Wagner as a musician were quite ignorant. At stake was not style but the survival of a language of expression and communication among people that had flourished between 1750 and 1850.

Rudolf Louis, writing in 1912 about the music of his time, observed that the natural tendency of "the young to underestimate the value of artistic form" had become extreme. Although Brahms's self-appointed successors were largely too academic, the composers who considered themselves followers of Wagner (and Brahms's true opposite Liszt) easily overlooked Brahms to their peril. Brahms's "masculine" character contained secrets, which could be unlocked. But the mechanism required a capacity to grasp his command of counterpoint and form—Brahms's "hard earned" and staggering command of the language of music. Not only to write music but to hear it, remember it, and respond to it required a discipline and training Louis regarded as all too rare. The enemies of music were "artistic dilettantes" and "professional experts" (by which Louis meant music journalists and historians) who did not possess the skills of music making but thought that writing about music was sufficient.[14]

Brahms, in all his work, wrote for an audience. The several genres he used all had a public. Often, as in the *Liebeslieder* and the later piano works, there was clearly a playing and listening audience. For both, comprehensibility was an overt goal. Brahms accepted that premise, but without concessions.

Brahms's often-quoted letter to Adolf Schubring regarding the imputed motivic unity of the *German Requiem* made clear that sophistication in compositional skill was not to be pursued at the expense of comprehensibility: "If I want to retain the same idea, then one should recognize it clearly in every transformation, augmentation, inversion. The opposite would be idle playing around and always a sign of impoverished inspiration." In discussing a particular set of variations, Brahms claimed that the bass line was the stable basis for his creativity. The elaboration of the melodic over a constant foundation achieved both comprehensibility as well as a proper avenue for original expression.[15]

If music was to be its own communicative medium, then subtlety in elaboration— the development across a long form of ideas and a new landscape of musical imagination and expression—had to carry the player and/or listener along. Therefore, from the start, a dimension of comprehensibility was required, although not through the linear sequences of Wagner. The comprehensibility was contingent on a deeper level of musical education. This conceit was only strengthened by the polemical example and perspective articulated in Schumann's critical writings. Brahms's ideal audience, whether in the short piano works, the *German Requiem*, the symphonies, the songs, or the chamber music, were individuals who could either play or follow him and, in Louis's words, "uncover the hidden soul of Brahms's world of sound."[16]

II. Music and Science

Without question, the most significant contribution to the relationship between science and music to occur in the second half of the nineteenth century was the publication of Hermann Helmholtz's *On the Sensations of Tone* in 1862. (A fourth edition appeared in 1877.) Helmholtz's subject included both the physics of sound and the physiology of perception. Helmholtz established the reigning definition of consonance (defined by equal temperament) and therefore dissonance. He dissected musical sound from the point of view of the source. He then analyzed the mechanism of perception and described what we hear and why. He spun a theory of the evolution of keys and tonality, and of the relationship between musical tones.

But Helmholtz drifted, despite his disclaimers, into the realm of aesthetics and the evolutionary history of musical systems. He took great pains to argue that the "modern" system of music was "not developed from a natural necessity, but from a freely chosen principle of style." Yet he regarded earlier historical periods as having less "perfect" systems, and concluded that "it has become possible to construct works of art, of much greater extent, and much richer in forms and parts, much more energetic in expression than any producible in past ages; and hence we are by no means inclined to quarrel with modern musicians for esteeming it the best of all."[17]

Helmholtz, in his conclusion to his work, avoided deriving aesthetics from empirical findings. But there was no doubt that the system of harmony of the nineteenth century had its justification in the physics of sound and the apparatus and process of perception. Helmholtz realized that art extended beyond nature. Two arenas were required to understand fully the links between art and nature: the psychology of perception and the philosophy of knowledge (epistemology), and philosophical psychology.

The power of Helmholtz's work was that it lent justification to those who saw in it a scientific vindication of a set of aesthetic, formal, and, in particular, harmonic procedures.[18] But at the same time, Helmholtz's genius and subtle awareness of the limitation of his empirical analysis—the limitations of scientific argument in establishing cause and effect—as well as his acute awareness of the problem of understanding aural perception and the consciousness of hearing, inspired the development of theory and research that justified the fundamental relativity and culturally determined character of musical systems and aesthetic norms.

The tradition of speculation begun by Helmholtz generated quite opposing schools of inquiry. In the history of twentieth-century aesthetics, this resulted in the radically opposed theories of Schenker, who argued the natural scientific basis of tonality, and Schoenberg, for whom, in the theory of the emancipation of the dissonance, perceptions of consonance and dissonance had purely historical and environmental determinant causes. An entirely new system of harmonic musical combinations could be developed. Schoenberg, however, continued to adhere to normative notions of the way music functioned in time and could be perceived to be derived from tonal practice. That permitted him to defend canons of form and structure and standards of judgment regarding musical craft, per se, above and beyond the logic of any specific harmonic system.

The impact of Helmholtz's book was extraordinary. It had a direct influence on the design of instruments, primarily the piano, especially through the relationship between Helmholtz and C. F. Theodore Steinway. Helmholtz seemed to have helped to solve the problem of how to build a stable instrument that could be tuned, remain reasonably in tune, and possess a rich, resonating sound. Steinway's famous duplex scale patent of the 1870s owed its origin to Helmholtz.

Helmholtz's work contributed significantly to the standardization of pitch and tuning in the late nineteenth century and to the establishment of an international standard tuning system (or the effort to do so). Brahms's colleague in Vienna, L. A. Zellner (for whom Brahms had little use), who was the longtime secretary of the Gesellschaft der Musikfreunde, lectured on aesthetics at the conservatory and organized an international symposium in Vienna in 1885 to establish standard pitch levels.[19]

Brahms, despite his dislike for theorizing, particularly about music, was no doubt aware of the intense interest in acoustics, hearing, and aesthetics surrounding him among his medical, scientific, and musical colleagues. Zellner's lectures and his fanatical efforts on the issue of pitch standardization reflect Helmholtz's influence and the conviction that there were links between aesthetic judgment, physiology (and therefore nature), and ultimately between the education and cultivation of the physiological capacity to hear. Aesthetic judgment in music became closely tied to the cultivation of natural properties, giving subjective perception, when fully developed, an objective basis, particularly in the matter of musical form, the use of time, and the harmonic structure of a work.[20]

The sociological implication was equally clear. Those who could develop their natural potential for musical discrimination were a superior lot. Musical cultivation was learned, perhaps not at high levels for all. As such, that learned skill was the sine qua non for judgment. A physiological and scientific basis for the judgment of the well-trained few over the many was, in Zellner's judgment, self-evident.

But beyond the arena of manufacture and the regulation of pitch, Helmholtz's work spurred a whole field of acoustical research. This research, throughout the nineteenth century, kept its links with the aesthetics and history of music. Furthermore, Helmholtz sparked a series of intense anatomical and physiological investigations into the design and function of the ear. How do we hear? Was there a physiological basis for not only how we hear, but how we discriminate and sort out sounds, particularly consonant from dissonant ones? In modern terms, as Noam Chomsky has argued concerning the innate capacity to fashion and grasp grammar and therefore language, the researchers of the nineteenth century sought to test the hypothesis that modern notions of harmony and beauty were not only the result of a progressive historical evolution but also the mirror of the natural physiological design and logic of the ear. Consequently, the field of psycho-acoustics was created.

In turn, the line of reasoning that asked questions about how we hear drifted into the more fundamental issue of what is being heard; about the relationship between object and subject, between perceiver and perceived. Particularly under the sharp scrutiny of Ernst Mach, who first wrote on Helmholtz in 1866 and who was an avid amateur musician (with a preference for the harmonium, one of the nineteenth century's most popular amateur domestic instruments), an entire epistemological theory evolved regarding perception and reality.[21] The intense preoccupation with music and hearing might be said, not entirely facetiously, to have altered the direction of modern science and been an essential historical precondition for relativistic mechanics and modern physics. Albert Einstein's notorious love of music (despite his dubious skills as a violinist) culminated a decisive seventy-five years of symbiotic contact between science and music.

The impetus behind Helmholtz's book and its consequence for music in the nineteenth century, particularly the perception of music, its character and history, can be gleaned from two leading popular tracts of musical aesthetics: H. A. Koestlin's *Die Tonkunst: Einführung in die Aesthetik der Musik* of 1879; and a book of 1882 by Brahms's friend Heinrich Ehrlich, *Die Musik-Aesthetik in ihrer Entwickelung von Kant bis auf die Gegenwart: Ein Grundriss*.[22]

Both Koestlin and Ehrlich began from the premise that their books, designed for the layperson, reflected the fact that, as Ehrlich wrote,

> music is, of all the arts, the favorite, perhaps the especially selected favorite of modern society. It constitutes the dearest ornament of domestic life . . . it is the most widespread and most practiced art. The greater public finds from it the most facile accessible distraction which possesses an elegant form; for the educated society music is an effective means of connection; high society likes to acknowledge

music as the most important ethical means of education, because music is the politically least dangerous art; many noble individuals consider music as the purest art.[23]

Ehrlich noted that the two schools of music in the nineteenth century— the absolutists and those who regarded music as connected to speech and the visual— placed extraordinary demands on the meaning of music. The formalists, the absolutists claimed for music a "meaning for the life of the soul" greater than in all other arts. Ehrlich wrote, "The phenomenon such as the following is not easy to explain: that today the majority of the public finds more pleasure in music than in all the other arts."[24] Yet music seemed to make fewer demands on thinking, making any serious evaluation of why this passion for music existed difficult. Ehrlich concluded:

This phenomenon just referred to can be explained only in the context of the entire cultural life, out of the relationship of the work of art with ideas of the time, and the reciprocal impact between artist and public, that today still is supported by other means than the pursuit of art alone.[25]

Ehrlich, among others, identified the recent research into the nervous system, starting with Helmholtz's theory of hearing. Ehrlich argued that it helped to explain the impact of music on the mind and "the legitimation of the historical development of particular nations, from which important works of music have emerged."[26] Ehrlich concluded that the scientific research of the recent past created an agenda for the aesthetics of music to use the knowledge of science to understand why people got excited about music. But to base aesthetics on a firm footing, enabling it to achieve sufficient clarity to forge a serious link between the development of aesthetic taste and the development of a moral sense, one had to create a science that could underpin aesthetic judgment. Having understood the science of subjective response, it was possible to build an independent but linked system of the rules of beauty, to define and link the beautiful with the good.[27]

Like Ehrlich, Koestlin was in search of answers, about not only the nature of music but also its impact on its public. Like Ehrlich, Koestlin sought to reconcile the objective findings about hearing with the apparent subjectivity of aesthetic judgment. However, Koestlin sided more clearly with the idea that the Helmholtz studies and their impact through later work (that of von Oettingen and Riemann) could justify a formalist, Herbartian aesthetic. That aesthetic might justify the autonomy of music even though it could also explain the success of the Wagnerian synthesis of music, words, and images. Koestlin wrote:

> The effort will be justified to take into consideration the construction of musical aesthetics in the first instance, and the particular nature of the material out of which musical art makes its forms, instead of, as before, taking concepts and claims from some other arenas and imposing them on the face of music. So perhaps we are close to that time when a satisfactory aesthetics of music will be available to us; that is, a presentation of the unique character and unique laws of our art which derives from the nature of sound and the particular existential conditions of the musical work of art.[28]

The direct impact of this mix of science and aesthetics was the triumph of the idea that music was autonomous among the other arts, perceived differently and bereft of content in the ordinary way. Within the well-known nineteenth-century debate between the Wagnerians and the followers of Liszt and the formalists, Hanslick, and others, in which Brahms somewhat reluctantly assumed the symbolic role of the "counter-pope," scientific speculation seemed to vindicate the anti-Wagnerians on two accounts. First, the evolution of music, by analogy with evolutionary theory, rendered instrumental music and the modern system of harmony the highest forms of development within a historical logic that was progressive and selective. The independence from the voice and speech was historical and reflected the increasing complexity of self-sufficiency of modes of sound production and modes of perception. In this sense, Wagner could be justified, if at all, only in so-called purely musical terms.

Second, the specific character of tones and their logic, as well as the receptivity of the human ear, as a triumph of evolution led to the judgment that music was the purest art form since it was the most abstract, the most spiritual in the sense that it was the most rational—divorced from raw daily experience. The formal compositional procedures that organized sound into art (e.g., harmonic relationships and rules of counterpoint) were located in the objective nature of music itself as well as in the selective evolutionary process that established a valid tradition.

Richard Wallaschek (1860–1917), a Viennese aesthetician and music historian who, after working in England, returned in 1895 and subsequently taught at the university and at the conservatory in Vienna, provided perhaps the best summary of the impact of scientific inquiry into hearing and musical sound on the aesthetic prejudices of the late nineteenth century when he wrote in 1886:

A comparison with the remarks made here about the musical work of art with the general remarks about the beautiful will reveal, with spontaneous logic, that through music the highest beauty can be achieved, because the forms that music provides are tied to no comprehensible content, but at the same time permit access to all—because musical forms reproduce in tones the general form of all experience to which spiritual activity is connected. Music constitutes the spiritual progress of modernity in comparison to antiquity in terms of the forms of perception. Music is the algebra of the arts.[29]

This credo corresponded closely with Brahms's convictions about the normative character of musical form and language. Brahms's much discussed concern with historical models was driven by an absolutist instinct: that music as an independent mode of human experience was at once tied to human experience per se—the emotions and thoughts that humans display and have expressed in all of history. That independent element of expression and perception experienced a gradual historical clarification. In this sense, progress in science was regarded on a par with progress in musical technique and aesthetics. The conceit of certainty was such, however, that the forms of musical art seemed clearly understood. The past had bequeathed objective standards on the way in which musical materials might be used, true rules of the grammar of musical language.

Originality and individuality expressed themselves within a normative framework in which a future was possible because the framework, based on objective physical and physiological phenomena, was well understood. As Brahms urged younger composers, serious training in the rules of that framework was indispensable if one wanted to write great music of the sort that Wagner and Schumann luckily managed to write without the proper fundamental training.[30] The historicism of Brahms's formal models and procedures—in sonata form and variation— was justified as an act of building on the truth, much as a scientist of Brahms's generation might build on proven hypotheses and then modify, elaborate, and revise that truth. In the modification—as in the case of Wagner and the occasional new discovery—the cumulative progress of knowledge and the expression of individuality could be reconciled.

When one fin-de-siècle critic compared a Brahms symphony to "a chemical and mechanical structure," the metaphor was not off the mark.[31] Brahms's aesthetic convictions and his self-image as a composer mirrored the culture of science in which he lived and in particular a contemporary conception of music, musical form, musical perception, and musical judgment widespread in German-speaking Europe. This conception was profoundly influenced by scientific speculation about the phenomena of music and their aesthetic implications. Brahms satisfied the widely held opinions and expectations among the educated, cultivated audience of Vienna and other major cities about what music was, and could do; about what was required to appreciate it; and why it was so alluring. His music, more than Wagner's, was self-consciously non-populist and reinforced the identification of cultivation and learning with aesthetic taste. Brahms's work underscored views about the nature of music and the necessity, if not exclusivity, of an education that empowered the elite individual truly to comprehend the purest and most objective form of art.

III. Theories of Sensation, Time Consciousness, and Habits of Listening, 1885–1905

Helmholtz's work spurred a new set of questions about how and why we perceive sounds, and how we conceive of the logic of time, and therefore retain and remember sequences of sound that possess their logic in associations with words or pictures. If Brahms's music, as has been suggested, played into the conceits of the successful cultivation of the understanding of objective musical elements and their combinations, then it was nearly inevitable that the fundamentals of that conceit of understanding itself would undergo critical scrutiny. The centrality of musical communication in the world of educated citizens in which Brahms lived was such that this critical enterprise entered at the center of epistemological discourse.

The journey from physics to psychology and then to philosophy can be traced in the work of Ernst Mach and Edmund Husserl. Both were citizens of the Habsburg Empire, and both experienced the lure of music as a mode of communication, in their social milieu and their own private lives. Through a look at their ideas, one can generate a speculative model of how the audience for Brahms's music listened—the player and listener alike—before access to mechanically reproduced music (i.e., before 1910) became widespread. The assumptions about perception, recall, judgment, and expectation with which Brahms worked as a composer can be revealed, albeit indirectly. The logic of his formal procedures can then be illuminated, if only from the outside.

In Ernst Mach's notebooks from the early 1880s, one finds the following fragment:

The spatial is reversible. It must be contingent on time. Music as a special instance; Music. The spatially reversible. The temporally irreversible; The same melody in different registers. The Third. Numerous ways. The form of sound. Conflict of sensations; The form of sound with the form of time. A tone is already a composite sensation. A mixed sensation.[32]

Mach's ruminations about the character of the perception of space and time led him finally in 1886 to the radical conclusion that in its subsequent elaborations would provide an impetus for Einstein's theory of relativity.[33] Mach denied the absolute character of space and time:

> The physiology of the senses, however, demonstrates that spaces and times may just as appropriately be called sensations as colors and sounds. . . . Nothing will be changed in the actual facts or in the functional relations, whether we regard all the data as contents of consciousness, or as partially so, or as completely physical.[34]

Mach opened up the radical possibility that scientific fact, as such, derives from the frame of reference of the perceiver, from the act of sensation. He did so by also denying the existence of a metaphysical ego, the "I," and therefore ending up with a monistic standpoint.

The appeal to nature as an external physical phenomenon was undercut. The perception of form and time duration, therefore, required an analysis quite different from that of Helmholtz: an analysis of how we mentally construct a sense of time. The center of Mach's argument in 1886 dealt with "The Sensations of Tone." Mach had greatly enlarged the research on the physiology of the ear. But his conclusion was that the perception of music was exclusively "a collateral product of [his] education . . . what we call talent and achievement . . . constitute but a slight departure from normal endowments."[35]

What Mach concentrated on was the notion that in music there was no absolute symmetry. Music possessed the spatial association of high and low but not right and left. Furthermore, a sense of order derived from the creation of a series of sensations and their remembrance. The logic of a series could not be derived from nature. Mach denied any scientific ability to prefer objectively one interval over another and broke any residual link between external physical reality and the aesthetic priority of consonance.

Furthermore, Mach speculated on the attention span and capacity to order a series of notes and intervals. He stressed the context of remembrance. For example, he cited the link between the interval of a fourth and the Overture to *Tannhäuser*. The hearing of the former could imply the latter, and vice versa. The aesthetic judgment of pleasure in sensation for

Mach was based on the fact that "the harmonic or the melodic addition of one to another affects agreeably only when the added tone reproduces a part of the sensation which the first one excited."[36]

In the discrimination of musical beauty, apart from references to the Helmholtzian overtone series in terms of how tones might be perceived by the ear, Mach distinguished between visual and aural perception, between the perception of space and time. Why can we consider a melody the same when it is transposed to a key where there are not even common overtone partials? Furthermore, one can distinguish common rhythm despite differential pitches that make two separate melodies. Rhythm is easier to distinguish than elapsed time or even tempo. The answer lay, for Mach, in the process of self-consciousness about orientation, about the mechanisms of selective self-representation in time and space. Mach's work constituted an effort to rescue the efficacy of science as a universal construct by retreating, so to speak, to the exclusive legitimacy of the act of perception. He generated a kind of legitimate, functional scientific impressionism.[37]

The dramatic shift of emphasis from the work of art to the hearer mirrored the historical reality. Any given work of Brahms was contingent not only on intent but on perceived meaning. Although Mach, in line with his social philosophy, sought to reduce the distance between the normal and the genius, Brahms sought to communicate with compositional procedures that could reach a highly developed discriminatory sensibility. The capacity to follow and recall long stretches of variation and thematic development required the capacity to orient oneself within the balances among formal integrity, the total duration of a work, and its larger harmonic structure. The relationship of detail to form, sequential logic to structure as recalled after an initial hearing—comprehending the irreversibility—became a challenge. So, too, was the capacity to perceive the distinctions between levels of form in a complex procedure which, as Schoenberg argued, eschewed evident aspects of musical symmetry (one thinks particularly of Brahms's playful use of rhythmic asymmetry). All this made demands on the listener's skill, given that mere "playing around" (*Spielerei*) was not at stake but deep inner communication through ordered musical sounds.

These Machian speculations show in the first instance the centrality of musical experience in the formation of scientific inquiry in the nineteenth century. But they indicate as well the self-consciousness in the nineteenth century of the extent to which a work of musical art was contingent on the hearer, on a symbiotic overlap between authorial intent and subjective perception. Brahms's adherence to known forms—Classical models and procedure—may have reflected the recognition that innovation within expectations framed by cultivated habits constituted a more valid and desirable means to assure correspondence between intent and result. The Wagnerian strategy not only simplified demands on the hearer but imposed a speech-based narrative structure and logic, eliminating a musical mode of expression. The purely musical communication was, for Mach, free of association but located—as Mach conceded that Schopenhauer correctly suspected—in a profound inner sensibility not necessarily accessible through ordinary experience or an imagination stimulated by words or pictures.[38]

Edmund Husserl, at the turn of the century, in his critique of Mach's theory of knowledge, went even further.[39] Beginning with Augustine, Husserl focused on the process of internal time consciousness beyond the conscious act of perception. Mental reproduction and recapitulative memory; the difference between hearing a sound and rehearing in one's mind; and the difference between memory and expectation were, in part, Husserl's subjects. Furthermore, the mental rehearing of sounds, the mental reconstruction of the present, and the difference between objective elapsed time and experienced time became troubling issues.[40] In Husserl's critical extension of the Helmholtz-Mach analysis, the internal psychic construct predominated over an external stimulus or sensation. But at the same time, the power of the mental creation of time, the inner expanse of subjective experience, became not merely evident but primary.

The experience of music was then subject to redefinition. Its social dimension—the shared elapsed time experienced by following a musical narrative—was implicitly compared to the intimate definition of music as heard (i.e., playing at home or hearing at a concert): the manner in which music can trigger internal expansive rehearing, recollection, and transformation, even in strictly musical terms. The music of Brahms, in its comprehensibility and also its complexity, lent itself to an elastic internal interpretation that, since the formalists of the early nineteenth century, had been one of the heralded dimensions of instrumental and so-called absolute music.[41]

One might be willing to speculate that the power of Brahms's innovative adaptation of expectancies from within his audience can be understood by looking at his use of time. Brahms, by eschewing speech-based narrative, created at least three levels of perceived time. The first was the time of the unfolding of the work, which proceeded in small units (not, like Bruckner, in large sections). The transformation of material began immediately, merging recollectable symmetries with evident alterations.

Second, there was the use of time divorced from the actual objective surface. This involved the clear units used by the composer (e.g., thematic material), the time of transformation (e.g., variation), the groupings of events (e.g., movements), which, extracted and reworked and compared by the listener, enabled radically different sensibilities of proportions and focal points—altered durations—within a work.[42]

Third, there was the perceived time, the experience of time by the listener, in performance and memory.[43] This dimension, created during hearing and primarily after, constituted a mixed accumulation of the three other elements. All were contingent on the assumed contact between Brahms and his audience, on Brahms's tacit assumption that intended or novel inferences from the work of art as experienced would be generated that could, despite the necessary process of individual appropriation and variation, approximate the intended experience.

Furthermore, by employing an evidently historicist framework, Brahms sparked the process George Kubler describes for art and architecture. By invoking fragments of the past, the recognition of discarded and retained elements from the past creates a dialectic of time perception: between a consciousness of the present with one of an imagination of the past. In the nearly archaeological invocation of recognizable traditions, Brahms, in his music, far from creating a static temporal or emotional experience, assumed a musical memory for his real and ideal listeners, and created experiences of the historical in the present.

This in turn provided a transformed and flexible reconstitution of the past for the listener. In the context of nineteenth-century Vienna, the musical experience interacted with at least the visual experience of historicism in art and architecture. The self-assertion of novelty on the part of Wagner, together with the historicist language of Wagner's poetry and the aesthetics of the scene painting, may have minimized Wagner's stimulation of inner-time sensibilities within the audience despite the other forms of response he generated.

The subjective time experience in Brahms's music became a means to sense a collective experience of historical time, recast and renewed in the present moment. The use of the historical in Brahms therefore can be understood as a strategy not of "aesthetic fatigue" but of contextualizing to highlight innovation and change. In the microcosm of each work, the present is set apart by the transformation of the evidently traditional.[44] As Heinrich Koestlin wrote about Brahms's music shortly after the composer's death, "The Romantic wealth of ideas is bordered by the discipline of Classical training, and contained by a hardnosed formal structure. The latter is unique, new, and not a simple repetition or recreation, but rather an organic progressive evolution and an entirely modern new formation."[45] In terms of the issues of internal time consciousness and its constitution, the Brahmsian exchange with a contemporary audience mirrored, in an authentic historical exchange, the direction and complexity of Husserl's contemporaneous framing of the issues of subjective time perception.

The density of temporal consciousness and the demands made on the powers of discrimination and remembrance by Brahms's music were severe, even by contemporary standards. In this sense, Brahms realized the ideology of absolute music by eschewing forms of musical realism and retaining the intimate communication associated with the prestige of chamber music. Likewise, Brahms sought to realize a strategy central to musical Romanticism, the cultivation of inner subjectivity. His success depended not only on the level of music education in his audience but on the acoustic and temporal environment in which he operated.

We forget too readily the vast stretches of ambient silence (punctuated not by regular background noise but by more random interruptions) in which the Viennese urban dweller lived and the concomitant space for musical contemplation. The urban environment operated with different expectations of volume and sound color. The absence of live performances and anything approximating today's means of reproduction placed a premium on powers of recollection and rehearing, as well as rereading musical texts in which imaginary sounds were present. This was true as well for the use of the piano for hearing orchestral works.

Apart from the silence and the aura of musical sound derived from its comparative rarity, the Brahmsian use of form and time, the micro-unit of change, and the larger coherences of which Schenker was fond of stressing, one must consider the reception of Brahms's music in terms of the clocks of everyday life. The pace of life and communication, the periodicity of the day (night and day), and the seasons, as well as the perceived value of time ratios—hour, minute, day, year, lifetime, and generational—were significantly different. Furthermore, the rarity of stable mechanical devices in the surroundings with constant power sources influenced time expectations (e.g., a motorcar as opposed to a horse-driven carriage, or a gaslight in relation to an electric current source).

A reasonable hypothesis is that the sense of intensity of time, as well as the tolerance for objective elapsed time (often referred to, in the Viennese context, as *Gemütlichkeit*), suggest that Brahms may have been aware that the writing of music, as it was likely to be experienced, permitted a contemplative intensity (beyond the references accessible by a musically educated audience), bounded by silence and a slower, more irregular daily clock of life than we are accustomed to today. The structure of society, as seen through the conception of time and its uses, was more discontinuous from our own than most musicological analysis has accounted for.[46]

Therefore the mode of perception and recollection, the comprehension of a Brahms work—given the clear hints of historical analogies provided by the composer—cannot be inferred exclusively from the text of music bequeathed to us. Nor can one infer the imputed meaning to the act of hearing and playing. The significance of the musical experience in the nineteenth century heightened the desire to understand the human constitution of time. Husserl's inquiry was an extension of a line of inquiry that had part of its source in issues of art and its perception.

NOTES

1. For a parallel characterization of the milieu in which Brahms worked, see Michael Musgrave, "The Cultural World of Brahms," in *Brahms: Biographical, Documentary and Analytical Studies*, ed. Robert Pascall (Cambridge, 1983), 1–26; Reinhold Brinkmann, *Late Idyll: The Second Symphony of Johannes Brahms*, trans. Peter Palmer (Cambridge, Mass., 1995); and Siegfried Kross, *Johannes Brahms: Versuch einer kritischen Dokumentar-Biographie* (Bonn, 1997). For a comparable piece on painting and Brahms, see my essay, "Brahms and Nineteenth-Century Painting," in *19th-Century Music* 14 (1990). See also Reinhold Brinkmann's brilliant essay, "Zeitgenossen: Johannes Brahms und die Maler Feuerbach, Böcklin, Klinger und Menzel," in *Johannes Brahms: Quellen-Text-Rezeption-Interpretation. Internationaler Brahms-Kongress, Hamburg 1997*, ed. Friedhelm Krummacher, Michael Struck, Constantin Floros, and Peter Petersen (Munich, 1999). More recent scholarship includes Daniel Beller-McKenna's *Brahms and the German Spirit* (Cambridge, Mass., 2004) and Margaret Notley's *Lateness and Brahms: Music and Culture in the Twilight of Viennese Liberalism* (New York, 2007).

2. J. V. Widmann, *Johannes Brahms in Erinnerungen* (Berlin, 1898), 58–59.

3. George S. Bozarth and Stephen H. Brady, "The Pianos of Johannes Brahms," in this volume.

4. See Leon Botstein, "Brahms and His Audience: The Later Viennese Years, 1875–1897," in *The Cambridge Companion to Brahms*, ed. Michael Musgrave (New York, 1999), 51–78.

5. *Neues Universal Lexicon der Tonkunst*, ed. Julius Schladebach and Eduard Bernsdorf (Dresden, 1856), 1:447.

6. See Werner G. Zimmerman, *Brahms in der Schweiz: Eine Dokumentation* (Zurich, 1983), 102–12.

7. This is evident if one reads his correspondence in *Briefe von Theodor Billroth*, ed. Georg Fischer (Hannover, 1897).

8. Ludwig Eisenberg, *Künstler und Schriftsteller Lexikon: "Das geistige Wien"* (Vienna, 1891), 646–50.

9. From Richard von Perger, *Denkschrift zur Feier des Fünfzigjährigen ununterbrochenen Bestandes der Philharmonischen Konzerte in Wien 1869–1910* (Vienna, 1910).

10. Hans Gál, *Johannes Brahms: Leben und Werk* (Frankfurt, 1961), 93.

11. From the perspective of the modern reader and concertgoer, this is an indication of both the rarity of live performances of orchestral works and the gradual acceleration in concert life. Vienna's leading impresario, Albert Gutmann, sponsored 16 concerts in 1890;

39 in 1896; and 86 in 1900. In the three-year period between 1894 and 1897, the end of Brahms's life, 37 percent were vocal recitals, 32 percent were piano recitals, 12 percent violin recitals, 15 percent chamber music ensembles, and 5 percent visiting orchestras. Seventeen percent of the recitalists played their own music. See Leon Botstein, "Music and Its Public" (Ph.D. diss., Harvard University, 1985), app., tables 1–3, n.p.

12. See Theodor Billroth, *Wer ist musikalisch?* (Berlin, 1898).

13. See Arthur Schnitzler, *Tagebuch 1873–1892* (Vienna, 1987), 27 and 128; and *Tagebuch 1917–1919* (Vienna, 1985), 417.

14. Rudolf Louis, *Die deutsche Musik der Neuzeit* (Munich, 1912), 159–62, 328–29.

15. Brahms to Schubring, February 1869, in Johannes Brahms, *Briefwechsel,* rev. edns. (Berlin, 1912–22; repr. Tutzing, 1974), 8:216–17. See the use of the same letter in Walter Frisch, *Brahms and the Principle of Developing Variation* (Berkeley and Los Angeles, 1984), 32.

16. Louis, *Deutsche Musik,* 161.

17. Hermann Helmholtz, *On the Sensations of Tone,* trans. and ed. Alexander J. Ellis (New York, 1954; orig. 1885), 249.

18. Ibid., 365–71.

19. See Max Kalbeck, *Johannes Brahms* (Berlin, 1904–14; rev. ed. Berlin, 1912–21; repr. Tutzing, 1976), 2:27–34; 388–89; also R. Hirschfeld and R. von Perger, *Geschichte der K.K. Gesellschaft der Musikfreunde in Wien* (Vienna, 1912), 191–94.

20. L. A. Zellner, *Vorträge über Akustik: Gehalten am Conservatorium der Gesellschaft der Musikfreunde in Wien* (Vienna, 1892), 2:113–14.

21. See Ernst Mach, *Einleitung in die Helmholtz'sche Musiktheorie. Populär für Musiker dargestellt* (Graz, 1866); and Leo Koeningsberger, *Hermann von Helmholtz* (Braunschweig, 1911), 182–87; and William M. Johnston, *The Austrian Mind: An Intellectual and Social History 1848–1938* (Berkeley and Los Angeles, 1972), 182.

22. On the relationship between Brahms and Ehrlich, see Kalbeck, *Johannes Brahms,* 1:73–75.

23. Heinrich Ehrlich, *Die Musik-Aesthetik* (Leipzig, 1882), 124.

24. Ibid., 2.

25. Ibid., 3.

26. Ibid., 4.

27. Ibid., 134–37 and 173–76.

28. H. A. Koestlin, *Die Tonkunst: Einführung in die Aesthetik der Musik* (Stuttgart, 1879), 260–61.

29. Richard Wallaschek, *Aesthetik der Tonkunst* (Stuttgart, 1886), 230.

30. See Gál, *Brahms,* 147–48; and Imogen Fellinger, "'Brahms's 'Way': A Composer's Self View," in *Brahms 2,* ed. Michael Musgrave (Cambridge, 1986), 49–58.

31. Philip H. Goepp, *Symphonies and Their Meaning: Second Series* (Philadelphia, 1902), 361.

32. Ernst Mach, "Auszüge aus den Notizbüchern 1871–1910," in *Ernst Mach: Werk und Wirkung,* ed. Rudolf Haller and Friedrich Stadler (Vienna, 1988), 171–72, 182.

33. See Gerald Holton, *Thematic Origins of Scientific Thought: Kepler to Einstein* (Cambridge, Mass., 1973), 223–25.

34. Ernst Mach, *Die Analyse der Empfindungen,* 6th ed. (Jena, 1911), 6, 28–30.

35. Ibid., 250–52.

36. Ibid., 230–34; see also Ernst Mach, *Populär-Wissenschaftliche Vorlesungen,* 4th ed. (Leipzig, 1910), 43–47.

37. See the interesting discussion of Ernst Mach in Katherine Arens, *Functionalism and Fin de Siècle: Fritz Mauthner's Critique of Language* (New York, 1984), 183–222.

38. Mach, *Die Analyse,* 214.

39. On Mach and Husserl, see Manfred Summer, "Denkökonomie und Empfindungstheorie bei Mach und Husserl—Zum Verhältnis von Positivismus und Phänomenologie," in Haller and Stadler, *Ernst Mach*, 309–28.

40. Edmund Husserl, *The Phenomenology of Internal Time Consciousness*, ed. Martin Heidegger, trans. J. S. Churchill (Bloomington, 1964); the slightly different German text is *Texte zur Phänomenologie des inneren Zeitbewusstseins 1893–1917* (Hamburg, 1985).

41. See, for a comparison on this subject, Stephen Kern, *The Culture of Space and Time 1880–1918* (Cambridge, Mass., 1983).

42. See Jonathan D. Kramer, *The Time of Music* (New York, 1988), esp. chap. 11.

43. See a comparable discussion for fiction in Paul Ricoeur, *Time and Narrative* (Chicago, 1985) 2:77–81.

44. George Kubler, *The Shape of Time: Remarks on the History of Things* (New Haven, 1962), 77–82.

45. H. A. Köstlin, *Geschichte der Musik im Umriss*, ed. Willibald Nagel, 6th ed. (Leipzig, 1910), 538.

46. See Norbert Elias, *Über die Zeit* (Frankfurt, 1988), 42–43, 126–27, 144–47.

Johannes Brahms, Solitary Altruist

PETER F. OSTWALD

Brahms was a Janus-like figure who looked backward, seeking inspiration from the older Baroque and Classical traditions, while at the same time he looked forward and seemed the embodiment of modernism. A man of many contrasts, Brahms was devoted to his homeland in north Germany, but chose to live in southern Europe. He adored his parents and enjoyed family life, but never married. He was a kind and generous man, but often adopted an extremely rude manner toward others. He was fiercely independent, yet would mourn bitterly the loss of friends and relatives. He amassed a small fortune, but always lived frugally and dressed like a poor man.

I became interested in Brahms while working on a psychobiography of Robert Schumann and trying to understand the role he played during the two and a half years Schumann was hospitalized and his wife could not, or would not, see him.[1] Brahms became a kind of human link between these two artists. He loved Clara and lived with her; he also loved Robert and visited him regularly in the hospital. He played the piano for both of them, spoke with one about the other, and conveyed messages back and forth. This linking function is beautifully symbolized in a composition Brahms wrote in 1854, his Variations on a Theme by Robert Schumann, op. 9, dedicated to Clara Schumann. This work begins with a Schumann melody for which Clara herself had once written variations; it continues with variations that sometimes resemble Schumann's musical style and at other times are uniquely Brahmsian.

It occurred to me that Brahms's way of interacting with and making music for the Schumanns may have had certain characteristics of what Winnicott, working with mothers and children, has called the "transitional object" and Volkan, observing states of bereavement, called a "linking phenomenon."[2] These technical psychoanalytic terms have come to denote such tangible physical items as clothing, dolls, toys, or other belongings that can carry personal meanings and thus are capable of temporarily allaying the anxieties produced by separation from a true love object. In terms of providing emotional gratification, transitional objects are less real than human objects but more real than fantasized objects. Art objects in that sense can become very powerful transitional or linking phenomena, valuable not only for individuals but for entire cultures.

Music, as I have suggested elsewhere, may be especially well suited for use as a transitional or linking phenomenon.[3] It has a unique capacity for soothing and comforting. It has both the concreteness of real events and the abstractness of symbols. Some composers seem especially gifted in exploiting these transitional qualities of music, and I would like to suggest that Brahms is a good example of such an artist. Not only did he create effective musical links for future generations, but he also manifested certain qualities of personality that I would consider "transitional."

Despite the voluminous literature about him, Brahms remains somehow remote and unfathomable. Perhaps that is the way he wanted it to be. Brahms seems to have resisted most efforts to get close to him. Those who tried to do it were rebuffed. Even Clara Schumann had to confess that nearly fifty years of acquaintance with this musician had given her no insight into his character or ways of thinking. Here was someone who habitually kept his feelings to himself, and he deliberately destroyed many manuscripts and other personal documents that might have revealed how his mind functioned.

For the clinician, such behavior can be frustrating as well as tantalizing. Does Brahms's reserve indicate the desire to hide something? Or was this a way of trying to get people more interested in him? My impression is that despite his efforts at anonymity, Brahms wanted to be understood. He seems to have suffered greatly at times, and he probably had a number of depressive episodes. But the basic textbooks about illnesses of great composers are not helpful in this regard.[4] In my review of the literature, I have been able to find only four authors who focus directly on his emotional condition. Lange-Eichbaum cites observations that depict Brahms as "obstinately depressive [*ein trotziger Melancholiker*] . . . sexually inhibited, immature, [and] with advancing age crotchety, pedantic, and helpless in practical matters."[5] Schauffler calls him a "schizoid personality."[6] Hitschmann describes his "marriage inhibition."[7] Geiringer, in the keynote address at the 1983 Library of Congress Brahms Conference, calls him "ambivalent."[8]

Each of these diagnostic hunches has something of merit. In addition, I would suggest that Brahms had something of the "avoidant personality" described in our modern diagnostic nomenclature, viz., hypersensitivity to rejection, unwillingness to enter into relationships that did not guarantee uncritical acceptance, social distancing, and low self-esteem. But how are all of these descriptive criteria to be understood in the context of his developmental history, particularly his musical development? In brief, he appears to have been hypersensitive and moody beginning in childhood, but music helped him to find ways of avoiding personal intimacy and thus prevent overstimulation throughout adolescence. Most of his adult life he was a loner, and he never married. Severe emotional crises were generally averted, and no serious breakdowns ever occurred. With Brahms there was also a very good fit between his personality, his talent, and his ambition—he never seriously attempted to compose an opera, for example—so that despite a number of career frustrations he always continued to work. Finally, to appreciate Brahms's generally favorable state of health, it should be pointed out that he had the advantage of a long-term relationship with an outstanding physician and surgeon, Theodor Billroth, who became his devoted admirer and undoubtedly exerted a therapeutic influence. Thus conditions that might well have become more overtly psychopathological seem to have been held in check, so that Brahms's depressive disorder and personality problems were muted, leaving residues of great music, loneliness, and altruism.

All his life Brahms had a way of avoiding intimate relationships with other people. Already as a child he was solitary and reclusive, preferring to be at the piano or to play with his favorite collection of toy soldiers, an interest that may have combined his need for order with sublimated aggression (as well as his love for his father, who belonged to a military band). Brahms's interest in military matters never subsided. All his life he was very patriotic. Enthusiastic about the Franco-Prussian War of 1870, he wanted to be sure "that the French [would] get a good beating," and he composed the *Triumphlied* for Chorus and Orchestra, op. 55, when they did.[9] Brahms greatly admired Bismarck, and knew many of his speeches and much of his writing by heart.

Solitary pursuits, in particular reading, occupied much of his time. One of his favorite books was the Bible, from which he also could quote at length. He was widely read in the classics, history, legends, Renaissance art, biographies of musicians, and poetry. Brahms resented bitterly any allusions to his lack of formal education, and he was proud of his ability to discuss literature and the arts with some of the leading German-speaking intellectuals.[10] He was an avid collector of rare books, musical manuscripts, and original autographs, including works by Mozart and Schumann. Over the years this came to be a valuable collection, over which he fussed like an orderly librarian, conscientiously keeping track of every sheet of music he ever lent out.

Some of the negative impression Brahms made on others may be attributed to the difficulty he had in using words. He often acknowledged this fault in letters containing apologies for the rough or clumsy way he would express himself—"I can't write letters, also can't write diplomatically."[11] He was often angry and self-critical for saying the wrong thing, and he would mock himself cruelly. Those who came to know Brahms well gradually came to realize that, as Niemann said, "His mockery and anger and humour were nothing but a 'lightning conductor,' a protection against his own soft-heartedness, of which he was afraid."[12]

A man of rigid habits, Brahms rose very early (at 5 a.m. in the summer), brewed many cups of strong black coffee for himself, and worked without stopping until midday. He then went to a restaurant, always the same one for the last fourteen years of his life in Vienna, Zum roten Igel (The Red Hedgehog). Then he would go for a long walk, preferably in the country. Toward the evening, he prepared himself to go to a concert or the opera. Afterward he had supper, often with friends and usually in an informal setting such as a beer hall. He could easily take a catnap and seldom seemed tired. It was difficult for others to keep up with Brahms; for example, while traveling he always had to be on the go, to walk faster, climb higher, and explore more places than anyone else. Like Beethoven, he moved around a great deal, frequently changing his residence until he finally settled down in 1872 at Karlsgasse 4, in a small furnished apartment. Yet his bags were always kept packed for a trip, and he would spend long stretches of time each year away from home. Brahms always preferred older houses, and when traveling he would stay in simple, modest inns where he could relax unobserved, mingle with the help rather than the guests, and not have to dress up. His tendency to wear ill-fitting clothes, to forget his tie and collar, and to look rumpled if not disheveled (but never dirty), was noticed already in his twenties, at the Detmold court, where Brahms sometimes appeared in public and even conducted concerts dressed in a way that would draw attention to his "bad manners" and thus offend his patrons. Later, in Vienna, he habitually wore trousers that were too short, and instead of an overcoat would drape a green blanket around his shoulders, held in place with an oversize safety pin.

To account for these character traits, and others yet to be described, I would like to suggest two possibilities, fully recognizing that proving or disproving such explanations will be impossible, considering that our subject cannot be brought into the laboratory for biological study or into the consultation room for a thorough psychological evaluation.

Brahms at the villa of Johann Strauss in Ischl, 1894 or 1895.

(1) *Bio-energetic factors*: I assume Brahms to have been afflicted with some type of mood disorder, possibly a bipolar or cyclothymic disturbance that he tried to control, more or less successfully, through strenuously compulsive musical activities, playing the piano, studying scores, composing, and conducting. We know this to be a not uncommon problem among exceptionally productive and creative individuals.[13] I have described the pattern in several other nineteenth-century composers, and such figures have unusually high levels of energy and are easily aroused.[14] Unless contained through activity and work, their abundant vigor and interest can spill over into uncomfortable states of (hypomanic) excitement, as it probably threatened to do when Brahms would become overly abrasive, jocular, and irritating. At the other extreme are states of exhaustion and fatigue, with which Brahms attempted to cope through caffeine and nicotine. A certain narrowing of interest may also conserve energy, and I suspect that after a long and exhausting day of struggling with musical problems, insufficient energy remained for him to attend to the "less important" matter of social conformance.

(2) *Psychological conflict*: Brahms may have been torn between disobedience and conformity. This polarization undoubtedly reflected the influence of his parents, who were so widely discrepant in age, social background, and cultural attitudes. In regard to his habits of dress, one of my favorite anecdotes is about Brahms leaving home as a teenager. His mother gave him a sewing kit, with careful instructions on how to use it. He never did. Any holes in his clothes he would mend with sealing wax. This was his way of rebelling, through simultaneous protest and submission. Indeed, it has been noted that in contrast to the carelessness in his physical appearance, Brahms manifested the utmost scrupulosity in polishing his musical compositions. No gap was ever permitted in the fabric of a work; there were never any "loose threads." Furthermore, I would suggest as an explanation for Brahms's deportment some internalization of the life style and personal characteristics of Ludwig van Beethoven and Franz Schubert, two composers he tended to idealize.[15] Brahms's early infatuation with Robert Schumann, and his lifelong interest in Clara Schumann, may also have led to a degree of identification with these musicians. If that was the case, then the internalized influence of Schumann would probably have had a balancing effect, tending to neutralize Brahms's identification with the lonely, eccentric, unmarried "mad genius" prototype. And that Clara did not permit a closer union and in the long run would not let him step into Robert's shoes, reflects perhaps her good judgment in recognizing that such a move would have been destructive to Brahms's great talent, which had to be nurtured in solitude and seemed to require certain eccentricities.

Needless to say, regular employment proved to be impossible for this artist who valued freedom and needed independence to do his creative work. Brahms used to say that he wanted to be appointed Director of the Hamburg Philharmonic Society, and he felt rebuffed and embittered when Julius Stockhausen (a singer and friend of Brahms) obtained the prestigious post instead. But every time an equivalent position in Berlin, Cologne, or another major city was offered to Brahms, he would find various reasons for turning it down, and when the Hamburg post finally was made available for him, he claimed lamely that it was now too late to accept it. Brahms did accept employment on a few occasions, but only briefly. At age thirty, he served as conductor of the Vienna Singakademie; ten years later he became artistic director of the Gesellschaft der Musikfreunde but resigned after three years. By that time he no longer needed a salary. Brahms was now earning sufficient income by giving concerts, and he gradually became fairly wealthy through the sale and publication of his compositions.

Self-imposed bachelorhood was another reason for his loneliness. Brahms would speak regretfully about this at times, and his song *Kein Haus, keine Heimat*, op. 94, no. 5, expresses very well the unhappiness of a lonesome man who, in the words of Friedrich Halm, has "no house, no home, no wife, no child. I'm like a straw blown by the wind." But there also were times when he tried to make a virtue of bachelorhood. For example, when offered the directorship of the Music Society in Düsseldorf (a post held earlier by Mendelssohn and Schumann), Brahms declined. In explaining why, he wrote to Billroth:

> My main objections are of a rather childish nature, and I must remain silent about them. Perhaps the good taverns and restaurants in Vienna, the disagreeable, rough Rhenish tone (generally in Düsseldorf), and— and— in Vienna one can remain a bachelor without any hindrance. In a smaller city an old bachelor is a caricature. Marriage is something I no longer want and—I do have some reasons to be afraid of the fair sex.[16]

No friendship did more to reduce Brahms's loneliness than that with Joseph Joachim, the violinist and composer who was two years his senior (and outlived him by a decade). "Frei aber einsam" (Free but lonely) was Joachim's personal motto; its initials *FAE* make a musical pattern that Schumann, Brahms, and Dietrich used in their jointly composed *F.A.E.* Sonata for Violin and Piano. Brahms also employed the theme elsewhere, for example in the first movement of his String Quartet in A Minor, op. 51, no. 2.

Brahms and Joachim often gave concerts together, and they maintained a lively correspondence for more than forty-one years, commenting on many musical matters as well as personal ones, such as their mutual dislike of gossip and their concerns about mental illness. Brahms held Joachim in very high esteem as a composer; in his typically ambivalent fashion he would regularly ask for technical advice, but just as regularly reject it. One source of difficulty in the relationship, alluded to earlier, was Brahms's discomfort with the violinist's need for physical expressions of affection. Apparently Joachim would try to embrace him, and while lying in bed would shed tears and beg his "dear Johannes" to come over to show his love.[17] An unconscious homosexual element in the relationship is also suggested by Joachim's delusion about his wife having an affair with Brahms's friend Simrock. Early in the course of the troubled Joachim marriage, Brahms had written a cradle song for the couple's son, who in his honor was named Johannes. This song Brahms later incorporated into his moving Songs for contralto, viola, and piano, op. 91. He had hoped that the music would bring about a reunion between Joachim and Amalie. It did not.

Sexuality clearly seems to have been a problem for Brahms. He was able to be affectionate with women, even demonstrative at times (as suggested by photographs, although these are mostly of the older Brahms and tend to show the women hugging him rather than vice versa). His habitual caution if not abhorrence in regard to physical intimacy may reflect traumatic childhood experiences, with parents who were unhappily married, often at cross-purposes, and perhaps abusive at times. His reserve toward women may also have been conditioned by the climate of sexual promiscuity in the Hamburg taverns where he had worked as a teenager. Hitschmann described it this way:

> Too early he came to know the active, frivolous, purchasable sexuality of the prostitute. He once told of scenes he had witnessed: of the sailors who rushed into the inn after a long voyage, greedy for drinks, gambling, and love of women, who, half-naked sang their obscene songs to his accompaniment, then took him on their laps and enjoyed awakening his first sexual feelings.[18]

One would have to assume that unconscious and even conscious fantasies have been incorporated into such reminiscences. Nevertheless, Hitschmann's imagery suggests that young Brahms may have been seduced into playing the role of an aphrodisiac puppet, a go-between whose physical androgyny might be stimulating to men as well as women. And at a very critical period in his life he entered into the sexually complicated relationship between Robert and Clara Schumann, trying to satisfy both partners, as well as himself, in a marriage that had failed. "I dream and think only about the marvelous time when I will be able to live with both of you," he wrote on 24 October 1854.[19] Two months later: "I wish the doctor would employ me as an attendant or male nurse. . . . I could write to you about him every day, and I could talk to him about you all day" (15 December 1854). And finally, as we know, he was in love with Clara: "I think I can no longer love an unmarried girl—at least, I have completely forgotten them; they only promise the skies, whereas Clara shows it to us open."[20]

Brahms did attract other women. Several members of a female choir he conducted in Hamburg adored him, and a singer from Vienna named Bertha Porubsky may even have encouraged him to move to that city. The relationship did not continue. However, when Bertha later married and had a child, Brahms composed his famous Wiegenlied (Lullaby), op. 49, no. 4, for her. A more substantial romance was with Agathe von Siebold, the daughter of a professor in Göttingen, introduced to him by Joachim. Brahms is said to have given her an engagement ring, and when Clara Schumann found out about this, she warned him not to marry Agathe. Brahms soon terminated this relationship, but not without considerable anguish, which he symbolized by means of an agitated theme spelling her name A–G–A–H–E in the first movement of his Sextet for Strings in G Major, op. 36.

Brahms often teased Clara about possibly marrying one of her daughters, but he found excuses: "If [Eugenie] retains only a tiny scar on her pretty face [from a minor injury], then surely I can't marry her, and nothing will tie me down" (15 January 1856). Julie Schumann, probably the prettiest of the girls, also interested Brahms for a while. When she got married in 1869 to the Italian Count Marmorito, he felt embittered and angry, unjustly, since he had never declared any intention to marry Julie. Brahms had recently composed his melancholic Alto Rhapsody, op. 53, and he now made a point of saying it was "a bridal song for the Countess Schumann, but with rage do I write such things—with anger!"[21]

Another attractive woman in his life was Elisabeth von Herzogenberg, and again Brahms's avoidance of physical intimacy is apparent. She had been his piano student, and he broke off the relationship after noticing himself to be uncomfortably sexually aroused in her presence. They remained on good terms, however, and he regularly sought to please Elisabeth by sending her his "trifles," as he mockingly called compositions like the "tiny little Piano Concerto [in B-flat Major], written with a small, delicate Scherzo."[22]

He also befriended a couple of contraltos. One was the buxom Hermine Spies, whom Brahms referred to jokingly as "Hermione without an O."

She premiered many of his most beautiful songs. The other was Alice Barbi, a friend in his old age. These must have been exceptional women to put up with his derisive, self-disparaging remarks to the effect that any woman who could find him appealing must be out of her mind! Brahms liked to pose for photographs as a presumably happy bachelor surrounded by attractive women. In unguarded moments, however, his eccentricities became only too apparent, and many of his casual remarks sound utterly disillusioned: "I have no friends! If anyone says he is a friend of mine, don't believe it."[23] It is often said that he frequented prostitutes. In Vienna Brahms was occasionally observed in the company of a streetwalker whom he seemed to know on a first-name basis. Whether such contacts actually led to physical intimacy is anyone's guess. I find myself in sympathy with the art historian Alessandra Comini's opinion (personal communication) that after pleasurably chatting and gossiping with these women for a while, Brahms probably went home to satisfy himself in private.

One of Brahms's most active defenses against isolation was a highly developed feeling of responsibility. The sense of obligation he displayed toward his own family and in his relationship with Robert and Clara Schumann has already been mentioned. His generosity in financial matters knew no bounds. He supported his parents, his siblings, his stepmother, and her children. He gave money lavishly to anyone, friend or stranger, who so much as requested it or seemed to be in need. Ruthless as he was toward mediocrity, he never stinted praise or direct helpfulness when it came to other musicians. He was genuinely impressed with the talent of Antonín Dvořák, found ways to get his compositions published, and even went to the trouble of copying scores for him. In the case of Richard Wagner, who on several occasions had made scurrilous statements about Brahms, he always behaved with utmost decency. Not that he had any sympathy for Wagner's extremism. On the contrary, Brahms had taken an early public position against the Liszt-Wagner camp. (He was also one of the few German composers who at that time did not make anti-Semitic remarks.) It was simply that Brahms respected Wagner as a composer of operas, the only musical form in which he himself had made no progress. Despite Clara Schumann's condemnation of *Tristan und Isolde*, Brahms judged this to be a "magnificent work," and he even assisted Wagner in a practical way, by copying orchestral parts for the premiere of *Die Meistersinger* in Vienna.[24]

In his thirty-year relationship with Theodor Billroth one also observes Brahms's altruism. These men had much in common: their background in northern Germany, their loyalty to their parents, their energy and creativity, as well as their abhorrence of emotional display. Billroth habitually condemned moodiness, which he thought was a form of stupidity. Like Brahms, he firmly believed that the best way to handle one's emotions was through disciplined work. But Billroth and Brahms also had their differences: the surgeon was a tall, stately man, eloquent in speech, socially tactful and gracious, as compared to the short, awkward composer with his shabby appearance and impossible manners.

Billroth was an accomplished pianist, a passable violist, and an amateur composer. He had written three trios, a string quartet, and a piano quartet, all of which he destroyed. To please his mother, Billroth had studied medicine instead of music. He was the most daring and innovative surgeon of his day, pioneering such operations as radical mastectomy, total thyroidectomy, and various gastrointestinal procedures. His marriage was not a happy one, however, and that may have been a factor in his sensitive understanding of the lonely, sexually inhibited Brahms. Both men adored children, and Billroth was heartbroken when his first son turned out to be a deaf, mute, and possibly autistic child. (The boy died when Billroth was thirty-seven; that was the year he befriended Brahms.) They took many vacation trips together and in Vienna saw as much of each other as the busy surgeon's schedule would permit. Brahms regularly invited Billroth to his rehearsals, and he offered him many new compositions to be premiered in his home. Needless to say, Billroth championed Brahms's music with utmost enthusiasm.

The friendship began to deteriorate after Brahms learned from an old letter that Billroth had made disparaging remarks about his lack of formal education—a touchy point. He then discovered that Billroth committed the unforgivable sin of applying his surgical technique to the manuscript of a string quartet Brahms had dedicated to him. (In his worshipful attitude, Billroth had cut Brahms's signature from the title page and glued it onto his portrait.) For someone who revered original manuscripts as much as Brahms did, this was a sacrilege that justified the end of a long friendship. (Their relationship would have ended soon enough anyway, for Billroth became ill, and died in 1894. Brahms wanted to publish Billroth's musical compositions in a posthumous edition, but the surgeon's wife objected to this plan.)

Nowhere is Brahms's generosity more apparent than in his behavior toward the old Clara Schumann.

> It angers me [he wrote her on 24 July 1888] that [among other things] you have these [money worries]—while I swim in money without even noticing it and without having any pleasure because of it. I cannot live otherwise, don't want to, and will not . . . and where my heart

demands it, I can be helpful . . . and do good without being aware of it. After my death, however, I won't have any responsibilities or special wishes.

Thus Brahms offered to send Clara 10,000 marks for the support of her children. "Just think what a great pleasure [it would] give me were you simply and nicely to say 'yes.'" Clara, characteristically, said "no." But Brahms found a way to give her the money anyway, by making an anonymous contribution to the Schumann Memorial Fund. He also took endless pains in helping Clara to edit her husband's complete works. That project led to many pathetic disagreements, caused partly by Clara's wish to suppress, and in some instances even to destroy, compositions by Schumann that she considered unworthy. Brahms was able to rescue Schumann's D-Minor Symphony from such a fate by having the original score published alongside its later, more thickly orchestrated version (op. 120). That infuriated Clara, whose coldness toward Brahms made him feel utterly rejected: "It is hard, after 40 years of loyal service (or whatever you might wish to call my relationship to you) to be thought of as nothing more than a 'bad experience'" (13 September 1892).

They soon forgave each other, however, and agreed to remain friends. Clara's terminal illness following a stroke in 1896 was heartbreaking for Brahms, and her death left him totally bereft. He said that she was "the only person [he] had ever really loved."[25]

One cannot measure a man of genius with the same yardstick used for normal people. Brahms may have had a depressive disorder and an avoidant personality. He often displayed obsessive-compulsive habits and an irritability and impulsivity that was upsetting to people. He became more eccentric as he grew older, and in the homes of his friends he was pampered like an overgrown child. An involutional melancholia in his mid-fifties probably interfered with both his creativity and his well-being, but he recovered with the sounds of Mühlfeld's clarinet ringing in his ears, only to be stressed beyond endurance by the death of his one and only Clara Schumann.

In terms of the theory of "transitional objects," which is so useful in explaining the childhood origins of shared pleasure, I would propose that there may also be "transitional personalities," people who do not attach themselves firmly to anyone, but who allow themselves to be used for purposes of aesthetic gratification by everyone. These individuals are able to endure great loneliness and even isolation without becoming psychotic. They may seem to be dualistic, and their behavior is paradoxical.

One notices, for example, their brittleness and their integrity, their ruthlessness and their amiability, their vulnerability and their security. The art (or science, or other original things) they produce is meant to create linkages, to establish new connections between people, even across generations and cultures.

Brahms may have been such a transitional figure. He rose from rags to riches but never outgrew the rags. He was complicated and intellectual, but also simple and boorish. Although he remained a stranger to many people, he was also a friend, able to transcend his painful loneliness through altruistic acts. As a composer of difficult music that is easy to enjoy, Brahms seems to have mastered "the interplay between originality and the acceptance of tradition [that is] the basis for inventiveness."[26] He was the kind of person who immerses himself so fully in his creative work that there is little time or energy left over for intimacy and the formation of families. One thinks of other geniuses for whom the whole world became a family, Beethoven, for example, or Michelangelo. Such men can change civilization. They give us new sounds, new visions, and new meanings. They achieve truths that become eternal.

NOTES

An expanded version of this article appeared as "Johannes Brahms—Music, Loneliness, and Altruism," in *Psychoanalytic Explorations in Music*, ed. Stuart Feder, Richard Karmel, and George Pollock (Madison, Conn., 1990), 291–320.

1. Ostwald, *Schumann: The Inner Voices of a Musical Genius* (Boston, 1985), 283–93.
2. D. W. Winnicott, *Playing and Reality* (London, 1971); V. Volkan, *Linking Objects and Linking Phenomena* (New York, 1981).
3. Ostwald, "The Healing Power of Music: Some Observations on the Semiotic Function of Transitional Objects," in *The Semiotic Bridge: Trends from California*, ed. Irmengard Rauch and Gerald F. Carr (Berlin and New York, 1989), 279–96.
4. There is scant consideration of such matters in the Brahms chapter in F. H. Franken, *Die Krankheiten grosser Komponisten*, vol. 2 (Wilhelmshaven, 1989); and no chapter about Brahms in D. Kerner, *Krankheiten grosser Musiker* (New York, 1973).
5. W. Lange-Eichbaum, *Genie, Irrsinn und Ruhm: Eine Pathographie des Genies*, ed. W. Kurth (Munich, 1961).
6. Robert Haven Schauffler, *The Unknown Brahms: His Life, Character, Works* (New York, 1933), 156.
7. Eduard Hitschmann, "Johannes Brahms and Women" (1949), repr. in *Great Men: Psychoanalytic Studies*, ed. Sydney Margolin (New York, 1956), 200.

8. Karl Geiringer, "Brahms the Ambivalent," *American Brahms Society Newsletter* 1/2 (1983): 5–6. Repr. in Geirlinger, *On Brahms and His Circle: Essays and Documentary Studies*, ed. George S. Bozarth (Sterling Heights, Mich., 2006), 3–6.

9. Kurt Stephenson, ed., *Johannes Brahms in seiner Familie: Der Briefwechsel* (Hamburg, 1973), 175.

10. See Michael Musgrave, "The Cultural World of Brahms," in *Brahms: Biographical, Documentary and Analytical Studies*, ed. Robert Pascall (Cambridge, 1983), 1–26.

11. Berthold Litzmann, ed., *Clara Schumann-Johannes Brahms: Briefe aus den Jahren 1853–96* (Leipzig, 1927), 1:597.

12. Walter Niemann, *Brahms*, trans. Catherine Alison Phillips (New York, 1929), 178.

13. Ruth L. Richards, "Relationship Between Creativity and Psychopathology: An Evaluation and Interpretation of the Evidence," *Genetic Psychology Monographs* 103 (1981): 261–324.

14. Ostwald, *Schumann*; "Anton Bruckner: Musical Intelligence and Depressive Disorder," in *Kongressbericht zum V. Gewandhaus-Symposium* (Leipzig, 1987); and "Gustav Mahler: Health and Creative Energy," in *Rondom Mahler* 8 (Amsterdam, 1988).

15. The identification with Beethoven was brought home to me by Alessandra Comini in "Ansichten von Brahms—Idole und Bilder," in *Johannes Brahms: Leben, Werk, Interpretation, Rezeption* (Leipzig, 1985), 58–65. Beethoven's slovenliness, rudeness, and disregard of social convention have been discussed psychoanalytically by Maynard Solomon in *Beethoven* (New York, 1977; rev. ed., 1998). Schubert's fluctuating sociability and withdrawal, his incessant involvement in things musical, and his ambivalence regarding women are also well known. See, most recently, Solomon, "Schubert and the Peacocks of Benvenuto Cellini," *19th-Century Music* 12 (1989): 193–206.

16. Otto Gottlieb-Billroth, ed., *Billroth und Brahms im Briefwechsel* (Berlin and Vienna, 1935), 222.

17. Private communication from Boris Schwarz at the International Brahms Conference, Library of Congress, May 1983.

18. Hitschmann, *Great Men*, 212.

19. Litzmann, *Clara Schumann–Johannes Brahms*, 1:24.

20. Artur Holde, "Suppressed Passages in the Brahms-Joachim Correspondence," *Musical Quarterly* 45 (1959): 314. Translation adapted.

21. Johannes Brahms, *Briefwechsel*, rev. edns. (Berlin, 1912–22), 9:77–78.

22. Brahms, *Briefwechsel*, 1:154.

23. Quoted in Niemann, *Brahms*, 180.

24. Brahms, *Briefwechsel*, 7:83.

25. Niemann, *Brahms*, 175.

26. D. W. Winnicott, "The Location of Cultural Experience," *International Journal of Psychoanalysis* 48 (1967):370.

Brahms the Godfather

STYRA AVINS

The title of this essay is not capricious. Brahms was godfather to at least sixteen children, a little-known facet of his life that accords strangely with his current reputation as a lonesome and solitary man. His first godchild, Johanna Cossel, was the daughter of his first piano teacher. Brahms was barely twenty years old when asked to fill this office, a sign of esteem, trust, and honor. Thirty-seven years later he agreed to stand godfather to the child of another of Cossel's daughters, Marie. In between were many little Johanneses and Johannas, plus one Felix and one Max Hermann. The earliest godchildren were born to his closest friends at that period of his life: Clara Schumann, Albert Dietrich, Julius Otto Grimm, Joseph Joachim, and Julius Stockhausen. Early admirers and colleagues joined the list: Avé Lallemant, Georg Otten, and Adolf Schubring (the latter a jurist and writer on music who very early recognized Brahms's talents in print). Later requests to stand godfather were from Joseph Viktor Widmann, Max Kalbeck, Julius Spengel, Friedrich Hegar (conductor of the Zurich Tonhalle Orchestra), his copyist William Kupfer, and Viktor Schnitzler (committee chairman of the Gürzenich Orchestra, Cologne).[1]

It is odd that Brahms's need for solitude has received so much more attention than his large network of personal connections, because his need for friends was great, and he had a talent for both making and keeping them. Some names are well known: Elisabeth and Heinrich von Herzogenberg, Joseph Joachim, Eduard Hanslick, Josef Viktor Widmann. But it is true that Brahms needed solitude: he needed it to compose. He made himself perfectly clear in an eloquent letter written from Thun, during the summer of 1887, to Helene, Freifrau von Heldberg, as he turned down an invitation to visit her and her husband, the Duke of Meiningen, at their enchanting palatial villa on Lake Como. He was working at the time on the *Gesang der Parzen*.[2]

Conflict is apparently of greater interest than harmonious relations, so it is the famous rifts with a few of his friends that are well known, rather than the long and active friendships with Franz Wüllner, Gustav Wendt, Klaus Groth, Ferdinand Hiller, Hans von Bülow, Theodor and Emma Engelmann, the von der Leyens, the Beckeraths (Alwin, Rudolf, and their wives); with the Fabers, the Fellingers, Theodor Kirchner, Eusebius Mandyczewski; with Ferdinand Pohl, Carl Tausig, Ignaz Brüll, Ludwig Deppe, Julius Spengel, Julius Stockhausen, Ernst Franck, Friedrich Hegar, Karl Reinthaler, Otto Dessoff, George Henschel; with Ottilie Ebner, and Luise Dustmann (more on them later).[3] Sometimes Brahms's friendship included offers of financial help. He supported the disabled Kirchner for years, and paid for the medical care of his friend the Beethoven scholar Gustav Nottebohm, staying with him as he lay dying in Graz. He once shared his own honorarium of 1,000 marks with Chrysander for their work on Six Duets by Handel, when the publisher would not agree to pay Chrysander individually. Years later he helped to make sure Chrysander received a large sum of money.[4]

This list—far from complete—would be longer if it included close friends from his youth, such as Julius Otto Grimm, Albert Dietrich, and Julius Allgeyer. But Brahms went a different way; and though those friends were not forgotten, his contacts with them diminished. The list would be longer still if it included members of his Viennese circle, for example, his walking buddies Julius Epstein and Anton Door, and two generations of the Wittgenstein family, in virtually all of whose homes he was a sought-after guest. One of the more fascinating documents related to Brahms is a visiting card on which he lists his engagements for the next several weeks. Of the eighteen scheduled, six are at the homes of various Wittgensteins.[5]

Brahms not only corresponded with his friends, he invited many of them to visit during his summer holidays; they went on walks and hikes and enjoyed good food.[6] Besides standing as godfather to some of their children, he sent Christmas and baptism presents, and dedicated music to a few of them. He visited them when he was on tour or went out of his way to do so. A dramatic example is the detour he once made, for no particular reason, to see Carl Tausig in Berlin. Tausig, the brilliant pianist with whom he had shared some high-spirited adventures, and who had introduced Brahms to the writings of Schopenhauer, had endeared himself to Brahms by frequently performing the *Paganini* Variations, op. 35, at a time when they were considered unplayable.[7] The extempore meeting would be their last; Tausig died shortly after of typhoid fever at age thirty-one.

Sometimes friends visited him in Vienna. Groth, Bülow, and Henschel spring to mind. Others joined him on his trips abroad, most famously Widmann, who wrote about their travels.[8] Brahms's sense of friendship is expressed in a letter he wrote to Engelmann, after learning of the death of Engelmann's sister-in-law: "I'll write further to Utrecht soon: through such news is one reminded that it isn't enough to think loving thoughts of one's friends; one should stay better in touch with them through frequent communication."[9]

If the deed was not quite up to the wish, one does have to ask how many readers of this essay have such a long list of real friends and can keep up with them in any consistent way. Brahms and Engelmann would exchange another hundred letters in Brahms's life, not including the many charming but unpublished letters that Emma Englemann wrote to the composer.[10]

One of Brahms's long-term friendships was with the irritable and brilliant Hans von Bülow. Unlike so many of the people Bülow antagonized, Brahms maintained his friendship despite Bülow's erratic behavior, never abandoning him despite his cranky outbursts. Neither Brahms nor anyone else could know that Bülow had been suffering since early manhood from a tumor at the base of the brain, the cause of his frequent and sometimes unbearable headaches.[11] When Bülow was finally too disabled to see people, Brahms relied for news on correspondence with his wife or with colleagues in Meiningen.

Even Brahms's business relations bear witness to his capacity for friendship: his major publishers, Melchior Rieter-Biedermann and Fritz Simrock, became his personal friends. Indeed, one could make the case that for the long term, he only willingly did business with people he could consider friends. Brahms was welcomed as a guest at the Rieter home when he traveled to Switzerland, living there for a time in 1866 and thereafter as a regular visitor. He joined father and daughter on more than one hiking trip. The Rieter-Biedermans let it be known to Clara Schumann that they would look favorably upon the marriage of their beautiful daughter Ida with Brahms.[12] His long relationship with Simrock, who served also as his banker and with whom he was eventually on "du" terms, is perhaps better known.[13]

It takes a certain impudence—well intentioned, of course—to write a biography, to claim to know another human being well enough to present one's own notion of the person to the world. Knowledge of place and time, the detailed use of documents, material placed in context, and some life experience on the part of the author are minimum requirements.[14] By these standards, Brahms has not often been well served. On topics such as his reputed misogyny, sexual orientation, relations with women, his friendships, and his early life, it is rare that reports are the result of searches into the archives or a broad knowledge of the time and place. Despite its indisputable and evident virtues, Max Kalbeck's enormous biography ranks among the problematic ones because there is often no way for the reader to distinguish fact from opinion and supposition, and because Kalbeck lacked the means to conduct the kind of archival work that we should now consider indispensable. The length of the biography, the scope and detail of the work, and the fact that Kalbeck knew Brahms during the last twenty years of his life have tended to make later biographers overreliant on it, assuredly the reason that so many misconceptions were repeated from one biography to the next over the decades.

Among the exceptional biographies two stand out. Although she didn't have access to the thousands of letters and many memoirs now available, Florence May's 1905 biography was based on direct personal contact, scores of interviews with people who had known Brahms, personal acquaintance with many of the people of Brahms's circle, and a good deal of common sense. Most important, she did not—apart from equating the condition of Brahms's birthplace in 1833 with its condition in 1900—make assumptions regarding matters she knew nothing about. The other biography written by an author who for the most part stood on his own two feet, is the less well known work of the Viennese musician and author, Hans Gál. As assistant to Mandyczewski during preparation of the complete Brahms edition published in the 1920s by Breitkopf & Härtel, Gál rubbed shoulders with many people who had known Brahms, including Mandyczewski himself. Well read in the published correspondence, he also produced a useful selection of about three hundred letters in an inexpensive paperback, the first time such a selection was made readily available.[15]

Brahms's reputed misogyny is a good starting place to examine the distortions that have arisen on account of incomplete information. Any number of biographies and articles state simply that Brahms was a misogynist.[16] What do the authors who subscribe to that view know about Brahms and his contemporaries? Do they distinguish between everyday male chauvinism and genuine misogyny, generally defined as the hatred of women? Ethel Smyth's well-known description of Brahms is caustic and convincing. She describes what she saw with wit, but only part of her remarks have been reported. "I think what chiefly angered me was his views on women, *which after all were the views prevalent in Germany, only I had not realized the fact.*"[17]

Brahms hardly fits the description of a misogynist. Smyth understood Clara Schumann and Elisabeth von Herzogenberg to be exceptions in his circle, but they were not. If she can claim ignorance—she could not have known about his many other friendships with women—modern commentators are not so easily excused. Take, for example, his lifelong friendship and affection for the singer Ottilie Ebner. Their acquaintance dated from the time of his earliest days in Vienna, when they were both struggling to make a career in music. Brahms came very close to proposing marriage to her, "saved" or prevented by her engagement earlier that very day to another man. When they first met, Ottilie was living independently, supporting herself by giving ten voice and piano lessons in a day and singing professionally at every opportunity. Brahms's attraction to her is notable because she was anything but the model of a *Hausfrau*; Kalbeck and others described her unkindly. But Brahms liked her very much, perhaps attracted by her fine voice or perhaps by her determination to succeed on her own merits by hard work. After her marriage and move to Budapest he stayed in touch, enjoying her company when he was on tour there. He took an active interest in her family, invited her and her children to visit him on holiday, and wrote forty letters to her which are collected in the biography her daughter wrote.[18] Ottilie owned the manuscripts of several of the songs from opp. 57 and 58, which she sang through with Brahms when they were first published, and which quite possibly were inspired by her return to Vienna.

Deeply depressed after the death of her firstborn son in 1870, Ottilie would not listen to music. For a long time after, Brahms came to her almost daily to "play for her, to distract her, and gradually to lead her back to her muse."[19] Years later, his friendly hand extended to her daughter Lilie. A gifted pianist (with an American Steinway Brahms loved to play), Lilie reported that when she came down with scarlet fever, Brahms visited frequently to keep her company and entertain her with his piano playing.[20] Upon her move to England, Brahms sent a recommendation to George Henschel on her behalf.[21]

Brahms wrote to Ottilie as easily as one would write to a favorite sister, at times even about personal matters close to his heart (the death of his father, for example). For her part, Ottilie was utterly unabashed by him, wrote him spirited and lively letters which she signed "Tilie," and showed her admiration for him and his music unaffectedly. The best mark of his friendship is the letter Brahms wrote to Joachim in 1893: "Frau Dr. Ottilie Ebner wishes to pay you a visit. She is one of my most valued friends, and furthermore a beautiful and serious musician of the rarest sort . . . [In meeting her] you will gain in every regard."[22] Ottilie and Lilie were among Brahms's last visitors when he was near death.

In fact, Brahms had so many female friends that only a few can be mentioned here. Many are names with which even Brahmsians will not be familiar. In response to her call for help, he gave the penniless singer Rosa Girzik practical aid, even offering her money to tide her over during a difficult period. That it occurred to the young singer to write to Brahms in the first place should be cause to question his reputation for misogyny. His reply to her was charming and encouraging.[23] A jolly friendship with Nelly Lumpe (Chrobak) stretched into his last years. He remained devoted to Amalie Joachim when many of her "friends" abandoned her. His friendship with Bertha Faber, dating from Hamburg in the 1850s, was lifelong; the birth of her second son provided the occasion for Brahms's famous Lullaby. Maria Fellinger was in his closest circle from the time of their meeting until his death. In both cases the husbands were welcome ancillaries to the friendship. Brahms enjoyed the company of Antonia Kufferath, flirted with Hermine Spies and Alice Barbi, admired Clara Simrock and Ellen Vetter.[24]

Brahms took the sixteen-year-old Marie Soldat under his protection and promoted her with great energy, exclaiming, after one of her performances of his Violin Concerto (she was the first woman to perform it in public), that she was worth ten men.[25] Once her career was thriving, he followed the course of her all-female string quartet with interest, applauding the Wittgenstein who paid for the women's valuable instruments.[26] Not only could Brahms turn a "greedy eye" toward young women, as Ethel Smyth describes so vividly, he could also be avuncular, flirtatious, friendly, and helpful.[27] The operative word is *also*. Were there women he did not like? Undoubtedly. There were *people* he did not like. In a sweeping judgment he claimed a dislike of female pianists—but then, there were Clara, Emma Engelmann, Ilona Eibenschütz, and surely others we have yet to learn about.[28]

One evening in 1887 he received Sidonie Grünwald-Zerkowitz-Koloktroni in his apartment. An obscure figure now, she was well known in educational and literary circles for her essays in which she promoted women's education and independence. At the time of her meeting with Brahms she was already famous for her book *Songs of a Mormon Woman* (later banned in Vienna). She did not consider herself a feminist, but was concerned over the double standard of sexual morality in Vienna, where men were free to engage in sexual adventuring before their marriages of convenience to women, whose lot in life she deplored. Perhaps it was Widmann who made the introduction, since he championed women's emancipation and their right to vote, and it is by a letter from Brahms to him that we learn of her visit.[29]

Two more female friendships deserve discussion here: that with the former actress Ellen Franz after she became Helene, Freifrau von Heldberg, morganatic wife of the Duke of Meiningen; and with Luise Dustmann-Meyer. Correspondence between the Freifrau and Brahms exudes warmth and informality as well as humor, and a real pleasure in each other's company, which is reinforced when we know how often Brahms was invited to the ducal residences and with what warmth he was received. One cannot get the sense of it without reading the letters themselves.[30]

Luise Dustmann may have been a friend, but she was also probably something more. One aspect of Brahms about which we know virtually nothing is his love life; often discussed anecdotally but without any hard evidence is Brahms's apparent lack of an active amorous liaison. Common "knowledge" has it that he relied solely on prostitutes for his sexual needs, prostitution being a staple of Viennese life.[31] The rumors may or may not be true. But it is unacceptable to assume that because we do not know of any romantic involvements, none existed. Luise Dustmann, prima donna at the Court Opera in Vienna from 1857 to 1875, the leading Donna Anna, Agathe, Elisabeth, Elsa, and Leonore of the day and Wagner's choice to be his first Isolde, is a continuing presence in Brahms's life. She has been quite overlooked, although it would not be difficult to make a case for a protracted liaison between them. Indeed, it is far easier to make the case than to deny it.

Kalbeck claims that Dustmann was one of the allurements that brought Brahms to Vienna in 1862, having fallen under her spell at that summer's Festival of the Lower Rhine. He says that she captivated him "by her voice and abilities" but neglects to say what her abilities were. One would like to know Kalbeck's source. He writes that Brahms was in danger of losing his heart to her, and that once he reached Vienna Luise's behavior toward him was even more seductive than at the Festival. "Certain it is that Brahms had an intimate friendship with her," Kalbeck writes, "and that until his end (Dustmann outlived him by two years), he remained her faithful friend."[32] She performed in Brahms's concerts, supplied him with opera tickets, studied his lieder with him, sang the premieres of over a dozen of his songs (including the famous Lullaby and the *Liebeslieder* Waltzes), and regularly received complimentary copies of his vocal music as they were published. Brahms was a frequent visitor to her apartment, which was within "astonishing proximity" to his own.[33] The two summered in the same obscure retreats at the same time, Tutzing and Pörtschach.[34] If Brahms had found her presence annoying, he could have done as he did in 1873 in Gratwein: picked up and gone elsewhere.[35] When Luise's voice lost its dramatic power, Brahms went to the trouble of helping her obtain concert engagements.[36] She wrote letters to Brahms that disclose more than a coquettish familiarity—they are like no others he received. Either these circumstances point to an unusual friendship on Brahms's part, or to something different.

Probably the most dramatic revision to the picture of Brahms which has developed through the process of detailed archival research concerns what we now know of Brahms's early life. The most widely circulated picture is also the most misleading: Brahms's birth and upbringing in poverty in the slum area known as the Gängeviertel, and his forced labor as a child piano player in brothels. None of his many biographers seemed to realize that their Gängeviertel of the late nineteenth and early twentieth centuries was far different from the neighborhood Brahms was born in. Documents establishing that the Brahms family moved away from the Gängeviertel before Brahms was a year old have been available for several decades, thanks particularly to research by Kurt Stephenson and Kurt Hofmann. Biographers at any time, however, might have done their homework and discovered that Hamburg's brothel ordinances prohibited anyone under age eighteen from entering them for any reason, under stiff penalties for the brothel owners, and above all, that piano playing and music in general was prohibited in them.[37] Nevertheless, a number of biographies and psychobiographies base their reading of Brahms the adult on the harm purportedly done him as a child.

Not surprisingly, someone with as rich, complex, contradictory, and many-sided a personality as Brahms is a natural subject for psychoanalytic musings. Despite some bold attempts, the results demonstrate the old problems: incomplete information, leading to assumptions and points of view that do not withstand deeper scrutiny. One difficulty is that psychoanalysts are rarely historians, and tend to make use not of a broad selection of current writing but a quote out of context or a biography that in itself may have an unspoken agenda. Such a biography is exemplified by Walter Niemann's popular work on Brahms, written in 1920, when Germany was reeling in the aftermath of the loss of the First World War and grasping for ways of reasserting the splendor of Germanic culture. That climate explains Arnold Schoenberg's claim that his development of the twelve-tone system would secure Germany's musical supremacy for the next one hundred years. Niemann's popular biography did its share by laying great stress on Brahms's North Germanness. He claimed knowledge that he had no way of having, since he had never met Brahms. His biography was inspired more by the urgent nationalism of the time than by any basis in fact—for example, his contention that Brahms increasingly took on North German traits and became more and more sparse with words as he aged, that his speech regained its North German color, and that he spoke his own words only with the greatest difficulty. Any reader of Richard Heuberger's *Erinnerungen*, who has thereby had the opportunity to hear Brahms virtually in his own words, will know that he had adopted Viennese figures of speech and had no problem expressing himself. Nevertheless, Niemann's biography, frequently reprinted and widely disseminated in its English translation, has often been quoted as a source of information for books and articles on the composer.[38]

An additional problem of existing psychological studies of Brahms is summarized by the authors of a paper for the journal *History of Psychiatry*, who take issue with the whole concept of psychoanalysis at a distance of place and time—the methodology necessarily used by those attempting to investigate Brahms's character psychoanalytically. Although they were writing about the psychiatrist Emil Kraepelin, not Brahms, their comment is widely applicable: "To engage in such retrospective, long-distance diagnosis and to subsume [X's] personality under the diagnostic categories of contemporary psychiatric systems is dubious in the extreme and may well reveal more about the convictions and interests of today's psychiatrists than about the historical 'patient.'"[39]

The double problem of insufficient information and questionable methodology has a direct bearing on recent explorations into Brahms's sexual identity. In an essay in the original version of *Brahms and His World*, published in 1990 and reprinted in the present volume, the late Peter Ostwald wrote, "Sexuality seems clearly to have been a problem for Brahms." In support, he quoted Eduard Hitschmann, author of "Johannes Brahms and Women," who gives what he claims is Brahms's account of sailors and prostitutes.[40] Neither a musicologist nor a biographer, Hitschmann was a Freudian psychoanalyst active in Vienna in the 1920s and '30s, specializing in frigidity. His account cannot come from any primary source, since for obvious reasons there are none. But Hitschmann does not hesitate to quote it as authentic, and Ostwald then uses that very passage to create his own diagnosis of Brahms. In this way a whole literature about Brahms has grown up. Ostwald's suggestion that, when the day was done, Brahms "probably went home to satisfy himself in private" can well be said to reveal more about the convictions and interest of at least one of today's psychiatrists than about the historical patient.

Suggestions of a putative if unconscious homosexual undertone to Brahms's relations with Joachim, alluded to by Ostwald and as a result by subsequent writers, suffer from the same problem. The surmise is based on an incident related to Ostwald by word of mouth, concerning Joachim's need for physical expressions of affection. Ostwald's source was the well-known violinist and musicologist Boris Schwarz. At the time, Schwarz was seventy-seven years old and possibly ailing (he died six months after their meeting). Without in any way injuring his reputation, one can suggest that his memory was probably not at its sharpest. The story is a garbled version of an account that appears in Kalbeck's biography of Brahms but whose ultimate source is Gustav Wendt, distinguished educator and head of the Karlsruhe Gymnasium, a longtime and well-trusted friend who, over a period of many years, faithfully visited Brahms on holiday. Wendt mentions his confidential conversation with Brahms about Joachim in his autobiography, *Lebenserinnerungen eines Schulmanns*. In his book, Wendt alludes discreetly to Brahms's confidential talks with him, writing, "Es war auf einem Spaziergang nach Schloß Schadau [in Thun] wo er mich über seine Freundschaft mit Joachim eingehend unterrichtete."[41] Kalbeck, who had access to Wendt's diaries and interviewed him directly, fills in the details. Here is Wendt quoting Brahms, as the incident appears in Kalbeck's biography:

> Joachim had the unhealthy inclination of feeling compelled to complain about his lot. . . . Even much earlier, when we had a lot to do with each other, he came often, sat on my bed, and asked even then if I liked him because he always doubted it. I specifically explained to him that we would always be the same to each other, but that that kind of question was utterly unbearable to me.[42]

It is instructive to compare what Wendt reported to Kalbeck with the ways in which those words have since been modified—one might say distorted—and spread further by other commentators who are quite possibly unaware of the context and words of the original.

Many other published ideas about Brahms show a want of familiarity with the details of his life: Brahms gave away money lavishly to anyone who asked for it (actually, his correspondence with Simrock provides details of concern and caution as he dispensed money to his family); he suffered from depression; he eventually quarreled with all of his good friends; he was unkempt (indeed, he was not fastidious and spurned the fashions of the day when he could, but knew how to dress for the theater and for his appearances at Court; he was hardly Beethovenesque); he fell apart after the death of Clara Schumann; and that he was routinely surly and rude. Of this last commonplace, readers of the Beckerath and Heuberger memoirs in the present volume may come away with another view. Once Freud's ideas became fashionable, the notion took hold that Brahms was unduly attached to his mother; this groundless assertion is readily contradicted by the documented evidence of his affection for and attachment to his father: by his actions, by his letters to his father, and by the forbearance Brahms showed him during the wretched period of the dissolution of his parents' marriage.[43]

Even the notion that Brahms was a lonely man needs to be scrutinized. There is a difference between being a loner, which he surely was, and being lonely, which he may have been at times—increasingly so toward the end of his life, but surely not perpetually so.[44] Brahms, as he said of himself, was an "Abseitler," an outsider, which is not the same thing as being lonely, and it is not always an unpleasant condition. People have differing tolerances for being outsiders, and some even enjoy it. Brahms's need to be alone has been mentioned earlier; and though he had a rich social life and there were ample scenes of enjoyment and good times, it is clear that an inner core of himself was always aware of darkness. In that, he may well have been a realist: death is the end for all of us. Some people are more conscious of that fact than others. As he wrote to a friend who objected to the threatening trombones in the Second Symphony, "I would have to admit . . . that I am a deeply melancholy person, that black pinions constantly rustle over us." Anyone who pictures Brahms therefore failing to enjoy his dinner, his beer, his coffee, his schnapps, his cigar, and his friends, would be mistaken.[45] It is also a mistake to claim that Brahms suffered from depression. On the contrary, that seems to be a state of mind he never battled, although as he put it to his good friend Theodor Billroth, he recognized the dangers of gloomy thoughts. He comments that one judges friends "according to the particulars" of what they allow one to see of them, "neatly wrapped and sealed"—by which measure, he tells him, Billroth may occasionally consider Brahms a very fortunate man. It is not Billroth who exerted a therapeutic effect on the composer, but Brahms who was able to cheer up Billroth when he was low.[46]

Much has been made of Brahms's troubled or broken relationships with some of his closest friends: Levi, Joachim, his early supporters Avé-Lallemant and Carl Grädener, with Billroth, and to some degree with Clara Schumann. Rarely do commentators focus on the partner in the relationship.[47] But as in so many matters, there are two sides to every story.

It is fair to say that Joachim was pathologically jealous. Until now we have known him primarily in the hagiography of Andreas Moser, but with the publication of Beatrice Borchard's monumental double biography of Joseph and Amalie Joachim we can begin to understand the problems faced by those in his immediate circle.[48] That Brahms refused to let loyalty to his oldest friend blind him to the injustice being done to his wife is witness to his unwavering sense of fair play, which indeed is what Brahms said to Joachim when contact was restored.

The difficulties of Brahms's relations with Clara Schumann were quite different. They resemble the crosscurrents of two people who have familial ties but are not quite on the same wavelength. She had her own complex constellation of expectations; Brahms was insensitive to many, and resisted others. And she had no sense of humor, no light touch, to help her to endure his perceived lapses. In the end, their irritations were always tempered by a mutual recognition of what they meant to each other, which sustained their love.

The eventual failure of Brahms's friendship with Levi is routinely explained as a result of his displeasure over Levi's increasing interest in the music of Wagner, but the event cannot be understood without knowing Levi's competitive nature and how he dealt with another Brahms friend, Franz Wüllner, when the two conductors were placed in professional rivalry in Munich through no fault of their own. Brahms tried to mediate between them, but in the end it is Wüllner who left town.[49] Whatever role Wagner's music played, the idea that Brahms's break with Levi primarily concerned the latter's growing interest in it cannot stand scrutiny. Wüllner led the premieres of *Das Rheingold* and *Die Walküre* and never ceased to conduct Wagner's music. Clara Schumann, whose implacable dislike of Wagner's music led her to refuse to attend concerts where it would be played, remained on friendly terms with Levi for years, something she could not have done had he given up his interest in Brahms's music. Brahms's stated reason for his declining friendship has to do with Levi's callous treatment of his manservant. Most likely there is no one reason, but an accumulation of several.

Brahms's diminished feelings toward Billroth had a quite different cause, a rather dramatic one, which had all the more impact because in all the years of their sometimes brilliant friendship, Billroth had only hard words to say about Brahms's father. With no understanding of the financial conditions of Brahms's youth, Billroth blamed Johann Jakob for not providing a better childhood for his son.[50] The climax came when, in a letter to Hanslick, Billroth blamed Brahms's rough edges on a generally deficient upbringing. By some appalling mischance this assault on Brahms's parents was forwarded by Hanslick to Brahms. Both he and Hanslick tried to make light of the business, but essentially Brahms never forgave Billroth. Equally regrettable, the old friend never learned the cause of Brahms's excessive rudeness at their next meeting or the coolness that followed. The men maintained contact to the end. But by the time Billroth died, the warmest period of their friendship was long over, as Brahms acknowledged bluntly when people sent him condolence letters.[51]

All biography is provisional. The vision of Brahms as a solitary man with few friends is widespread in the literature, but must inevitably give way to a rather different view as the thousands of letters he wrote and received become available, along with the large number of memoirs written by people who loved him and felt their lives had been enriched by knowing him. The past thirty years have seen a great surge in documentary information about the composer, due in part to a changed perception of biography and its legitimate concerns, and in part to a greater accessibility to those letters and memoirs.[52]

They remind us that there is no way to build a portrait of Brahms, nor even to comment on one aspect or another of his life, without creating— bit by bit—a mosaic from all those historical documents that concern him. Brahms's devotion to Hamburg, for example, cannot be understood without some knowledge of the history of the Free and Hanseatic City, which ingrained in its schoolchildren patriotic devotion to Hamburg as an independent political entity. That component of the composer's enormous disappointment at the snub he received from the Hamburg Philharmonic, which forever left its mark, is missing from the many accounts of Brahms I have read. So is the devastating and bloody history of the Napoleonic blockade of the city, which his mother lived through and which has everything to do with Brahms's distaste for things French. Accounts and analyses that make sweeping generalizations cannot do justice to anyone, let alone someone as deep, complex, and sometimes veiled as Brahms. The man who wrote the Lullaby, the *German Requiem*, and the *Liebeslieder* Waltzes at approximately the same time is not to be defined in brief. As Virginia Woolf wrote, "Yes—writing lives is the devil!" And the devil is in the details.

NOTES

1. A Lutheran godparent is responsible for the moral and Lutheran upbringing of the child should the parents be incapacitated.

2. Johannes Brahms, *Briefwechsel*, Neue Folge, vol. 17, ed. Hertha Müller and Renate Hofmann (Tutzing, 1991), 75–76. English translation in Styra Avins, *Johannes Brahms: Life and Letters*, trans. Josef Eisinger and Styra Avins (Oxford, 1997), 644–46. The Villa Carlotta, today a state-owned park of twelve acres located on the shores of Lake Como, is in much the same lush state as when Brahms knew it.

3. Peter Russell's *Johannes Brahms and Klaus Groth: The Biography of a Friendship* (Hampshire, 2006) is a recent and welcome account of a cordial and under-reported friendship.

4. On the honorarium, see Avins, *Johannes Brahms*, 576–77; on the large sum of money, 680–81.

5. Archive of the Brahms-Institut an der Musikhochschule Lübeck, Sig. Hofmann.

6. Reinthaler, Wendt, Kalbeck, the Engelmanns, Stockhausen, Henschel, Ebner, Dessoff are among many other friends.

7. Tausig was also Brahms's partner in the first public performance in 1864 of the Sonata in F Minor for Two Pianos, op. 34b, the two-piano version of the Piano Quintet.

8. See also Rudolf von der Leyen, *Johannes Brahms als Mensch und Freund* (Düsseldorf, 1905); and Kurt Stephenson, *Johannes Brahms und die Familie von Beckerath* (Hamburg, 1979). Both contain warm accounts of the friends' travels with Brahms.

9. Johannes Brahms, *Briefwechsel*, rev. edns. (Berlin, 1912–22; repr. Tutzing, 1974), 13:89.

10. Ibid., 7–8.

11. The headaches began in his early twenties. For a medical discussion, see J. Wöhrle and F. Haas, "Hans von Bülow: Creativity and Neurological Disease in a Famous Pianist and Conductor," in *Neurological Disorders in Famous Artists—Part 2*, ed. J. Bogousslavsky and M.G. Hennerici, *Frontiers of Neurology and Neuroscience* 22 (Basel, 2007), 193–205. For the most thorough discussion of Bülow's appalling suffering and the barbaric therapies he underwent, see Isolde Vetter, "Hans von Bülows Irrefahrt durch die Medizin. Mit Briefen und anderen unveröffentlichten Zeugnissen aus seinem letzten Lebensjahr," in *Beiträge zum Kolloquium: Hans von Bülow—Leben, Wirken und Vermächtnis*, ed. Herta Müller and Verona Gerasch, *Südthüringer Forschungen* 28 (Meiningen, 1994), 100–115. For a summary, see Styra Avins, "Sleuthing a Newly Discovered Letter from Johannes Brahms," *American Brahms Society Newsletter* 25/2 (2007): 1–4.

12. See Avins, *Johannes Brahms*, 224, 339, 342–43.

13. The most vivid demonstration of their friendship is their personal correspondence, collected in Kurt Stephenson, ed., *Johannes Brahms und Fritz Simrock: Weg einer Freundschaft* (Hamburg, 1961).

14. See Leon Edel's insightful *Writing Lives: Principia Biographica* (New York and London, 1984).

15. Hans Gál, *Brahms Briefe* (Frankfurt, 1979); and *Johannes Brahms: His Work and Personality*, trans. Joseph Stein (New York, 1963; orig. German ed., Frankfurt, 1961).

16. A brief sampling: Karl Geiringer, "Brahms as Reader and Collector," *Musical Quarterly* 19 (1933): 168; Robert Haven Schauffler, *The Unknown Brahms* (New York, 1933); and Ivan Hewett, writing of Brahms's "famous misogynist views" in "Behind the Beard," *Musical Times* 141 (2000): 61; and Jan Swafford in *Johannes Brahms: A Biography* (New York, 1997) and several subsequent newspaper and journal articles.

17. Ethel Smyth, *Impressions That Remained* (New York, 1946), chap. 24, esp. 235–36. My italics.

18. Ottilie Balassa, *Die Brahmsfreundin Otillie Ebner* (Vienna, 1933). Forty-seven of her letters were in Brahms's possession at his death.

19. Ibid., 55.

20. Ibid., 114.

21. Brahms to Frau Lilie Andrae-Ebner (Postmark: Ischl, 15/9/1895), unpublished postcard, Kneisel Hall, Blue Hill, Maine (Ann Stern bequest).

22. Brahms, *Briefwechsel*, vol. 6.

23. Avins, *Johannes Brahms*, 373.

24. Clara was the wife of his publisher Fritz Simrock, Ellen the married daughter of Josef Viktor Widmann. Brahms's letters to her are included in the volume of his letters to the father, Brahms, *Briefwechsel*, vol. 8. Antonia Kufferath, later the wife of Edward Speyer, a German-English banker, was the daughter of the Belgian conductor Ferdinand Kufferath, composer and admirer of Schumann. Brahms was on teasing terms with Antonia, a fine soprano. He dedicated the manuscript of 13 Canons, op. 113, nos. 1 and 2 to her. Their unpublished correspondence, preserved in the Speyer Autograph Collection, was kindly photocopied for me by the then-owner (since sold at auction in June 2003).

25. Michael Musgrave, "Marie Soldat 1863–1955: An English Perspective," in *Beiträge zur Geschichte des Konzerts: Festschrift Siegfried Kross zum 60. Geburtstag*, ed. Reinmar Emans and Matthias Wendt (Bonn, 1990), 219–330.

26. Avins, *Johannes Brahms*, 591 n. 19, and unpublished letters of the Wittgenstein family, collection of Marie Kuhn-Oser.

27. Smyth, *Impressions That Remained*, 263–64.

28. Such as Marie Jaëll, subject of an article by Marie-Laure Ingelaere, "The Transmission of Johannes Brahms's Music in Europe: Alfred and Marie Jaëll," *American Brahms Society Newsletter* 25/2 (2007): 5–7. Brahms kept seven of her letters. Ilona Eibenschütz has written a charming memoir about her connection to Brahms: Mrs. Carl Derenburg, "My Recollections of Brahms," *Musical Times* 67 (1926): 598–600. In addition to describing the pleasure he took in her playing, the memoir also portrays a Brahms quite recovered after Clara Schumann's death, in contrast to some claims that he was henceforth a broken man.

29. Brahms to Widmann (Vienna, 11 October 1887), in Avins, *Johannes Brahms*, 650–51. Sidonie Grünwald-Zerkowitz-Koloktroni (1858–1907) kept the names of her three husbands. Her next book was *Gretchen von Heute*, banned in Austria even as late as 1957! This is the briefest introduction to a remarkable woman, who was appointed professor of history and languages in Budapest while only in her twenties (Hungarian was not her native language, but she had learned it in two years and passed a state examination). Her later interests included promoting the reform of women's clothing in order to free them from the tyranny of Parisian fashion.

30. Brahms, *Briefwechsel*, vol. 17.

31. See Stefan Zweig, *The World of Yesterday* (Lincoln, Neb., 1964), chap. 3.

32. Max Kalbeck, *Johannes Brahms*, rev. ed. (Berlin, 1912–21; repr. Tutzing, 1976), 2:46, 65. Dustmann's letters bear out his contention.

33. Dustmann in a suggestive letter to Brahms, Archive of the Gesellschaft der Musikfreunde, D-B-7.

34. "Damals war Pörtschach ein sehr bescheidenes, fast unbekanntes Seeörtchen an der Straße gegen Klagenfurt" (At that time Pörtschach was a very modest, almost unknown little lake town on the road toward Klagenfurt). Hans Müller, "Johannes Brahms in Pörtschach," in exhibition catalogue of *Pörtschacher Johannes-Brahms-Wochen 1964*. Quoted in Willi Reich, *Johannes Brahms: In Dokumenten zu Leben und Werk* (Zurich, 1975), 126.

35. See the memoir in this volume by Richard Heuberger, "My Earliest Acquaintance with Brahms."

36. Brahms to Bernhard Scholz, November 1875, in Avins, *Johannes Brahms*, 488.

37. For brothel laws and other aspects of the myths surrounding Brahms's early years, see Avins, "The Young Brahms: Biographical Data Reexamined," *19th-Century Music* 24 (2001): 278–81. For the documentary underpinnings of the Brahms family life enormous debt is owed to Kurt Stephenson, *Johannes Brahms' Heimatbekenntnis in Briefen an seine Hamburger Verwandten* (Hamburg, 1948); and *Brahms in seiner Familie* (Hamburg, 1973); and to Kurt Hofmann, *Johannes Brahms und Hamburg* (Reinbek, 1986). Their archival work has opened a new chapter in Brahms biography, providing an admirable standard of rigor.

38. Walter Niemann, *Brahms*, trans. Catherine Alison Phillips (New York, 1929; original German ed., Berlin, 1920), 175. No other biography makes Niemann's claims except by reference to him. For a fuller discussion of the propaganda undertones of Niemann's biography, see Michael von der Linn, "Themes of Nostalgia and Critique in Weimar-Era Brahms Reception," in *Brahms Studies* 3, ed. David Brodbeck (Lincoln, Neb., 2001), 321–48; and Daniel Beller-McKenna, *Brahms and the German Spirit* (Cambridge, Mass, 2004), 172f.

39. Eric J. Engstrom, Wolfgang Burgmair, and Matthias M. Weber, "Emil Kraepelin's 'Self-Assessment': Clinical Autobiography in Historical Context," *History of Psychiatry* 13

(2002): 98. My thanks to William A. Frosch, M.D., who pointed me to this quote in his book review of Peter J. Davies's two-volume work on Beethoven's illnesses and character, *American Journal of Psychiatry* 159 (2002): 2126–27.

40. Eduard Hitschmann, "Johannes Brahms und die Frauen," *Psychoanalytische Bewegung* 5 (1933): 97–129. This article was later translated into English and included in a 1956 volume with a foreword by Ernest Jones, lending it considerable weight. It is cited in Peter Ostwald, "Brahms, Solitary Altruist," in this volume. It may be noted that Ostwald's article was written before the burgeoning advances in Brahms scholarship from 1983 on.

41. Gustav Wendt, *Lebenserinnerungen eines Schulmanns* (Berlin, 1909), 156. "It was on a walk to Schadau Castle [in Thun] that he informed me in detail about his friendship with Joachim."

42. Kalbeck, *Brahms*, 2:435.

43. For letters to his father, see Stephenson, *Brahms in seiner Familie*. For some translations see Avins, *Johannes Brahms*.

44. There is reliable evidence (from Widmann) that as Brahms grew older, he felt increasingly lonely.

45. Letter to Vincenz Lachner, August 1879, in Avins, *Johannes Brahms*, 552. Another great man wrote in a similar vein: "Freude an den kleinen Sachen / Heute weinen, morgen lachen / Wie es kommt, so nimm es hin / Dunkel bleibt der tiefre Sinn. (Joy in the little things / Cry today, laugh tomorrow / Take it just the way it comes / Dark remains the deeper meaning). Unpublished letter to a friend from Albert Einstein.

46. See Ostwald's contention in "Brahms, Solitary Altruist." See Brahms to Billroth, letters of 22 July 1886 and March 1890, in Avins, *Johannes Brahms*, 639 and 674.

47. Regarding Grädener, see my "Brahms Observed: Carl Georg Peter Grädener with Brahms in Vienna," *American Brahms Society Newsletter* 26/1 (2003): 1–5; and 26/2 (2003): 5–8. A welcome exception regarding Hermann Levi is found in Karl Geiringer, *On Brahms and His Circle: Essays and Documentary Studies*, ed. George S. Bozarth (Sterling Heights, Mich., 2006), 373 n. 33.

48. Beatrix Borchard, *Stimme und Geige: Amalie und Joseph Joachim: Biographie und Interpretationsgeschichte* (Vienna, 2005). Both Brahms and Clara Schumann were aware of Joachim's irrational jealousies and how they affected the running of the Berlin Conservatory. Letter from Brahms to Clara, 19 March 1874, in Avins, *Johannes Brahms*, 466–67.

49. The Levi-Brahms letters from 1875 to 1877 unfailingly mention Wüllner's situation. Wüllner and Brahms first met in 1853. Not only was their professional relationship friendly and successful throughout their lives, Brahms was a great admirer of Wüllner's son, Ludwig, and followed his career sometimes in person with much interest. On several occasions Brahms gave preference to Wüllner over Levi for the opportunity to conduct his new orchestral works, especially after 1877, the year Wüllner felt compelled to leave Munich. For more on the Brahms-Levi friendship, see Avins, *Johannes Brahms*, 411–13, 473–75.

50. Otto Gottlieb-Billroth, ed., *Brahms und Billroth in Briefwechsel* (Berlin, 1935; repr. 1991), 148f., where the circumstance is explored in some detail.

51. The adjective frequently used by acquaintances to describe the youthful Brahms as he appeared to them is *liebenswürdig*, lovable, endearing. There is no question but that the sarcastic and gruff Brahms known to Billroth was a result of life's buffeting, not Brahms's upbringing. Billroth made his own assumptions. See Avins, "The Young Brahms," 287.

52. As of this writing (April 2008) there are over 10,600 letters from and to Brahms listed in the catalogue under construction by the Brahms-Institut an der Musikhochschule Lübeck, in Germany.

Clara Schumann and Johannes Brahms

NANCY B. REICH

Today I have buried the only person I truly loved.
> —Brahms speaking to friends on the day of
> Clara Schumann's funeral, May 1896.

The friendship between Johannes Brahms and Clara Schumann has always been the subject of much speculation.[1] Those published accounts that sensationalize the "passionate friendship" (the title of a popular book on the subject) neglect the deeper personal and artistic bonds between the pianist and the composer.[2] Theirs was a many-layered relationship—a friendship that began in 1853 between a mature performing artist and a beardless young composer, and endured for forty-three years. As with Robert Schumann, Clara Schumann was for Brahms both muse and musician: the inspiration for much of his music and the sharer of his genius.

Clara Schumann was a working woman and an artist, one of the first of her kind. She began studying piano at age five with her father, Friedrich Wieck. She played in the Leipzig Gewandhaus at nine, made her formal solo debut at eleven, and carried on a succcessful professional career as a concert pianist for over sixty years. Her compositions, including a piano concerto, trio, and lieder, were published and performed throughout the nineteenth century. She married Robert Schumann after a long legal battle with her father (who disapproved of her choice), had eight children in fourteen years, and composed, concertized, and taught throughout her marriage. Her husband was hospitalized in 1854 after a suicide attempt and died two and a half years later, in July 1856. Widowed and left alone with seven children, she supported her family and resumed her work as a teacher and touring virtuosa.

Her concert career almost spanned the century, from 1830 to 1891. At age eighteen, on her first tour to Vienna, she was hailed as the peer of such giants as Liszt, Thalberg, and Henselt, and was named Königliche-Kaiserliche Kammervirtuosin (Royal and Imperial Chamber Virtuosa) by the Emperor of Austria, Franz Ferdinand I.[3] She proceeded to tour throughout Europe and England—from Moscow to Munich, from Liverpool to Lucerne—and was dubbed Europe's "Queen of Pianists."

The circumstances of her early life were both fortunate and tragic: fortunate in that she was born in Leipzig in 1819, at a time when cultural and mercantile life was renewing itself in a city with a tradition of middle-class enterprise and a glorious musical and literary history. Fortunate also was a family history of musicality: her own talents were largely inherited from her gifted mother, Marianne Tromlitz Wieck, daughter and grand-daughter of working musicians, who had originally come to Leipzig to study piano with Friedrich Wieck.[4] Marianne, too, had musical training and a career. During the eight years she was married to Wieck, she performed professionally as a singer and a piano soloist, helped out in Wieck's business, taught piano, and gave birth to five children. Clara's father, a difficult person but an innovative and creative pedagogue, devised the extraordinary musical training that would transform his daughter into a child prodigy and later virtuosa. A successful piano teacher, he was also a merchant of pianos and related materials. In his shop, he sold music, music books, and periodicals; he established a lending library of books and music; and he rented and repaired pianos. Clara was born in an apartment over the shop and reared to the accompaniment of piano music.

Wieck saw to it that Clara had an education second to none—daily piano lessons with him; theory and harmony with the cantor of the St. Thomas Church; voice with Miksch; and composition, orchestration, counterpoint, and fugue with other prominent musicians. Beginning at the age of six, Clara attended orchestra concerts in the Leipzig Gewandhaus and, on her girlhood tours between 1830 and 1838, almost every ballet and opera performance on the boards in Leipzig, Dresden, Berlin, Hamburg, Paris, and Vienna. This was an unparalleled education and probably unique for a female.

The tragic circumstances that shaped the girl and later the woman were family conflicts followed by divorce, in which custody of the five-year-old girl and her two younger brothers was given (as was the law at the time) to her dominating, tyrannical father, who arranged her tours and concerts and collected, kept, and invested the fees she earned.[5] Her marriage to Robert was shadowed by conflicts with Wieck, the man who had been her sole teacher and to whom she believed she owed her artistry.

Robert Schumann, who grew up in Zwickau, lived in the Wieck home during the time he studied piano with Friedrich. He heard Clara play when she was eleven, and she soon became a major interpreter of his works. Clara came to feel a responsibility to introduce Robert's works in both major and minor cities throughout Europe, since he, unlike most composers of his time, did not perform in public on account of a problem with his right hand.[6] Indeed, she premiered almost all of his piano music. To be sure, her husband had ambivalent feelings about her career: He loved and hated it at the same time, as we might expect. But Robert had no regular source of income until he was forty, and the family found that there were occasions on which it was necessary to dip into Clara's earnings for necessities like rent.

After Robert's death in 1856, Clara maintained her children, and later grandchildren, through her earnings as a concert pianist. With the help of Brahms and other friends, she edited the complete works of her husband (*Robert Schumanns Werke*, published by Breitkopf & Härtel), and she was sought out by students from all over the world. She knew well many of the great nineteenth-century musicians, including Chopin, Mendelssohn, Liszt, Wagner, Joachim, and Pauline Viardot. Brahms was her closest musician friend from 1854 until her death at the age of seventy-six.

Johannes Brahms came into the lives of Robert and Clara Schumann when they had been married for thirteen years. In 1850 Robert was appointed Municipal Music Director in Düsseldorf—his first salaried musical appointment. Brahms, who had just completed his first tour as a pianist, was urged by Joseph Joachim, who knew the Schumanns well, to visit Robert before returning home. Even as Brahms was making his way to the Rhenish city, however, Schumann's position as conductor was precarious; his mental illness, which was to culminate in a suicide attempt some five months later, was progressing alarmingly.

The coming of the young pianist-composer was a most significant event in the life of both Schumanns. In a biography of her father, Eugenie Schumann gave a description of his first visit:

> One day—it was in the year 1853—the bell rang toward noon; I ran out, as children do, and opened the door. There I saw a very young man, handsome as a picture, with long blond hair. He asked for my father. My parents went out, I said. He ventured to ask when he could come again. Tomorrow, at eleven, I said, my parents always go out at twelve. The next day at eleven o'clock—we were in school—he came again. Father received him; he brought his compositions with him and father thought that as long as he was there, he could play the things for him then and there. The young man sat down at the piano. He had barely played a few measures when my father interrupted and ran out saying, "Please wait a moment, I must call my wife." The midday meal that followed was unforgettable. Both parents were

Figure 1. Brahms in Düsseldorf in the autumn of 1853, drawn by J. B. Laurens.

Figure 2. Clara Schumann in 1854 or 1855, after Robert Schumann's hospitalization.

in the most joyful excitement—again and again they began and could not speak of anything but the gifted young morning visitor, whose name was Johannes Brahms.[7]

The friendship that ensued between Frau Schumann and the "gifted morning visitor" has been the stuff of myths and movies, but it is important to remember that the meeting had an enormous impact on the lives of all three artists. Although Robert knew Brahms for only a few months before being confined to a mental institution, an immediate sympathy with the musical ideals of the younger man led him to proclaim Brahms a "young eagle," "a mighty Niagara," "a genius," and "the true Apostle."[8] He urged the famed Leipzig music publishers Breitkopf & Härtel to take up the young man's work, and he himself published an article about Brahms, his famous "Neue Bahnen" (New paths), in the Leipzig *Neue Zeitschrift für Musik*—an essay that was to have repercussions for both men. In the latter, Schumann hailed Brahms in ecstatic language as "destined to give ideal presentment to the highest expression of the time," an artist "who would bring us his mastership, not in process of development, but would spring forth, like Minerva fully armed, from the head of Jove. And he is come, a young blood by whose cradle graces and heroes kept watch." Thus Schumann placed a heavy responsibility on the shoulders of the younger man.[9]

The coming of Brahms gave Clara Schumann the opportunity to share once again the thinking and work of a creative genius. The importance of this particular element of their relationship cannot be overestimated. From her earliest years, Clara had participated in the elite circles of Leipzig musical life. At nine, she was her father's "right hand"—the performer for the musical circle that met at the Wieck home, a circle that included the leading music publishers, editors, composers, and musicians of the day. She was applauded by Paganini, Spohr, and Spontini; Chopin, Liszt, and Mendelssohn dedicated works to her; and Goethe rhapsodized about her playing. Robert joined the Wieck circle when Clara was eleven. Soon, he entrusted her with introducing his music first to cognoscenti in Leipzig, Dresden, Vienna, and Paris, and then to a wider public.

Just as she could understand and interpret Robert's genius before it was generally appreciated, so could she understand that of Brahms; her musical instincts and understanding encouraged and inspired the young man who was destined to become the leading instrumental composer of his age. Her friendship with Brahms followed a lifelong pattern of close and reciprocal ties with the creative figures of her time.

For Brahms, the encounter with Clara Schumann was to affect the course of his life. The young composer arrived in Düsseldorf with a knapsack full of manuscripts and an imagination stimulated by German Romantic writers and poets, but with a limited acquaintance with cultivated, educated women. Clara was not merely Robert's wife and mother of his children; she was a musical partner who had entered marriage as a world-famous figure and thereafter maintained her vocation. At thirty-four, she had given birth to six surviving children and had just become pregnant with a seventh. Yet she was still a slender young woman, and though not conventionally pretty, she had an unusual beauty and strength. Not surprisingly, the twenty-year-old Brahms fell in love with her. In June 1854, he wrote to Joachim:

> I believe that I do not have more concern and admiration for her than I love her and am under her spell. I often have to restrain myself forcibly from just quietly putting my arm around her and even—I don't know, it seems to me so natural that she could not misunderstand. I think I can no longer love an unmarried girl—at least I have quite forgotten about them. They but promise heaven while Clara shows it revealed to us.[10]

Brahms was attracted to a number of women during his lifetime but never married. There is no doubt that no other woman could live up to this early ideal.

A few months after Brahms's first visit to the Schumann home Robert, who had suffered for years from bipolar disorder, began to experience other problems—including troubles with his hearing and speaking—that affected his conducting. He was asked to leave his position as Music Director in Düsseldorf, and this plunged him into severe depression. He attempted suicide in February 1854. On March 4, 1854, he was confined to a mental hospital in Endenich-Bonn, where he remained until his death two and a half years later.

From his hospital bed, Schumann asked for a picture of Brahms so that he might view it daily along with pictures of his family. There were times when he seemed to be in good health: he composed, he wrote to Brahms to request his latest works, and he responded to Brahms's compositions with joy and delight. But then he would break down again. In addition to bipolar disorder, we now know that Schumann was probably experiencing the final (tertiary) stage of syphilis, which he had contracted several years before his marriage. Though he was not diagnosed with syphilis at the time, notes recorded in the journal of Dr. Franz Richarz, director of the Endenich hospital, provide an indication of what Schumann was suffering.[11]

The relationship between Brahms and Clara Schumann deepened after Robert's hospitalization. For comfort and moral support, Clara turned to a group of youthful musicians, including Joachim, Albert Dietrich, and Julius Otto Grimm, who were devoted to her husband and his music. Among them, Brahms was the youngest and by far the most gifted, and because he had no regular employment, he was also the most available. As soon as he heard of Schumann's suicide attempt, Brahms rushed back to Düsseldorf. Declaring that he was prepared to dedicate himself to the Schumanns, he virtually sacrificed himself to the family for the next two years. He lived nearby and had a few pupils. But he spent much of his time at the Schumann home, playing their pianos, using their library, and helping to care for the children when Clara was away on concert tours. He and friends played for Clara when she was depressed. In a letter to a close friend, Marie von Lindeman, Clara confided, "If I did not have the true friend, Brahms, I don't know how I could carry on."[12]

Upon his arrival in Düsseldorf, Brahms took over the keeping of Robert's household books, following the example set by the meticulous husband and father. Beginning with the entry for 8 March 1854, and continuing until December 30 of that year, he noted (as Robert had) the costs for everything that pertained to the Schumann family: postage stamps, servants' wages (including pay for the wet nurse hired after the birth of Felix in June), rent, and school tuition for Marie, Elise, and Julie, as well as all monies earned or received.[13] In keeping such intimate records, Brahms became a member of the family circle. With those entries, he stepped into the shoes of the husband, an awesome responsibility for a young man of twenty-one.

Clara Schumann was forbidden by doctors from visiting her husband in the mental hospital because they were certain she would suffer at seeing him in his state, and they believed that a visit might have bad effects on him as well. Brahms, however, along with other family members and friends, visited Schumann many times and reported to Clara on his condition. Brahms's letters to Clara about Robert at Endenich were detailed and among the most heartfelt she received. Although his health went up and down, Robert remained in Endenich and Clara continued to give concert tours. By July 1856, however, his doctors realized that Robert was in a very poor state, and they asked his wife to visit him in the closing days of his life. On July 27, Brahms accompanied Clara to Endenich. They were joined by Joachim on July 29, the day of Robert's death.

After 1856, Clara Schumann and Brahms spent little time together but corresponded regularly.[14] They lived in widely separated cities and were kept apart by Clara's dizzying schedule of concerts, teaching, editing, and family responsibilities. They saw each other several times a year for short periods, often meeting while one or the other was on a concert tour or during summer vacations.

There was always some fear on both of their parts that their friendship might be misinterpreted. After Robert's death, Clara wrote a letter to her children in which she explained what Brahms had meant to her during the years of her husband's suffering and illness:

> You hardly knew your dear father; you were still too young to feel deep sorrow and so you could not give me any comfort for what I was suffering. Then came Johannes Brahms. Your father loved and honored him as he did no other person but Joachim. He came as a true friend, to share all my suffering; he strengthened the heart that threatened to break; he uplifted my mind, brightened my spirits where he could. In short, he was my friend in the fullest sense of the word.[15]

In May 1856, Brahms asked Clara to safeguard their letters in some way so that they would not be read by others.[16] By 1886 he had achieved international renown, and he guarded his privacy even more carefully. (His concern for privacy extended to his creative workshop as well: he regularly culled works and destroyed all sketches and drafts. He left orders—which were disregarded—that all letters found in his home after his death be destroyed.) Fearing exposure and perhaps misunderstanding of his intimate feelings, he asked that each return their letters to the other and that the letters be destroyed, a suggestion to which Clara reluctantly agreed.[17] (Fortunately, she held on to her favorite letters from him, so a goodly number of his early letters to her were saved.) When Clara began burning her own letters, her daughter Marie prevailed upon her to stop; thus most of the correspondence was preserved. Brahms, with no one to stop him, proceeded with his part of the bargain and threw his letters into the Rhine. Some thirty years after his death, the surviving letters were published under Marie Schumann's supervision, so a record of their friendship remains.

It is from this record that we know the depth of their feelings and the extent of their musical and personal interaction. Even in the letters published with family authorization, the emotions of the young Brahms burn up the pages. In June 1855, for example, he wrote:

> Deeply beloved Frau Clara, now the longed-for Sunday, for which I was so fervently waiting, is finally drawing near. If only it brings you

with it! I am actually shivering with expectation. It is becoming harder and harder to get used to being separated from you.[18]

Or, in May 1856: "I would like to be able to write to you as tenderly as I love you."[19] About this same time, and after a brief debate over his daring, he began to write *du,* the intimate form in German, in his letters to her; she may already have been using that form, since he was the younger person. They continued to use *du* to each other until the end of their lives. He was, it might be noted, the only man outside her immediate family whom she addressed in this way. Even with other close friends like Joachim, Clara always used the formal *Sie.* The correspondence shows that soon after Robert's death, the ardor with which Brahms wrote cooled, but the friendship—which had its share of generosity, anger, love, quarrels, and reconciliations—continued.

Among the significant ties between them were their common childhood experiences of enduring family tensions and financial insecurity. Like Clara, Johannes was subjected to angry quarrels when he was growing up, though his father did not leave his wife and home until his children were adults. Clara could understand, as few others could, the extent of Brahms's suffering when his parents separated. The circumstances of Clara's childhood were somewhat more comfortable than those of Brahms, but she had had neither a formal education nor a normal childhood. As a girl, she had to work, and her family's need for her earnings continued throughout her marriage and widowhood. Her daughter Eugenie referred to this when she wrote: "The thought that everything I needed had to be earned by Mama with the work of her hands often troubled me when I was a mere child, and it was always awful for me when I needed new clothes."[20]

Brahms lived with economic insecurity for many years; he, too, was sent out to work at an early age and played the piano at Hamburg restaurants and private fêtes as soon as his musician father realized that his talents could be turned to financial profit. Clara and Johannes discussed money matters such as rents, investments, fees, and honoraria without embarrassment, as between family members.

There were other bonds between them. In the early years, she was mother, sister, friend, and musical colleague to him. She introduced him to influential friends and musicians, wrote to publishers on his behalf, premiered his compositions, and arranged concerts tours for him. In November 1855 she organized two concerts for Brahms and Joachim in Danzig, in which she herself participated—thus lending her prestige to the two younger musicians. Those concerts included works by Bach, Beethoven, Schumann, and the young Brahms.[21] From that time on, she almost always included a Brahms work along with works by Schumann on her programs. She helped Brahms find employment and advised him on financial and musical matters as well as personal problems. She comforted him in his disappointments and gloried in his triumphs.

As the years passed, the correspondence shows that these roles reversed: Clara turned increasingly to Brahms for help and counsel. Although she had a large family and many friends, she asked Johannes for advice about her children—especially her sons—and discussed her own health and personal problems without hesitation. She requested his opinion about professional commitments such as concerts, programs, students, and teaching jobs. Although she was listed as the official editor of the collected works of Robert Schumann, a project on which she labored from 1879 to 1893, she made few editorial decisions until she had heard from Brahms. Busy as he was, he never failed her, listening and advising patiently. She did not always follow his advice, but she never stopped asking for his opinions.

Much as she loved the music of her husband, one suspects that Clara admired the music of Brahms even more. She felt that each new work was a gift to her. Writing about his Violin Sonata in G Major, op. 78, which moved her deeply, she exclaimed: "Many others could perhaps understand it and speak about it better, but no one could feel it more than I do—the deepest, most tender sides of my soul vibrate to such music."[22] Moreover, Brahms often solicited Clara's opinions about his works, and her letters to him include great praise as well as suggestions that he read carefully but—as Clara did with respect to his suggestions to her—did not always follow. When, in August 1882, she received a manuscript copy of his Piano Trio in C Major, op. 87, she was unable to play it on a decent piano but read through enough of it to write an enthusiastic response before turning to some critical suggestions:

> What a Trio! That was indeed a real musical treat! . . . Once again, a glorious work! There is so much that delights me in it and I long to hear it performed properly. I love each movement; how glorious the development sections are, how wonderful the way in which each motive grows out of the one before it, how each figure grows from the others! How charming the Scherzo is, and then the Andante with its graceful theme. . . . I have to tell you a few small points that have occurred to me.[23]

In turn, Brahms knew Clara's compositions well and spoke of them with respect, though as far as we know, he performed very few of her works on his concert tours. Nonetheless, he declared many times that Clara was always present in his music. In an early letter he wrote: "I do see you often, as good as in person; e.g., at the trill in the final passages of the Andante of the C-Major Symphony [Robert Schumann's Second, op. 61], at the pedal points of great fugues, when you suddenly appear as St. Cecaelia!"[24]

Thirteen of Brahms's works were dedicated to Clara, including his Piano Sonata, op. 2, which he dedicated to her only two months after they met. His first folk song collection, *Volks-Kinderlieder*, WoO 31 (1858), was dedicated to Clara's children and his Four-Hand Piano Variations on a Theme by Robert Schumann, op. 23 (1863), was dedicated to Clara's third daughter, Julie.[25] Soon after the birth of her last child, Felix (born in June 1854, when Robert was already in the hospital), Brahms presented Clara with manuscripts of what was to become his op. 9—a work that honored both Schumanns. When completed, it was published as Brahms's Variations on a Theme by Robert Schumann for Pianoforte, Dedicated to Frau Clara Schumann.[26]

In short, Brahms confided to Clara his hopes, dreams, fears, doubts, and—above all—his compositions. He valued her professionalism, experience, and musical sensibilities, and he respected her work as both performer and composer. In each of his letters, he described concerts he had attended or in which he had performed, and the two exchanged frank opinions on music and musicians. Almost everything he composed was sent first to Clara for comments, criticism, and reassurance. In December 1858, for example, he wrote regarding several manuscripts he had sent:

> Don't show these things to anyone, because there are some bad spots in the instrumentation [of his op. 13] that should not be seen by any eye but yours. You can be really critical; tell me especially what seems ugly, dull, etc. to you.[27]

This was written early in his career. But even at the height of his fame, Brahms had great self-doubts. In 1888, he explained that he had sent his new violin sonata (op. 108) first to Elisabeth von Herzogenberg, who had liked it very much indeed. Only then did he send it to Clara:

> Forgive me for not sending you the sonata first. But you won't believe my main reason!? I never consider a new piece capable of appealing to someone. So also this time, and I am also still very doubtful that you will sign Frau Herzogenberg's letter! But if you do *not* like the sonata when you play it through, don't bother trying it with Joachim, but send it back to me.[28]

Clara's generally ecstatic responses were often followed by the frank criticism and suggestions that Johannes requested. Despite all her other obligations, the opportunity to comment on the music of the younger composer was a task she accepted gratefully. She never failed to study the manuscripts and respond, knowing well he might not heed her suggestions but depended on her interest and involvement. She knew that other friends were also recipients of his manuscripts: Brahms sent his works to a trusted circle that included Joachim, Hermann Levi, the Herzogenbergs, and Dr. Theodor Billroth. But this circle changed over the years. Sooner or later, each of its members was alienated because of Brahms's famous lack of diplomacy, prickly sensitivity, or uncouth tactlessness. Only Clara Schumann remained a constant.

Although Brahms always solicited her comments on his new compositions, he was conscious of all her family problems and was grateful for her responses. She had already suffered through the death of her husband, the mental illness and incarceration of her son Ludwig, and the illnesses and deaths of three of her children who had died as adults.[29] One of the possible causes of Brahms's rudeness and gruffness (of which all of his friends and Clara often complained) was that he was—and yet was not—a member of her family. He longed to be taken into the Schumann family as a brother, husband, or son. Yet he was none of these. He expressed this succinctly in 1896, when he wrote the following in a letter meant to comfort Clara after hearing of the illness of her son-in-law, Louis Sommerhoff:

> It is the greatest good fortune to have a family and to live in a close relationship with people who are not only related by the bond of blood but who are also dear to us and beloved. You have enjoyed this beautiful happiness in full measure throughout a long life, yet I know you have paid for it dearly with much anxiety and pain. . . . But yet you would not want to exchange places with a lonely person who can no longer experience these things. . . . I hope to receive a card from you soon to relieve my anxiety.[30]

All in all, we learn a great deal about the friendship between Clara Schumann and Johannes Brahms from their correspondence. The published letters add up to more than a thousand pages, and many are still turning up. In addition, Brahms is mentioned in hundreds of letters that Clara wrote to family and friends, and he figures prominently in her diary as well. There were times when she expressed anger at his thoughtlessness and tactlessness, which affected so profoundly his relationships with others, including his lifelong friend Joachim. Indeed, a break between

Johannes and Clara seemed inevitable at one point in 1891, on account of a misunderstanding that began with an argument over publication of an early version of Robert's Fourth Symphony. It was resolved with these words, which Brahms wrote to Clara on her seventy-third birthday:

> Permit a poor outsider to tell you today that he thinks of you with the same reverence he always did and from the bottom of his heart wishes you—the dearest of all persons to him—a long life, everything good, and much love. Alas, I am more of an outsider to you than to anyone else. . . . But today I must repeat to you once again that you and your husband gave me the most beautiful experience of my life and represent its greatest treasures and its noblest moments.[31]

When news of Clara's death after a series of strokes reached Brahms shortly after his sixty-third birthday, he was struck with pain and anxiety. He rushed to the cemetery in Bonn where he attended her interment beside her husband—at the same grave where Brahms had also been among Robert's chief mourners. Soon after the funeral, he told the friends he was staying with, "Today I have buried the only person I truly loved."[32] Clara Schumann's death came on May 20, 1896. Brahms followed her eleven months later.

NOTES

1. Epigraph quoted in Gustav Ophüls, *Erinnerungen an Johannes Brahms* (Berlin, 1921; repr. Ebenhausen bei München, 1983), 16. Unless otherwise noted, all translations in this essay are my own.

2. Marguerite and Jean Alley, *A Passionate Friendship: Clara Schumann and Brahms*, trans. Mervyn Savill (London, 1956).

3. See Berthold Litzmann, *Clara Schumann: Ein Künstlerleben nach Tagebüchern und Briefen* (Leipzig, 1902–8), 1:190–91. In the sixth volume of the unpublished *Tagebuch*, located in the Robert-Schumann-Haus, Zwickau, one reads:

15 March 1838

To the piano virtuoso Clara Wieck, by the grace of God,

In consideration of her outstanding artistic skill and as a public gesture of the highest satisfaction with her artistic accomplishments, His Majesty the Emperor has decided with the highest cabinet approval on the thirteenth of this month to bestow the title of K. K. Kammer-Virtuosin upon her, a decision that this present decree confirms to his satisfaction.

4. Unless otherwise noted, all biographical information provided here is adapted from Nancy B. Reich, *Clara Schumann: The Artist and the Woman*, rev. ed. (Ithaca, N.Y., 2001).

5. Friedrich Wieck recorded Clara's entries in her diaries until she was able to write, and he retained control of them. As a result, Clara never wrote about her friends or her emotions until she broke with her father when she was eighteen and moved to Paris on her own.

6. See the discussion in John Daverio, *Robert Schumann: Herald of a "New Poetic Age"* (Oxford and New York, 1997), 77–79.

7. Eugenie Schumann, *Ein Lebensbild meines Vaters* (Leipzig, 1931), 357.

8. Joseph Joachim, *Briefe von und an Joseph Joachim,* ed. Johannes Joachim and Andreas Moser (Berlin, 1911–13), 1:84.

9. Robert Schumann,"Neue Bahnen," *Neue Zeitschrift für Musik* 39 (28 October 1853), trans. in Florence May, *The Life of Brahms,* 2nd ed. (London, 1948), 1:131–32.

10. Quoted in Artur Holde, "Suppressed Passages in the Brahms-Joachim Correspondence," *Musical Quarterly* 45 (1959): 314.

11. The journal was kept by the Richarz family descendants. Excerpts were first published in Marita Gleiss and Hannelore Erlekamm, eds., *Robert Schumanns letzte Lebensjahre: Protokoll einer Krankheit* (Berlin, 1994). A commentary and English translation by Judith Cherniak appeared in the *Times Literary Supplement,* 31 August 2001. The complete journal and related information appears in Bernhard R. Appel, *Robert Schumann in Endenich (1854–1856): Krankenakten, Briefzeugnisse und zeitgenössische Berichte* (Mainz and New York, 2006).

12. Renate Brunner, *Alltag und Künstlertum: Clara Schumann und ihre Dresdner Freundinnen Marie von Lindeman und Emilie Steffens* (Sinzig, 2005), 225.

13. For Brahms's entries, see Robert Schumann, *Haushaltbücher,* ed. Gerd Nauhaus (Leipzig, 1982), 2:649–55 and 683–84.

14. See Berthold Litzmann, ed., *Clara Schumann–Johannes Brahms: Briefe aus den Jahren 1853–1896* (Leipzig, 1927). Litzmann died before the letters were published; his work was completed and published by Marie Schumann, who had collaborated with Litzmann on the project. An English translation of most of the letters is available in Litzmann, ed., *Letters of Clara Schumann and Johannes Brahms, 1853–1896* (London, 1927). For translations and commentary on a number of the letters, see Styra Avins, ed., *Johannes Brahms: Life and Letters,* trans. Styra Avins and Josef Eisinger (Oxford and New York, 1997).

15. Litzmann, *Clara Schumann: Ein Künstlerleben,* 2:336–37.

16. Litzmann, *Clara Schumann–Johannes Brahms,* 1:187.

17. Ibid., 2:300–301, 315–16.

18. Ibid., 1:118.

19. Ibid., 1:188.

20. Eugenie Schumann, *Erinnerungen* (Stuttgart, 1925), 75.

21. May, *The Life of Brahms,* 1:194–95.

22. Litzmann, *Clara Schumann–Johannes Brahms,* 2:179.

23. Ibid., 2:258–59.

24. Avins, *Johannes Brahms,* 76.

25. Margit L. McCorkle, *Johannes Brahms: Thematisch-bibliographisches Werkverzeichnis* (Munich, 1984), 809.

26. *Variationen über ein Thema von Robert Schumann für Pianoforte, Frau Clara Schumann zugeeignet.*

27. Litzmann, *Clara Schumann–Johannes Brahms,* 1:230.

28. Ibid., 2:363, trans. in Avins, *Johannes Brahms,* 662.

29. Julie Schumann, Contessa Radicati di Marmorito, died of tuberculosis in 1872. Ferdinand, who had served in the army during the Franco-Prussian War, died in 1891 from morphine treatments given for an illness incurred during his service. Felix, born after his father was confined to Endenich, died of tuberculosis in 1879.

30. Litzmann, *Clara Schumann–Johannes Brahms,* 2:612–13.

31. Ibid., 2:476–77.

32. Cited in Ophüls, *Erinnerungen,* 16.

The Pianos of Johannes Brahms

GEORGE S. BOZARTH AND STEPHEN H. BRADY

The pianos Johannes Brahms encountered in Hamburg during his youth would have been essentially the same as the early Romantic fortepianos of Beethoven and Schubert. By the time Brahms wrote his final compositions half a century later, the piano had evolved to a state of construction—if not hammer design and voicing—virtually identical with the modern instrument. The two grand pianos commonly associated with Brahms—the Conrad Graf piano (no. 2616) presented by its Viennese builder to Clara Schumann in 1839 as a "reverential souvenir" and passed on to Brahms in 1856,[1] and an 1868 instrument by Johann Baptist Streicher lent to Brahms in 1872 for use in his apartment in Vienna and kept by him for the rest of his life—were both conservative for their times. In light of the advances in piano technology made internationally during the 1850s and '60s, Brahms's Streicher might be considered an anachronism and, by extension, the piano ideals of its owner old-fashioned. Yet Brahms's correspondence, concert programs, and other documents reveal a pianist performing on a wide variety of instruments, many demonstrating the latest advances in piano building.

Early in his career Brahms was at the mercy of the pianos provided to him by the venues in which he performed. Later in life he was in a position to request the type of instrument he required, and most often his wish was granted. But even then, the region in which he was appearing affected the type of piano he played. When in Vienna he performed mainly on instruments with "Viennese" actions by the foremost local makers, J. B. Streicher and Bösendorfer, and in Germany he asked for pianos by Bechstein (Berlin) and Steinway (New York and Hamburg), descendants from the English/French tradition of piano design.

These two different technologies had existed since the 1770s. Pianos with "Viennese" actions were characterized by lightness of touch, bright tone quality, rapid repetition, and swift, efficient damping. This type of action was developed by Johann Andreas Stein in Augsburg and adopted by Anton Walter, Nannette Streicher (Stein's daughter), Conrad Graf, and other builders in Vienna, and was still employed by Viennese makers during Brahms's time. In contrast, John Broadwood and his colleagues in England had perfected a piano with a different action and design that yielded a more powerful, sonorous, and resonant tone, but demanded a heavier touch and had a less reliable repetition. Sébastien Erard adopted the "English" model for his pianos, but, with his "double-escapement" action patented in 1808 and improved in 1821, he gave his instruments increased rapidity in repetition.[2] The actions in Bechstein and Steinway pianos evolved from Erard's invention.

The type of piano Brahms grew up playing at home is unknown. His child-hood friend Louise Japha recalled an instrument of poor quality—not surprising, given the family's modest means—and remembered the young musician frequenting the establishment of the Hamburg piano builders Baumgardten & Heins to practice on their instruments.[3] From Hamburg in October 1854 Brahms wrote to Clara Schumann that Baumgardten & Heins's square piano delighted him with its glorious sound: "I don't believe I've ever found such a songful tone."[4] One can confirm Brahms's obser-vation from the piano of this type on exhibit in the Brahms *Gedenkstätte* in Hamburg. The instrument is fitted with heavy brass string-termination bars similar to the *capo tasto* bars found on most modern grand pianos, which provide a rigid termination for the speaking length of the string and reflect the maximum amount of vibrational energy back into the string, thereby prolonging the duration of the sound and producing a "songful tone."

On March 24, 1859, Brahms gave the Hamburg premiere of his First Piano Concerto on a Baumgardten & Heins grand piano.[5] In April of the following year he again performed this work on one of their instruments, as part of a concert in Hamburg conducted by G. D. Otten.[6] At that time, Brahms offered advice to Joseph Joachim on the purchase of a Baumgardten & Heins square piano for a family in Hanover, noting that "the high price [of 340 Thaler] should not shock you; the instruments are really much nicer and more durable than others."[7]

During the 1850s and '60s, Brahms came into contact with grand pianos built in Paris by Erard, instruments that, with their double-escapement "repetition" action and beautiful tone, were preferred by most European concert artists, including Mendelssohn and Liszt, from the 1820s until mid-century.[8] Erard pianos were distinctive for their range of tonal shadings or colors, which changed with dynamic level as well as with register, and for the unusual clarity of their tone, particularly in rapid passages.[9]

In 1858 Brahms declined to premiere his First Piano Concerto in Hamburg because the only "decent" piano in the city, an Erard grand, could not be secured for the performance.[10] In 1865 he reported to Clara Schumann that he had played on "a beautiful Erard" in a concert in Zurich.[11] Brahms may have come to know the Erard piano at the home of Frau Schumann. According to the English pianist and Brahms biographer Florence May, in the spring of 1856, at the end of Frau Schumann's London concert series, Erard had given her a grand piano that continued to be her favorite for private use until 1867, when she was presented with an instrument by John Broadwood & Sons. May recalled that when Brahms visited Clara Schumann in Baden-Baden in the 1870s, he played duets with her on her Broadwood, although it was on her Erard that he performed his as-yet-unpublished third and fourth books of Hungarian Dances, "his eyes flashing fire the while."[12]

Between 1865 and 1874 Brahms performed in public on Erard pianos at least five times, playing his First Piano Concerto in Zurich, the *Paganini* Variations, op. 35, in Zurich and Winterthur, his Piano Quartets, opp. 25 and 26, in Basel and Zurich, and the Schumann Piano Concerto, op. 54, in Bremen.[13] The sound of Brahms's music performed on a restored 1866 English Erard (from the Finchcocks Collection, Goudhurst, Kent) may be heard on a recording by the English pianist Richard Burnett, assisted by Alan Hacker using a pair of Albert clarinets from the late nineteenth century and Jennifer Ward Clarke playing a "modernized" 1729 cello by Joseph Guarnerius of Cremona, fitted out mainly with gut strings.[14] Although the repertoire—the Clarinet Trio, op. 114, and the two Clarinet Sonatas, op. 120—dates from thirty years after the height of Brahms's involvement with Erards and might better have been played on an early 1890s Bösendorfer, Bechstein, or Steinway (as we shall see below), this experiment in the use of period instruments is nonetheless instructive. To begin with, the sound of the Erard is considerably less massive than that of a modern piano, with the result that dynamic balance between the piano and the other instruments is never a problem, the piano never overbearing. It must be said that at moderate and softer dynamics the middle and bass registers of this particular piano are a bit lacking in focus, yielding a somewhat "old upright" sound not desired by the piano's original builders (see the middle section of the second movement of op. 120, no. 2; an 1869 London Erard owned by one of the authors has no such deficiency). But at higher dynamic levels, and in the upper register at all dynamics, the color brightens and clears and the decay of the sound becomes quicker, so that fast passages can be played with an agility and clarity of articulation suggestive of Haydn and Mozart on period instruments. After hearing the demonic performance Burnett and Hacker give the opening Allegro appassionato of op. 120, no. 1, with the clarinet and piano perfectly matching each other's every gesture, and their highly articulated rendition of the finale of the same work, it is easy to understand why Brahms would have favored Frau Schumann's Erard to show off the colorful piano writing of his Hungarian Dances.[15]

The piano traditionally associated with Brahms's early years is the 1839 Graf that Clara Schumann gave him, probably not long after she had acquired her Erard and very likely before she moved from Düsseldorf to Berlin late in 1857. As noted earlier, the instrument had been a present from Conrad Graf to Clara Schumann. The piano stood in Robert Schumann's workroom and may well have been the instrument on which the twenty-year-old Brahms introduced his early compositions to the Schumanns in the autumn of 1853. To Robert, Brahms's sonatas were like "veiled symphonies," his playing "full of genius, transforming the piano into an orchestra of lamenting and jubilant voices."[16] A feature of Graf pianos, as well as many other earlier parallel-strung instruments, is variation in tone color according to register. Brahms capitalized on this quality in his early works (see, for instance, the beginning of the finale in the F-Minor Piano Sonata, op. 5) and apparently made the most of these orchestral effects in performance.

Yet, in comparison with Erards of the 1850s, the Schumann Graf was quite old-fashioned, and it is likely that Brahms viewed it as such. The range of the piano—six octaves and a fifth, from C_3 to g^4, is sufficient for nearly all of Brahms's solo piano music of the 1850s and '60s, and the three piano sonatas of 1852–53 would have excitingly explored this piano's very extreme registers (see, for instance, the opening theme of the F-Minor Sonata, op. 5, which employs both C_3 and f^4 at its climax).[17] Yet other early Brahms works demand the seven-octave keyboard (A_4–a^4) already typical of this time. In the First Piano Concerto, op. 15, and the *Paganini* Variations, op. 35, the highest notes are a^4, and the B-Major Piano Trio, op. 8 (1854 version), and several of the early songs descend to B_4. Moreover, the technology of the Graf, with its single-escapement "Viennese" action, all-wooden construction, and leather-covered hammers, is, except for a general increase in size and weight, virtually identical with that of Beethoven's famous Graf.[18]

Lacking permanent lodgings, Brahms entrusted the Schumann Graf to the care of his parents in Hamburg.[19] When he took rooms with Frau Dr. Elisabeth Rösing in Hamm, a suburb of Hamburg, in 1861–62, he apparently moved the Graf to her home, where he left it after taking up

Figure 1. Brahms at a Bösendorfer grand piano, 1860s.

residence in Vienna in the autumn of 1862. In February 1868 he wrote from Hamburg to Clara Schumann that Frau Rösing had been storing "Robert's grand piano" for a long time, but in a few months she would be moving to Hanover:

> I cannot, of course, leave it here; space is money. Yet you also have no room in Baden for such a dear but bulky memento. Yes, selling it here is also nearly impossible, as Heins informs me, and one would hardly want to think about [doing] that. If I lived here, I would not think of giving it away, but now I must come to a decision—and you?[20]

While residing with Frau Rösing, Brahms would have made use of the Graf for composing the *Handel* Variations, op. 24, the two Piano Quartets, opp. 25 and 26, and the F-Minor Piano Quintet, op. 34, as well as part of the First Cello Sonata, op. 38, and several of the *Magelone* Romances, op. 33. But as this letter suggests, its value to him was, by this time, mainly sentimental.

The immediate solution to the problem of where to keep the Graf seems to have been to store it with Baumgardten & Heins in Hamburg.[21] In 1871 Brahms's father took a new flat on the Anscharplatz in Hamburg, where he lived until his death the following year and where his widow, Brahms's stepmother, resided until 1883. At some point the Graf was moved into this apartment.

In February 1873 Brahms wrote to his stepmother that he would soon be sending for the piano, for it was to be displayed at the Vienna World Exhibition, together with the pianos of Mozart, Beethoven, and others, and in October he informed her that the instrument had arrived and was on display.[22] When the Exhibition concluded, Brahms gave the Graf to the Gesellschaft der Musikfreunde, where it took its proper place among the historic instruments in that society's collection.

The Schumann Graf is now on loan to the Musikinstrumentensammlung of the Kunsthistorisches Museum in Vienna.[23] Unfortunately, it can no longer be tuned, for the pinblock has cracked and the case is structurally unsound. In a recording of works by Clara and Robert Schumann performed on the instrument by Jörg Demus in the mid-1960s, one already hears an instrument in severe distress.[24] The sound is clangorous, filled with "false beats"—probably produced by irregularities in the worn-out strings—and poorly damped.[25] (The echo caused by the room or added by the recording engineers does not help matters.) A fairer idea of how the Schumanns' Graf sounded when new, and possibly still did when it was given to Brahms, can be gained from recordings by Demus on his own

1839 Graf, this one in excellent working order.[26] Here the sound is well focused, resonant but transparent, and ranges from delicate and harplike to robust. Differences in tonal color from one register to another are clearly in evidence and are put to particularly good use in "orchestral" works like Beethoven's *Diabelli* Variations. With leather-covered hammers and dampers, the attack is clean, the damping efficient. This instrument is truly a joy to hear, and one can easily imagine how exciting Brahms's earliest works would have sounded on it at the Schumanns' home in 1853.

After Brahms moved to Vienna in the early 1860s, he became intimately familiar with other Viennese action pianos, and in all of his public concerts there he performed on instruments by one or the other of the city's two preeminent piano builders, Johann Baptist Streicher and Ludwig Bösendorfer. The piano that Brahms chose for his apartment in 1872 was an instrument built four years earlier by Streicher, who was the descendant of an illustrious family of piano makers. At the turn of the century, Streicher's mother, Nannette, had built pianos on her own and in partnership with her husband, Johann Andreas Streicher, that were highly regarded by Beethoven. The pianos of Streicher's grandfather, Johann Andreas Stein of Augsburg, were praised by Mozart in 1777.[27] Among Viennese piano builders, a generally conservative lot, Johann Baptist was one of the most innovative. In 1831 he had patented a piano action that was neither "Viennese" nor "English," but of his own design and sharing features of both types.[28] In the 1860s Streicher experimented with the latest advances coming from America, and at the Paris Exhibition of 1867 he won a gold medal for an overstrung piano with a one-piece cast-iron frame modeled on a Steinway that had been exhibited in London five years earlier.[29] He also built pianos with "English" actions. In 1870 Clara Schumann performed a concert in Vienna on an 1868 Streicher with an "English" mechanism.[30] Meanwhile, Streicher continued to build instruments with "Viennese" actions that refined rather than revolted against tradition.

The earliest of the two-dozen documented instances of Brahms's performing in public on a Streicher dates from April 12, 1863, seven months after he first came to Vienna. The occasion was a Streicher *Soirée musicale*, held in a recital hall maintained by the firm to display its instruments. At the time, Streicher's major rival was Ludwig Bösendorfer, and concert programs and other documents from Brahms's first season in Vienna show him performing at least twice on Bösendorfer pianos—a chamber recital with the Hellmesberger Quartet on November 16, 1862 (the G-Minor Piano Quartet, op. 25), and his first solo recital on November 29 (including the

Handel Variations, op. 24, and the A-Major Piano Quartet, op. 26).[31] By October 1864, however, if not sooner, Brahms seems to have gravitated toward Streicher instruments. At the end of that month he wrote to Clara Schumann: "I have a beautiful grand piano from Streicher. With it he wants to demonstrate his latest achievements to me, and I believe that if he made a similar one for you, you would be pleased with it."[32] A letter from Frau Schumann to Brahms three years later suggests that the Streichers were courting her favor as well: "Frau Streicher wrote to me again. . . . Are the new instruments really so beautiful? She writes to me about them in such enraptured terms."[33]

During the years 1864–75, Brahms played Streicher pianos almost exclusively when in Vienna, and he recommended them to others coming to play there.[34] In October 1869, in anticipation of taking rooms in Vienna for the winter, Brahms wrote to Emil Streicher to inquire about having "one of your beautiful grand pianos" at his disposal, hoping that Streicher would "be inclined not to cure me of this agreeable habit," and in 1872 Streicher lent Brahms a grand piano, serial number 6713, for use in his new apartment at Karlsgasse 4.[35] This instrument remained with the composer until his death in 1897. Brahms's friends hoped to keep his apartment unaltered as a memorial, but in 1906 the building was torn down. Brahms's furnishings, most of which had belonged to his landlady, were first kept by the Gesellschaft der Musikfreunde but eventually went to the Historisches Museum der Stadt Wien. During the Second World War most of the furniture was destroyed and Brahms's Streicher was severely damaged. All that now remain are one leg and the music desk.[36]

Judging from photographs of Brahms's living room, his Streicher was a smaller piano, measuring in length approximately 6 feet 9 inches. Another 1868 Streicher, serial number 6668, a full-sized grand (7 ft. 9 in.) but otherwise quite similar in appearance to Brahms's instrument and typical of the pianos Streicher built in the late 1860s, is now part of the Frederick Collection in Ashburnham, Massachusetts.[37] Writing about this piano, Gregory Hayes has noted:

> With leather-covered hammers, Viennese single-escapement action, and parallel stringing, it presents a velvety but astonishingly clear and variegated sound. At low dynamic, it is as mellow as a modern instrument, but without the aural fog; at higher levels a chiff in the attack of each note allows for the possibility of *sforzando* without *fortissimo*. The aural gratification . . . is complemented on the technical side as well; simply put, it is easy to play. . . . Its action is lighter, faster, and a good deal shallower than that of a modern instrument. Lesser

Figure 2. The living room of Brahms's apartment at Karlsgasse 4, with his 1868 J. B. Streicher grand piano.

physical gestures—a snap of the wrist instead of an application of arm weight, for instance—beget more subtle musical gestures. Especially in mid-range (C to c¹) at low volume, the piano's own timbral characteristics reduce matters of voicing to a nuance rather than a preoccupation.[38]

Lynn Edwards and Edmund Michael Frederick provide further details:

This 1868 piano, while a modernized version of [Streicher's] earlier pianos, still has a wooden frame and parallel stringing. Its sound-board is larger, and the treble scaling is longer, than in earlier pianos, and it is fitted with two iron bars and a *capo tasto*. . . . This late instrument retains other features of the Viennese piano as well, including leather-capped hammers and Viennese action. Its range of AAA–a⁴ (seven octaves) and its length of 7' 11" [*sic*] are both typical for late nineteenth-century Viennese pianos.

Like early Viennese [parallel-strung] pianos, the 1868 Streicher has a relatively transparent tone which begins with a distinct articulation from the rather soft-surfaced hammers hitting the strings. The tone is more sustained and mellow than that of Viennese pianos of forty years earlier, the more lush, full sound having been gained, however, at the sacrifice of some clarity, delicacy, and lightness of touch. There is a distinct contrast in tone color between soft and loud which makes it relatively easy to separate a melody from its accompaniment, a capability which makes the Streicher particularly well suited to Brahms's combination of melody and polyphony. . . . The sound is generally sweet and gentle. It is not loud, but can sound thunderous in its fortissimo because it can so readily be played softly.[39]

Seth Carlin, who performed the *Handel* Variations, op. 24, and a group of short Brahms pieces on this instrument in a concert for the Westfield Center for Early Keyboard Studies in 1985, has described its tone as having "a grainy, woody quality—somehow more human or organic" than the modern piano. The treble he termed "angelic, sweet, bell-like," so that, for example, the "music-box" variation in op. 24 (variation 22) has a "celestial" quality not heard on modern instruments. Indeed, this Streicher, like other early pianos, has "a whole palette of timbres" that can be exploited in order to render most effectively the "orchestral" aspects of Brahms's piano writing.[40] This instrument can be heard on a recording of Michael Boriskin playing excerpts from the *Handel* Variations, released as an insert to the summer 1985 issue of *The Piano Quarterly*.

An 1871 J. B. Streicher grand piano (7' 9", no. 7119) from the Frederick Collection, played with great sensitivity and panache by Ira Braus (Centaur, CRC 2850), initially gives the impression of an instrument whose sound is so colorful as to be considered clangorous, and whose strings might be past their prime (part of this impression is created by too great room resonance). Yet the piano is newly strung, with stainless steel wire as near as possible in tensile strength to the original strings. The ears adjust rapidly, though, as Braus's performances of Brahms's final four collections of piano pieces, opp. 116–119, reveal the instrument's "orchestral" nature, with its rich tone colors varying greatly by both register and dynamic level. With an initial sound decay more rapid than a modern piano that subsides into an aural haze (a process called "stepped decay" by Braus), this Streicher adds a misty magic to such pieces as the E-Major Intermezzo, op. 116, no. 4, and the B-Minor Intermezzo, op. 119, no. 1. Braus exploits the instrument's full potential in his profound interpretation of the E-flat Minor Intermezzo that closes op. 118, from a celestial treble, through a rich midrange, down to a dusky, weighted lower register that enshrouds Brahms's "good basses" in a brooding timbre ideal for this and other of his "late" character pieces. Brahms's own playing was said to be passionate, but without "a trace of sensuality."[41] Braus captures this balance perfectly.[42]

The marked differences between mid- to late nineteenth-century Viennese grand pianos and their modern counterparts is further made clear in the side-by-side recordings of Brahms's two-piano arrangement of the Fourth Symphony, op. 98, by Hans-Peter and Volker Stenzel.[43] No matter how well articulated, sensitively shaded, dynamically graded, or texturally conceived they are, readings on instruments grounded in a sound ideal of homogeneity, like the two modern Fazioli pianos on this recording, seem monochromatic, and we are constantly reminded of all that Brahms's skilled use of his orchestral palette contributes. But perform his finely wrought arrangements on pianos of the late nineteenth century, like the ca. 1850 Bachmann and the 1872 J. B. Streicher paired here, and one begins to hear the close relationship between Brahms the pianist and Brahms the symphonist.

To the credit of the Stenzel brothers, their two performances are as different as the instruments on which they play. Whereas the Fazioli performance at times aspires to the fullness of the orchestral original (as in the coda to the first movement and in the climactic tuttis of the finale), during quieter moments and especially when textural layering is taking place (as in the opening of the slow movement) one keenly misses the colorings of the orchestral instruments. But distinct registral differences on the period instruments supply at least part of what is lost on the modern piano, and richer overtones and washes of pedaling fill in much of the rest, making possible sounds ranging from proto-impressionistic haze—ideal for creating Tovey's "hushed mystery" at letter H in the Allegro non troppo—to brassy clangor, with dark, rich basses, a variety of distinctive midrange tone colors, and an upper register variously flute-like and languid or percussively woody. The chief strength of the Fazioli pianos is a consistently well-rounded tone. The Stenzel brothers are fully attuned to the merits of their two different sets of instruments and offer convincing performances in both mediums.[44]

It is clear from Brahms's correspondence that he considered there to be important differences between Viennese and English action pianos and between various sizes of Viennese instruments. In April 1873 he wrote to his friend Adolf Schubring: "Today . . . I went to Streicher and tried all their grand pianos. I consider Streicher to be good and reliable. . . . You are accustomed to another [type of] piano, and the German [i.e. "Viennese"] action will seem strange to you. I like them very much in a room, and yet

I still cannot get used to the local grand pianos in the concert hall."[45] Brahms apparently admired the smaller Streicher grands, like the one in his apartment, and in general considered Streicher's instruments dependable, but he was not fond of the large, concert-size Viennese grands, including both Streichers and Bösendorfers. The Kunsthistorisches Museum houses two concert grands, by Bösendorfer (1877) and Streicher (1868; the one Clara Schumann used in 1870), that employ a modified "English" action. Both companies experimented with such actions—enhanced with a device for improving repetition—on some of their concert instruments, while in their smaller grands, under eight feet, they continued to use "Viennese" actions. The concert pianos may have necessitated this change, for it was characteristic of "Viennese" actions to become unwieldy as the hammers became larger. More than likely, it was to these concert grands with bulky "Viennese" actions that Brahms objected. Such an interpretation of his remarks is consistent with his predilection for Clara Schumann's Erard, with its double-escapement English-type action, and also with his subsequent admiration for Bechstein and Steinway concert grands, both of which employed repetition actions deriving from those built by Erard.

After the mid-1870s, Brahms played most of his concerts in Vienna on Bösendorfers. The last time he performed on a Streicher in public, according to available documents, was at a quartet evening on November 18, 1880, presented by Joseph Hellmesberger, during which Brahms and Hellmesberger's ensemble played the C-Minor Piano Quartet, op. 60. This shift in loyalty may have had as much to do with the decline of the Streicher firm as with any other factor. After Johann Baptist Streicher died in 1871, his son Emil continued the business as his illustrious forebears had, producing approximately 150 well-crafted instruments each year in a small shop. Although this strategy had worked well enough to earn the Streicher firm a formidable reputation during the first half of the century and to retain that standing well into the latter half, it proved not to be the best way to compete on the international scene against highly industrialized firms like Broadwood, Pleyel, Steinway, and Chickering, which were producing ten to fifteen times that number of pianos annually.[46] Nor could Streicher compete locally with Bösendorfer, which, in response to increasing demand, had moved to a factory in the Wiener Neustadt in 1860 and had, by 1870, already found that facility too small.[47] Although some pianists, like the Austrian composer Karl Prohaska, continued to play Streicher pianos in their Viennese recitals, Bösendorfer and other makers came to the fore. Finally, in 1896, Emil Streicher had to liquidate his firm.[48]

On the Italian Piano Quartet's recording of Brahms's three piano quartets (opp. 25, 26, and 60), where they use an 1880 Bösendorfer grand, one can enjoy the clarity that a parallel-strung instrument brings to Brahms's writing in low registers, as well as the beautiful effect that can be achieved by performing late-Romantic chamber music with restrained vibrato and detailed articulation.[49] Such moments as the muted beginning of op. 60 are magical. The quicker decay of the Bösendorfer's tone automatically creates nicely tapered slurs and phrase endings when pianists allow them to happen. Yet this particular Bösendorfer is not very colorful. The timbre of the ca. 1854 Bösendorfer that Steven Lubin plays on his recording of the Horn Trio, op. 40, stands in marked contrast.[50] The clear, at times almost brittle treble of Lubin's colorful instrument complements the tone of Stephanie Chase's 1742 Petrus Guarnerius violin, and its rather "covered," dusky bass register joins Lowell Greer's haunting natural horn in projecting moods of romantic gloom. Nowhere are these colors employed to better effect than in the trio's central Adagio mesto.

On several occasions in the late 1870s and '80s, Brahms performed private concerts for small groups of friends on pianos manufactured by Friedrich Ehrbar. In each case the musical gatherings were held in the Ehrbar salon and designed as trial piano four-hand performances of large-scale orchestral works: the Second Symphony in 1877, the Second Piano Concerto in 1881, the Third Symphony in 1883, and the Fourth Symphony in 1885.[51] At the time, Ehrbar's pianos were slightly more progressive in design and technology than those of Streicher and Bösendorfer. The 1874 production model housed in the Kunsthistorisches Museum has a Viennese action and a composite iron framework similar to those found in Streicher and Bösendorfer pianos, but it employs an overstrung bass, a feature not yet found on Streicher and Bösendorfer production models, and a side-to-side grain orientation in the soundboard, a feature that even today would be viewed as experimental.[52] Ehrbar was also one of the first Viennese makers to adopt the full iron frame for all of his instruments.[53]

Brahms's concert tours exposed him to a wide variety of pianos, both European and American. Judging from concert programs, the instruments he most frequently played when away from Vienna in the 1870s and '80s were Bechsteins, Julius Blüthners (Leipzig), and Grotrians (Th. Steinweg Nachfolger, Brunswick). Other pianos he encountered on his tours included instruments built by Bretschneider & Steinweg's Nachfolger, Heinrich Hüni (Zurich), Rud. Ibach Söhne (Unterbarmen), Jacobi (Switzerland), J. B. Klems (Düsseldorf), Knabe & Co. (Baltimore), Gebrüder Knake (Münster), van Lipp, Carl Mand (Coblenz), Steinway & Sons (New York and Hamburg), and van Trau.

Brahms's fondness for Bechstein and Steinway pianos when playing in Germany is well documented. As early as 1868 he played on Bechsteins in Hamburg, Dresden, and Berlin, the latter the home of Carl Bechstein's factory. At this time, Bechsteins were some of the finest and most popular instruments being produced. In many ways they were equivalent to the modern piano, utilizing an overstrung bass, a one-piece, cast-iron frame, and the Herrburger-Schwander version of Erard's double-escapement action. Bechsteins were noted for their strength and "velvety" tone.[54] In assessments sent to Carl Bechstein in 1868 and 1873, Hans von Bülow had noted that he found Bechstein instruments—"particularly in *piano* . . . less so in the *forte*"—to be "splendidly equal and pleasing in tone and easy to play," and that they provided "the playing-fields that I need for my fine shades of touch and tone" (which von Bülow found wanting in Bösendorfers of the time). His only qualms were about their repetition: "Incomparable as your pianofortes are in respect of nobility, fullness, and color of tone, not to speak of their splendid equalization and other advantages, they do leave much to be desired in their repeating mechanism"— a defect that had bothered von Bülow for many years and had "grown more marked of late."[55] In the early 1870s, Bechstein still used a single-escapement English action; by the end of the decade he had remedied the problem of repetition by adopting Erard's double-escapement action.[56]

When Brahms tried out his recently completed Second Piano Concerto in Meiningen for Duke Georg II in October 1881, the concert grand was a Bechstein. Hans von Bülow, who conducted on this occasion, reported to Carl Bechstein: "Maestro Brahms finds the new instrument quite excellent and very easy [to play]."[57] For the premiere of this "symphonic concerto" in Budapest in November 1881, Brahms used a Bösendorfer. But as he planned his tour of the concerto in Germany, he wrote to his conductors requesting either a Bechstein or an American Steinway. "Would you be so good as to inquire in Cologne or wherever whether one cannot send for a Bechstein or a Steinway," he asked Julius Otto Grimm in anticipation of the performance in Münster. "I will gladly pay the transportation costs. But I will not play again on some risky or questionable instrument."[58] Likewise to Julius von Bernuth for the Hamburg performance on January 6, 1882: "Since I do have to trouble you about a grand piano, I shall ask if I shall find a very good and *powerful* Bechstein (or American Steinway) waiting for me?"—the power of the instrument being a key factor in this particular concerto.[59] Brahms's willingness to accept a Bechstein or a Steinway virtually sight unseen testifies to how reliable he considered these instruments to be. According to the programs for his concerts in Germany, Brahms played Bechstein pianos more and more during the last fifteen years of his life.

Brahms's reference to "Steinways" in these letters was to the pianos of Steinway & Sons, New York and Hamburg, not "Th. Steinweg Nachfolger" in Brunswick.[60] When Heinrich Engelhard Steinweg and his family immigrated to New York in 1850 to found the Steinway & Sons dynasty, his eldest son, Carl Friedrich Theodor, remained in Germany to run his own piano factory. In 1865 he too moved to New York, however, selling his business to three of his workmen, who called the firm "Th. Steinweg Nachfolger." The following year, one of these partners, Wilhelm Grotrian, assumed sole proprietorship.[61]

The earliest documented concert on which Brahms played a New York Steinway took place in Mannheim on December 5, 1865.[62] By 1881, the year of the letters to Grimm and Bernuth, Steinway & Sons had opened a branch factory in Hamburg, making their pianos even more readily available in Europe. The action in the instrument they produced at that time was, for all intents and purposes, technologically the same as in the modern Steinway. Yet even in the case of Steinways, the sound varied significantly from modern instruments, due, at least in part, to differences in materials and approaches to voicing. According to Michael Lenehan, modern Steinway hammers are made so that "the felt that actually strikes the string . . . should remain soft and springy; the hardening [by impregnating the hammer with lacquer and lacquer thinner] should take place below the surface."[63] In contrast, at the turn of the twentieth century, according to William Braid White's manual for piano tuning, the interior of the hammer should be soft, providing "a cushion for the immediate contact with the string," and the striking surface "must not be mushy at the crown or actual place of contact."[64] Such a hard outer surface remains close to the tradition of leather-covered hammers. Jon Finson has described the 1892 Steinway grand used by Ignaz Paderewski for his 1892–93 American tour and preserved in the Smithsonian Institution as having "great clarity of tone, penetration, and a soft overall sound" and being "more acoustically efficient, emphasizing the fundamental tone of each note, with less pronounced overtones than a modern Steinway." Finson continues: "As a result, the pianist was able to produce sound with a lighter touch, and the sound was not so massive as that of a modern instrument."[65]

Finson's observations are borne out by sinewy performances of Brahms's two cello sonatas and Schumann's *Fünf Stücke im Volkston*, op. 102, on the "Paderewski" Steinway by Lambert Orkis, with Anner Bylsma playing the 1701 "Servais" Stradivarius cello.[66] The beauty and clarity of the piano's tone is remarkable. In these performances, lean, exquisitely articulated and phrased lines sketched with rhythmic intensity propel the Allegros, creating blithe rather than merely big climaxes. Shadows of sound fleet about the opening movement of the E-Minor Sonata; its central movement is interpreted as a minuet of the most delicate sort, surrounding a smoothly flowing "hesitation" waltz; and the counterpoint of the Bachian finale is finely etched. Likewise, the character of each of the four movements of the F-Major Sonata is sharply profiled. In 1892 Brahms encountered "a particularly successful Steinway" at the home of Ottilie von Balassa in Vienna and sang its praises to his friend Eusebius Mandyczewski, who later remarked to Frau von Balassa:

> So you are the fortunate owner of the best Steinway. Ever so many years ago Brahms came to me quite excited and told me that he played on a fabulous instrument at your home. It was marvelous, [and] did not at all have the sound of an ordinary piano.[67]

This description fits the magnificent "Paderewski" Steinway well.

Like any other pianist, Brahms valued excellence in his instruments. Their actions, whether "English" or "Viennese," had to be responsive, their tone beautiful and singing, and their construction reliable. Available documents demonstrate that, given a choice, Brahms favored the more technologically advanced instruments of his day. Although the Graf on which he composed keyboard music in the early 1860s was antiquated, the instruments he liked to play in public in his early years kept up with the times. Likewise, though he had an 1868 Streicher in his apartment in Vienna for the last two and a half decades of his life, and though he might still have considered it ideal for the more intimate of his piano pieces (opp. 116–119), the grand pianos on which he preferred to perform his two concertos late in life—Bösendorfers when in Vienna and environs, Bechsteins and Steinways when in Germany—incorporated many of the latest innovations. Nonetheless, it would be illogical to maintain that Brahms intended all of his keyboard music for the Steinway, just because in his final decade he found instruments by that maker that he especially liked. Recent recorded and live explorations of Brahms's keyboard music on period instruments that are excellently preserved or have been restored to a high standard, played by pianists who are sensitive to the assets of their instruments, are not misguided, as some maintain, and would certainly not "have astounded [Brahms] and engendered a sarcastic comment."[68] As the documentation introduced in this study has shown, Brahms considered, at various times in his life, the pianos of Baumgardten & Heins, Erard, Streicher, and Bösendorfer, as well as later instruments by Bechstein and Steinway to meet his high standards. Performing Brahms's music on late nineteenth-century pianos simply reflects a desire to play these works on the instruments he knew so intimately and loved, and for which he wrote so idiomatically. Yet in undertaking this endeavor, one would be well advised to remember that changes in Brahms's musical style reflect the considerable evolution of the piano during his lifetime, and to the end, with respect to his "ideal" in pianos just as in the style of his piano music, Brahms remained "the progressive."

NOTES

1. Stewart Pollens, "The Schumann/Brahms Conrad Graf Piano," *American Brahms Society Newsletter* 24/1 (2006): 1–2. Heretofore this piano was thought to have been a wedding present to Robert and Clara Schumann in 1840.

2. For a detailed account of the history of piano actions, see Rosamond E. M. Harding, *The Piano-Forte: Its History Traced to The Great Exhibition of 1851*, 2nd ed. (Old Woking, Surrey, 1978); and Michael Cole, *The Pianoforte in the Classical Era* (Oxford, 1998).

3. Max Kalbeck, *Johannes Brahms*, rev. ed. (Berlin, 1912–21; repr. Tutzing, 1976), 1:35. Similarly, while living in Düsseldorf in the early 1850s, Brahms practiced on instruments at Vilem's piano warehouse, from which Schumann had bought a piano for his wife on her birthday in 1833; see Max Kalbeck and Albert Dietrich, "Fragebogen für Herrn Hofkapellmeister Albert Dietrich," in *Hans Schneider Katalog 100* (1964): 11.

4. Letter of 21 October 1854, in Berthold Litzmann, ed., *Clara Schumann–Johannes Brahms Briefe* (Leipzig, 1927), 1:23. In November 1854, Frau Schumann performed several recitals in and near Hamburg. Brahms's comments were probably occasioned by a query from her about the availability of pianos. Brahms spoke of a *tafelförmigen Instrument*, because at the time Baumgardten & Heins had no grand pianos on hand. His recommendation was that she have J. B. Klems, a piano builder in Düsseldorf, ship an instrument to Hamburg. Brahms used a Klems piano for concerts in 1856 (1:191). For Brahms's repertoire in these and other concerts, see Renate and Kurt Hofmann, *Johannes Brahms als Pianist und Dirigent* (Tutzing, 2006).

5. Concert program, reproduced in Kurt Hofmann, *Johannes Brahms und Hamburg* (Reinbek, 1986), 31.

6. Concert of April 20, 1860; see Johannes Brahms, *Briefwechsel*, rev. eds. (Berlin, 1912–22; repr. Tutzing, 1974), 5:269; and Hofmann, *Pianist und Dirigent*, 60. On December 2, 1859, and February 10, 1860, Brahms played Schumann's Piano Concerto, op. 54, in Hamburg on a Baumgardten & Heins piano, and as late as February 14, 1868, he performed Beethoven's *Emperor* Concerto with the Hamburg Philharmonic using one of their instruments (Hofmann, 58–59, 103).

7. Letter of 18 April 1860, Brahms, *Briefwechsel*, 5:269.

8. See Cyril Ehrlich, *The Piano: A History* (London, 1976), 109; and Florence May, *The Life of Johannes Brahms*, 2nd ed. (London, 1948; repr. Neptune City, N.J., 1981), 1:208.

9. See David Wainright, *Broadwood, by Appointment* (London, 1982), 170–71.

10. Letter from Brahms to Clara Schumann, 28 February 1858, Litzmann, *Clara Schumann–Johannes Brahms*, 1:218. This letter provides a glimpse of musical politics in Hamburg: "So my concerto will also not be given here! All truly Hamburgish. Cranz will

not give me his Erard, but with the utmost amiability offers useless small ones [*unbrauch-bare Stutze*]. Aloys Schmidt and Alfred Jaëll were the last ones [to use Cranz's Erard?]. Otherwise there is no grand piano to be had." The following day he wrote to Joseph Joachim: "I am not allowed to use the only decent piano here, which is owned by Herr Cranz" (Brahms, *Briefwechsel*, 5:202). We thank Peter Clive (*Brahms and His World: A Biographical Dictionary* [Lanham, Md.: Scarecrow Press, 2006], 131) for calling the Joachim letter to our attention.

11. Letter of 3 December 1865, Litzmann, *Clara Schumann–Johannes Brahms*, 1:518.

12. May, *Brahms*, 1:208. In 1862, while presenting a series of concerts in Paris, Clara was given a second piano by Erard (Clive, *Brahms and His World: A Biographical Dictionary*, 131). On Brahms's famous recording of an excerpt from his First Hungarian Dance, see Will Crutchfield, "Brahms, By Those Who Knew Him," *Opus* 2 (August 1987): 13–21, 60; Helmut Kowar, Franz Lechleitner, and Dietrich Schuller, "On the Re-issue of the Only Existing Sound Recording of Johannes Brahms by the Phonogrammarchiv," *Phonograph-ic Bulletin* 39 (1984): 19–22; George S. Bozarth, "Brahms on Record," *American Brahms Society Newsletter* 5 (Spring 1987): 5–9; and Jonathan Berger and Charles Nichols, "Brahms at the Piano: An Analysis of Data from the Brahms Cylinder," *Leonardo Music Journal* 4 (1994): 23–30.

13. Hofmann, *Pianist und Dirigent*, 85–86, 109, 145.

14. Amon Ra Records, CD-SAR 37.

15. Hacker's Albert clarinet, which he describes in the liner notes as "very close to the design of Mühlfeld's Ottensteiner clarinets," is a delightfully multicolored instrument, played to its fullest by Hacker. The sound is not the plush Victorian one that many modern clarinetists try to produce, but consists of a thinner central sound sheathed in resonance to make it rich, but not overly so. Some of the most beautiful passages in the Clarinet Trio are when the cello, taking advantage of the "reedier" sound possible with gut strings, joins with the clarinet in passages of parallel octaves or tenths, the two instruments merging into one. Brahms's two cello sonatas, opp. 36 and 99, have also been recorded using a London Erard grand piano from ca. 1850 (by Olga Tuerskay, with Peter Bruns on a 1730 cello by Tononi of Venice; Opus 111, OPS 30–144).

16. Robert Schumann, "Neue Bahnen," *Neue Zeitschrift für Musik* 39 (28 October 1853): 185.

17. The notation we are adopting here for octave registers is that cited by the *Chicago Manual of Style* as widely used. By this system, C_3 stands for the C three octaves below middle C and g^4 for the G in the fourth octave above middle C.

18. Detailed specifications for the Schumann Graf are given in Deborah Wythe, "The Pianos of Conrad Graf," *Early Music* 12/4 (1984): 458–59; and in Pollens, "The Schumann/Brahms Conrad Graf Piano." This piano has four pedals: damper, *una corda*, and two moderators. Before the Graf left Düsseldorf, its hammers may have been replaced; on the lowest of the current hammers, written in pencil, are the date and name "30/9 [18]56. J. B. Klems." Pollens notes that further work was done on the piano in 1931, and the newer hammers may have been installed then (4). Although the replacement hammers are now entirely felt, traces of what appears to be glue suggest that they too were initially covered with a thin strip of leather, as was the practice from the 1850s on. Pollens has found a record in the Kunsthistorisches Museum that Jörg Demus removed the leather layer prior to making a recording on the piano in 1966.

19. See the letter to Brahms from his mother, 20 November 1858, in Kurt Stephenson, ed., *Johannes Brahms in seiner Familie: Der Briefwechsel* (Hamburg, 1973), 82.

20. Letter of 2 February 1868, Litzmann, *Clara Schumann–Johannes Brahms*, 1:576.

21. Litzmann, *Clara Schumann–Johannes Brahms*, 1:582. Frau Schumann considered letting her daughter Elise have the piano, but this apparently never came to pass.

22. Letters to Caroline Brahms of 23 February and 9 October 1873, Stephenson, *Johannes Brahms in seiner Familie*, 204, 209.

23. See Victor Luithlen, *Katalog der Sammlung alter Musikinstrumente*, Part 1, *Saitenklaviere* (Vienna, 1966), 49–50.

24. Harmonia mundi 1C 151-99 773/5; also released as 30 475 K and as 30 662.

25. In 1995 a conference was held by the Kunsthistorisches Museum to consider whether to attempt to restore this piano, but in the end it was decided that its structural problems were too great. Pollens, "The Schumann/Brahms Conrad Graf Piano," 4.

26. Beethoven's *Diabelli* Variations, on Archiv 2708 025; Schumann's lieder, with Elly Ameling, on Harmonia mundi 1C 065-99 631 (also released as 303 946 XK and, by BASF, as HB 293691); and selections from Schumann's *Fantasiestücke*, op. 12, on Harmonia mundi 1C 065-99 797 (also released as HMS 17 064, as 29 29069/7, and as 30 485K).

27. Letter from Mozart to his father, 17 October 1777, in Emily Anderson, *The Letters of Mozart and his Family*, 2nd ed., ed. A. Hyatt King and Monica Carolan (London and New York, 1966), 2:328–29.

28. Harding, *The Piano-Forte*, 319. An 1848 J. B. Streicher piano with this hybrid action has been available to the authors for study. Harding termed the action "Anglo-German."

29. Edwin M. Good, *Giraffes, Black Dragons, and Other Pianos*, 2nd ed. (Stanford, 2001), 239.

30. This instrument is now in the Kunsthistorisches Museum, Vienna; see Luithlen, *Katalog*, 54–55.

31. We would like to thank Dr. Otto Biba, director of the Archive of the Gesellschaft der Musikfreunde in Vienna, for placing at our disposal the large collection of nineteenth-century concert programs in the possession of his archive.

32. Brahms informed Frau Schumann that in eight days, on November 3 (see Hofmann, *Brahms Zeittafel*, 66), he would be trying out one of these "improved" Streichers in a public concert in Vienna with the violinist Ferdinand Laube, playing Schumann's D-Minor Violin Sonata, op. 121. Letter dated ca. 26 October 1864, Litzmann, *Clara Schumann–Johannes Brahms*, 1:471.

33. Letter of 11 January 1867, Litzmann, *Clara Schumann–Johannes Brahms*, 1:553. Friederike Streicher's letters to Clara Schumann have not been located, but seven letters from Frau Schumann to Frau Streicher, spanning the years 1856 to 1895, are owned by the Library of Congress.

34. See, for instance, Brahms's letter of December 1870 to the pianist Friedrich Gernsheim in Cologne, Brahms, *Briefwechsel*, 7:208.

35. Letter postmarked Baden-Baden, 20 October 1869, preserved in the Austrian National Library, together with five other missives from Brahms to Streicher dated 1869–79 (nos. 126/61-1 to 126/61-6), published in Felix von Lepel, "Sieben unbekannte Briefe von Brahms," *Signale für die musikalische Welt* 94 (1936): 510–11; and in Elisabeth Maier, "Die Brahms Autographen der Österreichischen Nationalbibliothek," *Brahms-Studien* 3 (1979): 23–29. As these letters show, Streicher also lent Brahms pianos while he was staying in Pörtschach during the summers of 1877 to 1879.

36. We thank Dr. Otto Biba for kindly providing this information. The extant furniture, including Brahms's writing desk, is now on display in the Haydnhaus in Vienna.

37. We would like to thank Patricia and Michael Frederick for providing us with detailed information about this and other historic pianos in their collection.

38. Gregory Hayes, "How Many Pianos Does It Take to Fill a House? The Frederick Collection," *Early Keyboard Studies Newsletter* 1/2 (1985): 4–5.

39. Lynn Edwards and E. Michael Frederick, "Two Nineteenth-Century Grand Pianos," *Early Keyboard Studies Newsletter* 1/4 (1985): 4–5.

40. Seth Carlin's observations were made in an unpublished interview with Virginia Hancock in 1985.

41. "In his playing, as in his music and in his character, there was never a trace of sensuality." Fanny Davies, "Some Personal Recollections of Brahms as Pianist and Interpreter," quoted in W. W. Cobbett, ed., *Cobbett's Cyclopedic Survey of Chamber Music*, 2nd ed. (London, 1963; orig. 1929), 182. What Davies did hear in Brahms's playing was "aspiration, wild fantastic flights, majestic calm, deep tenderness without sentimentality, delicate wayward humour, sincerity, noble passion." For more on Davies's observations, see Bozarth, "Fanny Davies and Brahms's Late Chamber Music," in *Performing Brahms: Early Evidence of Performance Style*, ed. Michael Musgrave and Bernard D. Sherman (Cambridge, 2003), 170–219.

42. This 1871 Streicher has also been used by Thomas Lorango for his recording of Schumann's Piano Concerto in A Minor, op. 54, with the New Brandenburg Collegium, Anthony Newman conducting (Newport Classics, NCD 60034; 1991).

43. Ars Musici, AM 1232–2 (1998). Praise is due to the Brahms Museum in Mürzzuschlag for its role in fostering this interesting project.

44. Emotionally charged performances of Brahms's two cello sonatas, opp. 38 and 99, by pianist Paul Komen and cellist Pieter Wispelwey on a Josef Riedel grand piano from Vienna, ca. 1865, and an anonymous nineteenth-century Bohemian cello also reveal how spirited the clearly articulated sound of leather-covered hammers on parallel-strung strings can render Brahms's virtuoso Allegros and how rich and full the romantic cello with gut strings can sound, even when played employing vibrato only as an ornament (*à la* Joseph Joachim's dictum).

45. Brahms, *Briefwechsel*, 8:224–25.

46. The production figures given here are taken from Good, *Giraffes*, 240.

47. William Leslie Sumner, *The Pianoforte* (London, 1966), 127.

48. Good, *Giraffes*, 240.

49. Symphonia, SY 94D26 (1994).

50. Harmonia Mundi France, 907037 (1991).

51. Kalbeck, *Johannes Brahms*, 3:178, 298, 451; Otto Billroth, ed., *Billroth und Brahms im Briefwechsel* (Berlin and Vienna, 1935), 356.

52. Luithlen, *Katalog*, 56–57.

53. Alfred Dolge, *Pianos and Their Makers* (Covina, Cal., 1911; repr. New York, 1972), 222.

54. Good, *Giraffes*, 251.

55. Letters of 1 March 1868, 15 September 1873, and 14 October 1873. Richard Maria Ferdinand du Moulin-Eckart, ed., *Letters of Hans von Bülow to Richard Wagner, Cosima Wagner, His Daughter Daniela, Louise von Bülow, Karl Klindworth, Carl Bechstein*, trans. Hannah Walter (New York and London: Alfred A. Knopf, 1931) 80, 138–39, 140. Von Bülow had a long and close association with Carl Bechstein. In 1856 he inaugurated the first grand piano that Bechstein built, and it was natural that the piano at the Meiningen Court, where von Bülow was conductor, would be a Bechstein.

56. Letter from Bülow to Bechstein, 24 August 1877, ibid., 166.

57. Ibid., 178.

58. Letter postmarked 18 November 1881, Brahms, *Briefwechsel*, 4:144. When Brahms had last played in Münster, in February 1876, the piano provided to him was one by Gebr. Knake. This is the "risky" instrument he now hoped to avoid. Brahms did not succeed, however; the piano used for the Münster performance of the Second Concerto (on January 18, 1882) was not a Bechstein but again one by Gebr. Knake. Hofmann, *Pianist und Dirigent*, 158–59.

59. Letter to Julius von Bernuth of 30 December 1881, in Styra Avins, ed., *Johannes Brahms: Life and Letters*, trans. Styra Avins and Josef Eisinger (Oxford, 1997), 586.

60. On the other hand, Brahms's request to Bernhard Scholz in February 1876 for use of "an American" piano in Breslau (Brahms, *Briefwechsel*, 3:305, quoted in Avins, *Johannes Brahms*, 11–12 and n. 6) is to a Knabe grand from Baltimore, not a New York Steinway, and his alternative suggestion, a "Steinweg from Brunswick," is to a Th. Steinweg Nachfolger instrument.

61. Sumner, *The Pianoforte*, 124. At least as early as 1874 Brahms had played on one of Grotrian's instruments, and on numerous later occasions he played instruments by this firm in concert.

62. Hofmann, *Pianist und Dirigent*, 86. Brahms played Schumann's *Fantasie*, op. 17, and his own A-Major Piano Quartet, op. 26.

63. Michael Lenehan, "Building Steinway Grand Piano I 2571: The Quality of the Instrument," *The Atlantic Monthly* 1150 (August 1982): 46, quoted in Jon Finson, "Performing Practice in the Late Nineteenth Century, with Special Reference to the Music of Brahms," *Musical Quarterly* 70 (1984): 461–62.

64. William Braid White, *Modern Piano Tuning and Allied Arts* (New York, 1917), 236, quoted in Finson, "Performing Practice in the Late Nineteenth Century," 462.

65. Finson, "Performing Practice in the Late Nineteenth Century," 462. Study of the composition of the materials used in the felt hammers and strings may also prove fruitful.

66. Sony, SK 68 249. Cellist Kenneth Slowik, together with violinist Marilyn McDonald and pianist Lambert Orkis (as The Castle Trio), has recorded Smetana's G-Minor Piano Trio, op. 15, and Dvořák's *Dumky* Piano Trio, op. 90, using this piano (Smithsonian Institution, ND 034).

67. Ottilie von Balassa, *Die Brahmsfreundin Ottilie Ebner* (Vienna, 1933), 114. Brahms also liked the Steinway owned by Edward Speyer. Clara Schumann felt that its action was too hard for her, but Brahms defended it. See Edward Speyer, *My Life and Friends* (London, 1937), 90; and Avins, *Johannes Brahms*, 753–54.

68. Avins, *Johannes Brahms*, 587. Moreover, Brahms did not play on "early pianos . . . simply out of necessity." These instruments were not "early" for him, but "contemporary,"

Brahms, the Third Symphony, and the

New German School

DAVID BRODBECK

I

During the first week of May 1883, Leipzig played host to the twentieth Tonkünstler-Versammlung of the Allgemeiner Deutscher Musikverein, the organization founded by Franz Brendel some years earlier to promote the musical avant-garde. The opening of the congress was marked by C. F. Kahnt, publisher of the *Neue Zeitschrift für Musik*, with a reverential greeting of the group's honorary president: "Welcome, thou most admirable master Franz Liszt, who, though deeply mourning for having recently lost Pollux and having now like Castor to pass through life's course alone, yet with thine presence honors this festivity, and with thine appearance places upon it a golden crown!"[1] Liszt's deceased twin brother was of course Richard Wagner, who had died three months earlier. The remainder of the festival, not surprisingly, reflected the tone set in Kahnt's salute: throughout the proceedings the late master of *Zukunftsmusik* was commemorated; the living one, celebrated.

Yet the presence of Johannes Brahms's work was by no means inconsiderable. Sharing a billing with a number of pieces by Wagner and Liszt were the Violin Concerto and the *Gesang der Parzen*. Brahms, with little taste for the Musikverein and its activities, declined to attend these concerts; he instead remained in Vienna, where on May 7 he celebrated his fiftieth birthday in the convivial company of his friends Eduard Hanslick, Theodor Billroth, and Arthur Faber. It was "a little *Trauerkommers*," as he put it to Billroth, that he wished to make of his own jubilee, in what may have been a cheeky reference to the Wagner commemoration that was taking place that week in Leipzig.[2] But from afar Brahms must have savored the ironic juxtapositions of his music with art of the New German School. This he ensured by means of a delightful deceit. By prevailing upon

Hanslick to plant a false announcement of his travel plans—the *Neue freie Presse* soon reported that "Johannes Brahms is departing at the end of this week for the music festivals in Leipzig and Cologne"—the composer could look forward to enjoying an irony of his own making. "It is not always necessary to be completely truthful—in regard to the change!" he explained. "But I have a strong hidden reason to read in print the world-historic occasion of my departure—and to have it read!"[3]

Brahms did soon depart for points north, although he bypassed Leipzig and headed directly to Cologne. There, on May 14–15, he celebrated his golden jubilee in public with performances, at the Lower Rhine Music Festival, of the Second Symphony and Second Piano Concerto. The Rhineland struck a resonant note, and after spending a few days visiting his friends Laura and Rudolf von Beckerath in their Wiesbaden apartment, Brahms settled into pleasant rooms for the summer in a nearby house that commanded a fine view of the great river and its valley below.[4] There, in the weeks that followed, he crafted his Symphony no. 3 in F Major.

To Max Kalbeck, the act of composing this work within sight of the Rhine seemed momentous. The river, steeped in nationalistic lore and memories of the composer's romantic youth, provided the fifty-year-old Brahms a natural setting in which to take stock of himself and his place in history, even to compose a "justification of his artistic existence."[5] The symphony does make one significant, if indirect, allusion to the Rhine: Brahms took both the prevailing hemiola rhythm and the main theme of the first movement from the opening Allegro of Schumann's *Rhenish* Symphony. But echoes of Wagner and Liszt, the composers to whom Brahms had recently been joined in the Leipzig concerts, resound quite as distinctly. Indeed, Brahms's references to all three composers speak directly to the question of his own musical *Anschauung* at age fifty. Through them we can begin to take the measure of the artistic justification that Kalbeck sensed underlay the whole.

II

Brahms's allusion to Schumann's *Rhenish* did not go unmentioned in reviews of the work's premiere by the Vienna Philharmonic, under the direction of Hans Richter, on December 2, 1883.[6] Ten days earlier, in a hearty toast made following the first performance of the two-piano version, Richter had likened Brahms's work to yet another Third Symphony, Beethoven's *Sinfonia eroica*.[7] Both critics and conductor were on to something here, inasmuch as the new symphony, from its very first page, calls both earlier works to mind (Example 1). Notably, Brahms's main theme, derived from

Example 1. (a) Brahms, Symphony no. 3, movement 1, mm. 3–6; (b) Schumann, Symphony no. 3 (*Rhenish*), movement 1, mm. 1–7; (c) Beethoven, Symphony no. 3 (*Eroica*), movement 1, mm. 3–8.

the *Rhenish*, is set over the work's famous motto (F–A♭–F), whose chromatic second note "threatens" the tonic (its mode, at any rate) in a way that recalls the effect of the famous "sore" C♯ that comes five bars into the main theme of the *Eroica*.[8]

We shall return to this last-named passage below, but it is another memorable moment in Beethoven's work—the celebrated early entrance of the horns just before the recapitulation—that must concern us here, since this is something to which both Schumann and Brahms responded in turn. What in Beethoven's hands produces a moment of powerful and decisive drama (mm. 390ff.) instigates in Schumann's work a leisurely episode (mm. 368ff.). Brahms, with both models before him, takes something from each. The process begins toward the end of the development (mm. 101ff.), where, following an extended *agitato* transformation of the second theme that pushes from C-sharp minor to a half cadence in G minor, the air is suddenly cleared. Following an unexpected turn upward by half step, the solo horn enters with the motto, exuding poise in a diatonic dress in E-flat major: here, in the key of both the *Eroica* and the *Rhenish*, this once pithy figure becomes a real melody, as Walter Frisch has observed, by means of a stepwise extension elided to its final note (Example 2).[9] A few measures later, and still in E-flat, the bassoons and low strings enter with yet another thematic transformation, not of the motto but of the main theme itself,

Example 2. Brahms, Symphony no. 3, movement 1, mm. 101–8.

which, in a new, quiet guise, is now made to recall the very passage in the *Rhenish* Symphony from which Brahms had most clearly derived this theme in the first place (Example 3). Only after taking all these preliminary steps does Brahms, so to speak, respond directly to Beethoven's stratagem by linking the development and recapitulation with two overlapping statements of the motto, thereby restoring to this decisive moment something of its original high drama (mm. 120–24).[10]

Example 3. (a) Brahms, Symphony no. 3, movement 1, mm. 112–14; (b) Schumann, Symphony no. 3, first movement, mm. 449–53.

As Brahms would have known, Beethoven evidently derived the opening gesture of the *Eroica* (mm. 1–2) from Haydn's String Quartet in E-flat, op. 71, no. 3, expanding on the earlier composer's gambit of setting a piece into motion with an isolated, forceful statement of the tonic chord by doubling the number of presentations.[11] Brahms's own subsequent expansion involved interpolating a neighboring vii⁷/V harmony between the two tonic chords (mm. 1–3), thus creating the striking progression that appears at the beginning of Schubert's String Quintet in C. Of special interest here is Schubert's use of the progression in a passage that deceives us into thinking we are hearing a slow introduction instead of the primary theme of the Allegro. Taking the opposite approach in his Third Symphony, Brahms uses this chord progression in a brief passage that seems at first to have all the earmarks of genuine "primary" material—here are not sharp, dry chords as in Beethoven, but richly scored and fully sustained harmonies as in Schubert—only in Brahms they elide with what turns out to be the "real" main theme in measure 3 (albeit one that, owing to its triadic descent, embodies elements of a cadence).

As Beethoven had borrowed his striking opening from a Haydn string quartet, so had Schubert modeled his unusual progression on the slow introduction of Haydn's Symphony no. 97 (mm. 1–4)—where, significantly, the progression begins with a single brusque opening chord but soon develops into something resembling a closing gesture. Haydn subsequently made good on the implications of this opening by using this material as the closing theme of his Vivace (mm. 97ff.). In the same way, Brahms's main theme does eventually appear in its natural habitat, recurring not only at the end of the first movement (where it is not quite fully closed melodically and metrically) but in the last pages of the finale (where closure is complete). Concluding this "history"—and thereby virtually exhausting the thematic possibilities—Brahms used Haydn's closing theme, together with the secondary theme of the *Eroica* (mm. 83–91), as a model for his own transitional theme (mm. 15ff.).[12] This tightly spun web of allusions to Haydn, Beethoven, Schubert, and Schumann, of course, would by itself have been enough to lend credence to Kalbeck's suggestion that Brahms's Third Symphony represented a kind of midlife justification of the composer's artistic existence.

III

Yet there is more. Brahms's treatment of the bridge in the first movement of his Third offers the first clue that at least a few strands in the web were reserved for Wagner. Here the modulation from the tonic to the second key is brought about by means of a real sequence: the model (mm. 15–22) moves from F to D-flat; the sequence (mm. 23–30) sets out in D-flat and thus comes around to the mediant, A. Since this eminently Wagnerian procedure is rarely encountered so openly in Brahms's oeuvre (least of all in his expositions), its unfolding here registers something of a surprise, especially as this follows on the heels of the theme derived from Schumann. Yet Brahms makes this sudden and unexpected orientation toward Wagner unmistakable in the conclusion of this section (mm. 31–35), wherein the general reference yields to a specific one that involves the Venusberg music from *Tannhäuser* (Example 4).

Wagner's "Chorus of the Sirens" at once concludes the famous Bacchanal and presents the first verses of the opera:

Naht euch dem Strande! Naht euch dem Lande, wo in den Armen glühender Liebe selig Erwarmen still eure Triebe!

Approach the strand! Approach the land, where, in the arms of glowing love, let blissful warmth content your desires!

Example 4. (a) Brahms, Symphony no. 3, movement 1, mm. 31–35; (b) Wagner,
Tannhäuser, "Chorus of the Sirens" (beginning).

This passage was not chosen idly. This seductive song of the sirens, this
invitation to enter into the Venusberg realm, may well be emblematic of
the temptations that Wagner's musical language must have exerted on
Brahms, a self-described *Wagnerianer*.[13] In Brahms's hands, the borrowed
material, transposed down a whole step to the key of A, is woven into an
even richer chromatic tapestry; the passage acquires an additional chromatic note, the lowered sixth scale-degree, and with that, in measure 31,
unfolds an aching augmented triad.[14] Yet this harmonic luxuriance did
not blind the composer to formal exigencies; by repeating the material in
mm. 33–35 in a lower register and with a written-out *ritardando*, Brahms
created an air of expectancy that is clearly in keeping with the nature of
a sonata-form transition (as also with the dramaturgical situation occurring at the end of the Bacchanal, with its gradually enveloping rosy light
that slowly obscures from view all but Tannhäuser and Venus).

   This Wagnerian context for the transition suggests an explanation for
the unusually strong arrival in A major well before the appearance of
the secondary theme (mm. 31 and 35, respectively). If the final four bars
of the transition are an invitation to delve into Wagnerian waters, then
the ensuing idyllic secondary theme (mm. 35–42) may be read as Brahms's

reply (Example 5). This only increases the significance of the drone bass underpinning the new melody: it is not merely an easy means of evoking a pastoral atmosphere, but a pointed one by which Brahms demonstrated the continuing viability, even in the post-Wagnerian world, of diatonic harmony, made sumptuous here by the many beautiful dissonant clashes that the tune creates against the pedal point, and also by the characteristically supple phrase rhythm of the passage. In other words, by juxtaposing chromatic and diatonic treatments of the same key, Brahms was able to demonstrate all the more effectively the rich possibilities remaining to be explored within the confines of traditional tonality.[15]

Example 5. Brahms, Symphony no. 3, movement 1, mm. 36–39.

This rejection of the Wagnerian style helps to explain why, of all the Wagner operas, Brahms chose to echo *Tannhäuser* (or, more properly, *Tannhäuser und der Sängerkrieg auf der Wartburg*), whose famed vocal contest debates the issue of the true nature of love. After all, he could scarcely have failed to see how the opera's contest between two *Minnesänger* of the thirteenth century parallels the real-life struggle over aesthetic matters waged in the music of nineteenth-century Germany's two greatest composers.[16] But despite Wagner's many public invectives against him, Brahms clearly respected his "adversary," and the whole passage seems calculated to offer a tribute to the style of a composer he genuinely admired, coupled with an assured demonstration of a more congenial alternative.

A similar claim issues from the second movement, wherein a pointedly diatonic primary group yields to frankly experimental material. The transition (mm. 24ff) focuses not on one tonality but on two (the dominant and submediant), which, astonishingly, are superimposed in the secondary group (mm. 41ff). The melody, once more in the clarinet and bassoon, begins in A minor, but the accompaniment, in the strings, sets forth clearly in G (Example 6). At measure 45 the matter seems to have been settled along conventional lines, as the two tonal planes converge on a coordinated half close in the dominant. That key is not sustained, however; the cadence is elided to a real sequential statement of the bitonal passage, transposed now by a fourth into the keys of D minor and C major. Likewise, the lovely and characteristic idea that follows at measure 51, with its metric displacement, subtle alternation of diatonically third-related keys, and melodic inversion, offers but a temporary return to normative means. Indeed, the greatest jolt of all is still to come, in the odd series of chords unfolded in mm. 57–62 (Example 7).

Example 6. Brahms, Symphony no. 3, movement 2, mm. 41–45.

Example 7. Brahms, Symphony no. 3, movement 2, mm. 57–62.

These harmonies make explicit what Brahms's earlier uses of real sequence and multiple tonal axes had only hinted at: the remarkable secondary group of the Andante offers another response to Wagner's chromatic idiom. Typically, Brahms's succession is grounded in the key of the local tonic (G); its root progression of IV–II–V could scarcely be more conservative. Yet the tonal flavoring is enriched, even made exotic, by the presence of several *Tristan*-like extended appoggiaturas, each of which contrives to form a lengthy altered chord. Thus the D♯ in mm. 57–58, the D♯ in mm. 58–59, and the G♯ in mm. 60–61, effect, respectively, a C-minor minor-seventh chord, a French-sixth built upon A, and another on D.

The tribute to Wagner seems genuine enough, but the idiom must have appeared to Brahms limited and uncongenial. And again it is the music into which the Wagner-like material passes that reveals sensibilities more purely Brahms's own (mm. 63ff). This section restates the familiar primary theme, at last unequivocally in the dominant, but varied now in an entirely characteristic manner. The new tenor register of the tune, the accompaniment in parallel sixths, the tonic pedal point, the background figures in triplets—each is a part of Brahms's stock in trade. But the really telling earmark seen in the varied form concerns the introduction of chromaticism. The melody does not recur in the naive guise presented in the exposition; its head-motive is split apart and worked over separately, eventually coming around to a chromatic inflection that subsequently leaves its mark on the theme's remaining motives (Example 8). Chromaticism per se, then, is no longer the focal point; here, instead, it is reined in and sublimated to that most venerable—and truly Brahmsian—of compositional procedures, variation.[17]

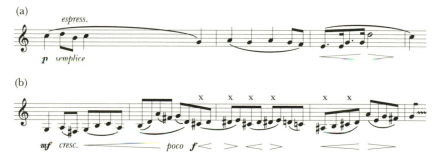

Example 8. (a) Brahms, Symphony no. 3, movement 2, mm. 1–4; (b) mm. 63–67.

IV

The echoing of Schumann and Wagner that I have sketched above sits well within the range of Brahms's normal working habits; each offers a tribute to the style of a composer he generally admired, coupled with an assured demonstration of a valid alternative. More startling is the evident influence on the symphony of Liszt, whose compositions seem never to have elicited from Brahms so much as a single word of praise. Yet before we can explore this possibility, it will be necessary to turn the clock back from the time of the twentieth Tonkünstler-Versammlung to that of the first, held during a period when Liszt's symphonic poems and program symphonies were at the height of their influence and prestige.

Brendel's announcement of the inaugural Tonkünstler-Versammlung, held in Leipzig on June 1–4, 1859, appeared in the *Neue Zeitschrift für Musik* on April 1 of that year, marking the twenty-fifth anniversary of the appearance of the journal's first number on April 3, 1834.[18] The opening-night concert included selections by Schubert, Berlioz, Mendelssohn, Schumann, Liszt, Wagner, and Robert Franz, but among this broadly representative group the emphasis lay on the side of the *Zukunftsmusiker*. As Brendel noted, "In designing this program, the determining aspect was to highlight the masters of the post-Beethoven era in their works, [both] the representatives of the most recent development, [and] at the same time those to whom the journal has since its founding occasionally devoted considerable attention."[19] All due respect was paid to Schubert, Mendelssohn, and Schumann, whose work had featured prominently in the *Neue Zeitschrift* during the 1830s and early 1840s. But it is clear that Berlioz, Wagner, and Liszt were privileged by virtue of their showing the "most recent development," while the absence of any of the more conservative composers of that generation, like Robert Volkmann or Ferdinand Hiller, is no less obvious.

Nevertheless, in his inaugural address the following day, Brendel lamented that the musical politics of the 1850s had now "reached a degree of animosity that recalled the religious fanaticism of earlier centuries in our history."[20] He argued that it was time "to take steps toward a reconciliation of the parties" and suggested that tensions might be defused by doing away with the controversial party slogan "Music of the Future," that "absurd and contradictory" (*widersinnig*) corruption of Wagner's conception of the collective "Artwork of the Future."[21] In its place he proposed the more prosaic (but, as it turned out, no less controversial) designation "New German School," whose locus he clearly placed in Weimar. By tacitly including the non-Germans Berlioz and Liszt (creators, respectively, of the program symphony and symphonic poem) along with the *echt* German Wagner as the school's leading lights, Brendel not only showed he had no real interest in healing the breach between the musical conservatives and progressives, but that he now had to justify a seeming contradiction of his own:

[Berlioz and Liszt] would never have become what they are today had they not from the first drawn nourishment from the German spirit and grown strong with it. Therefore, too, Germany must of necessity be the true homeland of their works, and it is in this sense that I suggested the designation New German School for the entire post-Beethoven development. We thus gain both in clarity as to grouping and in simplicity and meaningfulness as to the name. Protestant church music up to and including Bach and Handel has long been known as the Old German School. The Italian-influenced epoch of the Viennese masters is the period of Classicism, of the equal supremacy of idealism and realism. Beethoven once more clasps hands with the specifically Germanic North and inaugurates the New German School.[22]

Such talk—not to speak of Brendel's effort to underscore his view of music history by programming Liszt's "New German" *Missa solennis zur Einweihung der Basilika in Gran* and J. S. Bach's "Old German" B-Minor Mass on consecutive evenings—was bound to anger the young Brahms, who had by then come to very different terms with early music, the Baroque and Classical past, Beethoven, and "the entire post-Beethoven development." Above all, his pique was directed toward Liszt.[23] In August 1859 Brahms reported to his friend Joseph Joachim that "his fingers often itched to start a fight, to write something anti-Liszt," adding that Liszt's "compositions are getting worse and worse, e.g., the *Dante!*" A few months later, he likened Liszt's symphonic poems to the contagions of a "plague."[24] By the spring of 1860, Brahms and Joachim were working on a formal written "defense" (*Abwehr*) and circulating it among musicians who might be expected to join them in opposition to the party line of Brendel's journal.[25] In March Brahms thanked Joachim for sending him the first draft and reported on his own efforts to enlist fellow musicians who might join their cause. For his part, Joachim suggested that additional support might be found at the forthcoming Lower Rhine Music Festival ("this national meeting of praiseworthy musicians," as he put it, in a pointed dig at the Tonkünstler-Versammlung), which was to be held in Düsseldorf on May 27–29, 1860.[26]

In the midst of all this activity, Joachim reported that Clara Schumann had been invited to a rather different gathering, to be held in Zwickau on June 7–8 in commemoration of the fiftieth anniversary of her late husband's birth.[27] The widow had no interest in attending this *Erinnerungsfeier* (memorial ceremony), Joachim explained, because "the participation of the *Weimaraner* would have contradicted too much the wishes of her Robert."[28] In the public announcement of the Zwickau festival, which appeared in the *Neue Zeitschrift* and appealed for the participation of all who "had personally stood near the immortal Master," the matter was put more tactfully (or, rather, by way of a half-truth): "Frau Clara Schumann, whose participation had to be the committee's first task to win, has shown her lively interest in the festival, to be sure, but has declined to participate."[29]

Even as Brahms and Joachim continued to revise their protest and to solicit the support of others, a copy fell into enemy hands. On May 4 an anonymous parody ran in the *Neue Zeitschrift*; two days later, the leaked text itself appeared in the *Berliner Music-Zeitung Echo*, with the names of only Brahms, Joachim, Julius Otto Grimm, and Bernhard Scholz underneath (see Appendices 1 and 2).[30] News traveled slowly, however, and on May 15 Joachim reported in all innocence that Julius Rietz and several other musicians had agreed to join the protest, provided that "the blow" be deferred until after the Zwickau festival, at which, it was thought, a "provocation" would surely arise. And yet another week passed before Joachim learned of the premature publication and sent word of it to Brahms in Hamburg.[31]

The unauthorized publication of the "Manifesto" (*Erklärung*), as it finally was called, seems at first only to have strengthened the determination of the young men to proceed in their attack. Traveling with Clara from Hamburg, Brahms joined Joachim in Düsseldorf at the Lower Rhine Music Festival and arranged to meet there with Ferdinand Hiller, along with Scholz and Robert Radeke, to discuss what Hiller described as their "Declaration of War against Brendel's Newspaper."[32] Yet that was the end of it, as the older (and wiser) Hiller evidently convinced the two young men to take no further action, counseling, sensibly enough, that "the best means of struggle would be to create good music."[33]

Clara, Joachim, and Brahms traveled on from Düsseldorf together, avoiding the Zwickau festival, of course, and arriving instead for a holiday in nearby Bonn, where Brahms had arranged to spend the summer. There they undoubtedly would have read Brendel's report on the recent *Schumannfeier*, which appeared on 15 June 1860 in the *Neue Zeitschrift*. Predictably, Brendel took note of the three conspicuous absences, while seizing the opportunity to escalate the recent war of words:

> If something of a shadow was cast on the otherwise unclouded festival, it was the observation that some of Schumann's special friends and admirers had not come. . . . There is now a little circle of Schumann's admirers that seems to want to take his cult as its private possession. . . . The unquestionable one-sidedness that is implied by this, which is intensifying to the point of becoming pathological, is quite apparent, and no impartial person will agree with this faction if it maintains that the spaces in the temple of art are so limited that there is room only for itself and Schumann.[34]

In this heavy atmosphere—and perhaps with Hiller's recent advice in mind—Joachim and Clara Schumann encouraged Brahms to work.[35]

Indeed, within a few weeks he had completed the motet *Es ist das Heil uns kommen her*, op. 29, no. 1. Daniel Beller-McKenna has suggestively described this work, with its strong, direct evocation of the music of J. S. Bach, as a "telling response to Brendel's . . . appropriation of the Leipzig cantor [and, by extension, the Altdeutsche Schule] in his critical formulation of the 'New German School.'" Building on this idea, Nicole Grimes has suggested that Brahms's motet can be heard in terms of a general rebuke of Liszt's musical "aberrations," and perhaps even as negative commentary on Liszt's *Graner Festmesse*, which, as noted, Brendel had provocatively scheduled back to back with Bach's B-Minor Mass at the Leipzig Tonkünstler-Versammlung.[36] Of even greater interest here, however, is the possible stimulus to work coming from the recent Schumannfeier. Consider Clara's letter of 21 June 1860, which recalls Brendel's recent complaint about the "shadow" left by the trio's pointed absence from "the otherwise un-clouded festival": "A fine stormy sky can . . . pass into a symphony—who knows what already happened!?"[37]

Who knows, indeed? As I have suggested elsewhere, Brahms may well also have worked in earnest that summer on the opening Allegro of his First Symphony. However that may be—we know with certainty only that Brahms shared an early version with friends in June 1862—the unmis-takable allusions made in that score to Beethoven's Fifth stake Brahms's claim to a decisive place in Brendel's "post-Beethoven development."[38] At the same time, the music's many resonances with Schumann's Fourth Symphony and *Manfred* music can easily be understood as a defiant affir-mation of Brendel's complaint that Brahms and his circle were denying the New Germans any rightful claim to Schumann's patrimony and seek-ing "to take his cult as its private possession."[39] More surprising, perhaps, is the possibility that Brahms made an allusion as well to Wagner's re-cently published *Tristan* Prelude, but then again Wagner had never been a source of Brahms's anger throughout this episode.[40] By contrast, the absence from the First Symphony's allusive web of any strands from the "plague" of Liszt's symphonic poems and program symphonies takes no one unawares.

V

The surprise in this regard would not come until nearly a quarter-century and two symphonies later, when much of this history repeated itself with a few delicious twists. Just as, in the spring of 1860, Brahms had attended the "national meeting of praiseworthy musicians" gathered at the Lower Rhine Music Festival before pointedly skipping the Weimar-dominated commemoration of the fiftieth anniversary of Schumann's birth, so now, in the spring of 1883, he forsook the opportunity to hear his music played at the Tonkünstler-Versammlung that came during the week of his own fiftieth birthday but then gladly appeared at the selfsame Lower Rhine Music Festival a short while later.[41] The sense of déjà vu, moreover, extends from the biographical to the musical. Like the opening Allegro of the First Symphony, the new Third Symphony shows a renewed critical engagement with the music of Schumann and Wagner, and, of course, Beethoven himself.

Yet this time, in a way not seen in the earlier work, Brahms sets Liszt within his sights as well. It would go too far to suggest, with A. Peter Brown, that the Third Symphony, even with its use of thematic transformation and its presentation in the finale of several characteristic styles, constitutes "an extended symphonic poem." None of Brahms's large-scale compositions—for all the metaphorical readings that they seem rightly to invite—was *openly* programmatic in that sense.[42] No, the connection to Liszt has to do with form, not content. By dispersing the elements of a sonata form across an entire four-movement cycle, Brahms invites us to view the Third Symphony against the backdrop of Liszt's Piano Concerto in E-flat, which follows a somewhat similar path.[43] Here, however, Brahms offers no homage or even a respectful airing of artistic differences, but rather a "correction" —and, as we might expect, a none too gentle one.

Each of the four movements in Liszt's concerto can be reduced into one or another element of textbook sonata form. Thus the opening Allegro maestoso, in the tonic, offers a "masculine" primary theme-group; the Quasi adagio, in the submediant, presents a "feminine" contrasting theme; the Allegretto vivace stands as a scherzo but culminates in a grand transition that restates the primary material; and the finale brings about the rest of the "recapitulation," focusing on a march-like transformation of the secondary material but embracing other themes as well. In his own way, Brahms achieves a similar continuity across the entire span of his Third Symphony. Not only does the second movement (Andante, C major) incorporate the motto into the closing bars of its opening subject (mm. 21–23), but so, too, is this idea recalled in the finale. Although the third movement is not thematically united with the others, it forms a natural pairing with the preceding Andante by virtue of its leisurely tempo (*poco allegretto*), *romanze* character, and key (C minor). Taken together, these two intermezzi (both in the dominant) stand as a kind of a long-range secondary key center in the middle of the symphony.

Brahms's handling of both thematic material and the crucial pitch conflict between the notes A (the third of the tonic harmony) and A♭ (the middle note of the motto), joined at the very outset of the work, likewise reveals the underpinnings of a large-scale sonata form. The mysterious secondary theme of the Andante (mm. 41–50) is omitted from the reca-pitulation of that movement only to return in the finale, the "recapitulation" of the entire piece, where it serves as a mysterious interlude in the first group (mm. 19–29), forms the triumphant peak of the development (mm. 149–70), and, gently transfigured into a chorale along with the head motive of the main theme and the familiar motto, plays a central role in the coda (mm. 280–97). This last passage, in turn, prepares the way for the autum-nal return of the main theme of the opening Allegro, wherein the A–A♭ conflict is at last straightened out, as the minor mode yields unequivocally to the major.

This celebrated reappearance of the opening theme at the end of the symphony at once clinches the Lisztian background of the work and clari-fies a profound difference in the composers' attitude and approach. When we recognize that the march-like finale of Liszt's concerto is based upon the beautiful theme of his slow movement, we may be amused or offended, but not edified. In contrast stand the "strange and inscrutable" yet "won-derfully beautiful" final pages of the Third Symphony, whose effect is dependent upon everything that has transpired in the work.[44] In the sym-phony, the return of the opening theme in the finale seems at last to bring resolution to the many issues that Brahms had pointedly left unresolved. It "constitutes one of Brahms's most persuasive thematic transformations," as Walter Frisch has put it, "because it seems genuinely to embody all the thematic, harmonic, metrical, and formal processes that have spanned the symphony since the theme's initial appearance."[45]

The E-flat Concerto brings us back, finally, to the twentieth Tonkünstler-Versammlung of the Allgemeiner Deutscher Musikverein, held in Leipzig on May 3–6, 1883. Brahms avoided the affair, as we know, but his friend Elisabeth von Herzogenberg dutifully attended, and on May 5 she brought the composer up to date in a report about the "New German Musikverein days" that fairly dripped with smugness and sarcasm.[46] After mentioning the "atrocities and amateurishness" that marked some of the offerings, Elisabeth concluded by reporting on pianist Eugen d'Albert's perform-ance of Liszt's Concerto in E-flat:

D'Albert is in the hospital with measles. That is what comes of

oder ♭♩ ?

"It is all the same to us—
For what does it matter to us?
It matters nothing to us!"[47]

The musical incipit is, of course, the beginning of Liszt's concerto; the underlying text comes from a Viennese street song. We may well imagine that Brahms connected Elisabeth's humorous query concerning the final note of Liszt's opening phrase to the very different situation that obtains with the "sore note" in Beethoven's *Eroica* Symphony (see Example 1c). In that earlier work, as Brahms knew, it "matters" quite a lot (to recall the same street ditty) whether the last three notes of the main theme's opening phrase are E♭–D–C♯ (as in the exposition) or E♭–D–D♭ (as implied in the recapitulation). With the help of Elisabeth's letter, then, we gain access to yet another strand in Brahms's remarkable allusive web. That web, in turn, illuminates a larger biographical picture while belying the irony of Brahms's own humorous description of the work as "sheets of music from my youth."[48] Here the composer revisits a troubled earlier period in his life, one that had seen Brendel's infuriating address to the first Tonkünstler-Versammlung and the ineffectual Manifesto that followed in its wake. Now, at age fifty, and from his comfortable perch in a post-Wagnerian world, Brahms not only "effaces" Liszt from Brendel's "post-Beethoven development" but perhaps also lays claim to pride of place within it.

APPENDIX 1

Brahms and Joachim's Manifesto (as prematurely published 6 May 1860 in *Berliner Musik-Zeitung Echo*; translation adapted from Weiss and Taruskin, *Music in the Western World*, 385)

The undersigned have long followed with regret the activities of a certain party whose organ is Brendel's *Zeitschrift für Musik*. The said periodical constantly disseminates the opinion that seriously striving musicians are fundamentally in accord with the tendencies it champions and recognize the compositions of the leaders of this movement as works of artistic value; and that, in general, and especially in North Germany, the controversy for and against the so-called Music of the Future has already been fought out, and settled in its favor. The undersigned consider it their duty to protest against such a distortion of the facts, and to declare that, at least so far as they themselves are concerned, they do not recognize the principles that find expression in Brendel's *Zeitschrift*, and can only deplore or condemn as contrary to the most fundamental essence of music the productions of the leaders and disciples of the so-called New German School, some of whom put these principles into practice, while others keep trying to impose the establishment of more and more novel and preposterous theories.

> Johannes Brahms. Joseph Joachim.
> Jul[ius] Otto Grimm. Bernh[ard] Scholz.

APPENDIX 2

Parody of the Manifesto, as published 4 May 1860 in the *Neue Zeitschrift für Musik* 52 (1860): 179–80.

Dreaded Herr Editor! Everything is out![50]

A coup d'état is to be delivered, the whole of new music rooted out lock, stock, and barrel, and Weimar and Leipzig, in particular, struck from the map of the musical world. To this end a wide-ranging epistle was prepared and sent to selected right-minded persons of all countries, protesting in detail and very aggressively the increasingly spreading epidemic of the Music of the Future. The Board of Directors of this select group includes many selfless persons, traces of whose names, however, the most recent art history was unable to find. Nevertheless, in case the avalanche of signatories should be able to enlarge itself greatly enough, the storm shall thereupon suddenly break out. Although the hatchers of this musico-tragic finishing stroke enjoined the selected ones to the strictest secrecy, I succeeded nonetheless in examining the original, and I am pleased to be able to pass on to you in the following, dreaded Herr Editor, this timely, official document, all the while remaining

Your most devoted,
Fegweg[51]

PUBLIC PROTEST

The undersigned would like just once to play first violin and for that reason protest against everything that lies in the way of their requisite rise in the world—in particular, therefore, against the growing influence of the musical direction that Dr. Brendel has designated as the New German School, as, in general, against every spirit in new music. After the destruction of these things, which are most unpleasant to them, they will in its place hold out to all like-minded, well-disposed persons an immediate prospect for a Brotherhood for "Unstimulating and Boring Art." Sympathizing spirits are urgently admonished to join.

"The Staff Editors of the Music of Intelligence"
    (Undersigned:)
    J. Geiger. Hans Neubahn.
    Pantoffelmann. Packe.
    Krethi und Plethi.

NOTES

1. [C. F. Kahnt], "Zur zwanzigsten Tonkünstlerversammlung des Allgemeinen Deutschen Musikvereins in Leipzig," *Neue Zeitschrift für Musik* 79 (4 May 1883), 209.

2. Otto Billroth, ed., *Billroth und Brahms im Briefwechsel* (Berlin and Vienna, 1935), 348. The general reference here is to the traditional drinking celebration held by German *Burschenschaften* (student fraternities) in memory of their newly deceased members. We can well imagine that Brahms also had in mind the notorious *Trauerkommers* that was held in Vienna on March 5, 1883, in memory of Wagner. On this event, which was marked by strong expressions of anti-Semitism and subversive pan-Germanism, see James Deaville, "'Die Wacht an der Donau'?!? The Wiener Akademischer Wagner-Verein, Wiener Moderne, and Pan-Germanism," in *Wien 1897: Kulturgeschichtliches Profil eines Epochenjahres*, ed. Christian Glanz (Frankfurt am Main, 1999), 65–68.

3. Letter to Hanslick, quoted in Max Kalbeck, *Johannes Brahms*, rev. ed. (Berlin, 1912–21; repr. Tutzing, 1976), 3:380. The false report appeared in the *Neue freie Presse* (*Morgenblatt*, 3 May 1883): 6.

4. Kurt Stephenson, *Johannes Brahms und die Familie Beckerath* (Hamburg, 1979), 21–39.

5. Kalbeck, *Johanes Brahms*, 3:379–80. As Margaret Notley has observed, Kalbeck links the German nationalism that he sees expressed in the work to Brahms's discontent, as a mainstream German Liberal, with the conservative and Slavophile policies of Austrian prime minister Eduard von Taaffe's government; see Notley, *Lateness and Brahms: Music and Culture in the Twilight of Viennese Liberalism* (Oxford and New York, 2007), 42–43.

6. Critics Ludwig Speidel and Theodor Helm both drew attention to the source of Brahms's theme, while Hanslick made his point in more general terms: "I was unable to rid myself of the idea [then] and I am unable to suppress it here: it was as though Schumann were still living!" See Ludwig Speidel, "Konzerte," *Fremden-Blatt* (5 December 1883), 5–6; Theodor Helm, "Musikbrief aus Wien," *Musikalisches Wochenblatt* 14 (1883), 654; and Hanslick, "Concerte," *Neue freie Presse* (5 December 1883), 1–2, repr. in Hanslick, *Concerte, Componisten und Virtuosen der letzten fünfzehn Jahre, 1870–1885*, 2nd ed. (Berlin, 1886), 361–66 (at 365–66).

7. This anecdote was disseminated through Hanslick's widely read review (*Concerte, Componisten*, 362), and is corroborated in Richard Heuberger, *Erinnerungen an Johannes Brahms: Tagebuch-Notizen aus den Jahren 1875 bis 1897*, ed. Kurt Hofmann, 2nd ed. (Tutzing, 1976), 24.

8. Raymond Knapp remarks on the parallel between Brahms's A♭ and Beethoven's C♯, as well as a number of other features that the opening thematic groups of the two works have in common, in his article "Utopian Agendas: Variation, Allusion, and Referential Meaning in Brahms's Symphonies," in *Brahms Studies* 3, ed. David Brodbeck (Lincoln, Neb., and London, 2001), 152–53. We should note, however, that whereas Beethoven works out his "dissonance" within the opening movement itself, in a process that involves reinterpretation of the "sore" note as D♭ in the recapitulation, Brahms does not resolve his A–A♭ conflict until the very end of his symphony. For a suggestive comparison of the heroic narratives of Beethoven and Brahms, see Susan McClary, "Narrative Agendas in 'Absolute' Music: Identity and Difference in Brahms's Third Symphony," in *Musicology and Difference: Gender and Sexuality in Music Scholarship*, ed. Ruth A. Solie (Berkeley and Los Angeles, 1993), 335–36.

9. Walter Frisch, *Brahms: The Four Symphonies* (New Haven, 2003), 97.

10. When Frisch describes this moment as a "paroxysm" (ibid., 99), he might just as well be discussing the outburst that heralds the beginning of the recapitulation in the *Eroica*, but not the "real" beginning of the recapitulation in the *Rhenish* (mm. 412ff.), which is achieved through more conventional means.

11. Charles Rosen, *The Classical Style: Haydn, Mozart, Beethoven* (New York, 1971), 345–46.

12. See also Knapp, "Utopian Agendas," 141–43 (Examples 4.2 and 4.3); and Knapp, *Brahms and the Challenge of the Symphony* (Stuyvesant, N.Y., 1997), 93–96.

13. The best overview of Brahms's attitudes toward Wagner remains Karl Geiringer, "Wagner and Brahms, with Unpublished Letters," trans. M. D. Herter Norton, *Musical Quarterly* 22 (1936): 178–89; rev., with annotations, under the title "Wagner," in Karl Geiringer, *On Brahms and His Circle: Essays and Documentary Studies*, ed. George S. Bozarth (Sterling Heights, Mich., 2006), 359–75.

14. As Knapp has shown, Brahms alludes here not only to Wagner but also to Wagner's own model for the music in question, the end of the transition in the first movement of Beethoven's *Eroica*. In effect, he "cross-breeds" his version by combining striking harmonic features taken from each of his two sources (an augmented triad and triadic major-seventh chord from Beethoven, a tonic pedal point and diminished-seventh chord from Wagner). See Knapp, "Utopian Agendas," 142–45.

15. Knapp ("Utopian Agendas," 148–50) has argued that, in many respects, the Wagnerian allusion marks the actual beginning of the second group, noting that the ensuing dance theme, for all its outer differences from what comes before, retains the allusion's tonic pedal on A and moves to the same major-seventh dissonance (C♯ over D) before resolving similarly. But we might just as easily understand these continuities—as I have, in effect, done here—as a characteristic example of Brahms's "linkage technique." In any case, Knapp is surely correct in stressing the importance of this entire passage, not only to the movement's overall thematic processes, but to its allusive logic as well.

16. The dramatic confrontation in *Tannhäuser* was mirrored in the real lives of the artists in question. Wagner and Brahms carried on a protracted personal row over possession of the autograph of the "Paris" Venusberg scene, the very source of Brahms's recollection. See Geiringer, "Wagner," 363–65, 372–73; and Kalbeck, *Brahms*, 2:122–27.

17. Knapp has perceptive observations to make about variation as the central means by which, in the first movement, Brahms both spins his allusive webs and unfolds his internal (i.e., organic) thematic processes; see Knapp, "Utopian Agendas," 139–59 passim.

18. "Programm zur Tonkünstler-Versammlung in Leipzig vom 1. bis 4. Juni dieses Jahres," *Neue Zeitschrift für Musik* 50 (1 April 1859), 1–3. For a thoughtful and detailed account of the Leipzig Tonkünstler-Versammlung and of Brahms's negative reaction to it, see Nicole Grimes, "Brahms's Critics: Continuity and Discontinuity in the Critical Reception of Johannes Brahms" (Ph.D. diss., Trinity College Dublin, 2008), 41–62. See also the coverage of this period in the first edition of Kalbeck's biography: *Johannes Brahms, 1833–1862* (Vienna and Leipzig, 1904), 1:413–25, which is considerably more detailed than what appears in the comparable section of the revised version (Kalbeck, *Brahms*, 1:402–5).

19. "Programm zur Tonkünstler-Versammlung," 1.

20. Franz Brendel, "Zur Anbahnung einer Verständigung: Vortrag zur Eröffnung der Tonkünstler-Versammlung," *Neue Zeitschrift für Musik* 50 (10 June 1859), 265–73 (at 266).

21. Ibid., 267 and 271. As Brendel noted, Wagner conceived of the *Kunstwerk der Zukunft* as a fusion of all the arts, while those who spoke of *Zukunftsmusik* made music once more independent.

22. Ibid., 271–72. I adapt my translation from that published in *Music in the Western World: A History in Documents*, ed. Piero Weiss and Richard Taruskin (New York, 1984), 384.

23. For a convenient summary of Brahms's attitudes toward Liszt, see Imogen Fellinger, "Brahms und die Neudeutsche Schule," in *Brahms und seine Zeit*, ed. Constantin Floros, Hans Joachim Marx, and Peter Petersen (Laaber, 1984), 159–69.

24. Johannes Brahms, *Briefwechsel*, rev. eds. (Berlin, 1912–22; repr. Tutzing, 1974), 5:249; letter from Brahms to Clara Schumann of 27 January 1860, in Styra Avins, ed., *Johannes Brahms: Life and Letters*, trans. Josef Eisinger and Styra Avins (Oxford and New York, 1997), 212. See also Clara's letter to Brahms of 3 March 1860, in Berthold Litzmann, ed., *Clara Schumann–Johannes Brahms: Briefe aus den Jahren 1853–1896* (Leipzig, 1927), 1:302.

25. This development may be followed in Brahms, *Briefwechsel*, 5:262–84; and in Joachim's letter to Clara Schumann of ca. 13 March 1860, in *Letters from and to Joseph Joachim*, trans. Nora Bickley (London, 1914), 193–94. See also Grimes, "Brahms's Critics," 55–61.

26. Brahms, *Briefwechsel*, 5:266–67.

27. Helmut Loos, "Die Zwickauer Schumann-Feier von 1860," in *Schumanniana Nova: Festschrift Gerd Nauhaus zum 60. Geburtstag*, ed. Bernhard R. Appel, Ute Bär, and Matthias Wendt (Sinzig, 2002), 400–22.

28. Brahms, *Briefwechsel*, 5:270–71. Here Joachim is referring to a letter from Clara of 25 April 1860 (*Letters from and to Joachim*, 199–200).

29. *Neue Zeitschrift für Musik* 52 (25 May 1860), 200.

30. According to Hans von Bülow, the author of the parody was Carl Friedrich Weitzmann, who had sent his draft to Weimar, where it was toned down somewhat before being dispatched to Leipzig for publication in the *Neue Zeitschrift für Musik*; see Bülow's letter of 6 May 1860 to Felix Draeseke, in Hans von Bülow, *Briefe und Schriften*, ed. Marie von Bülow (Leipzig, 1896–1908), 3:312–13.

31. Brahms, *Briefwechsel*, 5:282–83, 284. For a full listing of signatories and those who had agreed to sign the Manifesto, see Avins, *Johannes Brahms*, 749–50.

32. *Aus Ferdinand Hillers Briefwechsel: Beiträge zu einer Biographie Ferdinand Hillers*, ed. Reinhold Sietz (Cologne, 1958–1970), 1:161.

33. Bernhard Scholz, *Verklungene Weisen: Erinnerungen* (Mainz, 1911), 142.

34. *Neue Zeitschrift für Musik* 52 (15 June 1860), 224.

35. Brahms, *Briefwechsel*, 5:285; *Schumann–Brahms Briefe*, 1:312.

36. Daniel Beller-McKenna, "Brahms's Motet 'Es ist das Heil uns kommen her' and the 'Innermost Essence of Music,'" in *Brahms Studies 2*, ed. David Brodbeck (Lincoln, Neb., and London, 1998), 31–61 (at 33); and Grimes, "Brahms's Critics," 60–61. Brahms introduced the term *Verirrungen* (aberations) in a draft of the Manifesto that was sent to Joachim on 8 May 1860 (Brahms, *Briefwechsel*, 5:278).

37. *Schumann–Brahms Briefe*, 1:312.

38. David Brodbeck, *Brahms: Symphony No. 1* (Cambridge, 1997), 9, 32–33.

39. Ibid., 41–50.

40. Both the *Manfred* Overture and the *Tristan* prelude were among the works performed in the opening concert of the Tonkünstler-Versammlung; see *Neue Zeitschrift für Musik* 25 (27 May 1859): 241. On the proposed allusion to *Tristan*, see Robert Fink, "Desire, Repression, and Brahms's First Symphony," *repercussions* 2 (1993): 75–103; reprinted with extended "Prologomena" in *Music/Ideology: Resisting the Aesthetic*, ed. Adam Krims (Amsterdam, 1998), 247–88.

41. In this light, we may suspect that Brahms's "strong hidden reason" for inducing Hanslick to publish the false report that he would attend the Leipzig congress reflects a determination to exact requital for Brendel's earlier journalistic dissimulation concerning the "lively interest" that Clara Schumann was said to have shown in the Zwickau *Schumannfeier*.

42. A. Peter Brown, "Brahms' Third Symphony and the New German School," *Journal of Musicology* 2 (1983): 451–52. Nevertheless, it should be noted that probably no other work by Brahms has elicited as many extramusical interpretations as the Third Symphony, by commentators from the composer's own time (e.g., Hermann Kretzschmar) down to

our own (e.g., Susan McClary). For a thoughtful account of all the larger issues that are raised here, see Knapp, *Brahms and the Challenge of the Symphony*, 271–91.

43. For an excellent account of Brahms's intriguing form (but without reference to any model that the composer might have had in mind), see Frisch, *Brahms and the Principle of Developing Variation* (Berkeley and Los Angeles, 1984),129–42. Although Frisch no longer made this claim explicitly in his later account of the symphony (*Brahms: The Four Symphonies*, 91–114), his discussion there of several long-range processes amounts to much the same thing. See also Robert Bailey, "Musical Language and Structure in the Third Symphony," in *Brahms Studies: Analytical and Historical Perspectives*, ed. George S. Bozarth (Oxford, 1990), 405–21; and Brown, "Brahms' Third Symphony," 439–49.

44. Here I quote from Hanslick's review, in *Concerte, Componisten und Virtuosen*, 364.

45. Frisch, *Brahms and Developing Variation*, 142.

46. Brahms, *Briefwechsel*, 2:2–5 (at 2).

47. Ibid., 2:5.

48. Letter of ca. 15 September 1883 to Fritz Simrock, in Brahms, *Briefwechsel*, 11:28.

50. The text here is "Alles is aus!" Throughout the rest of the original, the author plays upon this prefix, as in *ausgeführt, ausgerettet, ausholender, ausgearbeitet, ausgewählte, ausgeschickt, ausführlich, ausfallend, Ausschuß, Ausbundes, Außersichseiende, ausfindig, ausdehnen, ausbrechen, Aushecker, Auserwählten*—and not least of all, *Auskunftsmusik* (Music of Intelligence) in lieu of *Zukunftsmusik*.

51. The names of all signatories of this parody of a petition are old caricatures, from Fegweg (Sweepaway) to J. Geiger (J. Fiddler), Hans Neubahn (Johnny Newpath), Pantoffelmann (Hen-pecked husband), Packe (The mob), Krethi und Plethi (Everyman and his wife). Geiger and Neubahn would also have been understood as Joachim and Brahms.

The "Brahms Fog": On Analyzing

Brahmsian Influences at the Fin de Siècle

WALTER FRISCH

In a letter written in April 1894 to his friend Adalbert Lindner, the twenty-one-year-old Max Reger staunchly defended Brahms against his opponents. Although the music may at first be difficult to grasp, Reger noted, "Brahms has nevertheless come so far that all truly intelligent and sensitive musicians, unless they want to make fools of themselves, must acknowledge him as the greatest of living composers." Reger continued: "Even if Lessmann takes such pains to destroy Brahms and the Brahms fog (to use Tappert's term), the Brahms fog will survive. And I much prefer it to the white heat of Wagner and Strauss."[1]

Reger refers here to Otto Lessmann, editor of the *Allgemeine Musik-Zeitung* in Berlin from 1881 to 1907, and to Wilhelm Tappert, a prominent critic of Wagnerian sympathies. I have not located where Tappert coined the term "Brahms fog," or *Brahmsnebel*. Nor is it exactly clear what he, or Reger quoting him, meant by it. But the image is certainly an evocative one: the music of Brahms is seen as generating or being enveloped in a thick, dark mist; from the opposite camp comes the fiery glow of chromaticism and program music.

It is well known that during the last quarter of the nineteenth century much of Austro-German music was polarized between the Brahmsians and the Wagnerians, between the fog and the white heat. Most scholars and performers have been attracted more readily to the brighter glow, to the phenomenon of Wagnerism in European music. There has been less appreciation of how widely, and in what ways, Brahms's influence extended over the world of lieder and piano and chamber music.

"Brahms is everywhere," remarked Walter Niemann in an article of 1912.[2] Niemann, a devoted follower of Brahms (later to become his biographer), went on to survey briefly no fewer than fifty European composers whose piano music he said bore the unmistakable traces of the master's influence. Writing in 1922, Hugo Leichtentritt observed similarly that "from about 1880 all chamber music in Germany is in some way indebted to Brahms."[3] The same could be said of many of the thousands of lieder issued from the German publishing houses in the decades around 1900.[4]

There is no question that the Brahms idiom had tremendous prestige in these repertories. For one thing, as Niemann noted, some external elements of the style—the thick piano figuration, the rhythmic devices (two-against-three), the characteristic textures—were easily imitated. Indeed, to do so was apparently a point of pride among young composers. Alexander Zemlinsky, one of the most talented pupils at the Vienna Conservatory in the early 1890s (when the teaching staff was composed of such Brahms cronies as Robert Fuchs, Julius Epstein, and Anton Door), remarked in later years that "it was considered especially praiseworthy to compose in as 'Brahmsian' a manner as possible."[5] In 1893 the young Reger could actually boast to Lindner, "The other day a personal friend of Brahms mistook the theme from the finale of my second violin sonata [op. 3] for a theme from one of Brahms's recent works. Even Riemann [Reger's teacher] told me that I know Brahms really through and through." Reger went on to say, "Brahms is the only composer of our time—I mean among living composers—from whom one can learn something."[6] Reger's latter point is significant: Brahms represented, until his death in 1897, the most powerful and most respectable living model for younger German composers.

Just as one cannot easily measure the extent or scope of a fog, so would it be impossible and frustrating to tally all the composers who from the 1880s on fell under the sway of the Brahms idiom. (Some sense of the thickness of the fog can be gleaned by the number of musical works dedicated to Brahms. See Part IV of the present volume.) Even beyond any direct impact on musical style and technique—on the way music sounds— Brahms may have had a still farther-reaching effect on the whole concept of serious concert music in the twentieth century. Such, at least, is the provocative argument of J. Peter Burkholder, who suggests that with his self-conscious and complex historicism Brahms was seeking a place beside Bach and Beethoven in the "museum" of great music. Burkholder suggests that this attitude toward composition—in which one writes music chiefly to assure one's place in history—lies at the basis of musical modernism and has carried over into the present century.[7]

What I would like to trace in this essay is something more modest than Burkholder's bold picture: a vignette of some of the technical and expressive ways in which Brahms's music was appropriated by three of the most talented younger Austro-German composers coming to maturity in the

1890s: Alexander Zemlinsky, Arnold Schoenberg, and Max Reger. Even with such a restricted field, a comprehensive study of the phenomenon of Brahms's influence is not possible.[8]

Zemlinsky and Schoenberg present an intriguing contrast in Brahms reception. Although the former was the more impeccably trained and technically proficient composer—and as such can perhaps be seen as representative of many similar figures of his generation—it was in fact Schoenberg who probed more deeply into the essence of Brahms's music. Let us look first at Zemlinsky's song *Heilige Nacht*, which was published at the head of his first collection of lieder, op. 2, in 1897 (Example 1). The anonymous poem, a hymn of praise to the night, which cloaks everything in a cloak of tranquility—"even sorrow is sweet"—is of a type that attracted Brahms strongly.[9] The more specifically musical characteristics of Zemlinsky's song that derive from his study of Brahms can be itemized:

- the descending, broad triadic melody (mm. 1–4)[10]
- the strong stepwise bass line (especially mm. 1–6)[11]
- the arpeggiated figuration in the right hand of the accompaniment, which is in diminution of vocal rhythm and motives (mm. 1–8)[12]
- the dip toward the subdominant at the very beginning (mm. 1–2)[13]
- the sudden move, by third, from a G to an E-flat harmony in $^6_4$ position (mm. 6–7)[14]
- the extension or augmentation of "während der heiligen Nacht" to create an irregular three-measure phrase (mm. 24–26)[15]
- the final plagal cadence of the song (mm. 29–30)[16]

Despite their distinguished pedigree, these techniques fail to add up to a successful song. First, the phrase structure is too square: the rather rigid succession of two-measure units in the opening section, through measure 8, is scarcely concealed by the small modifications, such as in measure 6, where Zemlinsky repeats the words "dein Kuss" in order to extend the phrase another half measure. A subtler grasp of Brahmsian technique might have led to the kind of asymmetry and irregularity that Schoenberg delighted in pointing out in Brahms songs in his essay "Brahms the Progressive."[17] Brahms himself would never be guilty of undermining what is clearly supposed to be a magical moment, the shift to the E-flat $^6_4$ chord in measure 7, with an almost verbatim repetition of the opening theme. In Brahms such special harmonic expansions are almost always accompanied by—or coordinated with—a further-reaching melodic or thematic development.[18]

Example 1. Zemlinsky, *Heilige Nacht*, op. 2, no. 1 (1897).

Despite its surface resemblance to Brahms, the harmonic syntax of *Heilige Nacht* also betrays an un-Brahmsian awkwardness. The root-position IV chord in measure 2 is too emphatic; it virtually brings harmonic motion to a standstill. When Brahms employs a root-position subdominant near the beginning of a piece, it is more a harmonic inflection, imparting a delicate ambiguity.[19] Zemlinsky's actual cadence to F in mm. 8–9, though perhaps intended as a fulfillment of the opening gesture, is likewise unconvincing. The tonic has barely been reestablished in measure 7 when it is transformed into an augmented chord that is made to function as a dominant. The augmented sonority with an added major seventh sounds particularly bizarre in the prevailingly consonant context.

If I seem to have been too hard on what is in many respects an attractive song, it is because Zemlinsky seems to me to be very good at appropriating many of the stylistic traits of Brahms without really absorbing the fundamental compositional principles. This aspect of his art has been pointed out by Adorno, who in his excellent essay of 1959 suggested that Zemlinsky was a genuine eclectic, "someone who borrows all possible elements, especially stylistic ones, and combines them without any individual tone."[20] Adorno tries to strip the term "eclectic" of its pejorative connotation, arguing that Zemlinsky was in fact something of a genius in his "truly seismographic capacity to respond to all the temptations with which he let himself be inundated." I would argue here that his "seismographic" receptivity prevented him from really absorbing the essence of Brahms. He registered the aftershocks, so to speak, but failed to locate the source of the tremor.

This tendency can be seen in Zemlinsky's early chamber music as well, especially in the First Quartet in A Major, op. 4, composed in 1896 and published by Simrock in 1898. The first group of the first movement (Example 2) constitutes a virtual encyclopedia—grab-bag might be a more appropriate term—of Brahmsian metrical devices. Nowhere in the first group is the notated $\frac{6}{8}$ meter presented unambiguously. At the outset the measure is divided as if in $\frac{3}{4}$ (mm. 1–2). In the next measure the two lower parts move in $\frac{6}{8}$, the second violin in $\frac{3}{4}$, and the first violin somewhere in between. At the climax in mm. 9–12, Zemlinsky presents (although he does not notate) a dizzying alternation of $\frac{3}{8}$ and $\frac{3}{4}$ according to the pattern: $\frac{3}{8}$–$\frac{3}{4}$–$\frac{3}{8}$–$\frac{3}{4}$–$\frac{3}{8}$–$\frac{3}{4}$–$\frac{3}{4}$. After the fermata, the metrical roller coaster resumes its course.

In his commentary on this movement Rudolf Stephan has suggested that "rhythmic complications of this kind point to the model of Brahms, who, however, does not employ them in this (almost) systematic fashion."[21] Stephan's parenthetical "almost" betrays an appropriate diffidence. In fact,

Allegro con fuoco

Example 2. Zemlinsky, String Quartet no. 1 in A Major, op. 4, movement 1, mm. 1–13.

it is Brahms who is the more systematic, as a comparative glance at his Third Quartet in B-flat, op. 67, will show. Brahms, like his follower Zemlinsky, continually reinterprets the notated $\frac{6}{8}$ meter. But where Zemlinsky dives headlong into complexity and conflict, Brahms unfolds a gradual, subtle process (Example 3a). In mm. 1–2 he places accent marks on the normally weak third and sixth beats of the measure. In measure 3 these accents are intensified by *forzandos*. Only in measure 8 does Brahms introduce an actual hemiola. This hemiola serves an important structural function: it marks the first arrival on the dominant and the beginning of the B section of the

(a)

(b)

Example 3. Brahms, String Quartet no. 3 in B-flat Major, movement 1, mm. 1–12, 63–65.

ABA' design of the first group. The following transition unfolds unprob-lematically in $\frac{6}{8}$, but the conflict between duple and triple articulation of the measure finds new expression in the notated $\frac{2}{4}$ meter of the second group (Example 3b). As in the first group, the meter is carefully coordi-nated with the thematic and formal procedures: the arrival of $\frac{2}{4}$ coincides with a new theme and the confirmation of the dominant key area.

The implication of the above discussion may seem self-evident: no one could compose Brahms as well as Brahms himself. Yet my point is that a highly talented composer like Zemlinsky could master many of the most complicated Brahmsian skills without using them sensitively. He could *sound* Brahmsian without really *composing* Brahmsian.

The Brahms reception of the young Arnold Schoenberg presents a some-what different picture from that of his friend (and later brother-in-law) Zemlinsky. Schoenberg was almost completely self-taught until 1895 when he began to take private, informal lessons with Zemlinsky for about two years. Among his earliest surviving compositions are piano pieces, one completed work of chamber music, and thirty-two lieder that clearly show a Brahmsian stamp.[22] The Three Piano Pieces of 1894, among the earli-est firmly datable pieces, show him, somewhat like the Zemlinsky of the A-Major Quartet, exploiting Brahmsian metrical ambiguities with a vengeance. Although notated in $\frac{2}{4}$, the first piece unfolds from the begin-ning as if it were in $\frac{6}{8}$ (Example 4). As with Zemlinsky, this procedure seems somewhat arbitrary, unmotivated, as if Schoenberg is trying on some of Brahms's clothes for size.

But as he matured, Schoenberg seemed to look more deeply into mat-ters of Brahmsian technique and expression. The song *Mädchenlied*, set to a text by Paul Heyse (a favorite poet of the master), shows a different level of absorption of Brahms. The song, probably written in 1896–97 (the manu-script is undated), bears many of the outward aspects of Brahms's style (see the first strophe, Example 5): a modified strophic form, a broad triadic melody, and a primarily diatonic harmonic framework. Also reminiscent of Brahms (and to some extent of Dvořák) is the quasi-pentatonic opening melody, with its particular emphasis in measure 2 on the melodic sixth degree, B, and the harmony of B minor.[23]

But it is in the more subtle relationships between voice and piano and in the fluid phrase structure that Schoenberg's song reveals a more genuine Brahmsian inheritance. In the first two phrases, mm. 1–5, the accompaniment repeats a brief three-note motive, marked *x* in Example 5. In mm. 6–7 this motive migrates from the piano into the voice, at the words *süsse* and *kredenz dem*. This motivic transference forms part of a still more

Example 4. Schoenberg, Piano Piece (1894), mm. 1–7.

sophisticated exchange of material between voice and piano. As the voice reaches a half-cadence on the dominant in measure 5, the piano begins a restatement of what was originally the vocal theme, now in the dominant. From the second half of measure 6, this restatement begins to deviate slightly from the original (an exact transposition of the vocal melody of measure 3 would bring an E in the right hand on beat 3 of measure 6), but the contour and rhythms are fully recognizable through measure 7.

This piano statement of the melody actually overlaps with the conclusion of the first vocal phrase in measure 5 and the beginning of the next one in measure 6. There is thus an asynchronous relationship between voice and accompaniment, perhaps intended by Schoenberg as a musical corollary of the drunken beggars outside the tavern door. The voice and piano get back into phase in measure 8, for the final phrase of the strophe.

In *Mädchenlied* Schoenberg seems to have assimilated basic compositional principles much more completely than the Zemlinsky of *Heilige Nacht*. The same can also be said of his own D-Major String Quartet of 1897 in comparison with Zemlinsky's quartet of the preceding year (with which Schoenberg was undoubtedly familiar). Especially impressive in the Schoenberg work is the motivic technique of developing variation, in which one thematic idea is drawn from the preceding in a fluid, almost continuous process.

Example 5. Schoenberg, *Mädchenlied* (ca. 1896–97), mm. 1–12.

Example 6a shows part of the ternary first group of Schoenberg's first movement. Already in its second two measures the main theme begins to develop, as mm. 3–4 take shape as a free but recognizable retrograde of mm. 1–2. Measures 1–4 function as an antecedent, mm. 5–12 as an expanded consequent deriving quite clearly from what has preceded. The rhythm of four slurred eighth notes in measure 5 (marked *y*) develops from the second half of measure 3. The rhythmic profile of measure 6 derives from the figure (marked *x*) spread across the bar line between mm. 2–3, where the dotted quarter note has an accent. The consequent phrase develops the implications of that accent, as it were, by shifting it to the downbeats of mm. 6 and 8. In the brief B segment of the first group, beginning in measure 13, the eighth-note idea is further modified (*y'*). In pitch content

(a)

Example 6. Schoenberg, String Quartet in D Major (1897), movement 1: (a) mm. 1–17; (b) mm. 33–39.

Example 6 continued

the motive retains the neighbor-note motion of the consequent form
(mm. 5, 7, and 9).

This developmental process continues well past the first group, as is
shown in Example 6b, which presents the climax of the transition and the
beginning of the second group. Here *y* is presented *fortissimo*, then gradually "liquidated," as Schoenberg would later describe the process of reducing
a theme or motive to its basic elements.[24] The motive is then immediately
regenerated in the inner parts of the second theme, which begins in measure 39.

Schoenberg's strategy in this movement is clear: he seeks to saturate the
texture with motive *y* in its various forms. Instead of using "filler" or empty
figuration, he attempts to make all parts, and all moments, thematically
significant. These are precisely the kind of techniques that he and his pupils
would later admire and analyze in the music of Brahms. The D-Major
Quartet and the song *Mädchenlied* both demonstrate how early and how
well Schoenberg grasped these basic Brahmsian precepts.

In his later writings, Schoenberg would disparage the practice of composing "in the style" of a recognized master. He maintained that what
most people call "style" is only an external "symptom": "To believe, when
someone imitates symptoms, the style, that this is an artistic achievement—
that is a mistake with dire consequences."[25] In his early works Schoenberg
was himself somewhat guilty of adopting the symptoms of Brahms. But
what is admirable, and what sets him apart even from technically more

accomplished composers like Zemlinsky, is his concern with finding and appropriating underlying compositional principles, such as that of continuous motivic development. It is these principles to which he was to cling even as his "style" changed radically in the years after 1899.

Perhaps the only other composer of whom this might also be said—even though he moved in different directions from Schoenberg—was Max Reger. Reger, as we have seen above, was a Brahms-*Verehrer* from early on, and his devotion took extreme forms. In the summer of 1896, Reger, who up to that point had had no personal contact with Brahms, got up the courage to send the master a copy of his Suite for Organ, op. 16, a piece steeped in Bachian counterpoint and bearing the inscription, "Den Manen J. S. Bachs" (To the memory of J. S. Bach). Reger also asked Brahms to accept the dedication of a symphony in progress in B minor. Brahms replied: "Surely, permission is not necessary! I had to laugh, since you approach me about this matter, at the same time enclosing a piece with a startlingly bold dedication!"[26] Reger appears not to have finished the symphony. After Brahms's death the following year, he sought to pay homage in a different way. In the fall of 1897 he began work on a piano quintet in C minor that, although bearing a dedication to the critic Arthur Smolian, was, according to Lindner, "essentially dedicated to Brahms from the beginning."[27] Lindner suggests that woven into the main theme of the first movement is a motive containing the last three musical letters of Brahms's name, A–B♮–E♭.

More overt homage to Brahms is paid by two piano pieces composed around the same time. One, titled *Rhapsodie* and subtitled "Den Manen Johannes Brahms," is a large, turbulent work modeled closely on Brahms's Rhapsodies, op. 79. It was published in 1899 as op. 24, no. 6. The other piano piece, the very opposite in mood, is titled *Resignation* and subtitled "3. April 1897— J. Brahms †," the date of Brahms's death (on or shortly after which it may have been composed). It was published in 1899 as op. 26, no. 5.

Resignation is a *tombeau* for a master whom Reger admired, and from whom virtually his entire oeuvre springs (the other main source is Bach). Although it can hardly be taken as typical of Reger's music, the intentionally exaggerated "Brahmsian" spirit of the piece nevertheless makes it a wonderful specimen of Brahms assimilation by the younger generation of composers. In *Resignation* we can distinguish three levels of response to Brahms, which might be called quotation, allusion, and absorption. These can be considered not as exclusive categories, but as points on a spectrum of Brahms influence ranging from the very obvious to the almost undetectable or undocumentable.

Max Reger, 1902.

The piece ends with an unmistakable quotation of the theme from the Andante of Brahms's Fourth Symphony (Example 7a), which appears in its original key, E major, even though *Resignation* has been in A major up to that point. (It thus ends in the dominant!) Although the quotation in itself hardly represents a sophisticated degree of Brahmsian assimilation, Reger leads up to it by a wonderfully subtle process of allusion and absorption.

Example 7b presents the opening portion of the piece. (The piece as a whole has an ABA' form, like many of Brahms's late piano works.) Needless

Example 7a. Reger, *Resignation,* op. 26, no. 5 (1899), mm. 51–56.

to say, we find here many of the "symptoms" of Brahms's piano style, such as those described by Niemann in 1912: "passages in thirds and sixths, orchestral doublings, wide spacings, use of the deep bass register . . . [and] a tendency toward syncopated and triplet figures of all kinds."[28] But there is more as well, including allusions to at least three of Brahms's late Intermezzi: op. 116, nos. 4 and 6, both in E major; and op. 118, no. 2, in A major (Example 8). Reger's bass octaves recall Example 8a; the distinctly polyphonic texture, with active middle voices, is a feature of both 8a and 8c. Reger also reinterprets the opening gesture characteristic of all three Intermezzi: *Resignation* begins on an upbeat with a root-position tonic chord, which moves on the subsequent downbeat to a ii[6] (the chord is complete only when the middle-voice suspension resolves on beat 2). Brahms also has a tonic chord on the upbeat and then moves to some kind of "pre-dominant" chord: in Example 8a, vi[6]; in 8b, a passing chord over

Example 7b. Reger, *Resignation,* op. 26, no. 5 (1899), mm. 1–10.

A, then ii; in 8c, a IV$^6_4$. As in Reger, the precise formation of these down-beat chords is made initially unclear by appoggiaturas and suspensions.

In Example 8b these procedures generate considerable metrical ambi-guity. Our ear tends to hear the strong root-position chord as a downbeat, and the phrasing suggests a broad $\frac{3}{2}$ meter rather than the notated $\frac{3}{4}$. At the approach to the dominant in *Resignation*, mm. 6–9, Reger draws upon precisely these kinds of metrical ambiguity or conflict (as suggested in Example 7). As we listen (at least for the first time), mm. 5–6 suggest a $\frac{3}{2}$ hemiola superimposed over the notated $\frac{3}{4}$. But the downbeat of measure 7 does not, as we might expect, restore the notated meter unequivocally.

(a)

Example 8. Brahms Intermezzi: (a) op. 116, no. 4; (b) op. 116, no. 6; (c) op. 118, no. 2.

Instead, the implied $\frac{3}{2}$ measure is stretched, as it were, to accommodate the cadential approach to E through the circle of fifths, C♯–F♯–B–E. Reger now accelerates the harmonic rhythm, so that while the C♯ lasts a half note, or a full beat in $\frac{3}{2}$, the F♯ and B are only a quarter note each. The cadential goal, E, thus arrives on the notated last beat of measure 7. The two subsequent measures confirm E with the Phrygian approach through C-major and F-major triads. This cadence subtly foreshadows the actual quotation from Brahms's Fourth (Example 7a), with its prominent C♮s.

The Phrygian passage in the Reger prolongs the metrical ambiguity just long enough to bring the phrase to close on the notated second beat of measure 9, thus allowing for a varied restatement of the opening theme to begin in its proper place, on beat 3. The tonic now reappears modified by another Brahmsian gesture: the A enters half a beat too early, on the second half of the beat of measure 9, sounding deep in the bass underneath the prevailing dominant harmony.[29]

The kind of procedures involving meter, harmony, and phrase structure that are manifested by mm. 6–9 of *Resignation* fall under the category of absorption discussed above. Reger is making no quotation of, or allusion to, any specific passage in Brahms. Rather, he seems fully to have internalized or absorbed a number of Brahms's most characteristic compositional techniques. This is the kind of influence that Charles Rosen has identified as the most profound, where the study of sources or models for a particular work "becomes indistinguishable from pure musical analysis."[30]

In an editorial in the *Allgemeine Musik-Zeitung* of January 1891, Otto Lessmann, already mentioned above as a willful "destroyer" of the "Brahms fog," attempted to summarize developments and trends in German music during the decade of the 1880s. He lamented at length the passing of Wagner and Liszt, and pointed presciently to the emergence of the young Richard Strauss, who at that time had to his credit only a few daring tone poems. About Brahms, Lessmann had this to say:

> As a self-assured personality, Brahms raised his head proudly among the many Mendelssohn-Schumann epigones and struck out on his own path, which wound around the noble palace in which Beethoven reigned. That this path did not lead into unknown areas, that Brahms opened no new perspectives—this should be conceded to his opponents without hesitation. But is it really such a misfortune that on the broad path along which art develops there should be resting places as well as signposts?[31]

Such a patronizing assessment can irritate us today as much as it did the young Reger at the time. Although some critics of the fin de siècle like Lessmann saw Brahms as a dead end or "resting place," younger composers felt differently. The most talented of these, including Schoenberg, Reger, and even Zemlinsky at his best, found plenty of "signposts" in Brahms's music. One merely needed the inclination and skill to interpret them. As these composers matured, they adapted and eventually sublimated Brahmsian principles and techniques to forge some of the most impressive musical achievements of the early modernist period.

NOTES

Portions of this article appeared in Part I of my book *The Early Works of Arnold Schoenberg, 1893–1907* (Berkeley and Los Angeles, 1993).

1. Max Reger, *Briefe eines deutschen Meisters*, ed. Else von Hase Koehler (Leipzig, 1928), 39–40.

2. "Johannes Brahms und die neuere Klaviermusik," *Die Musik* 12/1 (1912): 45.

3. Hugo Leichtentritt, "German Chamber Music," in *Cobbett's Cyclopedic Survey of Chamber Music*, ed. Walter W. Cobbett (1929; repr. London, 1963), 449.

4. The best bibliographic source for this enormous repertory is Ernst Challier, *Grosser Lieder Katalog* (Berlin, 1885), for which supplements (*Nachträge*) were published every two years well into the twentieth century.

5 Alexander Zemlinsky, "Brahms und die neuere Generation: Persönliche Erinnerungen," *Musikblätter des Anbruch* 4 (1922): 70. See the translation of this excerpt in Part III of this volume.

6. Reger, *Briefe*, 33. The resemblance noted is probably between the theme of Reger's finale and that from the finale of Brahms's Cello Sonata in F Major, op. 99, no. 2, published in 1887.

7. J. Peter Burkholder, "Brahms and Twentieth-Century Classical Music," *19th-Century Music* 8 (1984): 75–83.

8. There is a fairly extensive literature on Brahms followers, although much of it remains on the general life-and-works level. See the encyclopedic bibliography in Imogen Fellinger, "Zum Stand der Brahms-Forschung," *Acta Musicologica* 40 (1983): 131–201; and "Das Brahms-Jahr 1983: Forschungsbericht," *Acta Musicologica* 41 (1984): 145–210. Especially valuable are the sections, in both articles, titled "Brahms und seine Zeit" and "Brahms' Weiterwirken."

9. At least twelve of his works are set to such texts, including *Abenddämmerung*, op. 49, no. 5; *Abendregen*, op. 70, no. 4; *Der Abend*, op. 64, no. 2; *An den Mond*, op. 71, no. 2; *Dämmrung senkte sich von oben*, op. 59, no. 1; *Gestillte Sehnsucht*, op. 91, no. 1; *In stiller Nacht*, WoO 33, no. 42; *Die Mainacht*, op. 43, no. 2; *Mondenschein*, op. 85, no. 2; *Mondnacht*, WoO 21; *O schöne Nacht!*, op. 92, no. 1; and *Sommerabend*, op. 85, no. 1.

10. Compare *Sehnsucht*, op. 49, no. 3, where the slow ascending arpeggios at the opening are inverted in the faster middle section. There are also ascending arpeggios at the opening of *Wie Melodien zieht es mir*, op. 105, no. 1, and *Maienkätzchen*, op. 107, no. 4; and a famous set of descending thirds in "O Tod," the third of the *Four Serious Songs*, op. 121.

11. Compare *Dein blaues Auge*, op. 59, no. 8.

12. Compare *Mein wundes Herz*, op. 59, no. 7.

13. Compare *An ein Veilchen*, op. 49, no. 2, where, however, the tonic root remains in the bass. See also the examples discussed below from Brahms's late Intermezzi.

14. Like Schubert before him, Brahms frequently shifts to key areas or chords lying a major third below. In both *Wie bist du, meine Königin*, op. 32, no. 9, and *Die Mainacht*, op. 43, no. 2, he moves from E-flat (via E-flat minor) to B major. In many instances he approaches the new area through its own $^6_4$ harmony, as in op. 57, no. 1 (*Von waldbekränzter Höhe*), measure 20.

15. Numerous examples of such phrase extension in Brahms songs were pointed out by Schoenberg in "Brahms the Progressive" (*Style and Idea*, ed. Leonard Stein [New York, 1975], 416–22). See the augmentation of the phrase "tonreichen Schall" in *An die Nachtigall*, op. 46, no. 4, mm. 5–7.

16. See the end of *Die Mainacht*, op. 43, no. 2.

17. In his *Style and Idea*, 418–22.

18. See, for example, the excellent analysis of the song *Feldeinsamkeit* in Christian M. Schmidt, *Johannes Brahms und seine Zeit* (Laaber, 1983), 146–54.

19. See my discussion of this aspect of the Andante of the Third Symphony in *Brahms and the Principle of Developing Variation* (Berkeley and Los Angeles, 1984), 88. Normally, Brahms's inflections toward the subdominant take place over the initial tonic root, as in *An ein Veilchen*, op. 49, no. 2.

20. Theodor Adorno, "Zemlinsky," in *Gesammelte Schriften* (Frankfurt, 1978), 16:351.

21. Rudolf Stephan, "Über Zemlinskys Streichquartette," in *Alexander Zemlinsky: Tradition im Umkreis der Wiener Schule*, ed. Otto Kolleritsch (Graz, 1976), 128.

22. There is no completely reliable inventory or catalogue of Schoenberg's early works. The best is Jan Maegaard, *Studien zur Entwicklung des dodekaphonen Satzes bei Arnold Schonberg* (Copenhagen, 1972), vol. 1.

23. Indeed, Schoenberg clearly had a specific Brahms song in his ear: *Ständchen*, op. 106, no. 1, whose first phrase concludes with the same 6–3–5 melodic shape, harmonized by a vi–I progression.

24. See Schoenberg, *Fundamentals of Musical Composition* (New York, 1967), 58.

25. Schoenberg, "Why No Great American Music?" in his *Style and Idea*, 178.

26. Reger, *Briefe*, 55.

27. Adalbert Lindner, *Max Reger: Ein Bild seines Jugendlebens und künstlerischen Werdens*, 3rd ed. (Regensburg, 1938), 146. Reger assigned the quintet the opus no. 21, but the work remained unpublished until 1922, six years after his death. It is printed in Max Reger, *Sämtliche Werke*, vol. 20, ed. Gunter Raphael (Wiesbaden, [1960]).

28. Niemann, "Brahms und die neuere Klaviermusik," 39.

29. For a discussion of the overlapping of dominant and tonic at similar moments of return in Brahms's Third Symphony, see Frisch, *Brahms and the Principle of Developing Variation*, 137–39.

30. Charles Rosen, "Influence: Plagiarism or Inspiration?" *19th-Century Music* 4 (1980): 100.

31. Otto Lessmann, "1881–91," *Allgemeine Musik-Zeitung* 18 (1891): 2.

Between Work and Play: Brahms as Performer of His Own Music

ROGER MOSELEY

At the beginning of the twenty-first century, we can hear Brahms's music wherever and whenever we like. But can we locate its source? The composer himself is long dead, even if his defiant gaze and formidable beard still haunt us. His printed musical texts survive, of course, taking up generous shelf space in libraries, music shops, and homes throughout the world, but their circles and lines will always remain mutely imprisoned on the page. Some have preferred this state of affairs, believing that musical notes are better seen than heard. The theorist Heinrich Schenker, for instance, believed that "a composition does not require a performance in order to exist," and that the "realization of the work of art can thus be considered superfluous."[1] Schenker was following the lead of Eduard Hanslick, Brahms's friend and critical ally, by locating musical works in a transcendent realm. For Hanslick, music ultimately consisted of "sounding forms set in motion" that floated free of the intentions and desires of the people who produced them, while Schenker went even further by claiming that music's true significance lay entirely beyond the auditory domain.[2] If, however, we want to register Brahms's music empirically, then we must allow for the intercession of human bodies and minds between the composer's conceptions and our perceptions. Collectively, these people constitute the legion of performers who have brought Brahms's notation to audible life for more than 150 years. They have transformed his circles and lines into an array of sonorous phenomena that unfold in music's eternal present while simultaneously acknowledging their origin in various strata of the past.

The role played by performers in the (re)production of European art music has been generally conceived in transmissive and mediatory terms under which performers form a bridge between the composer and listener. The success of a performance is thus often judged according to how faithfully it is thought to convey the composer's intentions, however indecipherable they might be. In this essay, I want to suggest other ways of constructing the relationship between composer, performer, and listener (or the aggregation of performers into an ensemble and listeners into an audience). To start with, what happens when two—or even all three—of these roles coalesce within one individual? A concrete example of this state of affairs survives in the form of Brahms's maddeningly indistinct piano recording of his own Hungarian Dance no. 1, WoO 1, made in 1889.[3] Conversely, there are intriguing instances where the implications of Brahms's music seem to exceed the agency of those who perform it, throwing up multiple personae. Some of them may be "embodied" by the musical gestures of instruments or voices, but others seem to invoke the presence (or absence) of the composer, address a specific listener, or even represent a broader historical or cultural force.[4] At such moments, Brahms's music can be heard to send a message through the medium of performance itself. Any attempt to locate the source of this communicative power has to contend with the multiple agencies of performers and listeners, even if we are always mindful of Brahms's shadowy figure behind the scenes.

To explore these issues and how they were manifested within Brahms's musical world, I will focus here on two instrumental works whose early performances featured Brahms as both composer and pianist: the Second Piano Concerto, op. 83 (1881), with which Brahms reinvented himself as a new type of keyboard virtuoso in a manner that belatedly responded to hostile criticism of the First Piano Concerto more than twenty years previously; and the Sonata for Piano and Cello in F Major, op. 99 (1886), which Brahms was prompted to write by (and which he subsequently premiered with) the cellist Robert Hausmann. I will rely on biographical information and historical evidence pertaining to the cultural status of musical performance in my discussion of the concerto, whereas my closer reading of the sonata will draw on recent theoretical attempts to understand musical performance in semiotic and gestural terms. My aim is thus to provide different contexts for the projection and interpretation of Brahms's music by illustrating how the composer's approach to performing his own works changed according to personal, public, and generic expectations, and how the traces left by these various forms of embodiment have continued to condition the responses of performers, listeners, and critics right up to the present.[5] Along the way, I hope to reveal and clarify some of the historical and aesthetic complexities that underpin conceptions of what it might mean to "play Brahms."

Putting Virtuosity to Work in the Second Piano Concerto

Debatable early experiences in Hamburg's taverns notwithstanding, Brahms made his public debut as a concert pianist at the relatively late age of fourteen.[6] The recital was only a modest success. His teacher Eduard Marxsen (to whom Brahms would later dedicate the Second Piano Concerto) recalled that his pupil's progress "was indeed remarkable, but not such as to give evidence of exceptional talent, only the results of great industry and unremitting zeal."[7] Despite (or perhaps because of) his natural short-comings, Brahms sustained ambitions of becoming a true virtuoso throughout the 1850s, and the work around which they coalesced was the First Piano Concerto, op. 15. The genesis of the concerto was notori-ously tangled: Brahms had started composing a sonata for two pianos before orchestrating it as a symphony. Ultimately, the genre of the con-certo seemed to offer a compromise between these rival conceptions while also presenting Brahms with the chance to star as the protagonist of his own musical drama.[8] A letter to Clara Schumann shows that this prospect had fired his imagination: "Do you know what I dreamt last night? I had turned my accursed symphony into a piano concerto and was playing it: a first movement, a scherzo, and a finale, terribly difficult and grand. I was absolutely transported."[9] But in 1859 Brahms's dream would turn into a nightmare when he finally performed the concerto in Leipzig. The critic Eduard Bernsdorf poured scorn not only on his writing for the piano ("Herr Brahms has deliberately made the pianoforte part of his concerto as uninteresting as possible") but also on his ability to play it ("Herr Brahms's technique as a pianist does not attain the standard that we have a right to expect of today's concert pianists").[10]

Such sour criticism stood in painful contrast to the adulation that had been lavished on Franz Liszt, the piano virtuoso extraordinaire who aban-doned the concert platform in 1847 in order to dedicate himself to composition. Brahms abhorred Liszt's music but unreservedly admired his pianism: "If you never heard Liszt, you really have nothing to say. . . . His piano-playing was something unique, incomparable, and inimitable."[11] Even Hanslick was spellbound by Liszt's cascades of notes and physical presence: "Not only does one listen with breathless attention to his play-ing; one also observes it in the fine lines of his face. . . . All this has the utmost fascination for his listeners, especially his female listeners."[12]

Conversely, while Brahms's works elicited Hanslick's approval, the crit-ic's response to how the composer performed them was decidedly cooler. When Brahms played the newly written *Handel* Variations, op. 24, at his Viennese concert debut in 1862, Hanslick made his reservations clear.

[Brahms] strives exclusively to serve the spirit of the composition, and he avoids almost shyly all appearances of self-important pageantry. Brahms has at his disposal a highly developed technique, which lacks only the final gleaming polish, the final energetic self-confidence that would permit us to call him a virtuoso. Brahms handles the most brilliant aspects of performance with a sort of casualness. . . . It might seem like a compliment to say that he plays more like a composer than a virtuoso, but such praise is not entirely unqualified. Inspired by the desire to let compositions speak for themselves, Brahms neglects—especially in performance of his own works—much of what the player is obliged to do for the composer. His playing resembles that of the astringent Cordelia, who would rather conceal her innermost feelings than expose them to the public. . . . Brahms handled his own works somewhat shabbily. His F-Minor Sonata, a composition so wondrously "sung to itself," was played by Brahms more "to himself" than in a clearly and crisply presented manner.[13]

By depicting Brahms as a servant and likening him to Shakespeare's demure Cordelia, Hanslick implied that he lacked the bravura and visual flair that characterized the Lisztian virtuoso. But Hanslick's critique also hinted at how this deficiency might be turned to Brahms's advantage: if Liszt's virtuosity was Faustian, Brahms's high-minded renunciation of showmanship placed him on the side of the angels. His Cordelian unwillingness to flatter and his devout dedication to the works he played could be construed as an index of a moral superiority capable of restoring virtue to debased virtuosity. Describing Brahms at the keyboard, his friend Joseph Viktor Widmann pursued these implications in nationalistic terms, emphasizing the *Innigkeit*—a term connoting both depth and intimacy—that Brahms's unlovely appearance concealed, and thus exemplified.

It is true, the short square figure, the almost straw blond hair, the jutting lower lip that lent the beardless youth a slightly sarcastic expression, were conspicuous and hardly prepossessing peculiarities; but his entire aspect was permeated by strength. The broad lionlike chest, the Herculean shoulders, the mighty head at times tossed back energetically when playing, the contemplative, beautiful brow glowing as if by an inner light, and the Germanic eyes framed in blond lashes and radiating a marvelously fiery glance.[14]

In the absence of Liszt's jaw-dropping legerdemain, the obstinacy of Brahms's "jutting lower lip" symbolized his determination to tackle the technical obstacles strewn in his path at the keyboard. The *Paganini* Variations, op. 35 (1862–65), exemplify this type of muscular, abrasive virtuosity, and in the light of his complex rivalry with Liszt, the circumstances surrounding their conception, composition, and early performance history are especially telling. After befriending the pianist Carl Tausig toward the end of 1862, Brahms presented him with "something to break [his] fingers over" in the form of an early version of the Variations.[15] By acquiring Tausig as a virtuosic proxy and offering him music based on Paganini's famous A-Minor Caprice, Brahms was flagrantly encroaching on Liszt's territory. Tausig had been Liszt's favorite protégé and was later to compose a number of symphonic poems; what is more, Liszt had dealt with the same theme in his *Études d'exécution transcendante d'après Paganini*, published in 1840, revised in 1851, and dedicated to none other than Clara Schumann.[16] Brahms's competitive intent was thus unmistakable. Considered both as musical literature and as substrate for performance, the *Paganini* Variations suggest that Brahms and Tausig combined to promote an anti-Lisztian doctrine of virtuosity that elevated effort above inspiration but preferred to mask that effort rather than to flaunt it. While Liszt conjured with special effects, Brahms and Tausig's only illusion was that there was no illusion: virtuosity was subjected to Brahms's rigorous compositional work ethic.

By 1868, the completion of the *German Requiem* marked the symbolic laying to rest of Brahms's virtuoso aspirations, along with the end of the financial insecurity that had sustained them. Thereafter the standard of his playing would steadily deteriorate, and he increasingly privileged the score over its realization. Thus when Florence May sought Brahms's advice on playing Mozart, he pointed to the score, saying, "It is all there"; on another occasion, he remarked, "When I play something by Beethoven, I have absolutely no individuality in relation to it; rather I try to reproduce the piece as well as Beethoven wrote it. Then I have quite enough to do."[17]

The austerity of this approach had ramifications for the fabric of Brahms's mature music; in Carl Dahlhaus's words, the perception of its qualities relied on

> a form of musical cognition based on the thematic process, a process in which every alteration infringed against the substance of the original. . . . A melody may be embellished without damage; a thematic process, however, must be interpreted, its latent structures made audible, before it can be comprehended.[18]

For Dahlhaus, the imposition of the virtuoso's personality through improvisation or ornamentation would imperil the audible logic of Brahms's thematic development, and thus the organicism of the work as a whole. Yet Dahlhaus's interpretation of the relationship between performer and composer is perhaps too binaristic. Brahms did not eliminate virtuosity from the discourse of his thematic arguments; rather, he reconfigured it, treating it as a minimum requirement for the performer while simultaneously transferring its attributes to the compositional realm. For those playing Brahms's music, fidelity to the text and virtuosity became one and the same, in that the latter was required merely to realize the former. A prime example is provided by Brahms's 1872 condensation of his Hungarian Dances from piano duet to piano solo. As Charles Rosen has pointed out, music that is fairly simple when distributed among four hands becomes a strenuous ordeal for two, and yet with ears alone one is hard-pressed to distinguish between the renditions of a pair of amateurs and a single sweating virtuoso.[19] In Brahms's more "serious" music, spontaneous embellishment by the performer was replaced by a hefty dose of written-out virtuosity from the composer in the form of a motivic density that had to be unpicked faithfully and unfussily. The pianist's task became subordinate and thankless in equal measure.

The ultimate measure of this task was Brahms's collection of 51 *Übungen* (exercises) for piano, WoO 6, written over several decades and gathered together for publication in 1893 as his last contribution to the piano literature.[20] The *Übungen* adhere to the utilitarian tradition of Muzio Clementi and Carl Czerny in their dissection of virtuosity.[21] Brahms suggested to his publisher Fritz Simrock that the cover should feature some unusual illustrations: "All possible instruments of torture should be represented, from thumbscrews to the Iron Maiden; perhaps some anatomical designs as well, and all in lovely blood-red and fiery gold."[22] If the *Übungen* were a grisly warning to the would-be virtuoso, they also demystified and codified virtuosity, breaking it down to its components in order to carve out a steep but scalable *gradus* to the summit of Parnassus, Brahms's "real" music. Brahms's writing down of his *Übungen* fixed the unscripted process of practice as a text; the exercising of Brahms's fingers was recorded in notation, and performance and score were thus brought together.[23]

The publication of the *Übungen* as a single set of exercises disguised the fact that they had emerged in parallel with the writing of Brahms's most challenging piano works. Although most of the *Übungen* were written in the 1850s and '60s, about twenty of the fifty-one exercises date from the early 1880s, and they were almost certainly practice aids for Brahms's performances of the Second Piano Concerto. The relationship between the exercises, written around the same time as the concerto, is evident in the type of figuration they share. The relationship is also audible in the concerto's musical figuration and syntax; in particular, Brahms's unusually heavy reliance on the sequential repetition of material in the concerto might be heard to draw on the lexicon of the exercise.

It is understandable that Brahms needed to write new exercises to lick his rusty technique into shape. The Second Piano Concerto is an ordeal for any soloist, and Brahms would perform it no fewer than twenty-one times over the winter of 1881–82.[24] Witnesses to his playing told of how he relished the difficulties of his own music. George Henschel remembered Brahms performing the notorious octave trills in the First Piano Concerto ("He would lift his hands up high and let them come down on the keys with a force like that of a lion's paw. It was grand!") and in 1892 Brahms wrote to Clara Schumann of "the peculiar appeal which is always connected to a difficulty."[25] But descriptions of Brahms's performances of the Second Piano Concerto raise serious doubts about whether he prevailed over its technical challenges. Brahms's playing was tolerated rather than celebrated; an anonymous contributor to the *Allgemeine musikalische Zeitung* echoed Hanslick's review of Brahms's Viennese debut in reminding readers that "we must remember that [Brahms] is primarily a composer. . . . Details lack finish, and his playing often seems somewhat colorless, but on the whole he grips the audience through his objective and stylish rendering."[26]

Privately, other members of Brahms's audiences were more forthright. The Irish composer Charles Stanford heard the composer perform his new concerto in Hamburg, and published a vivid account of it after Brahms's death:

> His piano playing was not so much that of a finished pianist, as of a composer who despised virtuosity. The skips, which are many and perilous in the solo part, were accomplished regardless of accuracy, and it is no exaggeration to say that there were handfuls of wrong notes. The touch was somewhat hard and lacking in force-control.[27]

Berta Geissmar, secretary to Wilhelm Furtwängler and Thomas Beecham, relayed what were presumably her mother's impressions of the composer's playing: "Brahms himself was not a good interpreter of his works. He played his concerto in B-flat major in the historic Rokokosaal of the Mannheim theatre and his clumsy fingers often hit the wrong notes."[28] Those closer to Brahms expressed similar reservations. Florence May had attended the rehearsal before the performance described by Stanford and "did not think Brahms's playing what it had been. His touch in *forte* passages had become hard, and he did not execute difficulties that before he had mastered with ease."[29] Clara Schumann confided to her notebook in 1882 that "Brahms plays more and more abominably—it's now nothing but thump, bang, and scrabble."[30]

Was the composer in denial of his shortcomings at the keyboard? Apparently not: May recalled that as early as 1871 "he was fully aware of his failings"—striking wrong notes and a hardness of tone—"and warned me not to imitate them."[31] Tausig was long dead, but had Brahms wanted a technically adept performance from a willing deputy, Hans von Bülow was on hand—indeed, Bülow conducted the rehearsal that May witnessed, and she openly wished that the two had swapped roles.[32] By 1885, even Liszt acknowledged that Bülow had performed the concerto "beautifully," whereas Brahms had played it "rather messily."[33]

One means by which Brahms compensated for his failing dexterity was his voice. His playing had been accompanied by a "gentle humming" since the 1850s, but in later years this noise transformed into what Ethel Smyth described as "a sort of muffled roar, as of Titans stirred to sympathy in the bowels of the earth."[34] Ferdinand Schumann was less poetic in registering "a sort of gasping, grumbling or snoring," which was "audible as far back as the tenth row," and Brahms's biographer Max Kalbeck once heard such extraordinary sounds accompanying Brahms's solitary piano-playing ("a growling, whining, and moaning, which at the height of the musical climax changed into a loud howling") that he thought the composer must have surreptitiously acquired a dog.[35] To adapt Roland Barthes, these sounds could be interpreted as the "grain" of Brahms's playing; they underpinned the fistfuls of notes both right and wrong, masking his inaccuracies and watermarking his soundscape with inimitable qualia.[36]

Brahms's grunting may have been designed to emphasize his masculinity: as a young man he was embarrassed by his high-pitched voice, and he tried to lower it, to somewhat unpleasant effect. Consciously or otherwise, he seems to have relished the greater resonance that his maturity (and probably his increased girth) afforded his voice, and thus his sense of male identity. It seems likely that his performance of the concerto took advantage of these properties, for when he met the pianist Ella Pancera, who played the Second Concerto in Vienna, he told her that his piece was "decidedly not for little girls."[37] But the gendered terms in which Brahms conceived the performance of his concerto take on a different form in relation to the practice of composition, as illustrated by a letter he wrote to Emma Engelmann: "What in the world doesn't the man intend and reflect upon when creating, or the woman while playing the piano?"[38] Although they may simply reflect widespread cultural prejudices, such remarks also hint at Brahms's identification of the private, inner world of composing with the masculine, and the public, visual elements of performance with the feminine.

In this context, it is telling that the features that most strongly marked Brahms's own style of performing were those that deflected interest from the ostentation of the virtuoso's body and its gestures. His listeners were on the one hand drawn within, treated to the rumblings of Brahms's inner workings, and on the other, steered away, forcibly reminded of his physical shortcomings. Ultimately, their attention was guided toward the music's metaphysical location. Richard Specht remarked on this paradoxical way in which Brahms's neglect of his audience somehow enabled its members to grasp the essence of the musical work: "The whole person was in this playing—and also the whole work: one seemed to possess it from that moment on, inalienably so. . . . He always played as if alone: he forgot the audience entirely, wholly immersed in his own world."[39]

If, as Stanford alleged, Brahms "took it for granted that the public knew he had written the right notes, and did not worry himself over such little trifles as hitting the wrong ones," then Brahms's disregard for the niceties of piano technique anticipated Schenker by the privileging of musical metaphysics over aural phenomena.[40] In pursuit of this aim, his execution of the concerto seems to have been calculated to create a discrepancy between score and performance. The misadventures of his fingers on the keyboard served to underscore the sureness of their grip on his pencil. The anonymous critic for the *Allgemeine musikalische Zeitung* described Brahms's playing as if the pencil were still in his hand ("he draws . . . in outlines, but in great outlines"), which chimes with Marie Schumann's description of his rendering of the concerto as "a spirited sketch."[41] By "despising virtuosity," as Stanford put it, Brahms was augmenting his compositional authority: he was putting virtuosity to work.

Regardless of whether they heard Brahms's pianism as a revelation or a hindrance, most audiences and critics responded enthusiastically to the concerto, leading Clara Schumann to write in her journal: "Brahms is celebrating such triumphs everywhere as seldom fall to the lot of a composer."[42] Positive responses to the Second Piano Concerto even spread to Brahms's performances of the First, as an anonymous review of an 1884 performance in Berlin demonstrates: "Maestro Brahms played his D-Minor Concerto wonderfully, especially with regard to the understanding of the work, since he obviously does not display the qualities of a professional pianist."[43] The reverential tone of this review stands in stark contrast to Bernsdorf's excoriation of Brahms's Leipzig performance twenty-five years earlier, even though sloppy piano technique was acknowledged in both cases. Brahms had transformed the criticism that Bernsdorf had hurled at him into praise of a higher order: any discrepancies between work and performance were firmly resolved in favor of the former. The Second Piano Concerto, and the circumstances under which Brahms presented it, thus had a powerful and lasting impact on the way its predecessor was performed and heard.

Brahms's biographer Walter Niemann grumbled about the unreasonable demands that Brahms made of the soloist throughout the Second Concerto:

> The pianist who plays this . . . concerto must to a great extent renounce his position as a virtuoso and become a mere journeyman at the piano, executing the pianistic toil imposed upon him by the composer with groans—and by the sweat of his brow. . . . One sees and hears the pianist striving and battling with things that are as extraordinarily difficult and unmanageable as they are exacting and fatiguing.[44]

For a contemporary pianist who did not happen to be Brahms, the concerto offered little more than an opportunity for martyrdom. But for those who came after him, Brahms's once-fearsome technical challenges eventually lost their power to intimidate, and recordings of both piano concertos now litter the catalogue. This process began even during his lifetime—after Brahms's final performance of the Second Concerto in 1886, he was happy to retreat to the conductor's podium while the Scottish-born Eugen d'Albert took over at the keyboard. Brahms was a great admirer of d'Albert, telling his friend Richard Heuberger that he no longer needed to play because he now had his own "court pianist."[45]

Brahms's two piano concertos thus expose the contingencies of writing and performing music in different ways. If the First evokes the *Sturm und Drang* of the young Brahms's musical and emotional trauma, it was also the site of a belated middle-aged triumph: the mature composer made up for the shortcomings of the youthful pianist. The Second also bears the fingerprints of Brahms in both capacities, but stacks the deck in favor of the composer. It quickly became a redoubtable warhorse that compelled subsequent pianists to attain a level of dexterity that had eluded Brahms himself, but their virtuosic obedience to his score demonstrates the ultimate subservience of the performer to the work.

Undercover Agency in the Sonata for Piano and Cello in F Major

Within the genre of the romantic piano concerto, issues of agency and drama tend to be delineated with sweeping gestures that reflect an elemental contrast between individual and community. The nature of this relationship can be depicted and construed in many ways, but most of them identify the soloist as a protagonist whose personality is defined, developed, and ultimately vindicated against the massed forces of the orchestra.[46] As mentioned above, this model has often been applied to Brahms's First Piano Concerto: the turbulence of the opening tutti sets the stage for a mighty struggle from which the piano eventually emerges triumphant. The temptation to cast the figure of Brahms in the piano's role is strong, especially in the light of his traumatic experiences with the Schumanns around the time of its writing, and his own performances of the concerto encouraged both friends and critics to identify his presence in the work under this rubric. But how might "Brahms" have manifested himself when performing works in other musical genres? Throughout his later Viennese years, Brahms was active as a conductor, accompanist, and chamber musician, and in each of these capacities his musical persona was projected and apprehended differently. The following attempt to reconstruct the premiere of his Sonata for Piano and Cello in F Major, op. 99, seeks to examine how Brahms's role changed when he was co-star rather than leading light.

Robert Hausmann (see Figure 1), Brahms's partner at the premiere, was a member of Joseph Joachim's famous quartet and taught alongside the violinist at the Berlin Hochschule. In the early 1880s Hausmann became close to Brahms. He pestered the composer for a second cello sonata after having successfully revived the first, op. 38 in E minor, in 1885.[47] Contemporary accounts of the two men's qualities as performers can help conjure up an idea of how they might have sounded when playing the new F-Major Sonata together, and an attempt to define the terms on which they interacted can similarly enrich our understanding of the sonata's syntax, structure, and gestural profile.

Fanny Davies, an English pianist who heard Brahms play his Piano Trio in C Minor, op. 101, described how he began the work by "lifting both of his energetic little arms high up and descending 'plump' onto the first C minor chord . . . as much as to say: '*I* mean *THAT*.'"[48] Her observation suggests an unambiguous attribution of agency: Brahms simply means what he writes and consequently does. Such rhetoric is easily applied to the piano's gruff roar at the outset of the first movement of op. 99 (see

Figure 1. Robert Hausmann and Johannes Brahms, photograph taken by Maria Fellinger (right) in 1896.

Example 1). But after this initial coup, the cello immediately assumes the limelight with its proud opening theme, while the piano recedes into a supporting role, providing little more than a metric and harmonic back-drop for the cello's flamboyant gestures. In these opening measures, the cello's bold monophonic line is concerto-like in invoking a solitary indi-vidual, perhaps even a heroic protagonist; in turn, the athematic tremolos in the first eight measures of the piano part might be understood to rep-resent what Robert S. Hatten has called, in his taxonomy of types of musical agency, a "depersonalized external force."[49] As Margaret Notley has shown, this relationship can also be understood within a philosophical and aes-thetic context (stretching from Hegel to Adorno) that links themes to the formal processes they undergo in terms that can be mapped onto the role of the individual within society.[50] But on close inspection, questions of agency and representation quickly become ambiguous. The cello's open-ing gestures may be bold, but they lack metrical grounding and repeatedly fall on weak beats, implying that its heroism is less confident than it appears. Rather than engaging in dialogue with the piano, the cello solipsistically muses on its theme in the manner of developing variation (mm. 9–20), a process that loses steam as the piano's energetic sextuplets slacken into six-

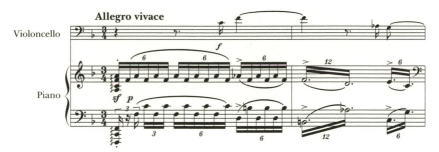

Example 1. Brahms, Sonata for Piano and Cello in F Major, op. 99, movement 1, mm. 1–12.

Example 1 continued

teenth notes.[51] For its part, the piano immediately undermines the cello's confident opening leap by shifting to a diminished-seventh harmony (a maneuver that brings to mind the opening of the Third Symphony, op. 90).[52] Similarly, the piano's single thematic contribution is offered as a counterpoint to the cello's theme, first in the right hand and then in the left. Boxed in Example 1, it sounds a minatory tone that hints at a threat to the cello's breezy optimism.

The self-assured second subject, shown in Example 2, brings respite while performing a neat dialectical inversion of the opening. The piano becomes the protagonist while the cello provides resolute accompanimental support in C major.[53] However, the two instruments do not pull together for long. When they swap roles once more, the piano's C-major chords give way first to A minor and then to E minor, as boxed in Example 2, which combine to push the cello toward the latter key while unsettling it to the extent that the ending of the phrase is breathlessly truncated in measure 45.

The turbulent section that follows leads to an impassioned "third subject" from the cello, illustrated in Example 3, that hovers around A minor, despite a disorienting whole-tone scale in mm. 54–55; once again, roles are exchanged, and it is the piano's firmly diatonic answer that clinches

Example 2. Brahms, op. 99, movement 1, mm. 33–45.

the cadence in this key, simultaneously revealing that both boxed chords in Example 2 have tonal ramifications beyond their immediate context.

This "third subject" sounds new, but some of its features can be traced back to the first theme: The cello's C–F fanfare has been inverted and augmented into a tritone, and the piano's agitated sixteenth notes, which outline a diminished seventh, are reminiscent of the opening tremolos. Most tellingly, the piano's cadential melody (boxed in Example 3) has been heard before as the counterpoint to the cello's initial theme (boxed in Example 1).

Rather than the piano and cello combining to reinforce the normative

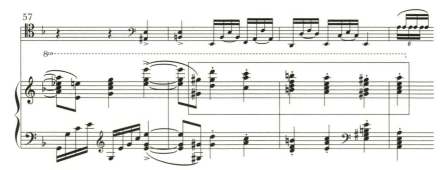

Example 3. Brahms, op. 99, movement 1, mm. 51–60.

dialectic of sonata form, then, their interaction results in a tripartite structure; instead of effecting a synthesis, the third element in this structure
seems to point out the unexpected implications of the first two, undermining the confident C major of the second subject while revealing a dark side
of the seemingly heroic first subject.[54] Moreover, the uncomfortable logic
of this third element seems to lie beyond the reach of either piano or cello
insofar as they act alone as principal or external agents, thus indicating
the presence of what Hatten calls a "narrative agent." This type of agent
takes the form of a "creative persona" who is "involved in ordering, arranging, and/or commenting upon the (sequence of) events of the story level."[55]

The firm hand of a narrative agent can also be felt in a passage that might
be categorized as a false recapitulation (a designation that already relies on
an awareness of narrative manipulation). As can be seen in Example 4, the
first subject returns in terms of key, harmony, and melodic outline, but it
is drained of gestural immediacy. The roles of piano and cello are reversed:
the cello struggles with the piano's tremolos while the piano sketches the
cello's opening theme in blank dotted half notes. The pianissimo dynamic
and *dolce* marking result in a hushed, almost minimalistic texture. Now little
more than an accessory, the cello is deprived of its ability to sing; instead,
it is pressed into fulfilling an uncomfortable and unidiomatic harmonic
function. Revealingly, the autograph score from which Brahms presumably played at the premiere has simple eighth notes on F written over the
awkward left-hand tremolo between F and low C at measure 112 of the
cello part (boxed in Example 4) that appeared in the first printed edition.
Although it is impossible to reconstruct the sequence of events that lay
behind these changes, the tremolo printed in the first edition is unambiguous. By considering an alternative, Brahms seems to have been thinking
about performing the sonata from a cellist's perspective, but he would
not ultimately allow such factors to threaten literal consistency within the

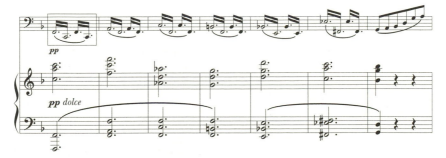

Example 4. Brahms, op. 99, movement 1, mm. 112–18.

Figure 2. Page 5 of Brahms's autograph score of the first movement of op. 99.

pages of the printed score.[58] In the autograph (see above), the tension between the conflicting demands of composer and performer is made manifest by the way the half-erased tremolo lurks behind the eighth notes written by Brahms's right hand in order to spare the cellist's left hand. The proposal and rejection of the alteration again opens up a space between Brahms as composer and performer, suggesting that what he first conceived—and ultimately published—was not necessarily the same as what he expected to hear.

Before returning to this idea, it is worth pursuing the presence of narrative agency into the coda (Example 5), where the tensions that first arose in the exposition are resolved with typically Brahmsian ingenuity and economy. First, the cello finds a middle ground between its opening gestures and the piano's pre-recapitulatory flattening out of the same theme (mm. 187–88); then, the piano revisits the second subject by way of the subdominant (mm. 193–95). Finally, both are brought together, as the texture and characteristic intervals of the first subject are melded with the thematic outline of the second subject, boxed in Example 6.

Example 5. Brahms, op. 99, movement 1, mm. 187–95.

Dialectical resolution is finally attained: the piano and cello have learned from each other at the prompting of the narrative agent, even though it seems that the cello had more to learn than the piano. But where can we locate—and how can we define—this narrative agent? For Fanny Davies and the audience at the sonata's premiere, the answer would have been sitting before them in the substantial form of Brahms himself. But how could Brahms's narrative agency and compositional ego then be distinguished from his agency as a performer?

Example 6. Brahms, op. 99, movement 1, mm. 203–7.

One answer lies in Hatten's fourth and final type of agent: the "performer-as-narrator," a persona that reflects the performer's influence insofar as he or she affects the listener's perception of other agencies within the work.[59] In the case of Brahms performing his own music, then, there is potential for slippage between Brahms as a narrative agent on the one hand and a performer-as-narrator on the other, not to mention his entanglement in the ambiguity between principal and external agency discussed above in relation to the unfolding of the exposition. Brahms, it seems, could shuttle between all these types of agency, showing their borders to be permeable: he could play the role of the piano or the pianist, but at moments such as the false recapitulation (Example 4), he was also uniquely qualified to assume the role of "the composer at the piano," a role that only he could play on stage but that continues to haunt any performance.

To complicate the matter still further, more discrepancies arise between notions of the ideal performance as mandated by the composer in the score and Brahms's documented characteristics as a pianist. Although the piano part of the F-Major Sonata is less demanding than the Second Piano Concerto, it still poses formidable technical challenges, and it is reasonable to assume that Brahms must have struck his fair share of wrong notes in performing it with Hausmann. Brahms's friend Elisabeth von Herzogenberg did not even have to hear Brahms playing his new cello sonata to imagine him "snorting and puffing away" throughout the scherzo; while she imagined the Barthesian "grain" of Brahms's voice with more amusement than distaste, it seems likely that Brahms's grunts and snuffles would once again have stood in for the musical gestures that his fingers could only approximate.[60]

But what of Hausmann's role? Brahms's demands on him were perhaps more exacting than on himself, for the cello part of op. 99 is held to be among the most difficult in the repertoire. And yet its difficulty is not immediately audible; it is typical of the awkwardness for which musicians over the years have cursed Brahms under their breath. As we have seen, Brahms paid little attention to matters of comfort and idiom, especially when it came to the publication of finished works. Hausmann might have been granted relief from the unwieldy left-hand tremolo in Example 4, but most subsequent cellists have had to confront it head-on.[61] This concession should not cast aspersions on Hausmann's technical abilities, however, which were of a very high standard, and Brahms knew that he could rely on humility and self-effacement from the cellist.[62] Hausmann's reputation in general and reviews of the premiere in particular suggest that he played with diligence and accuracy, although some critics thought these virtues were delivered at the expense of spontaneity and warmth.[63]

In the context of their collaboration, Hausmann's cello provided Brahms with something external that he could nonetheless appropriate. Brahms had briefly taken cello lessons as a young boy, and his orchestral and chamber works show that he was drawn to its potential for long-breathed melodies and ardent expression. But he was loath to give such emotion free rein; throughout his music, moments of melodic plenitude are tempered by formal and structural imperatives. This suggests one reason why the aging Brahms repeatedly turned to Joachim, Hausmann, and the clarinetist Richard Mühlfeld as musical proxies. All three were masters of their instruments, but none had a highly individualistic style, embraced virtuosity "for its own sake," or overstepped the bounds of good taste.[64] A thin line separated sentimentality and gruffness within Brahms's personality, and playing op. 99 with Hausmann allowed him both to growl and to croon, all the while providing him with an alibi should things get too embarrassingly personal. Thus it seems likely that Brahms sought refuge in Hausmann's agency even as Hausmann sought to divine Brahms's.

So what can we make of Brahms and Hausmann's imagined performance of op. 99, replete with both energetic grunts and tender lyricism? Although it would be fascinating to hear the real thing, I sense that it would also be somehow disappointing, too heavily laden with meaning and authority. I suspect that the nuances of agency raised here would be subsumed by the power of the composer's immediacy. After all, even today we hardly need encouragement to listen for Brahms's presence. Extrapolated from the score and repeatedly lionized by analysts and critics as well as performers, his agency is so strong that it threatens to render all other musical personae as puppets, whether they be the protagonists conjured up by his sonata-form dynamics or the dutiful performers charged with playing them.

A comparison of two recordings of the sonata illustrates the extent of Brahms's control and the drastic measures required to escape it. On their

RCA release recorded in 1984, Yo-Yo Ma and Emanuel Ax play with impeccable taste, technique, and musicianship, resulting in a wholly unobjectionable rendition; at times, however, it strikes me as overdetermined, excessively beholden to Brahms's agenda.[65] A brief passage in the scherzo offers a case in point (Example 7).

Example 7. Brahms, op. 99, movement 1, mm. 109–18.

The score here suggests that the cello should dovetail neatly with the piano, and Ma and Ax play it that way. The cellist follows obediently in the wake of the pianist, and the resulting circle of fifths is elegantly satisfying. Jacqueline du Pré and Daniel Barenboim, on the other hand, flagrantly disregard Brahms's dynamic, rhythmic, and agogic indications in their 1967 recording. Du Pré turns Brahms's echo into a defiant, impassioned declaration: she stretches time so far that Barenboim's ensuing hemiolas are in turn relegated to the status of an echo. In Hatten's terms, du Pré is an unapologetic protagonist as well as a "performer-as-narrator," whereas Ma and Ax minimize these aspects of their agencies.[66] And yet it might be that the reckless scraping of du Pré's bow is closer to the immediacy and physicality of Brahms's own "humming and snorting."

Perhaps the last word, or rather the last gesture, should belong to Robert Hausmann. Despite his sober reputation on the concert platform, Hausmann had a mischievous streak, as another photograph illustrates (Figure 3). Brahms is surrounded by his friends: Hanslick sits next to Brahms on the sofa while Mühlfeld flanks him on the other side. Meanwhile, Hausmann stands behind him, pretending to play the composer like a cello. Hausmann's cheeky gesture both confirms and belies his role as Brahms's faithful executant, suggesting that the performer might possess more power than the composer suspects. Brahms is as blissfully unaware of Hausmann's japery as he is of the recording that du Pré would make seventy years later. In their own ways, both cellists helped illustrate the inexhaustible riches of his music by "playing Brahms" in ways that the venerable composer could not have anticipated.

Figure 3. Brahms and friends, photograph taken by Eugen von Miller zu Aichholz in 1894.

NOTES

1. Heinrich Schenker, *The Art of Performance*, ed. Heribert Esser, trans. Irene Schreier Scott (Oxford and New York, 2000), 3. Brahms was reported to have said that Beethoven's *Fidelio* and Mozart's *Don Giovanni* were best enjoyed not at the theater but at home with the score. Robert Haven Schauffler, *The Unknown Brahms: His Life, Character, and Works* (New York, 1933), 217.

2. I refer to Hanslick's famous formulation in his aesthetic tract *Vom Musikalisch-Schönen: Ein Beitrag zur Revision der Ästhetik der Tonkunst* (Darmstadt, 1991), first published in 1854, according to which the content of music is "sounding forms set in motion" ("tönend bewegte Formen," 32). Despite his closeness to Brahms, there is no compelling evidence that the latter shared Hanslick's aesthetic perspective, but Hanslick's views have been enormously influential on the reception of Brahms's music nonetheless. The views of both Hanslick and Schenker can be understood within the context of a venerable strain of musical idealism that stretches from Plato to the present by way of the medieval concept of *musica universalis* (music of the spheres).

3. The cylinder recording is available on a CD issued by the Verlag der Österreichischen Akademie der Wissenschaften, titled *Brahms spielt Klavier: Aufgenommen im Hause Fellinger, 1889* (OEAW PHA CD5). On the cylinder's contents, see Helmut Kowar, "Zum Klavierspiel Johannes Brahms," in *Brahms-Studien* 8, ed. Kurt and Renate Hofmann (1990): 35–47; Jonathan Berger and Charles Nichols, "Brahms at the Piano: An Analysis of Data from the Brahms Cylinder," *Leonardo Music Journal* 4 (1994): 23–30; Michael Musgrave, "Early Trends in the Performance of Brahms's Piano Music," in *Performing Brahms: Early Evidence of Performance Style*, ed. Musgrave and Bernard D. Sherman (Cambridge and New York, 2003), 302–8; and Jonathan Bellman, "Performing Brahms in the *Style hongrois*," in Musgrave and Sherman, *Performing Brahms*, 329–30.

4. See, for instance, Paul Berry's insightful and imaginative reconstruction of networks of music and memory (involving Brahms as composer, the singer Julius Stockhausen as performer, and Clara Schumann as listener) that radiate from the song *Alte Liebe*, op. 72, no. 1, in "Old Love: Johannes Brahms, Clara Schumann, and the Poetics of Musical Memory," *Journal of Musicology* 24/1 (2007): 72–111.

5. In this sense, what follows could constitute a first step toward outlining what "carnal musicology" might bring to the study of Brahms: see Elisabeth Le Guin, *Boccherini's Body: An Essay in Carnal Musicology* (Berkeley and Los Angeles, 2006).

6. On the questionable authenticity of Brahms's recollections of playing in Hamburg's nighttime establishments, see Styra Avins, "Brahms the Godfather," in this volume; the exchanges between Jan Swafford, Avins, and Boman Desai in *19th-Century Music* (Swafford, "Did the Young Brahms Play Piano in Waterfront Bars?" *19th-Century Music* 24/3 [2001]: 268–75; Avins, "The Young Brahms: Biographical Data Reexamined," *19th-Century Music* 24/3 [2001]: 276–89; and Desai, "The Boy Brahms," *19th-Century Music* 27/2 [2003]: 132–36).

7. Quoted in Michael Musgrave, *A Brahms Reader* (New Haven and London, 2000), 18.

8. For a comprehensive account of the compositional history of the First Piano Concerto and factors influencing its reception, see George S. Bozarth, "Brahms's First Piano Concerto op. 15: Genesis and Meaning," in *Beiträge zur Geschichte des Konzerts: Festschrift Siegfried Kross zum 60. Geburtstag,* ed. Reinmar Emans and Matthias Wendt (Bonn, 1990), 211–47.

9. Letter of 7 February 1855, in Berthold Litzmann, ed., *Clara Schumann und Johannes Brahms: Briefe aus den Jahren 1853–1896* (Leipzig, 1927), 1:76.

10. Eduard Bernsdorf, *Signale für die musikalische Welt* (9 February 1859), 71–72. Bernsdorf's reaction was not atypical, as Brahms himself acknowledged: "The first rehearsal roused no emotions whatever among the musicians or the listeners. But for the second rehearsal, no listener showed up and not one musician moved a face-muscle. . . . I am plainly exper-

imenting and still groping. But the hissing was surely too much?" Letter to Joseph Joachim of 28 January 1859, in Max Kalbeck, *Johannes Brahms*, rev. ed. (Berlin, 1912–21; repr. Tutzing, 1976), 1:356; trans. in *Johannes Brahms: Life and Letters*, ed. Styra Avins; trans. Avins and Josef Eisinger (Oxford, 1997), 189.

11. Quoted in Kalbeck, *Johannes Brahms*, 1:90. To the poet Klaus Groth, Brahms was even more complimentary: "Of course, we are also capable of playing the piano, but none of us possesses more than a few fingers of his two hands." Quoted in Peter Clive, *Brahms and His World: A Biographical Dictionary* (Lanham, Md., 2006), 299. Clive's entry on Liszt (296–301) gives a succinct description of the long and complex relationship between Brahms and Liszt, showing that their mutual respect was genuine despite the aesthetic gulf that divided them.

12. Quoted in Henry Pleasants, ed., *Hanslick's Music Criticisms* (New York, 1988), 110.

13. Hanslick, *Aus dem Concertsaal. Kritiken und Schilderungen aus den letzten 20 Jahren des Wiener Musiklebens* (Vienna: Wilhelm Braumüller, 1870), 255–58; trans. Kevin C. Karnes in "Discovering Brahms," in this volume.

14. Joseph Viktor Widmann, *Johannes Brahms in Erinnerungen* (Berlin, 1898), 17–18; trans. by Dora E. Hecht in *Recollections of Johannes Brahms by Albert Dietrich and J. V. Widmann* (London, 1899), 94.

15. Letter from Brahms to Adolf Schubring of 25 June 1865, in Brahms, *Briefwechsel*, rev. ed. (Berlin, 1912–22; repr. Tutzing, 1974), 8:205; trans. in Avins, *Johannes Brahms*, 325.

16. Robert Schumann had written variations on Paganini's Caprice in 1832 (published in the *Études pour le pianoforte d'après les caprices de Paganini*, op. 3), but on the appearance of Liszt's set Schumann generously conceded the palm to the Hungarian. It seems that Brahms had been contemplating approaching Liszt's network of composers and virtuosos who gathered together under the banner of the New German School since 1860. In a letter to his publisher Melchior Rieter-Biedermann, Brahms bemoaned the fact that the only pianists capable of doing his First Piano Concerto justice were the least likely to take it on: "Almost all of the pianists able to meet its demands belong to the *neudeutsch* school, which doesn't tend to bother itself much with my things." Letter of 29 August 1860, in Brahms, *Briefwechsel*, 14:48.

17. Quoted in Musgrave, *A Brahms Reader*, 129–30. In general, Brahms's increased stature as a composer brought with it a concomitant lowering of his regard for performers. Despite Bülow's widely recognized qualities as a conductor and pianist and his dedication to Brahms's music, for instance, Brahms opposed the notion of a statue in Bülow's honor on the grounds that such memorials should be reserved for composers.

18. Carl Dahlhaus, *Nineteenth-Century Music*, trans. J. Bradford Robinson (Berkeley and Los Angeles, 1989), 138.

19. Charles Rosen, *Critical Entertainments: Music Old and New* (Cambridge, Mass., and London, 2000), 167–69.

20. The *Übungen* have recently been issued in a new edition by Johannes Behr with notes on execution by Peter Roggenkamp: *Brahms: 51 Übungen für das Pianoforte mit 30 weiteren, größenteils erstveröffentlichten Übungen* (Vienna, 2002).

21. Eugenie Schumann reported that Brahms "thought very highly of Clementi's 'Gradus ad Parnassum,'" and May also mentioned his reliance on it (quoted in Musgrave, *A Brahms Reader*, 132–33). Brahms also looked through Czerny's *Große Pianoforteschule*, op. 500, at the behest of Clara Schumann in 1880 (see *Brahms: 51 Übungen*, iii). It is notable that Liszt too turned to the prosaic form of piano exercise later in life. His *Technische Studien* were assembled between 1868 and 1873, but they were not published until after his death in 1886, and it is doubtful whether Liszt would have sanctioned their appearance in this form.

22. Letter of 12 November 1893, Brahms, *Briefwechsel*, 12:107. Brahms also warned Clara Schumann that his exercises could "do the hand all manner of damage." Letter of 22 December 1893, in Litzmann, *Clara Schumann und Johannes Brahms*, 2:535.

23. May commented on Brahms's predilection for "forming exercises from any piece or study upon which I might be engaged" rather than relying on the "ordinary five-finger exercises" (quoted in Musgrave, *A Brahms Reader*, 133). The tendency to conflate work and exercise has reached a new apex (or nadir) with Idil Biret's recording of the *Übungen* as part of Naxos's edition of Brahms's complete piano music (Naxos 8501201). Taking the reification of Brahms's music to such a logical extreme results in an uncanny sound-object shorn of meaningful musical context.

24. Over the winter of 1881–82, Brahms took the concerto on a tour that called at eighteen cities throughout Germany, Austria, and the Netherlands, involving no fewer than twenty-one performances. The following winter he took it to seven further cities. For the purpose of these early performances, Brahms entered detailed tempo indications into the autograph; typically, they did not survive into the published edition, which would remain unsullied by the residue of performance. See Robert Pascall and Philip Weller, "Flexible Tempo and Nuancing in Orchestral Music: Understanding Brahms's View of Interpretation in His Second Piano Concerto and Fourth Symphony," in Musgrave and Sherman, *Performing Brahms,* 220–43.

25. George Henschel, *Personal Recollections of Johannes Brahms* (Boston, 1907), 18. In his letter to Clara Schumann, Brahms was referring to the E-Minor Intermezzo, op. 116, no. 5 (letter of early October 1892, in Litzmann, *Clara Schumann und Johannes Brahms,* 2:479; trans. in Avins, *Johannes Brahms,* 698). The difficulties of Brahms's music generally adhere to Schenker's exacting criteria: "The composer may not throw in a technical problem merely to show himself and the performer in the pose of a musician easily overcoming difficulties—such pieces are generally written by the virtuoso-composers" (*The Art of Performance,* 77).

26. Anonymous critic, "Stuttgart," *Allgemeine musikalische Zeitung* 16/51 (1881): 810–11.

27. Quoted in Musgrave, *A Brahms Reader*, 125.

28. Berta Geissmar, *The Baton and the Jackboot: Recollections of Musical Life* (London, 1988), 8.

29. Quoted in Musgrave, *A Brahms Reader*, 125. The sympathetic Siegfried Kross contends that the lukewarm reaction to Brahms's playing was due to the rigors of his tour: he was burned out (*Johannes Brahms: Versuch einer kritischen Dokumentar-Biographie* [Bonn, 1997], 2:861). However, the tenor and frequency of such criticism suggest that Brahms's deficiencies were both notable and persistent.

30. Quoted in Robert Philip, "Brahms's Musical World: Balancing the Evidence," in Musgrave and Sherman, *Performing Brahms,* 351. In her memoirs, Eugenie Schumann recalled the "animosity" that was always latent in Brahms's playing: "I do not believe that Brahms looked upon the piano as a dear trusted friend, as my mother [Clara] did, but considered it a necessary evil, which one must put up with as best one could." *Memoirs,* trans. Marie Busch (London, 1927), 170.

31. Quoted in Musgrave, *A Brahms Reader*, 123.

32. Ibid., 125.

33. Quoted in Detlef Kraus, *Johannes Brahms: Composer for the Piano*, trans. Lillian Lim (Wilhelmshaven, 1988), 82. Liszt was in a good position to judge: he had asked to see the concerto when he met Brahms at a concert in 1882, and Brahms had been happy to comply (see Clive, *Brahms and His World*, 301). Liszt's response to the concerto was polite: "Frankly speaking, at the first reading this work seemed to me a little gray in tone; I have, however, gradually come to understand it. It possesses the pregnant character of a distinguished work of art, in which thought and feeling move in noble harmony." (Quoted in Karl Geiringer, *Brahms: His Life and Work* [New York, 1982], 150.) Liszt even tried to arrange a performance of the concerto in Zurich, but the orchestral parts were unavailable (see Clive, *Brahms and His World*, 301).

34. Quoted in Musgrave, *A Brahms Reader*, 124.

35. Richard Specht, *Johannes Brahms*, trans. Eric Blom (London, 1930), 306–7. See also Schauffler's description of Brahms's noises in "Brahms, Poet and Peasant," *Musical Quarterly* 18/4 (1932): 555.

36. See Roland Barthes, "The Grain of the Voice," in *Image, Music, Text*, trans. Steven Heath (New York: 1977), 179–89.

37. Quoted in Walter Niemann, *Brahms*, trans. Catherine Alison Phillips (New York, 1929), 319. Henschel reported that Brahms claimed to be able to tell the gender of a pianist by ear alone (*Personal Recollections of Johannes Brahms*, 41). Brahms affected to be contemptuous of women pianists: "I have a powerful prejudice against [them] and anxiously avoid listening to them." (Letter to Ferdinand Hiller of November 1876; trans. in Avins, *Johannes Brahms*, 502.) His respect for Clara Schumann tells a different story: she had performed the First Piano Concerto as early as 1861, which perhaps reveals as much about the differences between the two concertos as about the various forms of Brahms's misogyny. In any case, Florence May and Clara Kretzschmar (wife of the famous critic Hermann) flew in the face of Brahms's sexism by performing the Second Piano Concerto in 1888 and 1891, respectively.

38. Letter of 7 July 1881, in Brahms, *Briefwechsel*, 13:102–3, trans. in Avins, *Johannes Brahms*, 580.

39. Quoted in Pascall and Weller, "Flexible Tempo and Nuancing in Orchestral Music," in Musgrave and Sherman, *Performing Brahms*, 232. Specht's emphasis on Brahms's self-immersion echoes Hanslick's critique of Brahms's Viennese debut.

40. Quoted in Musgrave, *A Brahms Reader*, 125.

41. Marie's remark was recorded by her sister Eugenie: "To hear Brahms play his own things was not always satisfying, but highly interesting nonetheless. Marie once described his playing of his B-flat-major Concerto as a 'spirited sketch.'" (Quoted in Ulrich Mahlert, *Brahms: Klavierkonzert B-Dur op. 83* [Munich, 1994], 125.) The English pianist Fanny Davies also described Brahms's playing as "rugged, and almost sketchy." (Quoted in Bozarth, "Fanny Davies and Brahms's Late Chamber Music," in Musgrave and Sherman, *Performing Brahms*, 172.)

42. Quoted in Swafford, *Johannes Brahms* (New York, 1997), 469. Hugo Wolf's review struck a predictably sour note amid the chorus of approval (in Richard Batka and Heinrich Werner, eds., *Hugo Wolfs Musikalische Kritiken* [Leipzig, 1911], 113–14).

43. Anonymous critic, "Tagesgeschichte. Musikbriefe. Berlin," *Musikalisches Wochenblatt* 15/9 (21 February 1884): 111–12.

44. Niemann, *Brahms*, 319.

45. Quoted in Clive, *Brahms and His World*, 3.

46. On the myriad relationships between soloist and orchestra to which concertos can give rise, see Joseph Kerman, *Concerto Conversations* (Cambridge, Mass., and London, 1999).

47. See Kalbeck, *Johannes Brahms*, 4:33. Brahms went on to write the Piano Trio in C Minor, op. 101, and the Double Concerto, op. 102, with Hausmann in mind. For an overview of Brahms's relationship with Hausmann, see Friedrich Bernhard Hausmann, "Brahms und Hausmann," *Brahms-Studien* 7 (1987): 21–39.

48. Quoted in Bozarth, "Fanny Davies and Brahms's Late Chamber Music," in Musgrave and Sherman, *Performing Brahms*, 173.

49. Robert S. Hatten, *Interpreting Musical Gestures, Topics, and Tropes: Mozart, Beethoven, Schubert* (Bloomington and Indianapolis, 2004), 225–26. Since the ensuing discussion relies on Hatten's categorization of agency, I shall quote his definitions of them where relevant. The cello and piano here correspond to Hatten's Type 1 and Type 2 agents, respectively: "Type 1. *Principal agent* (actant, protagonist, persona, subject, voice): the individual subjectivity with which we identify, whether as performer or listener. Type 2. *External agent* (negactant, antagonist; *or* depersonalized external force, e.g., Fate, or Providence): that

agency which acts upon, or against, the principal agent." For an alternative perspective on issues of musical agency, see Eero Tarasti, *Signs of Music: A Guide to Musical Semiotics* (Berlin and New York, 2002), 140.

50. Margaret Notley discusses op. 99 in this context in *Lateness and Brahms: Music and Culture in the Twilight of Viennese Liberalism* (Oxford and New York, 2007), 76–80.

51. For a comprehensive overview of Brahms's application of this compositional technique, see Walter Frisch, *Brahms and the Principle of Developing Variation* (Berkeley and Los Angeles, 1984).

52. Kalbeck was the first to note the resemblance, along with that between the main theme of the sonata's finale and "Wir hatten gebauet," the student song Brahms quoted in the Academic Festival Overture, op. 80 (*Johannes Brahms,* 3:35).

53. The piano's dominance here is foreshadowed by the way it wrests control of the bass line in measure 31, taking advantage of the cello's inability to go any lower.

54. It is telling, however, that C major makes a brief attempt to reestablish itself via the piano in measure 57. This time, roles are reversed: the cello's harsh diminished fifth on the third beat of the measure pushes proceedings back toward E minor.

55. Hatten, *Interpreting Musical Gestures,* 226. The narrative agent constitutes Hatten's third type, and is distinguished from types 1 and 2 (which are embedded in a musical "story") through its concern with "a *compositional* play with musical events or their temporal sequence or relationship, inflecting their significance, or proposing a certain attitude toward them. This agency . . . provides a 'point of view' or filtered perspective. . . . The narrative agency is cued by shifts in level of discourse."

56. See also the opening of the slow movement, where the traditional roles of piano and cello are similarly reversed: the cello plods while the piano attempts an impossible crescendo (mm. 1–4).

57. See Notley, "Brahms's Chamber-Music Summer of 1886: A Study of Opera 99, 100, 101, and 108" (Ph.D. diss., Yale University, 1992), 280–82, for details of this alteration (and others).

58. Brahms made a similar amendment in mm. 56–57 of the piano part, where broken chords that were broad handfuls in the autograph became hair-raisingly difficult in the first edition for the sake of slightly more elegant voicing. (See ibid., 278.)

59. Hatten, *Interpreting Musical Gestures,* 226. The performer-as-narrator directs "the listener's attention (possibly overdidactically) to the structure and significance of events. . . . Commenting upon the events from the perspective of the individual point of view and prejudices of the performer as engaged participant in the 'telling' of the story. May (over-)emphasize the characterization of actants (Types 1 and 2), or (rhetorically) mark especially unusual (narrative) reorderings or disruptions of expected events or event sequence (Type 3)."

60. "I'd like to hear you play the scherzo, with its driving power and energy— I always hear you snorting and puffing away at it! Nobody else will ever do it justice as far as I'm concerned." (Letter of 2 December 1886, in Brahms, *Briefwechsel,* 2:131.)

61. Not all, however. On her EMI recording with Daniel Barenboim (*Brahms Cello Sonatas,* originally released on LP in 1967, digitally remastered and rereleased on CD as EMI 0724356275829), discussed in further detail below, Jacqueline du Pré takes the C an octave above the notated pitch. Perhaps she was using an edition such as that by Leonard Rose (New York, 1956), which tacitly transposes the C up an octave.

62. For an account of Hausmann's personality and musical style, see M. R., *Some Points of Violin Playing and Musical Performance as Learnt in the Hochschule für Musik (Joachim School) in Berlin During the Time I Was a Student There, 1902–1909* (Edinburgh, 1939), 83–102.

63. Notley quotes a review of the premiere by Robert Hirschfeld: "The cellist Hausmann pushes . . . objectivity as far as the mortification of feeling." ("Brahms's Chamber-Music Summer," 24.) She also cites Theodor Helm's tepid reaction: "Even then we had to com-

mend the artist on his truly classical playing, acquired in the very best school, while we also, nevertheless, did not fail to notice his lack of temperament and a certain academic-professorial bearing" (25). Wolf similarly complained that Hausmann's playing was "cold, affected, and (in our opinion) boring." (Review of 28 November 1886 in the *Wiener Salonblatt*, in *Hugo Wolfs Kritiken im Wiener Salonblatt*, ed. Leopold Spitzer and Isabella Sommer, [Vienna, 2002], 1:170–72.) Hausmann's scholarly self-effacement reminds us that types of agency may impinge on the performance of work even if they do not stem directly from the interpretation of the score: the cellist's disinterested approach to the work may have encouraged concertgoers to perceive him as a narrative agent—or even an agent of Brahms's agency!—rather than a protagonist.

64. On Joachim's musical personality, see J. A. Fuller Maitland, *Joseph Joachim* (London and New York, 1905); on Mühlfeld's, see Colin Lawson, *Brahms: Clarinet Quintet* (Cambridge and New York, 1998), 32–33.

65. Yo-Yo Ma and Emanuel Ax, Brahms Cello Sonatas (RCA Victor Red Seal 59415, 2004). Their re-recording of the sonatas for Sony (48191, 1992) comes across with greater flair, but retains many of its predecessor's fundamental characteristics.

66. Du Pré's agency as a protagonist and performer-as-narrator (Hatten's types 1 and 4) is so powerful that at times her performance seems to cast the sonata itself as an externalized type 2 agent (a negactant or antagonist).

Brahms, Max Klinger, and the Promise

of the *Gesamtkunstwerk*:

Revisiting the *Brahms-Phantasie* (1894)

KEVIN C. KARNES

On the first day of January 1894, the artist Max Klinger sent Brahms a remarkable gift in the form of his newest creation. That gift, a volume consisting of forty-one etchings and engravings interspersed with the complete scores of six of Brahms's vocal works, Klinger called the *Brahms-Phantasie*.[1] By the time Klinger unveiled his tribute to Brahms, he had achieved considerable renown as a visual artist. Indeed, as Hugo von Hofmannsthal declared, he was considered by some to be "the most original artist that Germany has the honor of calling her own."[2] But the *Brahms-Phantasie* was something more than just another volume of the artist's celebrated prints. It was a work to be seen *and heard*, either literally—when Brahms's scores are performed—or in the mind of the observer. It was a multimedia composition that extended the impressions made by two-dimensional images into acoustical space. As such, it constituted a novel realization of the composite art form that Klinger had described, in his theoretical writings, as *Raumkunst* or "spatial art." Inspired by Richard Wagner's attempts to unite music, poetry, and the visual arts into a *Gesamtkunstwerk,* or "total artwork," Klinger envisioned the *Raumkunstwerk* as an integral union of artistic media, literally filling the *Raum* (space) inhabited by the observer.

In recent years, the visual components of Klinger's *Brahms-Phantasie* have received considerable attention from art historians, and many have noted the indebtedness of Klinger's experiment to Wagner's theory of the *Gesamtkunstwerk*.[3] But the fraught relationship between Klinger's volume and broader lines of turn-of-the-century aesthetic and cultural discourse—its indebtedness to them and, more important, its critical commentary upon them—have been all but overlooked. In this essay, I consider a question that succinctly encapsulates many of the complexities inherent in this relationship. Namely, what can we make of the fact that Klinger chose *Brahms*, the notoriously conservative, even deliberately classicizing composer widely regarded by many contemporaries as Wagner's musical antithesis, as the supplier of his musical materials? In response to this question, I will suggest two things. First, by exploring the interplay of musical texts and visual images as they appear in Klinger's volume, I will argue that the *Brahms-Phantasie* constitutes an ambivalent critique of a vital yet largely forgotten line of late-century cultural criticism that regarded the Wagnerian union of artistic media as a means by which to foster transcendence of the individualistic concerns of the modern age and usher in a new, imagined era of humankind's spiritual unity. Then, by considering Brahms's own reception of the volume through the prism of recent scholarship in emblem studies, I will suggest that Klinger registered his critique of Wagnerian idealism in distinctly Brahmsian terms: by inscribing aspects of Wagner's expressive innovations within a deliberately classicizing form— in Klinger's case, not the classical symphony but the Baroque emblem book. In the end, I will argue that Klinger was not, despite the fantastical images conjured in his work, merely a "metaphysical dreamer" or a "magi who conjures enchanted art," as one contemporary critic charged.[4] Rather, his Brahmsian commentary on Wagner's legacy makes clear that he was also, at least at times, a critical, ambivalent modernist, whose work, in the words of another contemporary commentator upon it, was firmly "grounded in a critique of the present."[5]

The Promise of the *Gesamtkunstwerk*

Though it was the only one of Klinger's creations to make use of musical scores, the *Brahms-Phantasie* was hardly the artist's first attempt at Wagner-inspired multimedia work. Indeed, as one author has aptly put it, Klinger embarked upon a "path to the *Gesamtkunstwerk*" long before he began his work on the volume, and also before he formalized his theory of *Raumkunst* in his *Painting and Drawing* of 1891.[6] Having dedicated himself to the visual arts at an early age, Klinger made a stunning debut before the German public with a collection of etchings titled *A Glove*, which he exhibited to great acclaim at Berlin's Royal Academy of Art in 1878. For most of the following decade, he devoted the bulk of his attention to producing further volumes of prints, including *Eve and the Future* (1880), *A Life* (1884), and *A Love* (1887).[7] As early as 1883, Klinger had already attempted to realize what he would later characterize as his *Raumkunst* ideal in his work on a vestibule at the home of a patron, the Villa Albers in Berlin. There, Klinger painted walls and ceiling, even doors and mantle. He supplied sculpture and painted that as well, thus creating a completely crafted artistic *Raum* into which visitors to the villa would arrive.[8] In the coming years, Klinger found himself increasingly drawn to one aspect of that project in particular, painted or polychrome sculpture, and he completed his *New Salome* (greatly admired by Brahms) in the latter medium in 1893.[9] Klinger's best-known work of polychrome sculpture is his statue of Beethoven that formed the centerpiece of the fourteenth exhibition of the Vienna Secession in 1902, where it was surrounded by Gustav Klimt's *Beethoven Frieze* on the walls and accompanied, during at least one viewing, by a performance of a chamber arrangement of Beethoven's Ninth Symphony, scored and conducted by Gustav Mahler.[10]

Whereas the *Brahms-Phantasie* was unique in Klinger's oeuvre with respect to the materials used, it was, as only one among his many multimedia experiments, hardly out of place in relation to the artist's more general concerns. Moreover, if we take yet another step back from the particulars of its construction, we find that the *Brahms-Phantasie* also has a great deal in common with the creative efforts of many of Klinger's contemporary Germans with regard to its creative negotiation of Wagner's still-powerful legacy, and especially Wagner's widely underestimated theory of the *Gesamtkunstwerk*. For although the broad resonance of this theory has been largely forgotten in the decades since World War II, the late nineteenth century saw innumerable attempts among artists, philosophers, social theorists and even politicians to explore the promise of the *Gesamtkunstwerk* to transform not only artistic creativity but the individual psyche and society as a whole. As we will see, a number of themes that surface in this discourse are treated explicitly in Klinger's tribute to Brahms. And Klinger himself participated in this wave of Wagner-inspired, late-century theorizing in his aesthetic treatise *Painting and Drawing*, upon which he worked simultaneously.

In *Painting and Drawing* (1891), Klinger elaborated a narrative tale of the historical evolution of the visual arts that echoes closely Wagner's account of the historical development of music and drama in his *Artwork of the Future* (1849). Whereas the art of music, in Wagner's narrative, had once united dance and poetry in the drama of the ancient Greeks, so also color, for Klinger, had once united architecture, painting, and sculpture in the artworks of earlier peoples and ages, presumably extending back to Greek temple art. And just as the historic downfall of Greek society had spelled, for Wagner, the end of artistic union in the drama, so, too, Klinger linked the decline of earlier civilizations with the advent of colorless sculpture and unadorned architecture, and thus with the fraying of the ancient bond between the latter arts and painting.[11] "Today," Klinger wrote in words that could be taken directly from Wagner's book, "we have architecture and sculpture, painting and reproductive art, and even decorative and applied arts. But we lack a great, *composite* expression of our life's experience. We have arts, but no *art*."[12] Moreover, just as Wagner regarded the demise of Greek drama as both a cause and a reflection of broader societal decay, so, too, Klinger saw reflected in the explosion of once-unified composite art forms the alienation and creative impotence widely felt by modern man. "Alongside admiration and adoration of this marvelous, progressive world," Klinger wrote of contemporary German society, "we encounter resignation, little comfort, and the utter misery of the pitiful creature in his laughable smallness caught in a never-ending struggle between his desires and his capabilities."[13] What Klinger sought in his own attempts to "reunite" the arts in his so-called *Raumkunstwerk*, he explained, was nothing less than "what Wagner strove for and attained in his music dramas."[14]

Precisely what Wagner "strove for," however, was something that has escaped the attention of most recent commentators on the composer, namely, the refashioning of German and ultimately European society in such a way that the individualism and alienation characteristic of the modern age would be supplanted by a newly invigorated sense of social and spiritual communion. Significantly, in Wagner's view, the catalyst for such a transformation was the *Gesamtkunstwerk* itself.[15] Though Wagner's commitment to social reform seriously waned after his encounter with the philosophy of Arthur Schopenhauer in the early 1850s, the composer clung throughout his life to the notion that the creation and experience of the *Gesamtkunstwerk* would unite individual members of an atomized society just as it would reunite the separate arts once combined in Greek drama. The idea, as Wagner articulated it in *The Artwork of the Future*, was that the sort of multimedia work he envisioned was of such complexity that it could only be created by a collaborating team of artists, each bringing his unique expertise to bear upon the completion of the composite artwork. This was, of necessity, a communal endeavor, requiring cooperative effort for its creation and showcasing the fruits of collective labor in its every performance. "The great *Gesamtkunstwerk*," Wagner wrote on this point, "is recognized . . . as the necessary, collective work of the manhood of the future. . . . The individual spirit, striving creatively for its redemption in nature, cannot create the artwork of the future. Only the collective, infused with life, can accomplish this."[16]

Indeed, Wagner continued, the communal spirit required to create such an artwork constituted nothing less—and nothing other—than the one true and only meaningful "religion of the future." That is, it constituted a spiritually unifying alternative and antidote to Europe's fractious array of Judeo-Christian faiths. "The religion of the future is a religion of *commonality*," Wagner argued. "But we unhappy people, no matter how many among us feel ourselves driven toward [the creation of] the artwork of the future, will never experience this bond, *this religion of the future*, so long as we are *individuals* and *alone*. . . . The artwork is the living manifestation of religion. But religions are not invented by artists; they arise from out of the community."[17] In one of the composer's last published essays, an afterword to his "Religion and Art" of 1880, Wagner returned to this theme, declaring the nurturing of a sense of spiritual unity and its attendant social revivification to be the ultimate goal of all creative endeavors. "We recognize the cause of the fall of historic man, and also the necessity of his regeneration," Wagner proclaimed, speaking for like-minded artists. "We believe in the possibility of his regeneration and devote ourselves to its accomplishment in every sense."[18] Taken together, Wagner's writings on the *Gesamtkunstwerk* and its promise sketch out, in a characteristically oblique and fragmentary manner, a holistic, largely metaphysical system for the transformation of humanity and society, in which spiritual, social, and artistic unities are each both product and guarantor of every other (Figure 1).

Figure 1. Wagner's metaphysics of the *Gesamtkunstwerk*.

In the final quarter of the nineteenth century, countless European writers and intellectuals seized upon Wagner's theory of the *Gesamtkunstwerk* to advance a bewildering array of their own positions on artistic, social, and political issues. The young Friedrich Nietzsche, for one, saw in the *Gesamtkunstwerk* a model for the sort of unity that might someday be achieved in the sphere of German education. "It is entirely possible that Wagner will destroy the Germans' interest in occupying themselves with the separate, individual arts," Nietzsche wrote in 1874. "Perhaps in his wake we will even be able to formulate the image of a unified education, one that cannot be achieved by simply adding together separate skills and areas of knowledge."[19] For the Viennese poet Siegfried Lipiner, now all but forgotten but a major influence on Gustav Mahler and an important early disseminator of Nietzsche's ideas, the metaphysical implications of Wagner's statements were the greatest source of inspiration. In an essay of 1878 that anticipates Wagner's "Religion and Art," Lipiner closed with a declaration of the artist's spiritually unifying mission. Citing at length from the libretto to *Parsifal* and expressing a Schopenhauerian conviction in the essential identity of all being, Lipiner declared the following on behalf of all artists: "Trading the uniqueness achieved through individuation for awareness of one's unity with all that is, kneeling down as something transient and arising as the intransient: That is our motto."[20] Indeed, the popular enthusiasm for Wagner-inspired theorizing about the *Gesamtkunstwerk* and its seemingly limitless promise to transform individuals and societies was not limited to German-speaking Europe. In what would become one of the period's most notorious polemical exchanges, the anonymous British author of *Regeneration* (1896)—an answer to the sensational *Degeneration* (*Entartung*, 1895) by the Viennese critic Max Nordau—proffered Wagner's theory of the *Gesamtkunstwerk* as inspiration for a desired socialist refashioning of the whole of European society.[21] "The arts, after having demonstrated in the opera their solidarity and their independence," this anonymous author wrote,

> will leave that artificial shelter and take up their abode in our homes and in our civic buildings, in our streets and in our public places, in our arenas and in our temples. . . . The man who thinks and writes, the artist who paints or composes, the peasant at the plough, the miner in the bowels of the earth, all are contributing to further the advent of a new era when life, the work, the pleasure, and the worship of a regenerate race shall be exalted by the arts, and present a realization of what Wagner dreamed while he created.[22]

As Marsha Morton has recently shown in an insightful analysis of Klinger's theoretical writings, Klinger, too, was deeply concerned with the transformation of German culture. In elaborating his position on painting, drawing, and multimedia work, he also sought to effect a "regeneration" of sorts in the sphere of German art, which had, he felt, fallen shamefully behind the French and the Italian in terms of stylistic innovation.[23] What I shall focus on in the remainder of this essay, however, is the musical and visual imagery in Klinger's *Brahms-Phantasie*, and the ways in which these combine to lodge a powerful, ambivalent, and distinctly Brahmsian critique of the Wagnerian discourse just described. Although the thematic organization of Klinger's volume is a topic of continuing debate, that volume is, with respect to its musical content, clearly divisible into two halves.[24] In the first, the scores of five of Brahms's songs, all focusing on themes of love and loss, are provided with images that invoke the failure of an individual's endeavors to unite with another through love. In the second half of Klinger's volume, the complete piano-vocal score of Brahms's *Schicksalslied*, op. 54, is framed by images from the Prometheus myth, in a telling that reflects upon the futility of man's longing for atonement with a higher being, and also of the artist's Wagner-inspired aspirations to reshape his society from within. Though clearly attempts at precisely the kind of "reunion" of the arts for which Wagner called, the two halves of Klinger's *Brahms-Phantasie* elaborate in sound and image a pair of narratives that starkly reject both the social and the spiritual promises that Wagner's followers had come to associate with the *Gesamtkunstwerk*.

The *Brahms-Phantasie* (I): Love

The variety of failure that pervades both music and image in the first part of Klinger's volume is particularly significant in a Wagnerian context, for it was *love*, in Wagner's view, that would provide the spark to propel the transformation of contemporary society. As Wagner explained in *The Artwork of the Future*, it was the love of one human being for another that would ignite the communal spirit and inspire the collective labor required to construct the *Gesamtkunstwerk*. It was the renunciation, ignorance, and mistrust of love that spelled the unraveling of societies in *The Ring of the Nibelung*. And it was a vision of the metaphysical union of two individuals, achieved through the experience of romantic love, that inspired Wagner's creation of *Tristan and Isolde*.[25] Nonetheless, the failure of love and the unities it promises is starkly depicted in the first half of the *Brahms-Phantasie*. And that depiction is prepared by Brahms himself in the first song Klinger selected for his collection.

Klinger opens his tribute to Brahms with the following image (Figure 2): a man, accompanied by a figment of his imagination, poring over a trove of letters. Context is provided by Brahms's music, the opening phrases of *Alte Liebe* (op. 72, no. 1), in which, in a text by Karl Candidus, a "dark swallow returns from a distant land," and "the pious stork returns, bringing new luck."

Figure 2. Opening page of Klinger, *Brahms-Phantasie*, with Brahms, *Alte Liebe*, mm. 1–9.

Significantly, the "new luck" of which Brahms's singer sings is nothing truly new, but rather the "alte Liebe" or "old love" of Brahms's title—or, more precisely, the *memory* of an old love. And in typically Brahmsian, ironic fashion, this memory proves to be anything but comforting, as it brings the singer neither a recalled sense of fondness nor an imagined reunion with his beloved but a new taste of old pain. Brahms's song begins unremarkably enough, with his setting of the expectant first two lines. But as the poet proceeds to reveal to us the true nature of this "new luck," Brahms begins, ever so subtly, to pull the rug out from under our feet, with a handful of soon-to-become obsessive repetitions of the singer's opening motive (D–E♭–G–F♯), doubled at octaves in mm. 11–12 and articulated, jarringly, on weak subdivisions of the beat (Example 1), and with the beginnings of a prolonged modulation to the key of E-flat major, a key only distantly related to the song's tonic G minor:

On this spring morning, so gloomily overcast and warm,
it seems as if I'd encountered once again the pain of old love.

Example 1. Brahms, *Alte Liebe*, op. 72, no. 1: (a) mm. 1–3, (b) mm. 11–12.

As both song and poem proceed from here, the singer gradually loses his hold on reality. And Brahms, accordingly, casts us still further afield from the tonic, leading us through a seemingly aimless series of keys, only to emerge, unexpectedly, into the illusory safety of a false recapitulation at mm. 34–35 (Example 2):

It is as if someone touched me gently on the shoulder,
as if I heard a rustling like that of a dove's wing.
I hear a knock on my door, but there's no one outside;
I catch the smell of jasmine, but there is no bouquet.

Example 2. Brahms, *Alte Liebe*, mm. 33–35.

In the final stanza, the singer's descent into the abyss of memory is matched by Brahms's obsessive repetitions of the opening melodic motive, now articulated in three voices simultaneously (Examples 3a and 3b). In the song's final line, the singer is seized by longing for a path not taken and plucked emotionally from this world, hearing at the end only the opening motive, played in octaves by the piano (Example 3c):

> I hear a call from the distance, and feel an eye upon me.
> An old dream takes hold of me and leads me down its path.
> An old dream takes hold of me and leads me down its path.[26]

Example 3. Brahms, *Alte Liebe*: (a) mm. 37–39; (b) mm. 49–51; (c) mm. 55–59.

The second song in Klinger's collection, Brahms's setting of a Bohemian folk song here titled *Sehnsucht* (Longing) (op. 49, no. 3), Klinger illustrated with a pair of reflections on the psychological trauma of a lost relationship. On the one hand, the traditional text might be read as hopeful, consciously willing, against all odds, the eventual reunion of the singer with his beloved. And Brahms's setting of this text seems, if anything, downright pastoral (Example 4):

> Beyond these dense woods you tarry, my sweet beloved,
> far, oh so far away.
> Split, you cliffs, flatten out, you valleys,
> so that I might once again see, once again catch sight
> of my distant, my distant sweet girl!

For Klinger, however, the crucial line here seems to be the first: "Beyond these thick woods you tarry, my sweet beloved"—the key words being "you

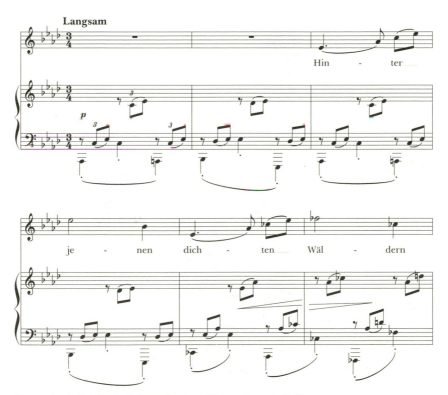

Example 4. Brahms, *Sehnsucht*, op. 49, no. 3, mm. 1–6.

tarry," you stay away. To match this, Klinger gives us an image titled *The Cold Hand* (Figure 3), in which a man, alone, tries to hold himself above the ground by grasping at branches, while touched by a spirit descending from above (the ghost of his beloved?), its "cold hand" laid upon his side.

Figure 3. Klinger, *The Cold Hand*, in *Brahms-Phantasie*, 7.

Klinger closes this meditation on longing with an etching, titled *Couple in the Flat* (Figure 4).

Figure 4. Klinger, *Couple in the Flat*, in *Brahms-Phantasie*, 9.

In this image, the solitude of the central figure is made explicit, for we have no *couple* at all, or at least none apparent. Is the man's partner fast asleep, somewhere in the bed behind him? If so, his solitary desolation, his sense of aloneness while nonetheless sharing his bed, is exquisitely portrayed. Or is his partner instead present only in his mind, perhaps having chosen, as Brahms's text suggests, to tarry somewhere beyond the woods?

The yawning chasm between appearance and reality is the explicit subject of Brahms's *Am Sonntag Morgen* (On Sunday morning) (op. 49, no. 1), the third song in Klinger's volume. Here Sunday morning arrives pleasantly enough on the surface. But, as the singer lets his straying lover know, "I know where you've been." As the song progresses, the layers of the lover's deception and the singer's public masking of his own failure pile one on top of the other. When "many people who saw you," he sings, told me what you'd done, "I laughed loudly," and even began to sing, only to return afterward to the solitude of my chamber, where I "cried through the night" and "wrung my hands raw." Klinger adorns these final lines with a marginal illustration of a man, submerged to the waist in water, barely—and probably only temporarily—saving himself from drowning by clutching at a bunch of reeds.[27] The final song in the first half of Klinger's volume presents the viewer with perhaps the most powerful image of emotional emptiness possible for a visual artist. Here Klinger gives us the complete score of Brahms's terse *Kein Haus, keine Heimat* (No house, no home) (op. 94, no. 5), confined in its entirety to the bottom half of a single page. "No house, no home, no wife and no child," the text runs, "I flit about like a piece of straw in the weather and wind. Tossed up and down, first here and then there—don't ask anything of me, world; what have I asked of you?" The singer's absolute aloneness is echoed vividly by Klinger, who leaves the entire top half of the page blank, as if waiting to be filled in. He provides not a single mark to accompany the singer in his life's meanderings; it is the only unadorned page in the whole of the *Brahms-Phantasie*.[28] As the art historian J. Kirk T. Varnedoe has remarked in his monograph on the artist (though without reference to "No House, No Home"), Klinger had "a judicious sense for the power of spaces left blank." Often, Varnedoe observes, these blank spaces "are important not only as formal elaborations, but also, and in fact primarily, as devices for increasing the meaning of the plates; they tell a second story, extending the narrative in time or reinforcing the emotion."[29] As the concluding gesture in this extended musical and graphic meditation on the failure of individuals to unite through love, the blank space of Klinger's visual silence speaks more loudly than any image could.

The *Brahms-Phantasie* (II): Prometheus

The second part of Klinger's volume, in which the complete piano-vocal score of Brahms's *Schicksalslied* is framed with images of the Prometheus myth, extends this meditation on irremediable isolation from the realm of the individual to broader social and spiritual arenas. For the image of Prometheus elaborated in Klinger's work could not be more different from that celebrated by Wagner and his followers. As Wagner explained, writing in *Art and Revolution* (1849), it was the performance of Aeschylus's setting of the Titan's tale ("the profoundest of all tragedies") that stirred the communal spirit of individual Athenians, inspiring them "to join themselves in the most intimate union with their being, their community, their god."[30] And in *The Artwork of the Future*, Wagner hailed Beethoven as a "second Prometheus," a "brotherly Prometheus" who would unite mankind through the medium of the choral finale of his Ninth Symphony.[31] Perhaps the most enduring late-century image of the Titan comes to us not from Wagner but from Nietzsche, who adopted Prometheus as a symbol of humankind's foreseen awakening to a Dionysian communal sensibility, to be realized through the power of Wagner's music dramas—as depicted in the title-page engraving in his 1872 book, *The Birth of Tragedy* (Figure 5).

Figure 5. Title-page woodcut from Nietzsche, *The Birth of Tragedy* (1872).

As in Aeschylus's classic telling of this ancient myth, so too in Klinger's graphic narration: the bringer of fire to man is punished with abduction and exiled to a mountaintop, where he remains tethered to a rock and tormented by eagles until eventually freed by Hercules.[32] But whereas Nietzsche's Prometheus emerges triumphant from his ordeal, his right foot pinning the tormentor-eagle to the ground and his gaze turned challengingly upward toward the heavens, Klinger's barely emerges at all—or rather, he comes out crushed by the experience (Figure 6).

Figure 6. Klinger, *Prometheus Unbound,* in *Brahms-Phantasie*, 37.

Where Wagner's Prometheus was a uniter of men, Klinger's is no such figure at all. Although the latter's followers look up expectantly and in evident disarray from the waters below (as seen in the lower left-hand corner of Figure 6), Klinger's Prometheus does not face them, and cannot even bring himself to rise. Our hero, Klinger seems to suggest, in bringing the light of knowledge to man, has been spiritually devastated by the unmistakable reminder of his own limitations, dealt by the gods. Though he might have succeeded in stealing fire from the heavenly abode, neither the Titan nor his earthbound followers will ever experience the enlightenment or untroubled sense of harmony and tranquility allotted to higher beings.

In this telling of the Prometheus myth, the model of Brahms's work for Klinger's is unmistakable. For though Brahms's *Schicksalslied* does not treat the Prometheus story directly, it constitutes an extended meditation on the very theme Klinger addresses: the unbridgeable gulf separating the human from the divine and the ultimate impossibility of achieving atonement in the spiritual realm. As Brahms's text by Friedrich Hölderlin runs:

You wander above in the light, on soft ground, blessed immortals!
Shimmering breezes of the gods touch you lightly,
like the fingers of the artist touch sacred strings.

The heavenly ones breathe like a sleeping child, free from care.
Chastely guarded in modest bud, their spirit blooms eternally,
and their blissful eyes gaze in quiet, eternal clarity.

But to us is allotted to rest at no abode.
Suffering humanity wastes away, falls blindly from one hour to the next,
like water hurled from crag to crag, year after year, downward into
   uncertainty.[33]

Brahms's setting of the first two strophes of Hölderlin's poem is a musical portrait of serenity: a slow, languid melody in E-flat major, accompanied by legato strings, with the choir singing in near-perfect homophonic unity. To set the third strophe, however, where Hölderlin contrasts the lives of the gods with humanity's life on earth, Brahms gives us a study in musical contrasts: a quick, jagged vocal line, with the homophonic texture giving way to imitative polyphony (mm. 193–251) and characteristically Brahmsian, disorienting hemiolas (mm. 145–53, 305–12), all in the contrasting key of C minor.

But in a notoriously ambiguous exercise of creative license, Brahms does not end his setting there. He follows Hölderlin's final strophe with a famously perplexing, wordless postlude, in which the opening music of the gods is transformed in orchestration (woodwinds take over the string parts) and recapitulated not in the tonic E-flat but in the key of C major. The key of C major is, of course, harmonically distant from the opening tonic, and thus Brahms composed, decades before many others would, a piece that, harmonically speaking, does not end where it began. An obvious model for such a tonal move—though I am not aware of any previous discussion of this possibility—is *Tristan and Isolde*, where a large-scale tonal shift from A minor to B major accompanies the transfiguration of the title characters, specifically Isolde's in her *Liebestod*. A "transfiguring" interpretation along these lines was in fact suggested by Eduard Hanslick, and it resonates as well with John Daverio's celebrated analysis of Brahms's piece.[34] As Daverio observes, however distant the concluding C major might be from the original tonic E-flat, the former is nonetheless the "major-mode equivalent" (i.e., the parallel major) of the C minor in which Brahms set the third, tragic "human strophe" of Hölderlin's text. Thus, Daverio writes, Brahms "supplies the mediation ('harmonic connection') between divine and human realms that is apparently absent in Hölderlin's poem."[35]

What Daverio suggests might indeed have had something to do with Brahms's intentions. But there is, I believe, another way to look at the ending of the piece—a way that is more closely in line with what Klinger heard in the work. To be sure, the postlude of the *Schicksalslied* gives the opening music of the gods over to the tonal world (broadly defined) of man. But in the transfer, the very foundation of that heavenly music—its key— has been lost. Indeed, even the sound of the melody is transformed through the act of instrumental rescoring. In this way, I would argue, Brahms's music acknowledges humankind's inevitably Promethean desire to win the gifts and sense of spiritual harmony enjoyed by higher beings. Yet it also reminds us that, whatever snatches of the heavenly abode we might steal, whether its fire or its melodies, we will always remain human, destined to remain tied to this mortal world (our human tonality, one might say) and bounded in our earthly endeavors by all of humanity's limitations.[36]

Klinger's *Brahms-Phantasie* as Brahmsian Critique

In giving us this powerful misreading of Wagner's image of the Titan, Klinger was also revisiting other, earlier castings of the Prometheus myth. For it is important to note that that myth had emerged as a prominent trope in the work of numerous German writers, including Herder and Lessing, long before Wagner had made it his own. It had found a seminal early treatment in Goethe's "Prometheus" of 1774, where the young poet proffered an image of the Titan that resonates with Wagner's and Nietzsche's.[37] Goethe's ode celebrates Prometheus's inner strength and unbounded creative gifts, and his nurturing of a race of men who would thumb their noses at gods and others who would limit the potential of humankind to reshape itself and the world:

Here I sit, shaping men
in my image,
a race destined, like I am,

to suffer, to cry,
to feel joy and to experience pleasure,
and to disregard you
as I have done.[38]

Reflecting upon this youthful ode from the perspective of later years, however, Goethe offered a corrective take on the poem's message and a different view of the lessons to be garnered from the Titan's fate. As the literary critic Oskar Walzel had already pointed out in Klinger's day, Goethe, writing in his notebooks, came to "recognize, in the destiny of Prometheus, the destiny of the artist, and he perceived his own fate in it." Indeed, the artist, like the Titan of myth, is a figure who strives, however in vain, to realize a sense of godly beauty and harmony in the phenomenal world. But as an ostensible mediator between humanity and the divine, the Prometheus-artist is also, by definition, separate and distinct from both. The artist, working alone on his creations and drawing strength and vision from within, must "reject the hand of man" in his efforts, "and in doing so," Walzel continues, "he isolates himself, in Promethean fashion, from the gods as well."[39] Thus, I would argue, we encounter Klinger's image of Prometheus unbound, his subjects looking up to him for guidance from the waters below. But unlike Wagner's promethean Beethoven, who rallied humanity with his "Ode to Joy," Klinger's Prometheus is isolated from his minions, and can only look within.

If we accept that Klinger, in his *Brahms-Phantasie*, cast a skeptical shadow over late-century theorizing about the promise of the *Gesamtkunstwerk* to unite humanity and reinvigorate society, then we should not fail to acknowledge that Klinger registered his critique of this Wagnerian discourse in distinctly Brahmsian terms. As many writers on the latter composer have shown, Brahms felt deeply ambivalent about Wagner's creative legacy, and he had a penchant for expressing his ambivalence by seeking to historicize Wagner's ostensibly modernist musical gestures within his own historically grounded compositions. We now appreciate, to take one example, how Brahms embedded Wagner's harmonic innovations within his Third Symphony, thus demonstrating how Wagner's novel harmonic language did not signal a clean break from historical practice but was wholly compatible with classical forms.[40] And we also understand Brahms's attempt to counter Wagner's self-serving appropriation of Beethoven's legacy by rewriting, in a purely instrumental guise, the latter composer's "Ode to Joy" in the final movement of his own First Symphony.[41] What makes the *Brahms-Phantasie* Brahmsian in this fashion is the formal guise of Klinger's volume, which recalls, in the manner of Brahms's symphonies, another historicizing artistic form: the Baroque emblem book. Such books were widely popular in German-speaking Europe throughout the seventeenth and eighteenth centuries, and they became the focus of renewed, intensive scholarly interest in the years around 1900. Often treating biblical or didactic themes, emblem books featured short texts, either literary or poetic, accompanied by discrete graphic images that reflect or comment upon the texts they accompany.[42] An example is shown in Figure 7, in which a reference to Matthew 8:23–27, which tells of Christ crossing the Sea of Galilee, is glossed poetically ("When suffering, death, wind and waves besiege you, strive to keep Jesus in your heart's ship") and accompanied by an image of a boat tossed upon stormy waters. Whereas Brahms had registered a critique of Wagner by inscribing Wagner's innovations within the framework of the classical symphony, Klinger also registered his ambivalence via a deliberately historicizing form. In the *Brahms-Phantasie*, the artist's images function in a manner analogous to those in emblem books, with poetic texts inscribed in Brahms's scores and embodied in his music.

Figure 7. Emblematic illustration from Johann Ulrich Krauß, *Heilige Augen- und Gemüths-Lust* (Augspurg, 1706).

Peter M. Daly observed in his classic study of the emblem in Germany and England that what distinguishes emblem books from other early-modern forms of illustrated literature is precisely the symbolic, inherently ambiguous nature of the relationship between image and text, a relationship that invites and even demands the observer's reflection—even speculation— upon the potential meanings of their juxtaposition. "Emblems," Daly writes, "are composed of symbolic pictures and words," and one assumes that "a meaningful relationship between the two is intended." Yet the "manner of communication is connotative rather than denotative" and "makes no assumptions about either the primacy of *pictura* or *scriptura*"—of image or text—"or the nature of the relationship between the two."[43] As another scholar of the emblem observes, "These pairings of image and text often carried an innate disruption of message, and pondering this distance between visual image, written text and their reverberating hidden meaning was the delight of the educated reader."[44] Indeed, the literary historian Daniel S. Russell has argued this act of all-but-compulsory interpretation lies at the heart of what he calls the "emblem idea" itself. "The emblem idea," Russell explains, "is more a way of seeing a work of literature or visual art than a distinct artistic form in itself . . . the entire emblematic mode comes across as a way of reading."[45]

Significantly, to engage in an emblematic reading of the *Brahms-Phantasie* seems to be precisely what Brahms did, though there is, admittedly, no evidence to suggest he was aware he was doing this. For, as Brahms's friend Max Kalbeck recalled in his biography of the composer, it was this "disruption of message," the "distance" between visual images and texts in Klinger's volume that drew Brahms so powerfully to it. And it was an active, imaginative engagement with the elusive yet clearly meaningful relationship between texts and images, Russell's "emblematic mode" of apperception, that Brahms found so intoxicating when he gazed upon the work. Kalbeck recounted:

> It was doubly enjoyable for me to have the pleasure of sitting next to [Brahms] and looking [at the *Brahms-Phantasie*] with him. He took his place at the piano, and we immersed ourselves—leaning over the lid—so deeply in its pages that we both completely forgot about lunch. He lingered for so long on each page and accompanied the images with such affecting remarks that the hours flew by me like minutes. And once he turned over the last page, he would turn back to the first with such enthusiasm, to uncover new subtleties and still more intimate charms, which had somehow remained hidden from us before.[46]

Sitting at the piano—and thus, surely, playing through its musical texts—Brahms and Kalbeck savored the emblematic nature of Klinger's *Raumkunst* experiment, just as they experienced its extension of visual images into acoustical space.[47] With this volume, Klinger strove to effect the very sort of reunion of artistic media for which Wagner and his late-century followers had called. Yet by crafting in sound and image narrative tales of insurmountable alienation from both humanity and the gods, he simultaneously registered profound skepticism with regard to Wagner's vision of a dawning spiritual utopia. Moreover, by inscribing his critique of the Wagnerian discourse within a form reminiscent of the Baroque emblem book, Klinger proclaimed his ambivalence toward Wagner's legacy in a thoroughly Brahmsian manner. To be sure, the *Brahms-Phantasie* proffers an image of modernity profoundly transformed by Wagner's achievements. But Klinger's modernity was one deeply rooted in German cultural history, limited in its spiritual achievements by the inherent frailties of human nature.[48]

NOTES

I wish to thank Stephen Crist, Steve Everett, Yayoi Uno Everett, Walter Frisch, Peter Höyng, Walter Melion, Michael Ouellette, Silvio dos Santos, and Janet Sonenberg, and members of the 2007–08 European Studies Seminar of Emory University's Graduate Institute of Liberal Arts for their invaluable comments on earlier versions of this essay. Unless otherwise noted, all translations are my own.

1. Max Klinger, *Brahms-Phantasie: Einundvierzig Stiche, Radierungen und Steinzeichnungen zu Compositionen von Johannes Brahms* (Leipzig, 1894). The most thorough account of the history of Klinger's volume is provided in Jan Brachmann,*"Ins Ungewisse hinauf . . ." Johannes Brahms und Max Klinger im Zwiespalt von Kunst und Kommunikation* (Kassel, 1999). The selection of musical works included in the *Brahms-Phantasie* was Klinger's.

2. Hugo von Hofmannsthal, "Internationale Kunstausstellung 1894," repr. in *Max Klinger: Wege zum Gesamtkunstwerk*, ed. Manfred Boetzkes (Mainz am Rhein, 1984), 96.

3. Much of the recent art-historical literature will be cited over the course of this essay. Among musicological studies to consider the *Brahms-Phantasie*, see esp. Walter Frisch, *German Modernism: Music and the Arts* (Berkeley and Los Angeles, 2005), 95–106; and Leon Botstein, "Brahms and Nineteenth-Century Painting," *19th-Century Music* 14/2 (1990): 154–68. On the *Brahms-Phantasie* as *Gesamtkunstwerk*, see, for instance, Manfred Boetzkes, "Wege zum Gesamtkunstwerk," in Boetzkes, *Max Klinger*, 9–12; and Karin Mayer-Pasinski, *Max Klingers Brahmsphantasie* (Frankfurt am Main, 1981), esp. 4–5.

4. Hermann Bahr, "Max Klinger," in *Renaissance: Neue Studien zur Kritik der Moderne* (Berlin, 1897), 217–22 (cited at 219).

5. Hans Wolfgang Singer, *Max Klingers Radierungen, Stiche und Steindrucke: Wissenschaftliches Verzeichnis* (Berlin, 1909), x. I borrow the terms *critical modernism* and *ambivalent modernism* from Allan Janik and Walter Frisch, respectively. Critical modernism, in Janik's terms, designates a pervasive attitude among turn-of-the-century German

intellectuals that encompassed "a critique of modernity that . . . was not a rejection of modernity pure and simple, but an immanent critique of its limits." In a related sense and with respect to the same historical culture, Frisch defines ambivalent modernism as "admiring and fostering the new" while simultaneously "clinging fervently to the past out of a sense that the past . . . was an essential part of the German character that could not be abandoned." See Janik, "Vienna 1900 Revisited: Paradigms and Problems," in *Rethinking Vienna 1900*, ed. Steven Beller (New York and Oxford, 2001), 27–56 (cited at 40); and Frisch, *German Modernism*, 7–35 (cited at 8).

6. Boetzkes, "Wege zum Gesamtkunstwerk"; Klinger, *Malerei und Zeichnung* (1891), repr. in *Malerei und Zeichnung: Tagebuchaufzeichnungen und Briefe*, ed. Anneliese Hübscher (Leipzig, 1987).

7. For images from these volumes, see *Max Klinger: Die druckgraphischen Folgen* (Heidelberg, 2007); Dieter Gleisberg et al., *Max Klinger 1857–1920* (Leipzig, 1992); J. Kirk T. Varnedoe and Elizabeth Streicher, *Graphic Works of Max Klinger* (New York, 1977); and Singer, *Max Klingers Radierungen*.

8. For photographs of the vestibule, see Boetzkes, *Max Klinger*, 60–63.

9. For a picture, see Boetzkes, *Max Klinger*, 16. Brahms expressed his admiration for *Salome* in a letter to Klinger of 18 October 1894; see *Johannes Brahms an Max Klinger* (Leipzig, 1924), 9.

10. For images and discussion of this exhibit, see Marian Bisanz-Prakken, *Gustav Klimt: Der Beethovenfries—Geschichte, Funktion und Bedeutung* (Salzburg, 1977); Jean-Paul Bouillon, *Klimt: Beethoven*, trans. Hanna Wulf (Tübingen, 1988); and Alessandra Comini, *The Changing Image of Beethoven: A Study in Mythmaking* (New York, 1987), 388–415. On Klinger's Beethoven statue specifically, see Barbara John, *Max Klinger: Beethoven* (Leipzig, 2004). Several scholars have suggested that Klinger's theory of *Raumkunst* might have directly influenced the work of the Viennese Secession; see, for instance, Bouillon, *Klimt: Beethoven*, 12–15; and Anna Harwell Celenza, "Music and the Viennese Secession: 1897–1902," *Music in Art* 29/1–2 (2004): 203–212. For a more general consideration of Klinger's notion of *Raunkunst*, see, in addition to sources cited in note 3, Elizabeth Pendleton Streicher, "Max Klinger's *Malerei und Zeichnung*: The Critical Reception of the Prints and Their Text," *Studies in the History of Art* 53 (1996): 228–49.

11. Klinger, *Malerei und Zeichnung*, 44–48; compare Richard Wagner, *Das Kunstwerk der Zukunft*, in *Sämtliche Schriften und Dichtungen*, 6th ed. (Leipzig, 1911), 3:81–86. See also Wagner, *Die Kunst und die Revolution* (1849), in *Sämtliche Schriften und Dichtungen*, 3:12–13.

12. Klinger, *Malerei und Zeichnung*, 48 (emphasis added).

13. Ibid., 33.

14. Ibid., 30.

15. Despite much recent work on the political and social idealism underlying Wagner's creative work, this aspect of his theory of the *Gesamtkunstwerk* has received little attention. It is noted in Frisch, *German Modernism*, 91–93; Ruth A. Solie, "'Tadpole Pleasures': *Daniel Deronda* as Music Historiography," in *Music in Other Words: Victorian Conversations* (Berkeley and Los Angeles, 2004), 161–68; and Bryan Magee, *Aspects of Wagner*, rev. ed. (Oxford and New York, 1988), 12–14. The most direct consideration of the topic of which I am aware is given by Timothée Picard, *L'Art total: Grandeur et misère d'une utopie (autour de Wagner)* (Rennes, 2006), esp. 37–41.

16. Wagner, *Das Kunstwerk der Zukunft*, 60 and 61. See also Wagner, *Die Kunst und die Revolution*, 40–41.

17. Wagner, *Das Kunstwerk der Zukunft*, 63 (emphasis in original).

18. Wagner, "'Was nützt diese Erkenntnis?' Ein Nachtrag zu: Religion und Kunst," in *Sämtliche Schriften und Dichtungen*, 10:263. For Wagner's mature image of a community united through the experience of art, see his "Religion und Kunst" (1880), in *Sämtliche Schriften und Dichtungen*, 10:249–51.

19. Friedrich Nietzsche, unpublished fragment (Winter–Spring 1874), in *Unpublished Writings from the Period of Unfashionable Observations*, ed. and trans. Richard T. Gray (Stanford, 1995), 320.

20. Siegfried Lipiner, *Über die Elemente einer Erneuerung religiöser Ideen in der Gegenwart: Vortrag gehalten im Lesevereine der Deutschen Studenten Wiens am 19. Januar 1878* (Vienna, 1878), 17–18. Lipiner's lengthy citations from *Parsifal*, the libretto of which was completed and published in 1877, five years before the opera, appear on 12–13.

21. Max Nordau, *Degeneration*, anon. trans. (New York, 1895); and *Regeneration: A Reply to Max Nordau* (London and New York, 1896).

22. *Regeneration*, 228–29. A valuable consideration of Nordau's work and the trope of degeneration in the turn-of-the-century discourse on Wagner and Wagnerism is provided in Thomas Grey, "Wagner the Degenerate: Fin-de-Siècle Cultural 'Pathology' and the Anxiety of Modernism," *Nineteenth Century Studies* 16 (2002): 73–92.

23. Marsha Morton, "*Malerei und Zeichnung*: The History and Context of Max Klinger's Guide to the Arts," *Zeitschrift für Kunstgeschichte* 58/4 (1995): 542–69.

24. A useful summary of this debate is provided in Brachmann, *Ins Ungewisse hinauf*, 121–24.

25. On love as inspiration for the creation of the *Gesamtkunstwerk*, see Wagner, *Das Kunstwerk der Zukunft*, 62 and 68–71. For a later, Schopenhauerian reformulation of these ideas, see Wagner, "Was nützt diese Erkenntnis," 259–60. A valuable discussion of themes of love and social transformation in *The Ring* is provided in Bryan Magee, *The Tristan Chord: Wagner and Philosophy* (New York, 2000), 102–25. On love and metaphysical union in Tristan and Isolde, see Eric Chafe, *The Tragic and the Ecstatic: The Musical Revolution of Wagner's* Tristan and Isolde (Oxford and New York, 2005), esp. 3–15 on Wagner's position generally, and 209–20 on the crucial dialogue of Act 2, scene 2; and Roger Scruton, *Death-Devoted Heart: Sex and the Sacred in Wagner's* Tristan and Isolde (Oxford and New York, 2004), esp. 125–59.

26. For further discussion of the motivic construction of *Alte Liebe*, see Paul Berry, "Old Love: Johannes Brahms, Clara Schumann, and the Poetics of Musical Memory," *Journal of Musicology* 24/1 (2007): 72–111.

27. For the image, see Singer, *Max Klingers Radierungen*, plate 197.

28. This fact has been pointed out in Frisch, *German Modernism*, 99. I am not aware of any reproduction of this page. For the original, see Klinger, *Brahms-Phantasie*, 14.

29. Varnedoe, introduction to Varnedoe and Streicher, *Graphic Works of Max Klinger*, xix–xx.

30. Wagner, *Die Kunst und die Revolution*, 11.

31. Wagner, *Das Kunstwerk der Zukunft*, 95.

32. For the complete cycle of six images, see *Max Klinger: Die druckgraphischen Folgen*, 132–35; and Singer, *Max Klingers Radierungen*, plates 202–6 and 228.

33. I have based my translation on that of John Daverio, who provides an insightful analysis of Hölderlin's text and its relation to Brahms's musical setting in "The *Wechsel der Töne* in Brahms's *Schicksalslied*," *Journal of the American Musicological Society* 46/1 (1993): 84–113.

34. Hanslick, in an 1872 review of the work, writes that the orchestral postlude "reveals to us the transfiguring power of music itself." This review is translated by Kevin C. Karnes in Hanslick, "Discovering Brahms (1862–72)," in this volume.

35. Daverio, "The *Wechsel der Töne*," 107.

36. Ursula Kersten has offered a different interpretation of Klinger's Prometheus that resonates with the one advanced here. In stressing the human frailty of Klinger's Titan, she emphasizes that Prometheus was unable to free himself from his mythical tethers and had to rely upon help from the demigod Hercules. See Kersten, *Max Klinger und die Musik* (Frankfurt am Main, 1993), 87–88.

37. On the Prometheus trope in German literature of the eighteenth and nineteenth centuries, see Joachim Heimerl, *Systole und Diastole: Studien zur Bedeutung des Prometheussymbols im Werk Goethes* (Munich, 2001); and Edith Braemer, *Goethes Prometheus und die Grundpositionen des Sturm und Drang* (Weimar, 1963). For a brief discussion in English, see M. H. Abrams, *The Mirror and the Lamp: Romantic Theory and the Critical Tradition* (Oxford, 1953), 280–82.

38. Johann Wolfgang Goethe, "Prometheus," in *Sämtliche Werke nach Epochen seines Schaffens*, ed. Karl Richter et al. (Munich, 1985), 1:229–31 (cited at 231).

39. Oskar F. Walzel, *Das Prometheussymbol von Shaftesbury zu Goethe* (Leipzig and Berlin, 1910), 38 and 40.

40. See David Brodbeck, "Brahms, the Third Symphony, and the New German School," in this volume.

41. See Mark Evan Bonds, *After Beethoven: Imperatives of Originality in the Symphony* (Cambridge, Mass., and London, 1996), 138–74; and Richard Taruskin, *The Oxford History of Western Music* (Oxford and New York, 2005), 3:716–29.

42. For general descriptions and analyses of emblems and emblem books, see Anthony J. Harper and Ingrid Höpel, eds., *The German-Language Emblem in Its European Context: Exchange and Transmission* (Glasgow, 2000); and Daniel S. Russell, *The Emblem and Device in France* (Lexington, 1985).

43. Peter M. Daly, *Literature in the Light of the Emblem: Structural Parallels Between the Emblem and Literature in the Sixteenth and Seventeenth Centuries*, 2nd ed. (Toronto, 1998), 8.

44. M. E. Warlick, "Art, Allegory and Alchemy in Peter Greenaway's *Prospero's Books*," in *New Directions in Emblem Studies*, ed. Amy Wygant (Glasgow, 1999), 113.

45. Russell, *The Emblem and Device in France*, 103 and 109.

46. Max Kalbeck, *Johannes Brahms*, rev. ed. (Berlin, 1912–21; repr. Tutzing, 1976), 4:335.

47. Citing Brahms's correspondence as further evidence of the composer's enthusiasm for an engagement with the *Brahms-Phantasie* and situating his analysis within a broader discussion of the Symbolist movement, Walter Frisch has recently advanced a complementary argument: that Brahms "clearly pick[ed] up on, and respond[ed] positively to, the Symbolist aspects of Klinger's works." See Frisch, *German Modernism*, 94. Some links between the "emblematic mode" of apperception and aspects of late nineteenth-century Symbolism are explored in Rainer Nägele, "The Laughing Tear: Constructions of Allegory in Modernism," in Wygant, *New Directions in Emblem Studies*, 77–91.

48. It should be noted that late nineteenth-century attempts to bridge the gap between Wagnerian and Brahmsian aesthetic positions were not confined to ambivalent critiques such as Klinger's and Brahms's own. For a thoughtful consideration of this issue, see Margaret Notley, "Late-Nineteenth-Century Chamber Music and the Cult of the Classical Adagio," *19th-Century Music* 23/1 (1999): 33–61.

PART II

RECEPTION AND ANALYSIS

Adolf Schubring
Five Early Works by Brahms (1862)

TRANSLATED, INTRODUCED, AND ANNOTATED
BY WALTER FRISCH

In the spring of 1862 a series of substantial articles about the music of Brahms appeared in Germany's leading music periodical, the Neue Zeitschrift für Musik, *which had been founded by Robert Schumann in 1834 and was now edited by Franz Brendel. Written by Adolf Schubring (1817–93), a judge by profession and music critic by avocation, the articles formed part of a larger series titled* Schumanniana, *in which Schubring tried to argue that Schumann's legacy lived on in a small group of composers he dubbed the "Schumann school." Schubring's articles on Brahms, spread out over five issues, constituted the first full-scale assessment of the composer, who was then only twenty-nine and had published only eighteen works (through the B-flat Sextet). Schubring analyzed each opus with considerable perspicacity, often resorting to detailed musical examples. He did not hesitate to criticize, but also lavished praise where he felt it was due. Even if we today, with the hindsight of Brahms's complete works, cannot share all his judgments, we must admire the thoroughness and vitality of his commentary. His articles, conceived essentially as an elaboration and vindication of Schumann's "Neue Bahnen" of 1853, form a crucial part of the reception history of the early Brahms. Schubring refers to places in the scores by page number in the first editions; where possible I have, through consultation of editions, tried to provide the corresponding measure number. Some measure numbers have been added to the musical examples, where a few other editorial emendations have also been made tacitly. The excerpts are taken from "Schumanniana: Johannes Brahms,"* Neue Zeitschrift für Musik 56 (1862): *93–96, 101–4, 109–12, 117–19, 125–28.[1] All endnotes are editorial.*

Introduction

In his musical testament and swan song, "Neue Bahnen," Robert Schumann wrote that he had always thought that, with music on the upturn in recent times,

> there inevitably must appear a musician called to give expression to his times in ideal fashion; a musician who would reveal his mastery not in a gradual evolution, but like Athene would spring fully armed from Zeus's head. And such a one *has* appeared; a young man over whose cradle Graces and Heroes have stood watch. His name is *Johannes Brahms*, and he comes from Hamburg, where he has been working in quiet obscurity, though instructed in the most difficult statutes of his art by an excellent and enthusiastically devoted teacher (Eduard Marxsen). A well-known and honored master recently recommended him to me. Even outwardly he bore the marks proclaiming: "This is a chosen one." Sitting at the piano he began to disclose wonderful regions to us. We were drawn into even more enchanting spheres. Besides, he is a player of genius who can make of the piano an orchestra of lamenting and loudly jubilant voices. There were sonatas, veiled symphonies rather; songs the poetry of which would be understood even without words, although a profound vocal melody runs through them all; single piano pieces, some of them turbulent in spirit while graceful in form; again sonatas for violin and piano, string quartets, every work so different from the others that it seemed to stream from its own individual source . . .
>
> Should he direct his magic wand where the powers of the masses in chorus and orchestra may lend him their forces, we can look forward to even more wondrous glimpses of the secret world of spirits.[2]

Like a second John the Baptist, Schumann felt himself called, indeed impelled, to deliver this enthusiastic prophecy (of which only the main utterances are reported here) and joyous message. He then concluded by predicting that he himself was destined soon to give up his magic wand; he called together his little band of followers: "There exists a secret bond between kindred spirits in every period. You who belong together, close your ranks ever more tightly, that the Truth of Art may shine more clearly, diffusing joy and blessings over all things."

And how did people receive the new gospel of John?

The Schumann circle, at that time rather small, was surprised and elated; and they had faith. The rest of the musical public, both conservatives and progressives, laughed and shrugged in disbelief. At the end of February 1854 the sad news came from Düsseldorf [of Schumann's suicide attempt]; and later, upon the publication of the seven Fughettas, op. 126, which showed traces of Schumann's mental illness, even many Schumannites shook their heads. Finally—it was about in the middle of 1854—the first works of Johannes Brahms were published. What astonishment, puzzlement, and bewilderment they generated: so difficult to perform, yet so clear in form, so new in content. At one moment they would be simply expansive, at another insanely colossal, at another demonically wild. At first people had difficulty making sense of the six cyclopean works forged by the young Vulcan (among them three sonatas), each one so different in character.

Scarcely had we taken these in when toward the end of the same year came a second smaller eruption. New bewilderment, for Brahms seemed to have entered another phase; he moved from ecstatic rejoicing to longing for the grave. But for some of us a *res severa* is true jubilation; we are accustomed to drill through the hard shell to get at the seed deep within. And so up to the work that has appeared most recently, the Sextet for Strings, op. 18, we continued to be amazed. We expected that each new work would be at least similar to the preceding one, yet were continually surprised by its complete novelty. We contemplated with increasing admiration the unusual path followed by this constellation newly risen to the musical heavens; it shone continually clearer and more splendidly.

Yes, these works are new, bold, large, and beautiful—but also very, very difficult to understand and to perform. The first sonata in particular is almost as difficult as the first movement of Beethoven's "Hammerklavier," whose main theme is in fact recalled by the opening. Yet the technical demands of Brahms's work go beyond even Beethoven. In his double counterpoint, his imitations in canon or contrary motion, Brahms does not restrict himself to two individual voices. Whenever possible he adds the third, fifth, or octave, and at the same time tries to charm us by adding a pedal point two octaves below. It is this uniting of the old contrapuntal art with the most modern technique that makes Brahms's two-hand piano works so difficult and prevents their wider dissemination. If Germany had a hundred musicians and music lovers who could master the three sonatas and the Scherzo, then surely not even half of this small number would be able to perform it with genuine understanding; they would not feel inclined to penetrate with sufficient depth into music that is as demanding spiritually as it is technically.

And so it has happened that these treasures have remained up till now virtually unknown by the general public. The song collections certainly offer no difficulty for performers, but they demand a pianist of delicacy and a well-trained singer who can feel deeply—thus a duo that is not too frequently encountered. Nor have the recently published orchestral and choral works yet found the recognition due them, despite their melodic beauty, their consistently clear form and style, and their relative accessibility to performers. I can solve this riddle only by suggesting that the routine of official concert life has accustomed the majority of different groups of listeners to applaud only those works that they have come to understand through years of repeated performance.

I once attended a fiasco at the first performance of Schumann's *Manfred* and Joachim's Overture to *Henry IV*. In order to avoid such a calamity it is necessary to perform a work the *first* time as if it were the twentieth time. Moreover, it is certainly possible that the novelty of Brahms's music and the unfamiliarity of his name have worked against any sweeping success. (A concert public is never quick to applaud the work of a composer who is not yet famous; they could make fools of themselves!) And finally, we can also blame in part the unfortunate fragmentation of musical Germany. Here, Guelphs! Here, Ghibellines! The battle cry is sounding, and the Schumann banner, which stands between the two warring parties, gets dragged into the fray. May God protect them! But I, who have sworn allegiance to the Schumann banner, will in the meantime await the verdict of the ultimate judge, Time (if I err, at least I err in good company). I will not become polemical, but will rather be thankful that friend Brendel has granted a welcome spot in his journal for me to unburden my heart occasionally and to begin without further ado my cursory discussion of Brahms's works. If I seem to place undue stress on many passages in the early piano works that overstep the bounds of beauty, if I focus on various flaws of declamation in the songs, it is only to demonstrate that I, despite great admiration of the young master, have kept my eyes and ears open for his faults and excesses, for errors which Brahms himself will surely have noticed, since he already avoids them in his latest works.

When he wrote Brahms's letter of recommendation, Robert Schumann seems—on grounds it would take too long to explore here—to have known only opp. 1–6 and perhaps individual pieces from opp. 7 and 10. He also makes passing reference to a few other works which have not yet appeared, such as string quartets and duos for piano and violin.

Even though the works published up to now are relatively small in number and very diverse in character, they nevertheless allow us to distinguish different phases and periods, or at least groups of related works. The most recent compositions, opp. 11 to 18, are like clear wine in comparison to the fermenting must of opp. 1–6. Between the two, opp. 7–10 appear as a kind of transitional group of less stable, more variable coloration.

Piano Sonata in C Major, op. 1

Of the works of the first period the C-Major Sonata is the boldest and stormiest. The construction of this sonata, and especially its first movement (there is a first part that is repeated, then a development and a reprise of the first part, and a long coda) offers no obstacles to understanding. Less easy to grasp at first is the thematic work, which Brahms employs not merely in the development section, but almost without interruption from the beginning to the end.

Let us try to clarify Brahms's thematic work in the first movement of the C-Major Sonata, insofar as possible without comprehensive musical examples.

From the brashly and boldly announced main theme *A*, in C major:

follows a gentle second one, *B*, in A minor:

Through two sequences this ascends to the high D and then from here descends again. The third main theme, C, oscillates in sorrowful tones between Aeolian and Phrygian:

These three main themes are now split up into their component motives and each of these smaller motives or motivic particles leads to other combinations, which are treated mostly by sequence.

From theme *A* are derived the following motives, which are the most obvious because they are at the original pitches:

the inversions:

and the freer reformulations and variations:

From theme *B*:

and finally from theme *C*:

Sometimes a theme is hidden among other notes; it is only adumbrated, as is theme *B* in the phrase:

Of the many canonic and contrapuntal shapes we can present here the following in simplified form:

Theme A

We see that Brahms is using the old thematic art of Haydn and Beethoven, and yet his work makes a very different impression from theirs. The use of imitation, increasing from the seventh, to the ninth, to the eleventh, gives the thematic work a strange character. When other voices are added as filler, the double counterpoint becomes ponderous and bloated, or at least loses that transparent simplicity which alone is suitable to the nature of arabesques. And since Brahms has already placed the most natural and pleasing of his thematic interweavings in the exposition, in order to bring about the necessary buildup in the development he must often have recourse to forced and harsh sonorities. Thus, especially in the development, he has repeatedly overstepped the limit of beauty. And thus it has happened that in his first sonata movement Brahms provides us with an image that is superb and original, yet overloaded with glaring contrast.

The following Andante (C minor, $\frac{2}{4}$) fully reconciles us with him again through its elevated simplicity. These are variations on the old German Minnelied "Blau, blau Blümelein." The first is distinguished by surprising harmonic progressions, whereas the second attracts us with its splendid double counterpoint, the third through a broad melody in the bass to which an intimate cantilena has been added, and the coda through graceful canonic imitation.

The third movement, Scherzo (Allegro molto e con fuoco, E minor, $\frac{6}{8}$) and trio (*più mosso*, C major, $\frac{3}{4}$), is the most ferocious thing Brahms has written. The mood is broken only briefly in the middle of the scherzo with the insertion of a small secondary phrase of more gentle humor; otherwise Brahms storms forth in a hunt that is roaring, grisly, ever wilder, *feroce, strepitoso*. Though scarcely less stormy, the trio presents something of a contrast, since it is more melodic and less demonic than the scherzo.

(In this scherzo Brahms uses as a main motive the pitch sequence

that becomes a hallmark of his later melodies; a great number of these melodies, however different in character, have this progression or its inversion as a motivic element. In a similar fashion, Beethoven in his first sonatas liked to use the rising fourth as the beginning of his main and secondary themes.)

The rondo-like finale (Allegro con fuoco, C major, $\frac{9}{8}$ and $\frac{6}{8}$) is once again truly human, but no less expressive. Here pulsates the irrepressible ardor of youth, his veins bursting with power and health. Particularly daring and audacious are the seventh and ninth chords [mm. 42–44] and the imitations on page 24 [mm. 51–57] which rise from the ninth to the thirteenth; also the defiant developments of the third (northern?) main motive [m. 107]. (If I could eliminate anything, it would be the cheap double counterpoint on the third and fourth systems of the final page [mm. 269–80], unworthy of a contrapuntist like Brahms.)

Young must matures in its own particular fashion; and the more unique it is, the nobler and more fiery the vintage becomes.

Piano Sonata in F-sharp Minor, op. 2

The thematic work in Brahms's first sonata consists chiefly of taking a theme that appears fully formed right at the beginning, then splitting it up into particles and combining these particles into new shapes in the manner of a mosaic. The Sonata in F-sharp Minor adopts the opposite procedure.[3] Its principal and subsidiary melodies originate from mosaic particles before our very eyes. And what is most astonishing is that all these melodies, so diverse in character, are all derived from one and the same basic motive, which attains its broadest development and melodic unfolding only in the finale:

This rather unremarkable fifth motive had already been used by composers from Bach to Bargiel (the Introduction to the Trio, op. 8). Before Brahms, other composers, for example Berger, Loewe, and the Munich composer E. Leonhard, had composed sonatas in the older form on one theme.* But these pieces failed because of the difficulty of combining diversity with unity; they became arid. Brahms has solved this tough problem in a truly ingenious way. He has managed to transform his basic motive more or less recognizably through rhythmic alteration, through displacement into other chordal inversions, and through exact or retrograde inversion, thereby creating themes and melodies of the most extreme contrast. It is impossible in this context to follow Brahms into all the hiding places of his creative workshop. But I cannot refrain from presenting at least the main motives of all four movements in simplified form and indicating with numbers the notes of the head motive from which they derive:

First Movement:

Andante: (inversion)

Scherzo, the same theme, rhythmically altered:

Trio, second inversion:

---

* I say specifically sonatas in the older form. Yet it would be inexcusable not to mention here the sonatas of the New German School, composed in a single movement and on a single theme, specifically the Liszt Sonata in B Minor, with its abundance of thematic transformations, and the Sonata op. 1 of Rudolf Viole. The latter also places the theme in retrograde.

Finale, with an upbeat:

The same, varied:

likewise:

likewise the theme of the small fugato:

the retrograde:

Now, any musician can learn these truly clever tricks, which precisely for that reason become valuable only when they are employed in the creation of a soulful and poetic artwork. But in the case of the F-sharp-Minor Sonata, which certainly fulfills this condition, the listener and player would be convinced of the artistry even if they were unaware of the thematic unity of all the movements. The C-Major Sonata might be given the subtitle "Youth must sow wild oats." By contrast, the second is characterized by a depth and strength of passion; it bears itself with a more sober dignity. In the first movement we see a battle (an inner one), a struggle between opposing forces that are at once closely related yet contrasting. The Andante, written in variation form, contains the same struggle, now between two orchestras of lamenting and rejoicing voices. And in the third movement this opposition arises once again, now divided between a defiant scherzo and a peaceful trio that frequently breaks out in more boisterous jubilation. At last there is reconciliation in the elegiac, gentle finale.

Several particularly ingenious places in the score are: in the first movement, the *crescendo* on pages 2 and 8 [mm. 2–4 and 125–29] ("Wisst ihr, warum der Sarg?"),[4] the hammering triplets on page 10 [mm. 176–78], and above all the *fortissimo* coda [mm. 179–98], which begins so energetically and defiantly, but whose certainty of victory is then unexpectedly called into question by the two final chords, played *una corda*. In the Andante, we might point to the final variation [m. 68]; in the Scherzo, the humorous transition from the trio to the reprise of the scherzo [mm. 64–72] and the Romantic sonorities on page 15, last system [mm. 42–47]; and in the finale, the grandiose chords on page 21 [mm. 119–42], which are spiritually allied with the description of Egypt in Schumann's *Paradies und Peri*.[5]

There are other bold moments, which tend to recall the wild spirit of the first sonata: in the middle of page 8 [mm. 131–38] (here [mm. 136–37] and in the parallel spot on page 2 [mm. 13–14], a $\frac{6}{8}$ time signature must be missing); the exceptionally difficult reprise of the Scherzo on page 17 [m. 89]; some harsh passages in the middle of page 20 [finale, mm. 71ff.] and on page 23 [mm. 179ff.], which may, however, be due to printing errors; and finally the grating imitations on page 26 [mm. 253–57] together with the following theme, which is doubled at the octave and accompanied with chromatic chords [m. 258].

Piano Sonata in F Minor, op. 5

The third sonata, op. 5 in F Minor, consists of five movements of very diverse quality. The first movement ($\frac{3}{4}$, Allegro maestoso, but better characterized merely as Maestoso, or simply Moderato) has the form of the four-part sonata movement and begins in truly splendid fashion with the motive:

The motives of all parts of the movement are derived from this basic motive, whose initial energy becomes dissipated when the subsidiary motives are extended, principally by means of augmentation. This is why Brahms has not succeeded in keeping us continuously spellbound in this movement. Although individual moments are outstanding, such as the *fortissimo* passages on pages 7 [m. 117], 8 [m. 137], and 11 [m. 200], the *misterioso* on page 8 [m. 131], the *pianissimo* on pages 4 [m. 37], 6 [m. 88], and 9 [m. 159], at others we are struck by a certain feebleness and stagnation. The more powerful the upward surge that has preceded, the more noticeable this impression becomes. The most important of the subsidiary motives derived from the basic motive shown above are as follows, arranged in the order of their appearance:

The second movement (Andante espressivo, A-flat major, $\frac{2}{4}$, alternating with two parts in D-flat major and in $\frac{4}{16}$ and $\frac{3}{4}$ time, and closing with a long coda in D-flat major, Andante molto, $\frac{3}{4}$, and Adagio, $\frac{4}{4}$, using a double pedal point on D♭ and A♭) is headed by some lines from Sternau:

Der Abend dämmert, das Mondlicht scheint,	The evening is coming, the moonlight shines,
Da sind zwei Herzen in Liebe vereint	Two hearts are united in love
Und halten sich selig umfangen.	And embrace each other blissfully.

This is program music, one of the most beautiful moonlight poems ever created. Words cannot describe the blissful caresses of the two lovers in the still night, the sweet scent that wafts over the entire scene. One must hear the poem, hear it and experience it, as it is sung by Clara Schumann, who often plays it in her concerts. In the summer night's dream depicted in Robert Schumann's *Humoresque*, op. 20, the nocturnal love scene is interrupted in truly humorous fashion by simple Philistines, before whose silly chatter and foolish laughter the lovers withdraw into a secret corner (pages 17–20).[6] By contrast Brahms has *his* lovers embrace to their hearts' content, repeat their most tender farewells, and even call out the last good-bye from a distance (see the last two systems on page 17 [mm. 137–43]: in the upper voice "Ade, ade," in the lower voice retreating steps). One lover is left behind alone: "In darkest midnight, he stands alone on his quiet watch." Everything is silent; quietly he hums the *Schildwachtlied* by Hauff: "His heart beats warmly, he thinks of distant love," and loudly, ever more loudly, he rejoices in the night: "She loves me truly, she is faithful to me."[7]

Jetzt bei der Lampe Dämmerschein	Now by the faint light of the lamp
Gehst Du wol in dein Kämmerlein	You go into your little room
Und schickst Dein Nachtgebet zum	And make your prayer to the
Herrn	Lord
Auch für den Liebsten in der Fern.	Even for your loved one far away.

The situation is now different from when his beloved came down to him; therefore the A-flat Andante closes with a pious Adagio in D-flat major.

I will leave self-proclaimed critics to cavil at details in this elevated song of love. To be sure, rules would forbid a melodic succession of five or six thirds (it is really a broken thirteenth chord); to be sure, the registral shift of the seventh chord from A♭ down to D♭ is somewhat peculiar (middle of page 15 [mm. 91–92]). But when something forbidden by the rules sounds good, and when the ear becomes accustomed to the unfamiliar, who wants to throw a stone? There was only one chord to which I could not become accustomed, the D-flat harmony at the beginning of the fourth bar on page 18 [m. 147]. Although I tell myself that the D♭ is nothing more than a pedal point, my ear still cannot tolerate it, because of the C that is sounded simultaneously in the tenor voice. Thus I now play the chord as:

Brahms may have felt it would be impossible to create anything more *poetic* than this solemn movement. Therefore in the following Scherzo he aimed less at poetic force than at clever contrapuntal play. Both in the scherzo (Allegro energico, F minor) and in the trio (D-flat major) he resorts to contrary motion truly *ex professo*. The latter makes its effect through its ardent melody, the former chiefly through its lively rhythm and elegant counterpoint.

Between the scherzo and the finale Brahms has inserted a short Intermezzo which is subtitled "Rückblick." This is spun out of motives already heard and is full of poetry and dramatic life.

The rondo-like finale is built in the following way: theme 1 [m. 1]; theme 2 [m. 39]; development of theme 1 [m. 71]; theme 1 [m. 104]; theme 3 [m. 140]; development of themes 3 and 1 [m. 195]; first coda, *presto*, based on theme 3 [m. 249]; second coda, *grandioso*, derived from theme 1 [m. 349]. Both main themes, and especially the first half of theme 1, are used in a great variety of contrapuntal combinations:

In theme 3 diminution and stretto play a particularly large role, of which a few examples can be given here:

After the Andante and Intermezzo, the finale is the most beautiful part of this sonata, full of the most charming humor and, from the middle onward, full of increasing vitality. One could if necessary ease the difficulty of the stormy spot on the bottom of page 34 [m. 226] by playing broken chords (from bottom to top) in triplets, or by leaving out the upper octave—as on pages 27 and 31 [mm. 25, 126]—and playing sixths.

Piano Trio in B Major, op. 8 [1854 version]

The trio for piano, violin, and cello, op. 8, belongs half to the transition period represented by opp. 7–10 and half to the earlier *Sturm und Drang* period.

No more than in his C-Major Piano Sonata is Brahms able to give the first movement of his first trio any unified shape. Here, as in the sonata, the same factors contribute to the failure: the padded counterpoint and the overloaded polyphony—and then chiefly the error that he draws from the main theme contrasting ideas that repel each other. Opposition within the theme is only appropriate in a humorous scherzo and trio; the rest of the sonata movements, on the other hand, require as themes merely *secondary* ideas, which do not conflict with the obligatory association and reduction of basic themes that culminate in the development section. This is also the reason why a scherzo and trio normally have no development section in common, but at most a coda that offers a truce or a kind of reconciliation between the two contrasting parts.

Brahms's first movement begins promisingly with a splendid cantilena in the piano, later given to the cello. But after a few measures the violin cannot resist throwing in a superfluous phrase like that of a canary—superfluous because it does not really belong to the theme and is not used in any later developments. The second group (page 4 [m. 63]) soon takes on a crabbed, grating quality, and still greater contrast is provided by the third (page 5 [m. 84]), which is more darkly brooding and unfolds mostly in canon. This is followed by the more idyllic, cheerful closing group. After this, brooding sextuplet figures return in the violin and cello; these are never used again and it is unclear whether the composer intended two or three accents. The sextuplets lead to the reprise of the first part, then to the development section, pages 7–12 [mm. 163–291]. Here it is principally the third and fourth themes that are developed in a humorous and ingenious way (only page 11 [mm. 262ff.] suffers from some rough spots and eccentricities); furthermore, the second theme is used as a principal accompaniment figure.

After the development section the glorious first theme resounds once again, but then up to the end of the movement Brahms bids farewell to beauty. Two new developments of the first and third themes surpass each other in bizarre eccentricities. First comes a four-voiced fugue on the third theme, which we described above as brooding [m. 354]. From the initial imitation on, this fugue becomes virtually opaque as the different lines trip over their own feet. This opacity increases in the very cramped stretto that follows after only four (quite harsh) imitative entries [m. 384]. Soon it is no longer possible to govern the troops, who have tangled themselves into a knot. The whole thing disintegrates into a frenzied rout (a canonically imitative episode [m. 396]), until the reserves of the first theme ride in to the rescue. But in the end they, too, are unable to resist the impact and are swept away in the general turmoil. Here passion and character celebrate their triumph, while beauty covers her face in sorrow.

The movement that follows is much more pleasing. It is really extraordinary how in the scherzo (B minor) demonic passion is kept so completely in check, held within appropriate limits by the powerful will of the master magician. And then in the trio (B major) a truly human geniality blossoms forth suddenly; in the second part it builds to the most blessed jubilation! After the repeat of the scherzo comes a gently flowing coda in B major, which resolves all the harsh contrasts.

The main theme of the Adagio suffers from the same rampant overabundance that we have already observed elsewhere. Two contrasting phrases, one gentler, one more robust, offer more solid support; yet their opposing qualities forbid any true unity or coherent overall impression, as happened in the first movement.

Beside the Scherzo the most brilliant movement is the finale, in which driving restlessness alternates with sorrowful laments. The opening reveille sounds almost eerie:

Although the movement storms and charges forward in ever wilder fashion, the composer always remains master of his passion, and he never oversteps the boundaries of ideal art.

Piano Concerto no. 1 in D Minor, op. 15

In the Concerto for Piano and Orchestra, op. 15, Brahms draws himself up to his full height before our very eyes. In his last sonatas and quartets, and in his *Missa Solemnis* and Ninth Symphony, Beethoven had crowned his own earlier achievements in these genres, composed in his first and second periods; and he carried these musical forms so far beyond his time and ours that the general public will still need a long time to absorb these works. (Even today, as we say, the Tenth does not understand the Ninth.) Only in his concertos did Beethoven remain stuck in his middle period. In his third period he never wrote a concerto, in which orchestra and piano would have had to become entirely equal partners, even though such a path was laid in the first movements of his E-flat-Major Concerto, and in parts of the G-Major and Violin Concertos.

And this is the path followed by Brahms, who rightly recognized where necessity was leading. To be sure, he has reached his lofty goal only in the Adagio and in the last half of the finale. The first movement is even more ambitious than the other two and in certain parts even towers above them; yet it suffers here and there from a certain roughness and harshness, and from the thick counterpoint with which we have often found fault before. One would not be wrong in placing the conception and first version of this work in an earlier period.[8] Specifically, the solo entrance on page 7 [m. 123] is very rough and angular. The clash between A and A♯ in the octaves played by bass and upper voice on page 14, system 2 [m. 282], does not sound good; it could have been easily avoided by means of another bass progression, for example B–F♯–A♯–B–D♯–G–B–B. The combining of the three themes on page 14 [m. 287] is not sufficiently transparent. At the beginning of the solo on pages 10 [m. 185] and 29 [slow movement, m. 87], orchestra and piano fall over each other's feet. Since in the piano reduction the orchestral parts are not indicated at this place, I demonstrate the beginning here to make my point:

It is this kind of heel-treading, sometimes quite bizarre, that we often encounter in Schumann (e.g., in the Andante of the Piano Quartet, page 29 [mm. 95–101]; and in *Paradies und Peri*, no. 21, page 92 [m. 173]). Bargiel also has it in his first Fantasy, op. 5, page 4. In none of these places do I find the effect beautiful; it always arouses in me a feeling of distress. These sunspots on the old master Schumann, which we learned to overlook and even to appreciate in him, should never be imitated by his followers.

We are reminded of Brahms's hazy second period by the passages on page 4, system 4 [mm. 49–51], and page 7, final system [mm. 131–41]; only at the third return of the passage on page 13 [m. 255] does it emerge in a fashion that is clearer and less surprising and mechanical. This occurs chiefly through the aid of the thematic accompaniment in the violas, which is not indicated in the piano reduction and goes as follows:

With the exception of these small details, which virtually disappear in the splendor of the work as a whole, the first movement is more gigantic than that of any other concerto known to me. Gigantic movements demand gigantic dimensions; it is thus appropriate that the movement covers twenty-three pages in score and goes well beyond the sonata form in its construction. The movement begins with an orchestral introduction (filling three pages in the piano reduction), which presents the four main themes and begins to develop the first two. The piano now enters and develops the third and second themes after one another and then (page 8 [m. 157]) a new fifth main theme, and finally the fourth. The piano is frequently interrupted by the orchestra, which competes for the thematic development.

If we take what has just been described as the first part [exposition] of a symphony movement, preceded by an introduction, then what begins on page 12 [m. 226] would be the development section. The much altered and partially truncated reprise of the first part begins on page 15 [m. 310]; it is followed on page 21 by a two-and-a-half page coda [m. 444].

I regret being unable to give here any comprehensive analysis of this magnificent movement, which is as great in its poetic conception as in its thematic development. I will restrict myself to pointing out that:

- Themes 2, 3, and 4 are conceived in double counterpoint to individual portions of the first main theme
- Later on, both halves of theme 2 are also placed in double counterpoint with each other.
- Immediately upon its first appearance, the same theme appears in two variants (page 3, bottom system [m. 26]; page 4, system 3 [m. 46]), then later in various altered forms (perhaps least recognizable on page 18 [m. 372]). Its two parts also appear later in double counterpoint (beginning of page 14 [m. 278]; page 18 [m. 372]; middle of page 21 [m. 444]).

In this movement there is no main theme, no secondary motive that is not combined with all the rest in astonishing ways. (Compare, for example, the motive in the last measure of page 4, second system [m. 45], with its diminution on pages 14 and 21 [mm. 278, 444].) Nowhere does Brahms merely write a phrase or figuration for its own sake; never does he seek aftereffects. His only concern is a process that moves from within to without. Even underneath the cascading triplets of the coda, the orchestra is playing the second half of theme 3 (or, one might say, the final measure of theme 5, for both are rhythmically identical):

Unfortunately, this is also not indicated in the piano reduction, although there is room for it.

This Allegro, which is, so to speak, as great and broad and deep as an ocean, is followed by a devout and solemn Andante, in which orchestra and piano compete to intone hymns in praise of the Highest, each one more ecstatic than the preceding. The score bears the inscription "Benedictus qui venis [*sic*] in nomine Domini." Moreover, Brahms uses for the most part motives from themes 2 and 5 of the first movement (more or less recognizable). These also appear in the rondo finale, which is livelier, and happier in its God, and in which the last third reaches truly dithyrambic energy. I give a few examples:

And I ask the reader to compare these main themes with the first two measures and the conclusion of theme 5 from the first movement (page 18 [m. 381]):

and with theme 2 as it appears on pages 4, 11, and 21:

At the end of the Andante, the G-major scale makes a very odd impression, especially the C♮ in the second bassoon against the tonic D pedal point (page 30, third system [m. 96]). It is all the more strange since the ear has accustomed itself to the C♯ which has been heard repeatedly earlier on. (Can we explain the C♮ here as Mixolydian?)

In the first third of the rondo finale the piano part predominates; but in the last two thirds, and particularly from the end of the second cadenza on, the most intimate blending of piano and orchestra makes for a magnificent symphonic duo. Nowhere, even with all the novelty and meaning of the poetic content, is the beautiful balance of parts violated and the transparency of the web destroyed. Even the (forbidden?) fifths on the fourth bar of page 38 [m. 184] sound good because they are completely justified by the motion of the two lines.

I take this symphony-concerto for the most significant work that Brahms has published up to now. In it is realized almost completely the ideal that I have set for Brahms. The more immediately likable opp. 16 and 18, which appeared later, may attract a circle of admirers more readily. But because of their very nature the Serenade and Sextet will not bear the least comparison with op. 15 as regards value, profundity, and grandeur.

NOTES

1. On the context of Schubring's "Schumanniana" series, and on the personal relationship between the composer and the critic, see Walter Frisch, "Brahms and Schubring: Music and Politics at Mid-Century," *19th-Century Music* 7 (1984): 271–81.

2. Cited from Robert Schumann, *On Music and Musicians*, ed. Konrad Wolff, trans. Paul Rosenfeld (New York, 1946; repr. 1969), 253–54.

3. Schubring does not seem to be aware (or at least does not indicate awareness) that the Sonata in F-sharp Minor was actually composed before every part but the slow movement of the C Major. Op. 2 was composed in November 1852. The slow movement of op. 1 was composed in April 1852, the rest in the spring of 1853.

4. A reference to the final song of Schumann's *Dichterliebe*, mm. 44–45.

5. Schubring may mean No. 25 of the oratorio, Peri's aria "Es fällt ein Tropfen auf's Land Egypten."

6. Schubring refers here to the third piece of *Humoresque*, in G minor, marked "Einfach und zart." This piece is interrupted by a faster Intermezzo in B-flat.

7. Schubring quotes here from a poem, "Treue Liebe," by Wilhelm Hauff. In the mid-nineteenth century this poem was fitted to a folk melody that bears a strong resemblance to the melody of Brahms's coda. The song can be found in Friedrich Silcher, *100 Volkslieder für eine Singstimme mit Begleitung des Pianoforte*, rev. Alfred Dörffel (Leipzig, n.d.), 76.

8. Schubring is, of course, right. The concerto originated as a sonata for two pianos in 1854. All of Schubring's page references in this review are to the solo piano arrangement of the concerto, or *Clavierauszug*, published in 1861. This would have been the only printed source (apart from individual orchestral parts) available to him at the time; a full orchestral score was not published until 1873. It is clear from this review that Brahms gave Schubring access to the autograph manuscript of the concerto, which is the only source that contains the "Benedictus" inscription mentioned by Schubring in his discussion of the slow movement.

Eduard Hanslick
Discovering Brahms (1862–72)

TRANSLATED, INTRODUCED, AND ANNOTATED
BY KEVIN C. KARNES

These five short selections from the collected writings of Eduard Hanslick (1825–1904) document the famous critic's first experience of Brahms's musicianship and his evolving appreciation for the composer's work over the course of the decade that followed. Hanslick's initial encounter with Brahms's pianism occurred on November 29, 1862, when Brahms appeared in a recital of his own works and those of J. S. Bach and Robert Schumann at Vienna's Gesellschaft der Musikfreunde. At that time, Hanslick later recalled, "the general public knew of [Brahms] only from Schumann's prophetic recommendation"—from Schumann's essay "Neue Bahnen" (New Paths), published in the Leipzig Neue Zeitschrift für Music *some nine years earlier.[1] As the first of Hanslick's essays below attests, Brahms's Vienna debut was a great success, and a close and enduring friendship between composer and critic developed almost immediately. By the following summer, the two were on familiar and affectionate* Du *terms.[2] And though Brahms occasionally griped about what he perceived to be Hanslick's superficial musical understanding, the two remained trusted companions throughout the rest of Brahms's life. As the composer wrote to Clara Schumann less than two years before his death, "I know of few people to whom I feel as sincerely drawn as to him."[3]*

The essays selected and translated here record Hanslick's responses to a wide swath of Brahms's music from the first two decades of the composer's career, from the F-Minor Sonata and First Serenade to the German Requiem *and* Triumphlied. *Together, they help to correct the persistent view of Hanslick (1825–1904) as an uncritical Brahms booster. Indeed, many of Hanslick's impressions were far from positive, especially regarding what he characterized as Brahms's overly pragmatic choice of thematic material. In addition to Hanslick's perceptive remarks about Brahms's music, these essays provide firsthand perspectives on Brahms's piano playing and the reception of his often challenging compositions by contemporary audiences. They also testify to Hanslick's sincere dedication to the notion that a critic must educate his public about the topics of his discourse (witness his lengthy detours into the genesis of Schumann's* Fantasie, *op. 17, and the history of the serenade as a genre), and also to his considerable learnedness as a historian of the art, as attested by the numerous explanatory footnotes that the preparation of this translation has required.*[4]

All five of the reviews translated below originally appeared on the pages of Vienna's Neue freie Presse *and were subsequently adapted by Hanslick for inclusion in what he called his "living history" of Viennese musical life: a series of volumes intended to narrate a history of recent musical events from the perspective of a listener.*[5] *They are taken, in the latter form, from* Aus dem Concertsaal. Kritiken und Schilderungen aus den letzten 20 Jahren des Wiener Musiklebens *(Vienna, 1870), 255–58, 259–61, 426–27, 427–28; and* Concerte, Componisten und Virtuosen der letzten fünfzehn Jahre. 1870–1885 *(Berlin, 1886), 51–54. All endnotes are editorial.*

Johannes Brahms (1862–63)

Johannes Brahms has now presented himself as composer and virtuoso before the public in a concert of his own.[6] Brahms's compositions do not number among those immediately understandable and captivating works that carry one along in their flight. Their esoteric character, nobly disavowing every sort of popular effect, combined with their significant technical difficulties, assures that a broad embrace of these works will be much longer in coming than Schumann delightedly prophesized for his darling as a parting blessing.[7] In Vienna, none of Brahms's larger compositions had previously been performed, and among his smaller works we had heard only a set of (unpublished) Hungarian Dances played by Clara Schumann.[8] Thus the appearance before the Viennese public of this blond, St. John visage of a composer was indeed a novel thing.

At the present time, it would be a questionable undertaking to try to size up Brahms's talent and effectiveness. Even for those who have made his works more completely their own than we have, it is by no means easy to orient oneself with respect to Brahms. It is not as if the composer were still working in the rush of first fermentation. Some time ago, mature creations already followed upon the heels of the best of his youthful works, whose wild genius drew us in at once irresistibly and forbiddingly. What progress has been made in the way of achieving a free and secure technical mastery, and what an increase of moderation and formal clarity can we observe when we compare the two frothy piano sonatas to the Variations in F-Sharp Minor and, more recently, to the two piano quartets, the *Handel*

Variations, and so forth![9] Thus no one can speak of him as a beginner. It's just that Brahms's recent works present us with question marks and riddles whose answers and solutions will only be found in his next creative period. And those answers will be decisive. Will Brahms's originality of invention and melodic strength keep pace with the development of his harmonic and contrapuntal art? Will the natural freshness and youthful energy of his early works, such as we find contained in the precious vessels that Brahms has created thus far, continue to blossom in an untroubled way and open up even more beautifully and freely? Is the foggy miasma of brooding reflection that frequently clouds his latest creations the harbinger of a penetrating ray of sunshine to come, or of a still duskier, more inhospitable twilight?* The future—the near future—will provide the answers.

At the present moment, Brahms is a significant phenomenon—indeed, perhaps the most interesting phenomenon of all. With respect to the form and character of his music, he draws sustenance, first and foremost, from Schumann, though certainly more in the sense of an inner relatedness than of formal imitation. Only with the greatest of difficulty could a figure like Brahms resist the influence of the Schumannian spirit, which penetrates undeniably and decisively the musical atmosphere of the present.† Above all else, Brahms's music shares with Schumann's a sense of chastity, of inner nobility. There is no hint of vanity or preening affectation. Everything is sincere and true. But Brahms's work also shares with Schumann's a sovereign subjectivity bordering on esotericism, a brooding quality, a turning away from the outside world, a sensibility turned inward. In fullness and beauty of melodic invention, Schumann towers over Brahms. But Brahms frequently matches him in richness of a purely formal sort, and it is here that we encounter Brahms's greatest strength. From Schumann he acquired the brilliant modernization of the canon and the fugue. But the common well from which they both have drawn is *Sebastian Bach*. Already in Brahms's first set of variations—on a theme by Schumann—we encounter an extraordinary strength of formal invention at work. The variation sets that followed, on an original theme and on a Hungarian melody, stand at approximately the same level. But Brahms surpassed them all with his twenty-five variations on a theme by Handel.[10]

---

* In Brahms's new songs as well (for one and two voices), we find nothing comparable to the freshness and uplift of his first set, op. 3.

† A prophetic word from Schumann might be appropriate here. In a letter of 1840 to a friend, he noted that he found it petty of [Gottfried Wilhelm] Fink to have ignored, consistently and for years, all of his compositions in his musical newspaper [*Allgemeine musikalische Zeitung*]. "I'm not annoyed because I want to see my name in print," he remarked, "but because of the fact—of which I'm convinced—that mine is the music of the future."

Thus far Brahms's talent has found its most marvelous expression in variation sets; above all, they demand formal richness and a unity of mood— precisely Brahms's most distinctive qualities. In Brahms's concert, it was indeed the *Handel* Variations that elicited the liveliest applause. (I cannot stop thinking about the second and the twentieth, two exemplary studies in brilliant harmonization.)

The reception of the A-Major Piano Quartet was not as auspicious. In that work, the shadowy side of Brahms's creativity comes distinctly to the fore. For one thing, its themes are insignificant. Brahms is fond of choosing his themes for their contrapuntal utility rather than for their inherent worth in and of itself. The themes in the quartet sound dry and bland. To be sure, he does explore, over the course of the piece, a plethora of inspired relationships between them. But overall effectiveness is impossible if one does not have meaningful themes. Furthermore, we fail to perceive any great, forward-striving train of development in the work. Instead, we witness an incessant joining together and taking apart, a sense of preparing for something without any goal in sight, of promise without fulfillment. In each movement we find motives well suited for episodic treatment, but nothing capable of carrying an entire piece. Having heard the quartet only once, we are naturally capable of registering only our initial impressions, not of describing the work itself. And there is no doubt that a more exacting study of this work, as with Brahms's music in general, would bring many of its good qualities to light. But such a study would hardly do much to alter one's impressions of the liveliness and effectiveness of the piece, for those things rely upon clear, plastic melodies and a powerful sense of intensification and development, of striving toward a *single* goal. Like other new works by Brahms, the Piano Quartet reminds us disturbingly of Schumann's *final* period, just as Brahms's earliest works remind us of Schumann's *first* period. Only to the pure Schumann of the ripe, crystal-clear middle period has his favorite student offered us nothing comparable thus far.

Generally speaking, Brahms's piano playing reveals the nature of his artistic personality accurately and in highly beautiful ways. He strives exclusively to serve the spirit of the composition, and he avoids almost shyly all appearances of self-important pageantry. Brahms has at his disposal a highly developed technique, which lacks only the final gleaming polish, the final energetic self-confidence that would permit us to call him a virtuoso. Brahms handles the most brilliant aspects of performance with a sort of casualness—as, for example, when he plays octave passages with such a loose wrist that the keys are grazed sideways rather than struck from above. It might seem like a compliment to say that he plays more like a composer than a virtuoso, but such praise is not entirely unqualified. Inspired by the desire to let compositions speak for themselves, Brahms neglects—especially in performance of his own works—much of what the player is obliged to do for the composer. His playing resembles that of the astringent Cordelia, who would rather conceal her innermost feelings than expose them to the public.[11] Violence and distortion are, for this reason, absolute impossibilities in Brahms's playing, determined as it is, in its sensible moderation, not even once to extract the fullest possible tone from the piano. But we would prefer not to make too much of these small shortcomings on the part of the pianist, given how insignificant they seem in comparison with the irresistible, soulful charm of his playing. This pleased us most profoundly in Schumann's *Fantasie*, op. 17.

The fantastical magic of this work, one of the most remarkable from Schumann's *Sturm und Drang* period, had never before been conjured in Vienna. Liszt, to whom the piece is dedicated, never performed it in public. (This is part of the great debt to Schumann of which Liszt cannot be absolved, and which he later acknowledged and regretted with admirable candor.) When composing the *Fantasie*, Schumann originally had in mind a contribution to the Beethoven monument in Bonn, intending to title its three movements "Ruins," "Triumphal Arch," and "Garland of Stars." When he abandoned this idea, he denied his disciples a veritable feast for the interpretative "arts."[12] How uncannily would imaginative musicians have heard Beethoven's entire biography in the work, which now, without such titles, stands silently before such attempts. On the other hand, the motto by Friedrich Schlegel that Schumann appended to his *Fantasie* seems highly characteristic, for it points, in an unintended way, to a *musical* point of departure for the work:

Durch alle Töne tönet im bunten Erdentraum
Ein leiser Ton gezogen, für den, der heimlich lauschet.[13]

Through all the tones there resounds, in a colorful earthly dream,
a single soft tone for the one who secretly listens.

This "tone" is the passionate motive that permeates the first movement above the peculiar buzzing and boozing of the bass, and that, aside from a few echoes, falls silent in the second movement, only to surface once again in the third, where it builds slowly from harplike strums to a soft transfiguration.

We cannot imagine a truer or more deeply affecting realization of this work than the one brought to us under Brahms's hands. How contentedly we listen to Brahms's playing! As soon as he touches the keys, we are overcome by the sense that *here plays a true and genuine artist, a man of spirit and soul and unpretentious self-awareness*. Brahms seemed to be in especially good form. In cannot be said that every passage glittered brilliantly and that every articulation was razor sharp. His technique is like a strong, well-bred man who strolls about somewhat carelessly dressed, who has more important things on his mind and in his heart than constantly tending to his outward appearance. But Brahms's playing is always compelling and always moves the heart. How powerfully and finely he played Bach's Chromatic Fantasy and Beethoven's Variations, op. 35, on the E-flat-major theme from *Prometheus* that the composer later took up in the *Eroica*! Yet once again, Brahms handled his own works somewhat shabbily. His F-minor sonata, a composition so wondrously "sung to itself," was played by Brahms more "to himself" than in a clearly and crisply presented manner. The outer movements, despite all their beautiful details, are too formless to make a distinct impression, and the listener is put off by the conspicuous reminiscence from Mendelssohn's C-minor trio in the Scherzo. The Andante, however, belongs among the most intimate in the modern piano repertoire. Of greatest interest was Brahms's performance of Schumann's F-Minor Sonata, op. 14. It might well have been the first public performance of this work, which must be counted among the most passionate, most characteristic, and probably most obstinate fantasies of Schumann's first period. It originally appeared, at the whim of a publisher, under the heading *Concert sans orchestre*, which accurately describes neither the substance nor the form of the piece. Conceived as a sonata from the start, the title was changed to *Sonata* in the second edition, and the previously suppressed Scherzo was reinstated.[14]

Serenade no. 1 in D Major, op. 11 (1862)

In Brahms's serenade for large orchestra (D major), we became acquainted with one of the most delightful orchestral works of recent times. Here again, a reaching back to old, nearly vanished musical forms is attempted in the modern age. Lachner and Raff write "suites"; Brahms writes "serenades." Serenades—also *Cassationen*, *notturni*, and *divertimenti*—belong among those musical character-pieces of the previous century. During that period, every prince and wealthy nobleman had a small orchestra charged with playing music in the park on summer evenings. It was even more pleasant in the cities. In the time of Haydn and Mozart, the streets and squares of Vienna resounded at night with soft music commemorating the following morning's name day celebration for someone's beloved—or, if the lover had good sense, for the name-day of her stern mother. Mozart wrote many such serenades, some for winds and some for full orchestra. This was indeed occasional music, with the event at hand helping to determine the form and character of the piece, its orchestration, and so forth. Serenades consisted of six to eight movements, among which two or three were minuets. Spohr's *Notturno* for winds may have been the last exemplar of this genre, which accompanied so humanely our grandfathers' affairs of the heart. What led Brahms back to the serenade was certainly not some archaeological urge to restore an old form, but rather an attraction to—a feeling of affinity for—its poetic content. From out of this gilded serenade there drifts the scent of dried flowers, transporting us magically back to a beautiful time long passed. Brahms's serenades—I will not deny that he composed them in a poetic atmosphere, in a gentle, happy mood—revive the sweet significance of this old night-music, only in modern music's more profound guise.

The present serenade consists of six movements. In its dimensions, it surpasses the symphony. This expansion, however, is not grounded in some overly grandiose content like that which prompts some composers to explode the usual form of the symphony, such as we find with the five-movement symphony of a Berlioz.[15] To be sure, the serenade strings together more movements than a symphony, yet those movements are not only shorter but also less demanding by nature—more monochromatic, more bourgeois, we might say. Indeed, it is precisely in this quality that we find justification for the serenade in the present day and the future. With Beethoven, one became accustomed to regarding, as the highest measure of a symphony, its content. It should be filled with passionate struggles and sublime pathos. Since Beethoven, we have lost touch with the notion of a symphony as a frame for modest images, as an asylum for pleasant states only touched upon lightly rather than churned up by struggles and passions. Today, whoever does not feel himself possessed by both Faust and Hamlet and whoever is not gripped by "the wailing of the whole of humanity" had better not become involved with a symphony. With his four symphonies and planned sinfonietta, Schumann hinted, ever so subtly, at the need to consider, alongside the great and impassioned symphony, its delightful counterpart, the "little symphony."[16] We regard the serenade, whose construction can assume the most multifarious forms, as the playground of idyllic dreams, of beloved thoughts, of lightness and gaiety. It is the symphony of tranquility. Brahms conceived of it in this way, and he created it in the most charming manner.

A contented, evening calm is draped gently over the whole, moved only lightly by joyful hopes and sweet longing. The mood is not self-consuming or one of solitary brooding, but one sung forth in verse, as it were, and, with a certain festiveness, proffered to the Queen of Hearts.

The six movements of Brahms's serenade are not of equal worth. Among the themes in the first movement, the first is more usable than original or meaningful, whereas the second makes a more distinct impression. The whole movement has a certain freshness, but also—in the development— a great deal that sounds forced and deliberate. Nonetheless, the poetic conclusion sets things right in the end. The Scherzo that follows, complete with trio, is perfectly splendid. The music streams forth in a soft, uninterrupted flow, magically illuminated by the colorful light of the orchestra. The Adagio is animated by a gentle, dreamy feeling which, though elaborated over a long period of time, never loses a sense of beautiful moderation. The first minuet (the second actually stands in for the trio, after which the first is repeated) is for us the pearl of the entire work, and perhaps the most beautiful thing that Brahms has written. The warm coloring—with only flute, clarinet, bassoon, and pizzicato cellos—and the naïve charm of the melody lend this movement, above all the others, the characteristic aura of night-music. This is a warm garden-serenade, full of moonlight and the scent of lilacs. The second scherzo is less meaningful and has more than the requisite similarity to the scherzo from Beethoven's Second Symphony. We do not count ourselves among those dreadful reminiscence hunters who exclaim, with every D-minor chord, "Aha! *Don Juan!*" We do not fault Brahms for the echoes of Beethoven's "Scene by the Brook" that one hears in the Adagio of his serenade.[17] But the second scherzo's lack of originality disturbs us enough to make us think that the movement would best be struck from the work. In a lively, marked rhythm, only without the proper buildup, a cheerful Rondo brings the serenade to a close.

German Requiem, op. 45 (1867)

The Gesellschaft concert also brought forth, again under Herbeck's direction, a still-unpublished *German Requiem* for chorus and orchestra by Joh. Brahms. The entire six-movement composition was not performed, only its first half.[18] The text consists of biblical passages that speak of the ephemeral nature of earthly things and of the hope for something beyond. The work is like a magnificent musical memorial service, intended more for the church than for the concert hall. The *German Requiem* is a work of extraordinary significance and great mastery. To us it seems like one of the ripest fruits to have grown in the style of Beethoven's last contributions to the field of spiritual music. Since the requiem masses and mourning-cantatas of our classical composers, hardly any music has portrayed with such power the shudder of death and the solemnity of transience. Here, the harmonic and contrapuntal art that Brahms acquired in the school of Sebastian Bach and infuses with the breath of our time completely recedes, from the listener's perspective, behind a powerful expressiveness that swells from touching lamentation to the crushing horror of death. How grippingly does the first movement, "Selig, die da Leid tragen" (Blessed Are They That Mourn), arise upon the wings of its soft and yet surprising harmonies, sometimes drawn from the deep cellos and trombones and other times wafting out quietly from the harp like an apparition. And yet, this is merely a prelude to the monumental tragedy of the second, B-minor movement, "Denn alles Fleisch ist wie Gras" (For All Flesh Is as Grass), in which the horror of decomposition is brightened only by the transfigured smile of a twinkling eye. This is the most substantial of the three movements, and it would have made an even greater impression upon us had it concluded with the final, resounding repetition of the principal theme in B minor. The B-major allegro appended to it, "Die Erlösten des Herrn" (The Ransomed of the Lord), seems more like a distinct addition than an organic conclusion.

The third movement does not measure up to the first two in terms of greatness of conception, yet it surpasses them both in terms of contrapuntal artistry. It does not, however, make such a clear, harmonious impression as the others. Indeed, it besieges the listener with impressions of a sometimes rather forced kind—a difficult position to assume after all the preceding excitement and exertion. The movement starts off with a baritone solo, "Herr, lehre mich doch, daß es ein Ende mit mir haben muß" (Lord, make me know mine end), which finds support—in a tone of deepest mourning—in the choir's response. The D-minor Andante finally gives way to D major and a four-voice, figural passage, "Der Gerechten Seelen sind in Gottes Hand" (The souls of the righteous are in the hands of God), above a tonic pedal. This pedal has the merciless length of seventy-two common-time measures (*tempo moderato*), sustained by basses (tuned down to D), horns, trombones, and timpani articulating unbroken sextuplets rather than rolling.[19] The passage indeed looks impressive in the score, but the composer misjudged its audible effect. At one point, the booming pedal becomes so entwined in the tangle of singers' voices that one can no longer make it out. And the incessant hammering of the timpani puts the listener in a state of nervous agitation that throttles all aesthetic appreciation. One listener compared the effect of this pedal to the disconcerting feeling one gets when driving through a very long tunnel. On the other hand, if the pedal were sustained in the *organ*, then the passage would lose this alarming quality, which detracts so greatly from the success of the movement. Although the first two movements of the *Requiem* were, in spite of their dusky seriousness, received with unanimous applause, the fate of the third was quite dubious. Brahms need not worry about it; things can change with time. Moreover, it is understandable that such a difficult work, spun exclusively from thoughts of death, can expect to garner no popular success and will leave much of the public at a loss. But we believe that protestations must be mixed with appreciation for the greatness and seriousness of the composition, which surely demands respect. This seemed not to have been the case with the half-dozen gray-haired old-school fanatics who committed the sin of responding to the applauding majority and the bowing composer with sustained hissing. That such a requiem could inspire such a breakdown of decency and decorum in a Viennese concert hall was, for us, a most regrettable surprise.

Sextet no. 2 in G Major, op. 36 (1867)

Finally, in their seventh *soirée*, the Hellmesberger Quartet Society brought forth something new: a sextet for two violins, two violas, and two cellos (G major) by Johannes Brahms. The work was given a very respectable reception, even if it did not speak to us so directly and warmly as Brahms's earlier B-flat-Major Sextet, whose clarity and blossoming freshness eclipse this new creation.[20] This latter begins with an extremely beautiful theme, well suited to all the metamorphoses of development. The whole first movement (the most significant of the whole, as was the case in the B-flat-Major Sextet) deserves the title "a brilliant piece of work in true Beethovenian spirit." The piece flows forth nobly, ernestly, and compellingly, infused with quiet yet deep emotion, flowing forward in a single lucid stream. A few harmonic rough patches toward the end could not disturb our joy. The Scherzo begins not with any distinctly original melody but with a little two-penny rhythmic figure, quietly and monotonously giving way to longer notes, just as we find so frequently with Schumann. But at just the right moment, a rushing trio in waltz tempo brings rhythmic life, sparkle, and brightness to the movement.

As products of brilliant, even profound combinatorial reasoning, the following two movements are no less significant than those that came before them. Only a musician possessing mastery over all the secrets of harmony and of art itself can exploit such relationships with this degree of surefootedness. But in terms of their immediate impact upon the listener, who can derive only an exhausted kind of enjoyment from such musical thought work and reflection, both of these movements sound tired and cold. In the broadly spun-out Andante (a kind of free variation set without a theme), there arise individual, distinct figures with significant and captivating physiognomies—most notably in the first, chromatically descending variation. But as the piece progresses, the impression it makes becomes ever more colorless, nonsensical, and incomprehensible. In the finale, the warm, living pulse of the music is lost entirely, and in its place a kind of drab reflection hammers away, mechanically and tediously. This is an abstract sort of music making, with restless combinatorics and brooding [*Combiniren und Grübeln*] pursued until one's head begins to ache. In its lack of sensuous beauty, rhythmic life, and melodic luster, the finale reminds us of many a truly unpleasant work from Schumann's final period. We report our first impressions as we experience them. But our respect for Brahms is too great and sincere to let the first impression have the last word. It is quite possible that hearing this work again and having a look at the score (we could not get hold of one) would show the final two movements of the G-Major Sextet in a more proper, more favorable light.

Triumphlied, op. 55, and *Schicksalslied,* op. 54 (1872)

Along with the *German Requiem*, Brahms's *Triumphlied* for eight-part choir, orchestra, and organ belongs among those magnificent works that place Brahms among the ranks of the great masters. In both, we find realized those wonderful effects that Schumann predicted "when Brahms waves his magic wand over the united forces of chorus and orchestra."[21] Here Brahms found his true footing, and he constructed such a tower upon that foundation that no living composer could follow him. In the area of spiritual music in the grandest sense, nothing has appeared since Bach's Passions, Handel's oratorios, and Beethoven's *Festmesse* that stands so close to those works in magnificence of conception, sublimity of expression, and power of polyphonic composition as Brahms's *Requiem* and *Triumphlied*. Influences of all three masters—of Bach, Handel, and Beethoven—are at play in Brahms. But they have been so dissolved within his blood and have reemerged as part of such a unique and independent individuality that one cannot derive Brahms from any of these three alone. One can only say that in him something of this tripartite spirit is resurrected in modern form.

Originally, the *Triumphlied* bore the subtitle "Auf den Sieg der deutschen Waffen" (To the victory of German arms), and this glorious occasion is clearly commemorated, for all time, within the work itself. It was not Brahms's desire to declare any overt bias, but one cannot suppress it in a work whose text was written over a thousand years before the Battle of Sedan.[22] The words are taken from Chapter 19 of the Book of Revelation. The first of the three movements for double choir that together comprise the *Trimphlied* sets the words "Hallelujah, Heil und Preis, Ehre und Kraft sei Gott unserm Herrn!" (Hallelujah, salvation and praise, honor and strength belong to our Lord God!), the principal motive of which repeats exactly the notes that set "Heil dir im Siegerkranz" (Salvation is yours in the circle of victors), but with a completely different rhythmic and harmonic setting. The rejoicing trumpet fanfare in D establishes the Handelian character of the piece from the start, fusing a healthy strength of expression to the highest art of composition.

"Lobet unsern Gott, alle seine Knechte und die ihn fürchten, Kleine und Große; denn der allmächtige Gott hat das Reich eingenommen" (Praise our God and all who work for him and fear him, small and great; for the almighty God has entered into the kingdom): these are the words upon which the second movement is built. Toward its end, the movement gives way to a rolling melody introduced by soft triplets, setting "Laßt uns freuen und fröhlich sein" (Let us rejoice and be happy)—a melody whose mild, blissful expressiveness is raised to the level of true transfiguration by the wonderful concluding *piano*. The third and final movement, which, after the lyricism of both preceding choruses, passes by in a dramatic and epic manner (though measured and quick), is introduced in an extraordinarily effective way. It begins with the baritone solo, "Und ich sah den Himmel aufgethan und siehe, ein weißes Pferd; der darauf saß" (And I saw heaven open, and behold, a white horse; and he who sat upon it), after which soloists from both choirs chime in with "Der darauf saß, hieß Treu und Wahrhaftig und richtet und streitet mit Wahrhaftigkeit und Gerechtigkeit" (And he who sat upon it is called Faithful and True, and in truthfulness and righteousness he judges and makes war). "Und er tritt die Kelter des Weines," it continues with wonderful power, "des grimmigen Zorns des allmächtigen Gottes" (And he will tread the winepress of the fury of the wrath of God the Almighty). Then the soloist takes over again: "Und hat einen Namen geschrieben auf seinem Kleide und auf seiner Hüfte, der also lautet: *Ein König aller Könige und ein Heer aller Herren!*" (On his robe and on his thigh he has a name inscribed: *King of kings and Lord of lords!*) After this, the "Hallelujah" enters again in a somewhat altered rhythmic guise. Swelling to an ever more powerful climax, this brings the entire work to a close in greatest rejoicing and glorious splendor.

Incidentally, we cannot count ourselves among those who place the *Triumphlied* at an equal or higher level than the *German Requiem*. To begin with, such a comparison is rendered nonsensical by the completely incomparable scope of the two works. The larger scale of the *German Requiem* goes hand in hand with greater stylistic diversity and vocal richness, and with an alternation between choir and soloists that provides for points of rest in an extremely effective way. In the *Triumphlied*, such resting places are almost completely lacking. Moreover, the melodies of the *Requiem* seem to pour forth more richly, clearly, and distinctly, which enables that work to make a more immediate and profound impression upon the uninitiated listener. To be sure, the *Triumphlied* also makes a marvelous impression, but it is more demanding and, in its combinatorial art, more difficult to grasp. It is best, however, to attempt no such comparisons. We are blessed to possess two such powerful works, two such towering contributions to our modern musical literature!

Brahms's *Schicksalslied* for chorus and orchestra (op. 54) is another tone poem of profound content and evocative uniqueness. Admittedly, Hölderlin's beautiful poem does not appear particularly well suited for a musical setting with respect to either its content or its versification. Indeed, it could only attract a composer as serious—and so consistently drawn to ideas of greatness and immortality—as Brahms. The first two strophes of the poem extol the blessed peace of the Olympian gods, who "droben im Licht schicksalslos athmen" (draw breath in the light above, free from care).[23] The choir sings these strophes in a nobly and broadly resounding adagio (E-flat major, $\frac{4}{4}$ time). In contrast, the poem's third strophe describes the pitiful lot of man, to whom it "gegeben ist, auf keiner Stätte zu ruh'n" (is allotted to rest at no abode). With deeply distressing eloquence, and without obscuring the monumental style of the work with genre-specific gestures, the composer sets this contrasting section in a gloomy allegro (C minor, $\frac{3}{4}$ time). How vividly and with what supremely simple means is the fall "von Klippe zu Klippe" (from crag to crag) portrayed! And how the voices' long pause on the word *Jahrlang* (Year after year) bores into the listener! The poet concludes in this state of hopelessness, but not so the composer. In an extremely beautiful poetic turn that reveals to us the transfiguring power of music itself, Brahms turns back, after the choir's final words, to the solemnly slow music of the beginning, and in a lengthy orchestral postlude dissolves the confused tribulation of human life into a blessed peace. In a touching manner understandable to all, Brahms realizes this turn through the means of pure instrumental music, without the addition of a single word. Thus instrumental music, in this instance, provides a sense of completion and expresses what words no longer can—a curious complement to the inverse process heard in Beethoven's Ninth Symphony. In style and mood as well as in its resonance, Brahms's

Schicksalslied reminds us of his admirable *German Requiem*. It portrays the same Christian worldview, only in Greek form.

NOTES

1. Eduard Hanslick, *Aus meinem Leben* (Berlin, 1894), 2:14. The two had met once before, at the Lower Rhine Music Festival in 1855; see *Aus meinem Leben*, 1:260–61. Schumann's essay, written to introduce Brahms to the musical world after the young composer paid his first visit to the Schumanns' Düsseldorf home, appeared in the *Neue Zeitschrift für Musik* 39 (28 October 1853): 185–86. Several translations have been published, among them the one in Oliver Strunk, *Source Readings in Music History*, rev. ed., ed. Leo Treitler (New York and London, 1998), 1157–58.

2. Styra Avins, ed., *Johannes Brahms: Life and Letters*, trans. Styra Avins and Josef Eisinger (Oxford and New York, 1997), 283.

3. Letter of 27 August 1895; trans. in Avins, *Johannes Brahms*, 728.

4. On the pedagogical role of the music critic in Hanslick's Vienna, see Leon Botstein, "Listening through Reading: Musical Literacy and the Concert Audience," *19th-Century Music* 16/2 (1992): 129–45.

5. For further discussion of Hanslick's "living history" project, see Kevin C. Karnes, *Music, Criticism, and the Challenge of History: Shaping Modern Musical Thought in Late Nineteenth-Century Vienna* (Oxford and New York, 2008), chap. 2.

6. Though dated 1862 in *Aus dem Concertsaal*, Hanslick's discussion makes clear that the essay was completed at some point during the following year, for it conflates two separate performances by Brahms, one given on November 29, 1862, and the other on January 6, 1863. In the first, given at Vienna's Gesellschaft der Musikfreunde, Brahms played his A-Major Piano Quartet, op. 26 (with members of the Hellmesberger Quartet); a toccata in F major by Bach (presumably his own transcription of BWV 540); Schumann's *Fantasie*, op. 17; two unspecified songs; and his own Variations and Fugue on a Theme by Handel, op. 24. (The promotional flyer for this concert is reproduced in Avins, *Johannes Brahms*, 261.) In his concert of January 6, Brahms performed a selection of his songs with Marie Wilt as well as four works discussed in Hanslick's essay: Bach's Chromatic Fantasy and Fugue; Beethoven's Variations in E-flat Major (*Eroica*), op. 35; Schumann's F-Minor Sonata, op. 14; and his own F-Minor Sonata, op. 5. On the latter performance, see Max Kalbeck, *Johannes Brahms*, rev. ed. (Berlin, 1912–21; repr. Tutzing, 1976), 2:33–34; and Florence May, *The Life of Johannes Brahms*, 2nd ed. (London, n. d.; repr. St. Clair Shores, Mich., 1977), 337–38.

7. An apparent reference to Schumann's "Neue Bahnen" (New Paths).

8. Probably one of the several "Ungarische Tänze" discussed by Brahms and Clara Schumann in correspondence going back to 1854. As Margit McCorkle notes, Schumann reportedly performed Hungarian dances by Brahms at concerts given in Düsseldorf, Budapest, and Vienna in 1858. (*Johannes Brahms: Thematisch-bibliographisches Werkverzeichnis* [Munich, 1984], 497.) Hanslick attended Schumann's 1858 recital in Vienna but did not report on any music by Brahms being performed (*Aus dem Concertsaal*, 164–67). It is possible that material from the dances in question later surfaced in Brahms's six volumes of Hungarian Dances for two and four hands (WoO 1, 1869–80).

9. The sonatas to which Hanslick refers are presumably two among opp. 1, 2, and 5:

No. 1, op. 1, in C major (1853); No. 2, op. 2, in F-sharp minor (1852); and No. 3, op. 5, in F minor (1853). Hanslick also refers to Brahms's Variations on a Theme of Schumann, op. 9 (1854); Piano Quartet no. 1 in G Minor, op. 25 (1861); Piano Quartet no. 2 in A Minor, op. 26 (1862); and *Handel* Variations, op. 24 (1861).

10. Hanslick refers to Brahms's *Handel* Variations, op. 24; *Schumann* Variations, op. 9; Variations on an Original Theme, op. 21, no. 1 (1857; pub. 1862); and Variations on a Hungarian Song, op. 21, no. 2 (ca. 1853–57; pub. 1862).

11. A reference to Shakespeare's *King Lear*.

12. On the history of this work and its conception as a contribution to a fund-raising effort on behalf of the construction of the Bonn monument, see Nicholas Marston, *Schumann: Fantasie, Op. 17* (Cambridge, 1992), chap. 1.

13. At Schumann's request, the *Fantasie* was published with Schlegel's quatrain, from his "Die Gebüsche" ("The Bushes," from the cycle *Abendröte* or *Sunset*), printed on the verso of the title page.

14. On the compositional and publication history of Schumann's op. 14, see John Daverio, *Robert Schumann: Herald of a Poetic Age* (Oxford and New York, 1997), 150–51.

15. A reference to Berlioz's *Symphonie fantastique* (1830).

16. Hanslick's reference to a planned sinfonietta is obscure; it is possible that he is thinking of Schumann's incomplete G-Minor Symphony or one of the two uncompleted symphonies in C minor, all of which Schumann left as sketches.

17. "Scene by the Brook" ("Szene am Bach"): the second movement of Beethoven's Sixth (*Pastoral*) Symphony.

18. At the time of the Viennese premiere of the *German Requiem* on December 1, 1867, Brahms had deemed the work complete with six movements. Only the first three, however, were performed on this occasion. In 1868–69, Brahms added an additional movement for soprano solo (the present fifth movement, "Ihr habt nun Traurigkeit") and published the resulting seven-movement work as op. 45 in 1869.

19. Thirty-six $\frac{4}{2}$ bars in the edition, by Eusebius Mandyczewski, published in *Johannes Brahms: Sämtliche Werke* 17 (mm. 173–208). The tonic D is sustained by trombones, tuba, contrabassoon, timpani, cellos, and basses.

20. Hanslick refers to Brahms's Sextet no. 1, op. 18 (1860). The Second Sextet, reviewed here, was published in 1866.

21. A loose quotation from Schumann's "New Paths" (1853); See also Schumann, "Neue Bahnen," 186, trans. in Strunk, *Source Readings*, ed. Treitler, 1158: "Later, if he will wave with his magic wand to where massed forces, in the chorus and orchestra, lend their strength, there [will] lie before us still more wondrous glimpses into the secrets of the spirit world."

22. The work was apparently conceived in response to the siege of Paris by German troops in the autumn of 1870. On its genesis and political context, see Daniel Beller-McKenna, *Brahms and the German Spirit* (Cambridge, Mass., and London, 2004), chap. 3.

23. Hanslick misquotes Friedrich Hölderlin's text set in the *Schicksalslied*, conflating the first distiches of the first and second strophes: "Ihr wandelt droben im Licht / Auf weichem Boden, selige Genien! . . . Schicksalslos, wie der schlafende / Säugling, atmen die Himmlichen" (You wander above in the light, / on soft ground, blessed immortals! . . . The heavenly ones breathe / like a sleeping child, free from care).

Hermann Kretzschmar
The Brahms Symphonies (1887)

TRANSLATED BY SUSAN GILLESPIE
INTRODUCED BY KEVIN C. KARNES

Hermann Kretzschmar's analyses of Brahms's symphonies exemplify perfectly those aspects of his writing that aroused the notorious scorn of the theorist Heinrich Schenker during the interwar years—a repeated and high-profile censure that cast a pall over Kretzschmar's work that has only recently begun to lift.[1] In the essays translated here, we encounter Kretzschmar's personifications of instruments and themes, his descriptions of moods that the latter seem to conjure or embody, and his explications of musical processes in dramatic, narrative terms. But as Schenker's own early essay on Brahms translated elsewhere in this volume attests, such hermeneutic strategies of explication were common in the late nineteenth century among German critics seeking to elucidate the effectiveness and worth of Brahms's challenging music to uninitiated audiences. Indeed, Kretzschmar penned his essays on Brahms's symphonies with precisely that goal in mind.[2] Having received degrees in composition and music history from the University of Leipzig in 1871, Kretzschmar (1848–1924) moved to Rostock in 1877, where he lectured at that city's university and directed the Rostock Konzertverein and Singakademie. Brahms's music figured prominently in Kretzschmar's concerts with those organizations; in his first three seasons with the Konzertverein, he programmed the First and Second Symphonies and the German Requiem.[3] At each of his concerts he distributed elaborate program notes, complete with examples in musical notation, intended, as he wrote, "to prepare the audience for the performance of unfamiliar or difficult works."[4] All four of his essays on Brahms's symphonies originated as such program notes, which he collected and published in 1887 under the title Führer durch den Konzertsaal *(Guide to the concert hall). By the time of his death, Kretzschmar's guide had been expanded to two volumes and revised repeatedly. Extremely popular throughout German-speaking Europe, it was enlarged still further, posthumously, by others. The selections translated here are taken from* Führer durch den Konzertsaal, *vol. 1,* Sinfonie und Suite *(Leipzig, 1887), 276–93. All endnotes are editorial.*

The Brahms Symphonies

Brahms, who emerged from the circles of the Romantics, embodies the enduring principle of the Romantic tendency: the principle of mixed moods and rapid movement in the life of the emotions. But Brahms surpasses all previous representatives of musical Romanticism in the versatility of his spirit, acquired in the course of a wonderfully purposeful and energetic development, and in the objectivity, stringency, and diversity of his style. Among all the symphonic composers of our century, Brahms is the only one who equals Beethoven in the logic and economy of his structure, the unbroken expansiveness of his material and creations, and his lofty disdain for convention. Therefore, his works, and naturally his symphonies in particular, are not always easy to enjoy. Difficult, above all, is his First Symphony.

Symphony no. 1 in C Minor, op. 68

The First Symphony resembles the Beethoven Fifth in its character and in the progression of its ideas. It, too, leads the way from struggles and difficult times to clarification and joyful freedom of the soul.

The first movement begins with a slow introduction (Un poco sostenuto, C minor, $\frac{6}{8}$), which prefigures the following great Allegro in brief strokes. Like the latter, it flares up passionately, draws breath, and expresses hopes; in it, the thematic motives of the Allegro already begin to emerge. The underlying chromatic theme, in which the violins struggle up to the heights accompanied by the menacing bowing of the double-basses, is the same one that will have preeminent significance for the structure of the symphony as a whole:

This theme appears at the beginning of the symphony and provides the compositional basis for most of it. It reaches spiritually and bodily into the second and third movements; the first movement is built entirely on it. In the form

it appears now as the upper voice, now as the bass, functions within the fabric of the counterpoint as a secret *cantus firmus*, and serves as a loyal, guiding spirit in both good and bad moments. It sounds the warning signal and soothingly bids the storm of the passions to subside. The actual main theme of the Allegro is the following:

This theme supports the demonic scenes of the movement, which are expressed with great energy, power, and rigor, but relatively briefly. More insistent, and almost more decisive as far as the overall effect of the Allegro is concerned, are those passages in which the despairing mood of struggle softens and gives way to milder, gentler sentiments. The transition to the second theme is wondrously beautiful—the gradual emergence of calmer movement, the appearance of plaintive motives, the tone of longing, in which the above-mentioned chromatic theme emerges to lead the imploring voices. The entire passage bears the stamp of authenticity. The second theme, whose first phrase

gives a good sense of the whole, concludes this peaceful turn of events. In a spiritual as well as a technical sense, it, too, seems to derive from the chromatic leading motive of the symphony. A charming dialogue follows between the French horn and the clarinet, carried on almost entirely in the simplest, most natural tones; regrettably, it is of brief duration. The violas summon the chorus of instruments back into passionate action with a rough rhythm:

From this emerges the motive

that will play an important role in the development of the movement. In the development section, the two great *piano* passages stand out. In the sudden, deathly stillness they introduce, and in their quiet, half-hidden domination by somber thoughts, they have a transcendental quality. The first one is followed by a scene of strength and piety. The old motives of defiance come together as if joining in song:

The second *piano* entry leads into a passage that strikes the agitated tone of the introduction more strongly and emphatically than before, and makes the transition to the recapitulation with the most terrifying expression of inner outrage. This passage is one of the most powerful achievements in the pathetic style and is simultaneously a masterpiece in the art of making transitions. The recapitulation takes its normal course. But after leading the demonic forces of the movement to a still higher, unheard-of level at the end of the first group of themes, the music breaks off as if in natural exhaustion. The chromatic theme is expanded into touching melodies of lament, and the movement comes to an elegiac and melancholy close.

The second movement of the symphony (Andante sostenuto, E major, $\frac{3}{4}$) betrays the lingering oppressive influence of the first. However much it tries to avoid the previous Allegro in its key and in its purposeful search for consolation and peace, some of the terrifying elements of the former overtake it nonetheless. They find expression in the violent crescendos, in the abrupt modulations of individual themes; in fact, the Allegro even sends some of its motives literally into the slow movement. The chromatic passage of the fifth bar appears in the first theme:

and the painfully reiterated

appears in the conclusion of the second group of themes.

In individual passages, the tone of childlike trust comes through in an extraordinarily touching way, for example, in the coda of the first theme:

It appears with even more engaging liveliness in the play of sixteenth-notes offered by oboe and clarinet as the second theme. The conclusion of the Andante, where the French horn and solo violin together take up the last-cited consoling theme, creates the effect of true *musica sacra*.

The third movement of the symphony (Un poco allegretto, A-flat major, $\frac{2}{4}$) is far removed in its character from the scherzo that is traditional in this position. It is conceived in strict accord with the spirit of the first movement; its cheerfulness is therefore muted, as it might be during a happy interlude that follows a series of sorrowful days. The sadness is evident in the second theme, in particular:

At the *forte* there is an accent of pain. The basic tone of this movement is childlike sincerity. This is expressed by the principal theme, particularly in its second half:

It is even more evident in the trio, a graceful alternation of woodwinds and violins on the theme:

There is much natural sound in the gentle bell-like tone of the winds, along with an original talent for instrumentation that in Brahms often finds expression in formulations of the utmost simplicity. The conclusion of the movement, quiet and half unexpected, is in complete accord with the discreet character of the composition.

The finale (Adagio, C minor; Andante–Allegro, C major, *alla breve*) begins with a return to the passionately sorrowful mood of the first movement of the symphony. The introductory Adagio commences with melancholy strains:

The violins try energetically and desperately to distract from the path of melancholy, in a phrase that is very sharply characterized by pizzicato and *stringendo* and that reappears at critical points in the Allegro. In vain! The imagination strays agitatedly in a dark circle; at the motive

the orchestra reaches a state of open revolt. The timpani give out a terrifying roll. Then the French horn appears, like a peaceful messenger from heaven, with the following melody:

We are in the Andante, the second part of the introduction. The mood softens, becomes more elevated, and prepares for the mighty, joyful hymn with which the principal section of the finale, the Allegro, begins:

A long and folklike melody develops out of this first section. This melody serves as the primary bearer of representation in this movement.[5] Among the other ideas that combine with this melody, the most important is the wavering:

The energetically cheerful motives:

the fervent theme:

and the melancholy:

also take on passing significance.

The section gives a grandiose, dramatically spirited picture of a mood of victory that strides over all obstacles and swells to dithyrambic jubilation.

This finale is as vivid and lively in its cheerful moments as in its somber ones; it expresses a powerful quality.[6] The most brilliant and moving passages in the Allegro are probably those in which the horn melody from the Andante reappears.

Symphony no. 2 in D Major, op. 73

Brahms's Second Symphony in D major, published at the end of 1877, is stylistically one of the author's most Romantic creations, in which pastoral motives and Anacreontic ideas occur in close proximity with ghostly strains. From the point of view of its musical composition, it is inferior to the First Symphony. Its outline is more deliberate, and at several points it reveals the junctures where additions and insertions have had to be made. In its content this symphony is related, in a distinguished modern form, to the imaginative world of the earlier Viennese School. Its basic tone is cheerful, and even in the melancholy portions of its Adagio, spiritual grace and a peaceful frame of mind hold sway.

The first movement of this symphony (Allegro non troppo, D major, $\frac{3}{4}$) resembles an agreeable landscape into which the setting sun casts its sublime and somber lights. It contains a far greater number of independent musical ideas than this scheme requires, and some of these numerous secondary ideas appeal strongly to the memory. The central theme of the movement consists of an amiably candid, warmhearted dialogue between French horn and woodwinds:

The violins shadow the conclusion with soft triadic figuration; the trombones punctuate it with chords of dark solemnity. The transition section, whose middle part is based imposingly on fragments of the first theme, introduces two new motives, first a gay one:

and finally a teasing one:

The beginning of the second theme

betrays some influence of Mendelssohnian sentimentality. It is followed in the closing thematic group of the exposition section by a number of powerful ideas, among which the following two examples are noteworthy:

and

In the overall impression made by this symphony, the last theme stands out, intensified by vigorous imitations. The development section, which is relatively brief, is characterized by the use of contrast to create a fantastic effect. The recapitulation comes abruptly and with charming variations. The coda of the movement is among the most beautiful parts of the symphony. It is the product of immediate inspiration. The French horn leads with a peculiarly hesitant and searching melody, and the violins and woodwinds, aiding each other by turns, repeat in abbreviated form the most appealing and graceful things they have encountered on their previous long journey.

The second movement of the symphony (Adagio non troppo, B major, *alla breve*) is introduced by the cellos with a melody that begins as follows:

For a long time it seems to be seeking the key that will enable it to break out of a melancholy circle. Finally its sorrowful glances light upon a friendly image that seeks to lead the imagination back to youth, with its happy days of play and graceful dance:

A third part, dominated by the theme

deepens the gloomy mood with which the movement began, until a passionate climax is reached. The development, which is based on themes 1 and 3, is dominated by this tone of agitation. Nor does the conclusion permit the sweet melody of the $\frac{12}{8}$ rhythm to return; rather, it lets the sorrowing theme of the cellos vanish in a dreamily pleasant light.

The main part of the third movement (Allegro [recte Allegretto] grazioso, G major, $\frac{2}{4}$; presto, $\frac{2}{4}$; presto, $\frac{3}{8}$) has the same naive character of melody and instrumentation as the original minuet of Brahms's D-Major Serenade. The principal theme of the movement begins as follows:

The harmonization and instrumentation of this modest, lovely melody are of equal simplicity. The second group is essentially nothing but a rhythmic reformulation of the main theme:

It is strengthened by the addition of a very weighty subsidiary theme:

In this theme, as in the $\frac{3}{8}$ bars

that take the place of the trio, the humor takes on the guise of Hungarian music.

The finale of the symphony (Allegro con spirito, D major, *alla breve*) recalls the shimmering colors of Cherubiniesque Romanticism. It is high-spirited and overflowing with life, like the Haydn symphonies. In the style of that master, even the fantastically lively principal theme

begins with a suspenseful *piano*, which is followed, after a striking transition, by a ringing *forte*. The first subsidiary theme is the following:

The pleasantly familiar atmosphere of the second theme

is strongly supported by a series of subsidiary thoughts, some patriarchally strong, others, with their easy eighth-note figures, flirtatious. An intimate, enthusiastic episode based on the theme

provides the graceful centerpiece of its development section.

Symphony no. 3 in F Major, op. 90

The Third Symphony of Brahms, which was published in 1883, paints the picture of a powerful nature. It accomplishes this project in an unusual manner, inasmuch as the locus of its conflicts is at the end of the composition.

Stylistically, this symphony differs from its predecessors in its even greater clarity of articulation. It shows us the composer advancing steadily along the path of a noble popularity. The subjective aspect of development recedes more and more into the background; the ideas and their representation cleave to a sphere that is understandable and comprehensible to everyone. This Third Symphony of Brahms may perhaps represent the point of departure of a new epoch in the history of the symphonic art. For it seems to initiate the break with Beethoven's method of treating the movements, shifting the compositional emphasis from the development section to the themes, from elaboration and artful continuance to original invention. One stately theme follows on the heels of another. The majority of the melodies, it is true, are extended, and a practiced facility is required to grasp them— a task that is made easier by their extraordinary formal clarity.

The first movement, whose basic characteristic is a robustly spirited cheerfulness, is introduced by two bars whose melodic motive

takes an independent role in the development of the movement. It sets off the theme groups and expands at times into great, expressive melodies. The principal theme of the movement flares up combatively, now in major, now in minor, and develops an unusual energy by means of its quick succession of pauses and terse movement, its great strides and slow forward motion:

The subsidiary theme,

which follows immediately, is one of numerous episodes in this movement that seek to lull the powerful elements of the composition to sleep with gentle feelings. But to no avail: They are followed by yet bolder expressions of spiritual strength. The most seductive in this group of Delilah-figures is the second theme,

which proves to be extraordinarily rich in transformations. Elements derived from this theme can be found as leading voices in both the playful and the heroic scenes. In the development section it appears in minor and establishes the serious character of this section. A *sostenuto* in E-flat, based on the principal theme, provides the climax and at the same time completes and closes the development section. The coda takes the powerful phenomenon of the principal theme, raises it once more to a higher level, and then, with magical beauty, makes the transition to a state of rest. With a last soft quotation from its first bars, in a manner that recalls the opening movement of Beethoven's Eighth Symphony, the Allegro comes to an elegiac close.

The Andante of the symphony (C major, *alla breve*) is an unpretentious piece of poetry in a devout mode, a composition whose self-contained, unified, and dispassionate bearing finds scarcely any rival in the more recent symphony since Beethoven. The greater part of the movement is based on the theme

which is developed in a series of free variations that alter little in its character but offer the most glorious shifts of ornamentation. For just a moment a plaintive tone is struck:

But this melody, which formally plays the role of the second theme, is not further exploited. Only its consequent phrase, which ends in a mystical play of soft dissonances, returns at the end of the movement.

Beginning with the third movement (Poco allegretto, C minor, $\frac{3}{8}$), the character of the symphony becomes gloomier. Its principal theme rather resembles one of Spohr's melodies

and presents the image of a graceful dance, like the reflection of a beautiful past. This is the passage in the principal section where the music displays its greatest charm. It is introduced by the cello motive

and painted in the hues of recollection and dream. In place of the trio there is a middle section (in A-flat) that the winds fill with a tone of pleading and resignation:

It closes with a Beethovenesque phrase.

The fact that the third movement did not become a fiery scherzo results, as in Brahms's First Symphony, from the general poetic plan of the symphony. This third movement serves to prepare the way for the passionate and often darkly agitated Finale (Allegro, F minor, *alla breve*). The latter is the focal point of the work. Here the heroic element of the symphony must prove itself in contest with harsh and unfriendly opponents. The movement begins in a darkly fantastic manner—scuttling figures, then a pause and complete standstill of rhythmic activity:

The tone becomes even eerier and more oppressive with the entrance of the trombones and the veiled theme that follows:

Immediately after this, the long drawn-out arc breaks off, and the situation takes on a definite aspect of struggle. Wild and defiant, the violins break in with:

The cellos sing in joyful victory:

In the development section there are several climaxes based on this passage of conflict. One of the most significant is the point at which theme B enters at full strength, in opposition to the fanatical figures of the violins. A notable and meaningful call from the bassoon calms the stormy waves. The composition moves into a *sostenuto*, which has all the beauty of a sky filled with rainbows. The dark themes A and B now exude quiet and peace, and, as the conclusion of the symphony approaches, the heroic theme of its first movement reappears like an apparition transfigured.

Symphony No. 4 in E Minor, op. 98

Brahms's Fourth Symphony, published in 1885, has been described by many connoisseurs as the composer's most significant work in this genre— a judgment based largely on the conclusion of the work. Here, for the first time, Brahms expresses the most unique and powerful part of his individuality, emphatically and in a clearly recognizable way, in the sphere of the symphony—the singer of the *German Requiem* stands before us! Stylistically, this symphony follows the path of its predecessor. It even surpasses the Third in the simplicity and clarity of its basic musical ideas and in the disposition of its movements, which confine themselves to a few principal groups of themes. The symphony opens in a simple narrative tone, and the first movement, in particular, almost resembles a great stylized song.

The opening theme begins without preliminaries:

It is a long melody whose cloudy horizon brightens from time to time, only to assume a still gloomier character and an often painful accent. The accompanying theme (in the cellos) and the second theme,

which proceeds by barely perceptible steps to its delicately fading conclusion, are close companions of the elegiac main figure that dominates this movement. They live on beside it in gentle diffidence, pose resigned questions, and rest, darkly brooding, on long chords. Immediately after the conclusion of the great E-minor melody comes a chivalrously gay countertheme, whose various transformations

give this movement its original stamp. Now powerful and commanding; now affectionate and gentle, teasing and secretive; now far, now near, now hurried, now peacefully expansive—its appearance is always surprising, always welcome, bringing joy and giving dramatic force to the progress of the movement. Here, too, as in the opening movement of the Third Symphony, the development section is kept very brief and is essentially content to express the elegiac elements of the poetry somewhat more forcefully. As simple as the whole structure of the movement seems, it is extraordinarily rich and artful in its details. Each voice has an independent melodic life. The principal choir of instruments and the accompanying one relate to each other antiphonally throughout most of the movement, making the effect fuller without being obtrusive.

The second movement (Andante moderato, E major, $\frac{6}{8}$) continues the elegiac ideas of the first movement. Its relationship to the first is like someone recalling a story from earlier days, in connection with a subject that has just been brought up. Its principal theme

is introduced by several *unisono* bars and has the unvarying tone of old romances; some of its cadences also include turns of phrase characteristic of medieval music. In the middle of the movement, where the triplets begin, the music casts off its tone of neutral narration, exhibits joyful involvement and enthusiasm, and breaks out in heartfelt lamentations.

The third movement (Presto [recte Allegro] giocoso, C major, $\frac{2}{4}$) has the same archaic ornamentation as the Andante. This is especially evident in the conclusion of the countertheme, in minor,

Presto

which is treated only fleetingly. This is a presto whose cheerfulness is not absolute. It repeatedly touches on frightening elements. In the muffled and deeply penetrating chords of the principal theme

in its hastening, restless rhythms, in its suddenly pulsing energy, in the predominant harshness of its character, the movement directly recalls the composer's demonic piano ballads (op. 10), which are among the most poetically significant of his early works.

The finale (Allegro energico e patetico [recte passionato], E minor, $\frac{3}{4}$) presents more obstacles to formal understanding than any other part of the symphony, due to the sheer volume of material it contains. From the standpoint of idea content, it is one of the most serious and high-minded symphonic movements in existence.

It begins with a series of heavy chords, to which the trombones add threatening colors and accents. All the themes that are presented following this entrance have an anxious, alarmed, and searching character. Among them, the following

Allegro

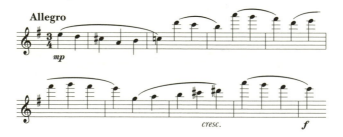

is to be regarded as the principal theme. It returns several times during the movement; however, it is not exploited in the usual manner of the development section. The leading element in this moody group of ideas is a long flute solo, which, true to its melodic and rhythmic nature, creates the image of an unstable frame of mind. After it comes the turning point: the harmony suddenly changes to E major; the rhythm becomes broad and peaceful; clarinet and oboe begin to sing consolingly and devoutly:

The trombones solemnly express the elevated ideas of a requiem:

The composition leads to the sphere where suffering and joy fall silent and the human bows before the eternal. In the natural sublimity of its conclusion, the Fourth Symphony of Brahms is one of the most magnificent and soul-stirring works of symphonic literature.

NOTES

1. For Schenker's view of Kretzschmar, see, for instance, his "Beethoven's Fifth Symphony (Continuation)" (1923), trans. William Drabkin, in Schenker, *Der Tonwille: Pamphlets in Witness of the Immutable Laws of Music, Offered to a New Generation of Youth*, ed. William Drabkin (Oxford and New York, 2004–5), 1:193–95.

2. On Kretzschmar's work in relation to various trends of hermeneutic discourse in nineteenth-century music criticism, see Ian D. Bent, ed., *Music Analysis in the Nineteenth Century* (Cambridge, 1994), 2:22–25.

3. Karl Heller, "Das Rostocker Jahrzehnt Hermann Kretzschmars," in *Hermann Kretzschmar: Konferenzbericht Olbernhau 1998*, ed. Helmut Loos and Rainer Cadenbach (Chemnitz, 1998), 64.

4. Kretzschmar, *Führer durch den Konzertsaal*, vol. 1, *Sinfonie und Suite* (Leipzig, 1887), iii.

5. Where I give *representation*, Kretzschmar uses the term *Darstellung*, literally "portrayal." This is only one of a number of terms that he borrows from the visual arts. Kretzschmar's use of the term *Bild* (image or picture) in the following paragraph is another example. (*Trans.*)

6. Where I give *vivid*, the German term is *anschaulich*—another expression drawn from the realm of visual experience. Its root is *schauen*, "to look." The use of the word *anschauen* in a nineteenth-century German text would very likely have brought to mind the terminology of Goethe, who used *anschauen* quite systematically to express the irreducible concreteness he held to be common to scientific observation and artistic form. (*Trans.*)

Heinrich Schenker
Brahms's A Cappella Choral Pieces, op. 104
(1892)

TRANSLATED, INTRODUCED, AND ANNOTATED
BY KEVIN C. KARNES

Heinrich Schenker's review of Brahms's choral pieces, op. 104 (1889), appeared in serialized form across three issues of the Leipzig Musikalisches Wochenblatt *in August and September 1892. It was the third published essay by a writer who would go on to become one of the most influential music theorists of the twentieth century. In this review, we find few hints of the sorts of analytical work for which Schenker (1868–1935) would later become famous—though as Allan Keiler has pointed out, there are indeed a few hints.[1] Nonetheless, we encounter a young composer and critic whose passion for analysis had already been stoked by his sense that in Brahms's music, unique among that of living artists, one hears traces of a glorious German musical tradition stretching backward in time through Beethoven and Mozart to Johann Sebastian Bach. Indeed, for Schenker to remark as he did on Brahms's* Nachtwache II *(op. 104, no. 2) that "one might suspect J. S. Bach" if Brahms's name were not appended to the title page was, for the critic, to bestow upon Brahms the highest praise imaginable.*

In this review, we witness the twenty-four-year-old Schenker engaging in excited, sometimes breathless discussions of Brahms's mastery of melodic construction and of the moods conjured by his melodies. We also encounter Schenker's Wagner-like fascination with music's ability to express the emotional significance of poetic texts more vividly than words alone can, and with the power of motivic development and replication to mirror the dynamic complexities of human thought and feeling. Throughout, Schenker's discussion is deeply rooted in a German hermeneutic tradition that evolved from the work of the philosopher and theologian Friedrich Schleiermacher (1768–1834) and pervaded the Romantic discourse on the arts. His technical descriptions of the music's unfolding are accompanied, at nearly every stage, by attempts to describe the meaning of that music and the probable creative intentions of the composer.[2]

Though Schenker and Brahms crossed paths occasionally during the latter's final years, the two were hardly on intimate terms. After 1900, Schenker's analytical and theoretical work would take him far afield from the sorts of interpretive statements and strategies explored in this early essay, but his deep respect and fondness for Brahms's music remained unchanged to the end. Schenker's review originally appeared as "Kritik. Johannes Brahms. Fünf Gesänge für gemischten Chor a capella, Op. 104," Musikalisches Wochenblatt *23 (1892): 409–12, 425–26, 437–38. It is reprinted in* Heinrich Schenker als Essayist und Kritiker. Gesammelte Aufsätze, Rezensionen und kleinere Berichte aus den Jahren 1891–1901, *ed. Hellmut Federhofer (Hildesheim, 1990), 14–26. All endnotes are editorial.*

Nachtwache I

There are six voices in the choir: soprano, first and second altos, tenor, first and second basses. The melodic construction makes clear that its invention was inspired from the start by an antiphonal exchange:

"Soft tones of the breast, awakened by the breath of love"

The deliberate retention of the antiphonal structure—the whole choir comes together only to express the point "Trag ein Nachtwind euch seufzend in meines zurück" (Let a night wind bear you back, sighing, to mine) and four measures before the end—enables the choir to represent, as it were, two individuals, embodied in the soprano and the tenor. The other voices exhibit little individuality in a melodic sense and, functioning harmonically, merely support the melody. This homophonic texture, embedded within the antiphonal structure (this arrangement is probably to be regarded as the most extreme concession to the element of individuality in the poem that the choir could possibly make), corresponds marvelously to the idea of the distich. That is, if one will give me the right to assert that the thin layer of reflection spread over the poetic content refers to a single individual of a particular intellectual disposition, then the homophonic texture in the choir seems, at the very least, quite justifiable.

Leise Töne der Brust,	Soft tones of the breast,
Geweckt vom Odem der Liebe,	awakened by the breath of love,
Hauchet zitternd hinaus,	whisper forth tremulously
Ob sich euch öffn' ein Ohr,	if an ear or loving heart
Öffn' ein liebendes Herz,	should open to you;
Und wenn sich keines euch öffnet,	and should none open,
Trag' ein Nachtwind euch	let a night wind bear you back,
Seufzend in meines zurück.	sighing, to mine.[3]

Not every lover knows how to express his "soft tones of the breast." And if one such expression takes on the unique character of the individual who utters it, then it cannot possibly be the case that several individuals can evoke this same character in their own utterances, otherwise that character would lose its uniqueness as such. Thus it seems to me that the poetic idea must exclude the possibility of polyphony in the choir. For the most part, Brahms holds himself to a homophonic framework in this piece. And for the reasons just discussed, I would chastise him for tending toward polyphony in a few spots, in contravention against the poetic idea—as we find when he sets "whisper forth tremulously," "if a loving heart should open," etc. Furthermore, the system of two individuals, each represented in a homophonic manner (about which I spoke above), seems to me to reveal an independent idea on the part of the composer, going beyond the idea of the poet. It is like two lovers who have not yet confessed their love for each other, but who, separated by a great distance, dedicate to each other their "tones of the breast awakened by the breath of love." It is as if their tones and sighs cross paths in the air that separates them. One will consider this impression of mine a mere hypothesis in which I, for my part, find an explanation for the two individuals. Without it, the division of the choir would remain inexplicable to me, since the content of the poem seems by nature to revolt against it.

Since Brahms perceived the poetic content like an event unfolding before him and acknowledged the driving force of feeling that gradually implanted into the scene (so to speak) the idea of things following each other in time, so he responded to these hints, rooted in reality, in the form of tone painting—a tone painting that seems, as it were, motivated directly. And so, for instance, we find the musical setting of "hauchet zitternd hinaus":

"whisper forth tremulously"

and the words "trag ein Nachtwind euch seufzend, seufzend":

"let a night wind bear you back, sighing, sighing"

The intensification of feeling, with the crescendo building to forte, becomes readily perceptible with the words *Ob sich euch öffn' ein Ohr* (if an ear should open). But I wonder whether Brahms could not compel the psychological sense of time to overcome the form of the poem at the words *Öffn' ein liebendes Herz* (if a loving heart should open). In spite of the pentameter and in spite of the hexameter, these words belong together with those that came just before them, and certainly within the context of the same intensification of feeling. And so, a forcible separation, as we hear it, cannot be carried out. So why was it?

Nonetheless, this piece must be considered worthy on account of its absolute musical beauties, which I could regard somewhat one-sidedly, and even more so because of the truthfulness of its fundamental mood, which is that of its creator in the best sense. Finally, it is worth noting that Brahms has set this same distich as a four-part canon for women's voices (op. 113, no. 10).

Nachtwache II

A six-part choir (soprano, first and second altos, tenor, first and second basses), and a masterwork down to the smallest cell! If the melody and harmony did not give Brahms away immediately, one might suspect J. S. Bach in the free and meaningful polyphony, in the powerful solemnity, and in the broad rush of harmonies.

In brilliant ways, Brahms mixes, in the first part of the piece, epic and lyrical elements when he foists upon the united choir of soprano, altos, and tenor—which declares to us its impression, already emerged into feeling: "Ruhn sie? rufet das Horn des Wächters drüben aus Westen" (Do they sleep? Thus calls the horn of the watchman from the West)—the motive of the watchman, proclaimed in the basses, as if under the pretext of actuality:

"Do they sleep? Do they sleep?"

And so the world of mood floats above the world of reality. Especially remarkable in this respect is the composer's determination that mood take priority over tone painting in the horizontal line. Even more remarkable, perhaps, is the way in which Brahms has portrayed, through rhythmic means, the form of the question, "Ruhn sie? . . . rufet das Horn":

"Do they sleep? Do they sleep? Thus calls"

And now, when the horn "aus Osten" is heard and "Sie ruhn!" answers back, the melody turns, as if instinctively, in the opposite direction:

"and from the East, the horn"

And again one hears, in the second bass and tenor, and finally in the second alto, the motive of the horn in the affirmative form of the inverted leap of a fourth, like an element of reality emerging from out of the fabric of mood!

Sie ruhn!

"They sleep!"

The first part comes to a close without having changed the fundamental tonality (E-flat major). In this way, I believe, the nature and character of the inversions, which have played such a significant role in this setting, have been made more conspicuous in the best sense of the word, and have been brought more closely in line with the feeling. But one must admire the consequences of this aspect of construction even more when one looks at one of the means by which Brahms does justice to the relationship between the two distiches of the poem: between the one that is inquiring and the one that is responding. In order to set the inquiring first distich before the responding one (namely, the second, as indicated by both mood and idea) in the most effective way possible, Brahms strove, using every means at his disposal, for vivid uniformity and energy in the first distich, which is precisely the consequence of the E-flat-major tonality.

Ruhn sie? rufet das Horn	Do they sleep? Thus calls the horn
des Wächters drüben aus Westen,	of the watchman from the West,
Und aus Osten das Horn	And from the East, the horn
Rufet entgegen: Sie ruhn!	answers back: They sleep!
Hörst du, zagendes Herz,	Do you hear, timorous heart,
Die flüsternden Stimmen der Engel?	the whispering voices of angels?
Lösche die Lampe getrost,	Extinguish your lamp confidently,
hülle in Frieden dich ein.	and let peace envelop you.

In the second part of the piece, one hears—just as readily and likewise psychologically motivated—A-flat major, C-flat major, and A-flat minor taking turns, until E-flat major once again asserts its hereditary right to rule, so to speak.

And now one wonders and takes pleasure in all the wonders and pleasures that be! At the boundary between the two large sections of the work, it is necessary to color and strengthen the organism of moods and thoughts, and even, in a certain sense, to call it newly to life. At this moment, Brahms lets the choir sink from forte to piano, with the words "They sleep!" at the end of the first section. He lets the new idea enter at this piano, thus letting go of the tone that concluded the old mood and bringing in the new one! Is it not, at this point, as if the moods and thoughts meet each other in the midst of the stillness of the piano? And doesn't some sense of the earlier harmony almost seem to live on in this new tone?

Then, the voices enter one after the other, as if each wanted to ask, "Do you hear, timorous heart"? And they come together to complete the question with the words "the whispering voices of angels." The melody of this short, three-measure phrase is closely related to the preceding section, as I will show below.

The way the passage loses itself in the key of A-flat major (I say *loses itself* because of its gentle gliding over the C-minor triad, and because of the F triad that saturates the first part of the second measure); the rhythm and the sequence of harmonies, and especially the placement of the tonic and dominant triads together; the melodic line at the word *voices* and the dynamic intensification of the melody to a gentle height with this word—how willingly all of these elements are bound together in order to serve the poetic idea, which seeks to capture and hold down, as it were, a more remote thought with the gentle strength of the mood. All of these things are furthermore united in order to satisfy the form dictated by the poet, with its fine and soft questioning, just like that of his own imagination!

The magic of this mood disappears very quickly, and a new idea, more clearly based in actuality, makes its appearance. But Brahms, with the most perfectly characteristic will, as if he served that of the poet alone, lifts this idea up into a transfiguring light. In groups and individually, the voices call one after another: "Extinguish your lamp confidently." The warmth and depth of a happy confidence emerge, and all the voices sing, softly but with full strength, "let peace envelop you."

Already [we observe] the brilliant use of the G♭ in the first group of voices, which leads us, for the very first time, into the free world of polyphony and reveals, all at once, the so peculiarly beautiful C-flat-major tonality! To be sure, the motive that appears with the words "extinguish your lamp confidently" is hardly new.[4] But what freedom in the transformation of the leap of the fourth, with its gradual augmentation in the soprano! New motives and melodies bring us the words "let peace envelop you" in both free and strictly imitative figures that chase each other in the lively voices. But here one also hears, clearly and frequently, the old motive of the horn resounding throughout in the form of the answer (especially in the two basses), as if it wanted to set us, once again, firmly upon the floor upon which we stood earlier.

Now I will address the melodic construction. Indeed, it is this that lends the work a sense of Romantic magic by virtue of its unique quality, and in whose womb the seeds of all the harmonic gestures that lend the piece its distinct physiognomy grow. Take a look at the following structures:

"Thus calls the horn of the watchman from the West"

and

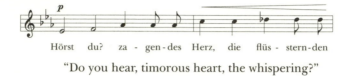

"Do you hear, timorous heart, the whispering?"

Characteristic of both is the interval of a second, which pushes its way into the purely harmonic series of tones without destroying its own harmonic sense.

At the end, the melodic construction of the soprano is as follows:

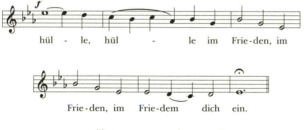

"let peace envelop you"

How characteristic is its descent into the depths, and the elementary decomposition of the triad in measures 3 and 4!

Finally, I ought to comment upon the contributions made to the effectiveness of the piece by rhythm and harmonic structure. But who can assess these? One will permit me merely to remark, in a descriptive way, upon a few things related to this issue. In the first four measures, the tonic triad appears on the first beat and the dominant triad on the third. In the next two bars, the subdominant triad usurps the place of the dominant in order to make way for the close of the first section of the piece in its proper place. Eight measures before the end, we have a C-flat-major triad on the downbeat, an A-flat-minor triad on the second beat, and an E-flat-major triad on the third. But seven measures before the end (that is, in the very next bar), the first two beats of the measure are dominated by a B-flat-major triad functioning as the dominant of the E-flat-major chord reached on the third beat. And it is precisely this latter sonority that will, in its own key, usher in the future! A crisis of melody, dynamics, ideas, and tonality occurs on this third beat of the measure. And what a brilliant accomplishment this is! Like an aftereffect of this crisis, the E-flat-major (tonic) triad is permitted to occupy, once again, the third beat, while the subdominant takes the first for itself. Only later does the tonic push its way forward, until it reaches the one place that truly reflects its significance.

And the amazing work that I've just described is only twenty-one bars long!!!

Letztes Glück

The most remarkable thing about this six-part choral work is the freedom with which the poetic idea has created its own musical form corresponding precisely to itself. As in the poem, the brightness and gentleness of the *Frühlingsträume* (dreams of spring) oppose the serious shadow of the autumnal, and the delicate, graceful energy of the color represented by "der bei den späten Hagerosen verweilende Sonnenblick" (the ray of sun lingering on the late, wild roses) is tinted by the sweet-sad melancholy of "eines letzten, hoffnungslosen Glückes" (a last, hopeless bliss). The music vividly portrays these contrasts through means peculiar to it. A perfect congruence is apparent in the ordering of the four tonalities that govern the work: F minor and A-flat major, F major and F minor. The melody is likewise divisible into four groups, which only increases the vividness of the ideas expressed. One will allow me to say the following about the motivic replications and repetitions appearing in the melody. In one's experience of a mood imparted through the senses or only indirectly through the imagination, opposing feelings seem to combat each other, but in reality one feeling exerts a lasting effect upon the next. Ultimately, all of these feelings work together, contributing to the overall character of the mood. In order to re-create the complicated nature of a mood that one will readily consider "unified," motivic replications and repetitions, if operating in the service of ideas, can function like materials for binding together skillfully assembled thought constructions, since they can replicate certain effects of one idea within opposing ones. It is possible (ultimately every individual must decide for himself) that the partial repetition of the first melodic group in the fourth part of our piece portrays perfectly the idea of the "letztes Glück" (last bliss), since it implies a connection with the image, "leblos gleitet Blatt um Blatt still und traurig von dem Bäumen" (lifelessly, leaf after leaf glides quiet and sorrowfully from the trees). It is equally possible that similarities in the melodic construction of the two middle sections also bring these closer together, with symbolic strength, so to speak. All of this is possible within the mind of each individual, even if it goes beyond the intentions of the composer, who would perhaps claim only a formal function for the similarities and repetitions in his melodic construction, as one generally does in purely instrumental music. It is indeed tone painting when "leblos gleitet Blatt um Blatt" is rendered musically in this way:

"Lifelessly, leaf after leaf glides"

Verlorene Jugend

There are five voices in the choir: soprano, alto, tenor, and two basses. This five-voice texture is required by the canon, which appears between the soprano and the alto one time and between the first bass and the soprano another. The other voices content themselves with interpreting the canon in a clear and unambiguous manner. The idea of a canonic setting is not required by the poem, however. Rather, it is a spontaneous musical luxury.

Within the canon, there are motives of a typically Brahmsian type:

"My youthful days, where have you gone so quickly?"

The poet's broad apostrophe to youth—a warm apostrophe indeed—lifts the composer from the D-minor tonality of the canon upward to D major, but carries him well beyond the usual convention of symmetry. And so we have the following turn, a characteristic expression of Brahms's melodic style:

"Youth, precious youth, you have fled from me"

I consider the close of the D-major section to be Schubertian:

"unheeding was my mind!"

The clarity of the melody and the plasticity of its structuring are heightened by the dynamics, which aid the composer with their manner of rising and falling.

Brahms has provided the tempo indications *lebhafte, doch nicht zu schnelle* (lively, but not too fast) for the first section of the piece and *ein wenig gehaltene* (a tad restrained) for the second. The latter should be regarded as an intensification of the former rather than its opposite. To me, the most characteristic aspect of the composition is revealed in these indications. For it seems to me that the composer has not found an expression of heavy resignation in the poem. Rather, it seems that he saw both a picture and the mood of a mature personality, whose seriousness is only the result of self-reproach on account of his "achtlos verlorene Jugend" (unheeding, lost youth). To my mind, what is expressed in this piece is more like the fleeting nature of a thought than the persistence of a deeper mood.

On its own, the music is pure Brahms. One could include it on a program with a hundred other compositions, and it would declare "who my master was."

Im Herbst

If our master is inspired by thoughts of transience and eternity as they
verge upon him, so too those thoughts seem to intensify his strength to an
unusual degree. Though I may be having unwelcome visions, it seems to
me that they wish to reveal their own immortality to him. So long as the
poem draws nourishment from this most powerful stuff that depresses us
all (transience), Brahms casts a pall of tones over the poem without shed-
ding a tear. But when the last strophe arrives with its narrower, pettier,
even feeble content, it seems to me that Brahms loses his inspiration.
Brahms (a serious reader) divides the poem into six strophes of four lines
each. In these strophes, the first phrases always depict the most general
image, and the subsequent phrases reveal the content—the source or cause
of the mood and image—in greater detail. Look at how Brahms portrays
the relationship between the first phrases and subsequent ones:

"Gloomy is autumn. And when the leaves fall"

Or, in another place:

"Man becomes humble. He sees"

How clearly does the fifth scale degree in the melody hint at the note that follows, and yet the phrase ends in such a resolute way! Elsewhere, we encounter a motive with this characteristic rhythm:

"the heart also sinks"

which, at the same time, superbly serves the cause of psychological truth in its inversion:

"he foresees the end of life, as of the year"

The soprano retains the lead throughout. But at times the other voices go beyond mere harmonic commentary insofar as they acquire a distinct, characteristic sense of their own, in imitation of a motive related to the image portrayed. (See the middle voices in measures 3 and 4, 8 and 9, 11–16, etc.) The soprano also has occasional painterly moments, as with the words "nach dem Süden wallen" (migrate southwards) and "Blinken entströmt" (gleaming pours forth). The light of a mild, reconciled sort of wisdom seems to have illuminated Brahms's feeling when he thought of the man "der die Sonne sinken sieht, des Lebens, wie des Jahres Schluss ahnt" (who sees the sun set and foresees the end of life, as of the year). What quiet dignity greets the C-major tonality, entering as C minor departs! In contrast, the music expressing the point of "des Herzens seligster Erguss" (the most blessed outpouring of the heart) seems to me to slide downward from the heights. This is where Brahms, to my mind, placed himself before the greatness of his great conception and his great music, in relation to which my own impressions can and must orient themselves. Incidentally, Brahms is right; such a powerfully thinking and powerfully feeling man cannot possibly portray and dissolve such a rich and substantial mood in a tear.

NOTES

1. See Allan Keiler, "Melody and Motive in Schenker's Earliest Writings," in *Critica Musica: Essays in Honor of Paul Brainard*, ed. John Knowles, 188–91 (Amsterdam, 1996).

2. On Schleiermacher's contributions to hermeneutics and their applications in nineteenth-century music criticism and analysis, see Ian D. Bent, ed., *Music Analysis in the Nineteenth Century* (Cambridge, 1994), 2:2–8. For a discussion of the Wagnerian qualities of Schenker's review, see Kevin C. Karnes, *Music, Criticism, and the Challenge of History: Shaping Modern Musical Thought in Late Nineteenth-Century Vienna* (Oxford and New York, 2008), chap. 3.

3. My translations of the poetic texts are based upon those by Lionel Salter, published with the recording *Brahms: Choral Works*, Philips, CD 432 512–2, 1992.

4. At this point, the published text refers the reader to the line "and from the East the horn," rather than to "extinguish your lamp confidently." However, Schenker's discussion makes clear that this is a mistake. The G♭ to which Schenker refers appears in measure 13, and the C-flat-major triad in measure 14; the text "extinguish your lamp confidently" appears in measure 13, with the G♭. At this point, the soprano's melodic line is, as Schenker observes, indeed not new. It is a transposition of the soprano line at measure 5, which sets "and from the East the horn"—thus, a possible cause for the error. I have corrected this mistake in the translation.

Max Kalbeck
Brahms's *Four Serious Songs,* op. 121 (1914)

TRANSLATED BY WILLIAM MILLER
INTRODUCED AND ANNOTATED BY KEVIN C. KARNES

Max Kalbeck's essay on the Four Serious Songs, *the last of Brahms's works published during his lifetime, appears in the fourth and final volume of the author's monumental Brahms biography of 1904–14. That study, which Kalbeck began almost immediately after the composer's death in April 1897, remains a principal point of departure for much present-day Brahms research. Kalbeck's essay on op. 121 provides a clear indication of why this is so. The biographer's discussion is remarkably rich, making extensive use of his unparalleled access to primary sources: it features the first publication of Max Klinger's letter to Brahms of 1896, which Kalbeck obtained from Klinger himself, and also the first detailed description of Brahms's sketches for the fourth song in the collection.[1] It also displays Kalbeck's widely noted penchant for vividly evocative analytical elucidation. The crux of Kalbeck's argument here is that the* Four Serious Songs *were not composed for the artist Klinger, to whom the collection is dedicated, or (as is often presumed) as a tribute to the recently departed Clara Schumann, but in memory of Brahms's one-time student and close friend, Elisabeth von Herzogenberg. Along the way, Kalbeck advances a pair of theories about the genesis of the set that remain widely accepted today: that the composition of* Wenn ich mit Menschen, *the fourth song in the collection, was tightly bound up with Brahms's work on a pair of uncompleted songs on texts by Gottfried Keller and Friedrich Rückert; and that Brahms had once toyed with composing the cycle as an orchestral cantata.*

A native of the Habsburg town of Breslau (now Wrocław, Poland), Kalbeck (1850–1921) became acquainted with Brahms at some point in the late 1870s, probably through his work as a music critic, and he cultivated a close if somewhat one-sided relationship with the composer shortly after moving to Vienna in 1880.[2] A talented poet and translator in his own right (Brahms set two of his poems to music), Kalbeck was perhaps Brahms's staunchest advocate in the Viennese press, regularly lauding

Brahms's music on the pages of the liberal daily Neues Wiener Tagblatt *and thus drawing considerable scorn from a host of Wagnerian colleagues. The selection translated below is drawn from Kalbeck's* Johannes Brahms, *rev. ed. (Berlin, 1912–21; repr. Tutzing, 1976), 4:441–60. All endnotes are editorial; all citations of secondary sources in Kalbeck's notes, which are retained at the foot of the page, have been modernized.*

The *Four Serious Songs*

Brahms left us several written statements about his *Four Serious Songs*, the maestro's final work, designated opus 121. These statements—sometimes running parallel to, other times diverging from his verbal remarks—might seem to contradict each other. At first glance, the contradictions appear to be profound. However, a closer look does away with them completely. The first thing one notes is the jovial, almost frivolous tone with which Brahms speaks of the "godless *Schnadahüpferln*," the "*Schnadahüpferln* of May 7," or simply the "*Schnadahüpferln*," as if it were obvious that he could only be referring, with this term, to the *Four Serious Songs*. He used this south-German expression, which refers to a certain trivial variety of dance tune and folk song, not only in his letters to Simrock, with whom he often joked and teased, but also with others. It is clear to anyone familiar with Brahms's sense of humor, however, that he did not mean to denigrate the composition with such remarks. Indeed, he intended precisely the opposite. For in this case, where the theme is the deepest and most serious contemplation of the common fate of all men, to venture outside the realm of art and indulge in solemnities would have gone against the grain of Brahms's temperament, which was resistant to all forms of affectation. The more his own feelings became involved while setting these biblical texts, in which the terrible is so calmly articulated, the less he wanted to reveal to others just how deeply the words had affected him. Indeed, he had made the words his own, singing them forth from the innermost reaches of his heart.

In order to orient ourselves, we must return to the assertion, frequently cited in the previous chapter and repeatedly stressed with particular emphasis by Brahms, that he had composed the songs as a birthday gift to "himself and only to himself." There is no doubt that he considered their composition a private matter at first, consistent with the desire he expressed upon his penultimate farewell to Clara Schumann, in February 1895, to compose "nothing more for the public, but only for himself."[*] In all likelihood,

---

[*] Kalbeck, *Johannes Brahms,* 4:391–92.

at least a part of op. 121 had already been completed by then. Significantly, the fourth song has no apparent formal connection to the other three (it was written in May 1896), and indeed changes the character of the whole by virtue of its positive outlook. Below, we will suggest that it was precisely this fourth song that Brahms wanted to keep from the public's view, and we will offer our view about why.

It is possible, of course, that Brahms had reservations regarding the first three songs as well—perhaps on account of their "godless" texts, or (more specifically) because of the glorified status he granted those texts. And we must not dismiss the possibility that it was my own encouragement, on his birthday (my encouragement born of a secret wish), that the work be brought before the public, which led to his quick change of mind about the matter.* He had long wanted to honor Max Klinger, the creator of the *Brahms-Phantasie*, with an enduring token of his gratitude. He still felt indebted to the artist, who had visited him again in the spring of 1896.[3] When Klinger's beloved father died and his son was deep in mourning, the *Serious Songs* provided a most eloquent testimony to Brahms's own sympathy and grief. They had also comforted him when he scattered flowers for the memories of all those who had been snatched away from him in recent years. In them, he gave voice to a powerful lamentation for those who lay sick and dying before him, a voice that enables even the last innocent, martyred wretch to sing in the chorus of the world's sorrows, reaching up to the ear of the Almighty. On July 23 he wrote to Klinger:

Dear revered friend,

What will you say when sometime soon you receive a few little songs by me, dedicated expressly to you! But while working on them I often thought of you, and of how deeply the momentous words, heavy with meaning, might affect you. Even if you are a reader of the Bible you may well be unprepared for them, and surely so with music. Well, in any case, I wanted to convey my sincere greetings to you, something I have often wanted to do since those days in Vienna—but writing paper comes to my hand with such difficulty!

I think back very affectionately to your friendly family life and to your mother, for whom you are now the best comfort. Commend me to her most kindly, and be greeted mostly warmly by your

J. Brahms[4]

---

* In any case, he immediately adopted the argument I had made, adding, in the above-mentioned letter to Simrock of 8 May, the conditional statement that "the police could forbid it . . . *if the words were not all in the Bible*."

Fourteen days later, on July 7, the following letter was sent to Marie and Eugenie Schumann:

> If you soon receive a score titled *Serious Songs*, rest assured that it has not reached you in error. Regardless of the usual custom of writing your names at the top of the page in such cases, these songs indeed concern you quite personally. I wrote them during the first weeks of May. Similar words have often occupied me. I thought that I had no need to fear worse news about your mother. But something often stirs and speaks deep within a person, almost unconsciously, and sometimes it manifests itself as poetry or music. You cannot play through the songs now, because their words will be too painful for you. But I ask you to view them as a funeral offering for your beloved mother, and then to put them aside.[5]

The *Serious Songs* were not composed while "thinking of Clara," as Litzmann claims based on this letter.* Indeed, Brahms confesses the opposite. He wrote that he was often occupied with song texts of this kind and had believed that he did *not* have to fear worse news in the first week of May. It was, perhaps, a voice—*unconscious* even to him—that had driven him to set the text. His recent pain, and even more his tenderness and tact, had led him, once he had learned the truth of the situation, to ask the daughters of the departed to consider the collection of songs "a funeral offering for [their] beloved mother." If the work were truly a funeral offering, the name of Clara Schumann (or her daughters) would undoubtedly be found on its title page rather than "Max Klinger."

Brahms took the texts of the first three serious songs from his old boyhood Hamburg Bible of 1833, copied down in his oft-mentioned quarto-notebook.[6] Hardly calmed by the tribulations of his deeply aggrieved heart, which had been afflicted by the political events of 1888–90, he yearned for new solace when terrible sickness and death struck members of his intimate circle in quick succession and robbed him of his sister and best friends.[7] The *Serious Songs* could just as well be considered offerings at the graves of Elisabeth von Herzogenberg, Billroth, and Bülow as they could for Clara Schumann, who died after the songs had been composed.[8] There is no doubt that the mourning Brahms thought about the latter suffering friend on more than one occasion, but images of many beloved people, stricken with sickness and death, appeared before him whenever he contemplated the books of Job, Ecclesiastes, and Sirach.

* Berthold Litzmann, *Clara Schumann: Ein Künstlerleben nach Tagebüchern und Briefen* (Leipzig, 1902–8), 3:609.

The verses taken from the book of Sirach (41:1–4), "O Tod, wie bitter bist du" (Oh death, how bitter you are), occupy the first section in the quarto-notebook, following excerpts from the first book of Kings, 1:11–14 ("Und es geschah des Herrn Wort zu Salomo" [And the Lord's word to Solomon was heard]), etc., where God's promise is affirmed during the construction of the temple. A *nota bene* flags the chapter "Solomon's Wisdom," in which the ruler of Israel, "a mortal man like all the others," pleads to God for enlightenment. To this Brahms adds: "the prayer of a king." His intention is clear; he wanted to use his art to aid the young German emperor, to hold up a reflection of a classical regent to him.* This notation was apparently made around the time of the emperor's first speeches and Bismarck's resignation.[9] Separated only by a stroke, excerpts from the Old Testament and Apocrypha follow. Many of these excerpted passages were never set to music. "Do not fear death!" declares Sirach. "Remember that the Lord rules over all men, both those who came before you and those who will come afterwards." And from Ecclesiastes, before the verse "for it befalls men," the text states "I said in my heart: concerning the children of men, may God test them so that they come to see that they too are like beasts." Neither passage inspired a musical echo in Brahms, yet he jotted both of them down.[10] Indeed, they do not reach the heights of the verses to which he composed music; they almost seem as if they were added by a pious editor. "As it is with a Greek sculpture," said Klinger to Brahms, "others would have added much more. But only the succinctness of what is essential gives a thing its value."

When Brahms recorded the sentence, "Thus I saw that there is nothing better than that a man rejoice in his work," he could not help but add a pregnant exclamation point, in parentheses, after the word *rejoice*.[11]

At this point we make a remarkable discovery: the verses from Corinthians, which contain the text of the last of the *Four Serious Songs*, do not follow immediately after the others but appear after a break of two blank pages and are completely different from the others with respect to ink and handwriting. They stand "on a different page and constitute a wondrous chapter."[12] This same separation can be seen in the manuscript copy of op. 121, in possession of the Gesellschaft der Musikfreunde.[13] This suggests that the fourth song was, from the very beginning, not intended as the conclusion of the cycle. It could hardly have been the last song composed, even though the date, "May 7," is clearly written in large print beneath it. This is not meant as the date of the song's composition, but of

---

* The arrangements were already set; verses 1–12 of the ninth chapter had already been divided for composition. Verses 3, 5, 6, 8, and 9 were to be omitted.

the completion of the cycle as a whole! The second song must have traded places with the first, as numbers written on the manuscript in blue ink testify. This renumbering became necessary when Brahms decided to juxtapose the weighty dirge of the first movement with the uplifting res-urrection song of the last, so that the cyclical form of the work thus achieved would attain a sonata-like—or, shall we say, a symphonic—character. This raises the possibility that the finale was at one time intended to fulfill a different, separate mission. And the unique example of a sketch page preserved in the composer's estate elevates this speculation to certainty.

A striking testament to the interplay of inspiration and labor, unequaled among the maestro's few sketches left to posterity, this browned, dusty manuscript page provides us with the answers we long for to persistent questions, and it also presents us with new riddles. The twenty-line page is covered on both sides with a swarm of notes and bar lines, sometimes scrawled in pencil, sometimes in ink. On the front, we find an orchestral score with numerous corrections. The assignment of the (contrapuntal) lines to the various instruments is not at all regular but somewhat *ad hoc*. The opening is as follows:

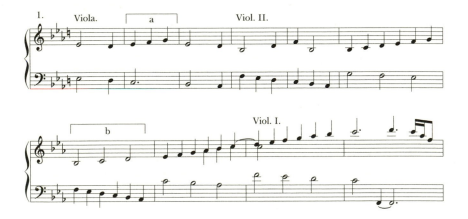

As one can see from the natural sign at the beginning of the first measure, this opening, in E-flat, is the continuation of a composition in A-flat major; but nothing remains of the preceding, torn-out page. The work proceeds in a similar fashion for forty-five measures. The forty-sixth bar prepares, with three chords derived from Examples 1a and 1b,

for the transition to a secondary theme in B-flat major:

For comparison, if we take a look at these four measures from the second of the *Four Serious Songs*,

the striking similarity between the transition (Example 3) and introduction to "Da waren Tränen" (There were tears; Example 4) catches the eye immediately. The variant assigned to flutes and bassoons in Example 3 is nearly identical to the vocal passage "Tränen, derer" (Tears, of those). In the bottom-most line of the score, we encounter this line in the bass:

It calls to mind the beginning of the *grave* "O Tod" (Oh death; op. 121, no. 3).

These examples are sufficient to establish that Brahms once intended to create an orchestral work in which motives from the *Four Serious Songs* were present. Recalling the Violin Sonata, op. 100—to take only the most obviously analogous case—might lead us to believe that in this sketch, too, he attempted to compose a kind of fantasia from preexisting songs whose melodies are presented in entirely new thematic combinations. This is possible. But then, when we turn the page over, we see that the back also has writing upon it. And examining this leads us to an entirely different conclusion.

On the back of the manuscript page, we find a nearly complete sketch for the last of the *Serious Songs*. The principal themes of the E-flat-major and B-major sections are presented in immediate succession, as if the one were supposed to follow directly upon the heels of the other. But it was perhaps a sudden desire to hold on to the sublime idea of the second theme that prevented the writer from continuing along this path. While he was jotting down, in hurried and thickly packed pencil marks, the notes to *Wenn ich mit Menschen—und mit Engelszungen redete* (If I speak with the tongues of men and of angels), the loudest bells of his heaven rang out. The voice sang "Wir sehen jetzt durch einen Spiegel" (We now see in a mirror), and he grabbed hold of the celestial tones before they could drift away.[14] This same passage is repeated a second time; the scintillating E-flat-major theme, which blazes like a burning bush and greedily devours the words thrown into it, then breaks off again as the wonderful continuation of the B-flat-major melody declares "Jetzt erkenne ich's stückweise" (Now I understand it in part), and "Stirb und werde!" (Die and become!) is pronounced and sung more harrowingly then it ever has been before.[15] After this comes the melodic phrase that was transferred from one section to the other: "So wäre mir's nichts nütze" (Then it would be of no profit to me), in the form:

But oddly, the anacrusis ("So") is missing, and a different text underlies the melody! We can decipher the verses as follows:

Nun in dieser Frühlingszeit	In this springtime
Ist mein Herz ein klarer See.	my heart is a clear sea.

The phrase repeats itself in the elusive bass, and two verses accompany it:

Und im Quelle badest du,	And in the spring you bathe,
Eine Nix im goldnen Haar.	a mermaid with golden hair.

Even more astonishing is the third combination of text and music, into which the principal theme is interwoven. One has to see it to believe it:

Under these instrumentally conceived strettos are the words

Ich zog auf meinen Lebenswegen	On my journey through life
Dem Schimmerlicht des Glücks	I encountered the shimmering
entgegen.	light of happiness.

The verses written under the music of Example 6 belong to Keller's poem "Nixe im Grundquell" (Mermaid in the spring); those that appear under Example 7 are derived from the first of the *Trauerlieder* (Mourning songs) by Rückert. Keller writes:

Nun in dieser Frühlingszeit	In this springtime
Ist mein Herz ein klarer See,	my heart is a clear sea;
Drin versank das letzte Leid,	in it sank my last sorrow,
Draus verflüchtigt sich das Weh.	my pain vanishes coming out.

Spiegelnd meine Seele ruht,	Mirrored, my soul rests
Von der Sonne überhaucht,	in the warm breath of the sun,
Und mit Lieb' umschließt die Flut,	and the water lovingly embraces
Was sich in dieselbe taucht.	that which dives into it.

Aber auf dem Grunde sprüht	But from the seabed
Überdies ein Quell hervor,	bubbles a spring,
Welcher heiß und perlend glüht	glowing hot and sparkling
Durch die stille Flut empor.	through the still water above.
Und im Quelle badest du,	And in the spring you bathe,
Eine Nix' mit goldnem Haar;	a mermaid with golden hair;
Ober deckt den Zauber zu	the water above, deep and clear,
Das Gewässer tief und klar.	cloaks the magic below.

We must reproduce the poem in its entirety in order to experience the inexpressibly tender heart, filled with childlike piety, that lies behind the sweet sense of secrecy. For the composer, these fragments alluded to things about which only he knew, and he thought to create a memorial to them, as he did for others of the sort, by reserving a consecrated place for them in his work. The melodic arches (Example 8a) are derived from the transitional phrase (Example 6), which had formerly seemed somewhat suspicious to us on account of its almost trivial-sounding quality.

These arches constitute a transcendental bridge upon which sensual love is elevated to a love that goes far beyond the sensual [*auf welcher die sinnliche zur übersinnlichen Liebe fortschreitet*]. We are reminded of the F-sharp-major passage in the Andante of the Second Piano Concerto and its playing out.* There, as here, we find the same mood of isolation from the world, the ecstatic intoxication of renunciation. And there, as here, we find that a mnemonic device, a learning tool borrowed from older songs, brings about this magic. Along with the song from which he took it, Brahms would have committed this phrase (Example 6) to oblivion with merciless but deserved criticism had it not exerted a magical power over him. That power emanates from the image of a woman, an image that bathed in the spring

---

* Kalbeck, *Johannes Brahms*, 3:284–87.

of his soul. The allure of this deeply concealed magic was so compelling that he could not resist setting Keller's words to this bit of music, even though they were hardly needed. They were just as unnecessary as the two lines from Rückert's mourning song, which speak of the "shimmering light of happiness." Only in the first light of day did the poet realize that his happiness in fact resided in the evening-light now vanishing behind him ("wie bin ich denn vorbeigekommen?" [how, then, did I arrive here?])

Along with *Todessehnen* (Longing for death; from op. 86), with its recollection of the Andante of the B-flat-major Piano Concerto, the two doubtlessly composed yet never published songs in question belong, textually, to the new portfolio that Brahms had with him in Pörtschach in 1877–79.[16] That was the beautiful, unforgettable season that he spent with "the mermaid with golden hair," "the graceful head haloed with golden splendor,"[17] when the sun shone down upon the zenith of his love and passionate letters and manuscripts flew back and forth between him and Elisabeth von Herzogenberg.* We knew for some time that Brahms, seeing clearly the hopelessness of his suffering, was living in self-denial. But now we can see, for the first time, four years after the passing of his beloved Elisabeth and shortly before his own death, just how deeply these feelings had taken root in his heart. What he could never admit to the living, he confessed to the dead. In the story of his love for Elisabeth von Herzogenberg, this carefully concealed final chapter is the most poignant.

The end of the fourth song, with the words "Aber die Liebe ist die größeste unter ihnen" (But love is the greatest of these), incorporates the final measures of the Daumer-Hafis *ghazal* "Wie bist du, meine Königin, durch sanfte Güte wonnevoll" (My queen, how sublime you are in your sweet benevolence) in the key of that song, E-flat.[18] Also corresponding to the *ghazal* is the harmony, with the dissonant A in the bass:

* Cf. Kalbeck, *Johannes Brahms*, 3:132 and 138.

And the bass itself, in the *ghazal*, corresponds to this melodic descent in the fourth song:

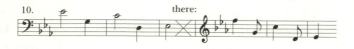

After considering these examples we can no longer speak of coincidence. The song originated in conjunction with op. 32, which Brahms wrote in Vienna in 1864, when he was the music teacher of the sixteen-year-old Elisabeth.

It is also worth nothing that the first part of the song, indicated first with "Andante" and then with "con moto ed anima" (it is usually played too fast), is linked thematically to the orchestral piece sketched on the back side of our manuscript page, namely through this motive:

(See Examples 1a, 1b, and 2!)

The three notes now serve as a ritornello and act as a prelude to the singing voice; they continue underneath it in a modified rhythmic form—as we already saw in Example 7, measures 3 and 4—and mark off the sections of verse. To be sure, the thematically interpreted motive that comes directly after the third song (*O Tod*) is no less strange than the key in which it appears: E-flat after E major. But although Brahms's remnant of a plan, undertaken and then discarded, accounts for the completely different nature of the fourth song, it does not conflict with the aesthetic basis of the rest of the piece, even though the fourth song is separated here from its original intended purpose. Indeed, the character of the finale, fitting for the apostle Paul, not only allows for his sudden throwing away of the string arrangements but explicitly demands it. The rigid, bleak, and merciless pessimism of the Old Testament encounters the New Testament's message of salvation, the gospel of all-believing, all-hoping, all-suffering love that teaches us unbounded, merciful, ideal optimism. The rational philosopher has bumped up against the limits of empirical science and human cognition, and now the mystic and the ecstatic, the artist and the poet, overcomes these things in a flight of fantasy. The three notes (Example

11) hold their own. Their motive resounds like a fanfare of horns, trumpets, and trombones, and the apostle, glowing with zeal, delivers his powerful sermon, which falls like fire from the sky.

This detailed examination was necessary, for only through such a consideration can we form hypotheses capable of supporting claims made with a high degree of certainty. The composition of the *Four Serious Songs* can thus be said to have unfolded in the following way.

After Elisabeth von Herzogenberg passed away on January 7, 1892, Brahms immersed himself in her letters. His departed friend spoke to him as she had before, and the transfiguring power of death restored her beautiful image to its untarnished brilliance. His grief over her death, which was never felt more deeply than when he heard her husband praise his compositions, was augmented by remorse and even more painful emotions that embittered him to an unreasonable degree. We get a sense of this in a jotting from 19 March 1892 (drafted even earlier), in which Brahms explains that he wanted to share the immortal bequest of the departed, the treasure trove of her letters, with no one, not even her husband, of whom he was now even more jealous than when Elisabeth was still alive.[*] In time he came to feel remorse, as he became distressingly aware of having been unfriendly to her, of having neglected her and of not having inquired about the physical afflictions that had stricken her. Her angry shadow stepped before him and threatened to obliterate his dimly recalled image of earlier, happier times. He was ashamed of his inconsiderateness and determined to reconcile with the offended, to quiet the unsated hunger in his heart and to provide her, once again, with what was once her daily bread: an exquisite example of his art. He did not want to make it easy on himself; rather, he sought to create a work incomparable to any of his others—a symphonic cantata, different from Gustav Mahler's C-Minor Symphony (which Koeßler showed him in manuscript, at the request of the composer residing in Unterach, during one of his last Ischl summers) but illuminated and seized by a similar "primal light" (*Urlicht*), which washed over him in "eternal, divine life."[19] During the creation of the draft, the yet-to-be-written melodies of the three Old Testament songs were already on his mind; he had been carrying their texts around with him for years. The clarinet works composed in the interim delayed the completion of his plan, which he wanted to carry out "only for himself."[20] In 1894 or '95 he took up once more the work he had temporarily set aside. The "Preis der Liebe" (Price of love), Paul's letter to the Corinthians, was to be the text of the baritone solo, which was conceived as the finale of a work with

[*] Johannes Brahms, *Briefwechsel*, rev. eds. (Berlin, 1912–22; repr. Tutzing, 1974), 2:261.

one or more orchestral movements. But if the union of symphonic and songlike material ultimately did not please him, if this original plan somehow went awry, Brahms stood by his more general one. Once he had completed the first three songs in the first days of May 1896, he composed the version of the fourth that we are familiar with today, and he recognized its suitability as the concluding movement in the cycle without seeing the rhapsodic nature of its transplanted beginning as a hindrance.

Like the sun appearing once more in full glory from behind twilit clouds just before sunset, so arose Brahms's genius once again before it was snuffed out, presenting us with the wonder of his vision: a credo of worldly and heavenly wisdom that he, the creator of the *German Requiem*, composed from Holy Scripture in accord with his taste and intellect. Here as elsewhere, the Protestant made full use of his inherent right to engage freely in biblical research. His philosophical and religious doubt sought assuagement in the last place one might expect it to be found, in the word of God. But this will in fact surprise only the ignorant, who do not understand that "The Book of Books" is truly deserving of that title. Everything that moves the hearts and minds of men is found on its pages. It is the godliest book precisely because it is the most human. In the renowned and notorious forty-sixth chapter of the appendix to Arthur Schopenhauer's *The World as Will and Representation* there is nothing more powerful than what the "Preacher Solomon" says on its every page.[21]

As mentioned earlier, Brahms derived the text for the first two of the *Serious Songs* from the much-studied Koheleth or Ecclesiastes. The author of Ecclesiastes chose the most prosperous, most powerful, and wisest king of Israel to give voice to his sad experiences and bleak observations. In the third variation of the main theme ("*Vanitas, vanitatum vanitas!*") Solomon comes to the dispiriting conclusion that man is no better than the beasts: "wie dies stirbt, so stirbt er auch" (as the one dies, so dies the other).[22]

And now we must consider the music. The bass voice, quiet and *andante*, floats above the cavernous fifths and octaves of the accompaniment in a melancholy D-minor ($\frac{4}{4}$ time). This is the way Goethe heard the lemurs sing as they dug Faust's grave.[23] Swaying to and fro with imperturbable calm, like some callous, inevitable fate, the vocal line swells twice with personal feeling. But destiny remains unchanged. The modern musical lyricist penetrates the cool, objective discourse of the ancient maxim-giver with revealing sympathy. Soundless lightning illuminates the breaking storm. *Andante* is replaced by *allegro*, the time signature changes, the eighths rush forward in hurried triplets ($\frac{3}{4}$ time). A wind rises up, gathers the dust into clouds, and blows them upward, carrying with it every living thing. Now thunder rolls with Promethean anger; the Titan has stolen Cronus's arms in order to destroy the god with his own weapons.[24] Blow after blow falls: "Wer weiß, ob der Geist des Menschen aufwärts fahre?" (Who knows whether the spirit of man travels upward?) Only the tempest answers, with the triplets of the four-bar interlude lashing out in descant. The sharp, downward-falling blows begin to dull and become ever more despondent with the continuation of the question, once again pronounced: "Und der Odem des Viehes unterwärts unter die Erde fahre?" (And the spirit of the beast descends down to the earth?) It is as if the usurper of divine power had discovered a secret that destroys both gods and men. The Titan turns into a dwarf, his faintheartedness becoming resignation. Thoughts of labor (recall Brahms's exclamation point in his songbook!) through which man forgets all his sufferings, appear to him in a friendly major key. But such thoughts cannot reassure him, for he does not know for whom he labors and why. "Wer will ihn dahin bringen, daß er sehe, was nach ihm geschehen wird?" (Who shall make him see what is to come after him?) The descending chromatic scale does not bode well, and the singer finishes only to begin yet again, just like the preacher in Ecclesiastes. Both must begin a new chapter in the same old book of sufferings.

The theme of the second song (G-minor, *andante*, $\frac{3}{4}$ time) casts deep shadows in the bass. The lonely figure proceeds with his own doppelgänger as a companion, as if he needed a witness to the misery he is to encounter in his wanderings. "Ich wandte mich und sahe an alle, die Unrecht leiden unter der Sonne" (I turned and saw all the injustice that is perpetrated under the sun). Soon the burning eyes of the seer fill with tears, which flow together with the tears of the downtrodden in a single wail, touching the hearts of all who hear it. The music conveys inexpressible compassion. From out of the words of this text, which seems to feel none of it, compassion pours forth like some mild, heavenly dew that brings fruit to the hard earth. The giver of consolation, for whom the unfortunates vainly groan under the weight of gleeful tormentors, is near, but is not recognized as such; enveloped in shadows, the wandering preacher has followed them closely from the beginning. Soon this unconscious feeling will emerge into consciousness and draw him out of his dark hideaway. A grand pause of two quarter notes announces his presence. "Da lobte ich die Toten, die schon gestorben waren, mehr als die Lebendigen" (Thus I regarded the dead who have departed more fortunate than those who still live). A second, longer grand pause of four quarter notes portends the crushing realization that has been gradually taking shape in the mind of the preacher. The music anxiously holds its breath before the terrible word arrives, as if it dares not speak it aloud for fear of those powers that rule over life. Referring to both the dead and the living, the consequent of the preceding phrase contains the text "Und der noch nicht ist"—pause—"ist besser als alle Beide" (And he who has not yet been—is better than both of the others). This sentence touches wondrously upon a choral ode by Sophocles. It is nearly the same sentence that Sophocles gave to the chorus in *Oedipus at Colonos*: "not to be born," etc.* With the pause, Brahms praises divine oblivion as the requirement for this most desirable of fates and sets "the denial of the will to live," like Schopenhauer, in a warm and comforting major key.[25] The inconceivability of a state in which we are ignorant of all the evil under the sun transfigures the closing of the song with a magical, ominous gleam.

And now the idea of death is introduced. The shadows emancipate themselves from the melody and appear by themselves in the third song, based on Sirach, in a *grave* tempo in E minor ($\frac{3}{2}$ time); it proceeds to a major key in the central *alla breve* section. "O Tod, wie bitter bist du!" (Oh death, how bitter you are!) cries the poet, and the composer lends even more weight to this apostrophe by giving us half notes in the slowest tempo, using the pauses in the vocal line to frame important chord changes in the accompaniment, and by immediately repeating the words of the doubled phrase at the end of the first section.[26] How vividly, characteristically, and elaborately the music approaches and takes hold of its subject matter without threatening the tone of the piece or doing violence to its form. It conveys these effective scenes with almost dramatic vitality. The melody strolls along easily and self-contentedly, like a happy-go-lucky youth taking a walk: "der gute Tage und genug hat und ohne Sorgen lebet, und dem es wohl gehet in allen Dingen und noch wohl essen mag" (to a man who lives at peace with what he possesses, to one who is prosperous in all things and has plenty to eat). But suddenly it breaks off—the peaceful mortal stumbles and stands rooted to the ground, as if he had come across his own killer or funeral procession: "O Tod! O Tod!" And now, in the parallel scene in major, death is greeted as a friend to mankind, as Pausanias, who brings rest and quiets pain![27] From the friendly E major of the softly hued harmonic background there emerges the sharply outlined figure of a wretched old beggar, who, shaking from hunger and cold, can hardly hold himself upright with his crutch. And at the same time the deepest compassion is awakened for the needy one, "der da schwach und alt ist, der in allen Sorgen steckt und nichts bessers zu hoffen, noch zu erwarten hat" (who is old and weak and consumed by troubles, but who hopes for and expects nothing better.) Never has charity been so profoundly extolled, never has compassion been so eloquently preached as in these broken

---

* Cf. Kalbeck, *Johannes Brahms*, 3:480.

tones, steeped in the heart's blood. Come, brother, alongside our father who is death; we shall unburden ourselves of life, or else die together! . . . "O Tod, wie wohl tust du!" (Oh death, how well you work!) resounds softly in an inversion of the initial melody.

The *caritas* of Jesus and his disciples in a turbulent world of hate and strife, the compassion for which one cries out in the face of death at the hands of the raging *bellum omnium contra omnes*, the charity for which the egotistical self makes sacrifice and joyfully gives praise—this cardinal Christian virtue, misinterpreted and abused by charlatans, sophists, and religious pretenders, forms the link between the first three and the last of the *Four Serious Songs*.[28] When members of the early Christian community, as students of different teachers, were at odds with one another at Corinth and engaged in sectarian feuds, the apostle Paul reminded them of the principles of unity and love. This song, which sets the oft-cited text of Paul's first letter to the Corinthians, constitutes the sublime peak of the entire set, which seems to lead up to it as in a continuously ascending line, until it cloaks itself in the light of a higher world of glistening towers surrounded by dawning, mystical golden clouds. Like the strumming of harps and the clashing of swords, there is a rushing quality to the fanfares of the introductory bars and in the powerful voice of the heathens' great apostle—sharp and plain like a blade of ice yet as loving and persuasive as enticing string music—as it makes its captivating entrance. With what fiery zeal the music seizes the apostolic sermon! With what angry contemptuousness does it do away with the rubbish of conventional formalities! How precisely it incorporates the discourse of the speaker, and how it permeates the rhetorical masterwork of his tripartite, three-tiered principles! Brahms set the period structure of the address in its proper light, so that every eye could behold the art therein and every heart could glow with passion as it asks the questions: How can these beautiful words, ringing like heavenly bells, be of help? And how can faith that moves mountains, doing good deeds, and practicing self-sacrifice, how can these things help if love plays no role? A forgotten Christianity, true Pauline Christianity, in which grace is achieved not through prayer, not through faith, and not through deeds, is resurrected in these tones. The image of the apostle surges ever higher. The Raphael of music has painted him as the speaking and singing counterpart to the cartoon drawn for Pieter van Aelst's tapestry, in which Paul preaches to the heathen philosophers in Athens about "the unknown God."[29] He stands firm, by himself, like "a column radiating divine spiritual power."[30] A few bars go by, and, as always, Brahms constantly alters the music's expressive qualities with the simplest of means in order to bring out the profound content of the shifting rhetorical devices. He then comes back to the same refrain with the same *ceterum censeo*, a refrain that endeavors to reveal the basis of both fleeting and eternal salvation through love. During his fiery address the apostle is seized before our eyes, as it were, by the movement of the heavens—as if by passing clouds—and gives us a glimpse of the hereafter. We are blessed, along with him, by his vision. We experience firsthand this miracle, of which Paul writes: "I knew a man in Christ; fourteen years ago (whether within or out of the body, I do not know; only God knows) he was lifted up to the third heaven. And I knew this man (whether it was within the body or outside of the body, I do not know; only God knows), who was lifted up to paradise, where he heard unspeakable words that no mortal can utter."* Broken chords accompany the song of the enraptured and transfigured apostle, who reads the dark words of revelation through the looking glass of God. We shall see, face-to-face, and recognize, on the most fundamental level, the image reflected back at us in this mirror—as we see in this fragment:

The burning pain of man's inadequate knowledge is felt in the dissonant chords of the three measures cited above, particularly in the beginning of the third, just as a fissure in the poet's heart yawns open among all creation. But the following "dann aber" (then, however) pours soothing balm over this festering wound and portends its healing.

It is well worth having lived, loved, practiced self-denial, suffered, and atoned for the sake of this B-major section. And when, at the end, this divine love thinks back to earthly things with celestial laughter, recalling the Daumer-Hafis *ghazal* and its sublime queen, we know who stands at the topmost rung of Jacob's ladder, leading us to paradise.

* 2 Corinthians 12:2–4.

NOTES

1. On Kalbeck's research trip to northern Germany in the spring of 1897 and his meetings with Klinger in Leipzig, see Sandra McColl, "Max Kalbeck: Excerpts from the Diary of 1897," in *Brahms Studies* 3, ed. David Brodbeck (Lincoln and London, 2001), 1–18.

2. For a thoughtful evaluation of Kalbeck's relationship with the composer, see Michael Musgrave, "Brahms und Kalbeck. Eine mißverstandene Beziehung?" in *Brahms-Kongress Wien 1983*, ed. Susanne Antonicek und Otto Biba, 397–404 (Tutzing, 1988).

3. On January 1, 1894, Klinger sent Brahms a copy of his newly completed work, the *Brahms-Phantasie*, a collection of forty-one etchings and engravings interspersed with the complete scores of five of Brahms's songs and the piano-vocal reduction of Brahms's *Schicksalslied*, op. 54. Klinger and Brahms had corresponded—at first through Brahms's publisher Fritz Simrock—since the early 1880s, and a mutual respect quickly developed. They first met in Leipzig in 1886. Kalbeck's reference to Klinger's visit with Brahms in the spring of 1896 is unclear; no documentary evidence survives to suggest that such a visit took place. Perhaps Kalbeck has in mind Klinger's visit to Brahms's Vienna home in April 1894. On the biographical circumstances of their relationship and a complete list and description of their known correspondence, see Jan Brachmann, *"Ins Ungewisse hinauf . . ." Johannes Brahms und Max Klinger im Zwiespalt von Kunst und Kommunikation* (Kassel, 1999), 23–53. For further discussion of Klinger's *Brahms-Phantasie*, see Kevin C. Karnes, "Brahms, Max Klinger, and the Promise of the *Gesamtkunstwerk*: Revisiting the *Brahms-Phantasie*," in this volume.

4. Brahms's letter to Klinger, which Kalbeck copied from the artist, was later published—with the date given as 28 June rather than 23 June as Kalbeck reported—in *Johannes Brahms an Max Klinger* (Leipzig, 1924), 11. It is translated and discussed in Styra Avins, ed., *Johannes Brahms: Life and Letters*, trans. Styra Avins and Josef Eisinger (Oxford and New York, 1997), 733–34. The translation given here follows that on p. 734 of Avins's study, with the paragraph break shifted to its location as Kalbeck gives it. For Kalbeck's account of receiving this letter from Klinger, see McColl, "Max Kalbeck," 13–14.

5. Clara Schumann died on May 20, 1896. She was survived by three daughters—Marie, Eugenie, and Elise—and her son Ludwig.

6. The volume to which Kalbeck refers is Brahms's manuscript notebook of biblical texts, presently located at the Wienbibliothek im Rathaus (formerly the Wiener Stadt- und Landesbibliothek) in Vienna. Its contents are described in George S. Bozarth, "Brahms's Lieder Inventory of 1859–60 and Other Documents of His Life and Work," *Fontes Artis Musicae* 30/3 (1983): 109–10. Brahms's Bible is preserved in the Brahms archive at the Gesellschaft der Musikfreunde in Vienna.

7. By "political events," Kalbeck presumably means the coronation of Emperor Wilhelm II on June 15, 1888, and the resignation of German chancellor Otto von Bismarck, at Wilhelm's insitence, on March 18, 1890. Kalbeck will return to these events below.

8. Elisabeth von Herzogenberg died on January 7, 1892; Theodor Billroth on February 6, 1894; and the conductor Hans von Bülow on February 12, 1894.

9. Kalbeck refers to Emperor Wilhelm II.

10. The passages are from Sirach 41:3 and Ecclesiastes 3:18.

11. From Ecclesiastes 2:24.

12. In fact, only one blank page, rather than two, separates the text of the fourth song from that of the other three in Brahms's manuscript booklet of biblical texts; see Bozarth, "Brahms's Lieder Inventory," 109–10. Kalbeck's quotation is a playful rewording of a passage from the "Witch's Kitchen" (*Hexenküche*) scene in Johann Wolfgang von Goethe's *Faust*, Part I.

13. The sketches for the fourth song in the collection are preserved in the Brahms archive of the Gesellschaft der Musikfreunde in Vienna. They are described in Margit

McCorkle, *Johannes Brahms. Thematisch-bibliographisches Werkverzeichnis* (Munich, 1984), 485 (Autograph C).

14. The text of the fourth song in the set, *Wenn ich mit Menschen,* is from 1 Corinthians 13:1–2 and 12–13.

15. "Stirb und werde!": a line from Goethe's poem "Selige Sehnsucht." *(Trans.)*

16. Kalbeck refers to Brahms's use of the same melodic line in the third movement of his Second Piano Concerto, op. 83 (mm. 59–63, in clarinet), and in his *Todessehnen,* op. 86, no. 6 (mm. 37–41, in voice), the latter composed in Pörtschach in 1878.

17. The second of the two quotations in this passage is from Elisabeth von Herzogenberg's characterization of Brahms in an exchange of December 1877, cited in Kalbeck, *Johannes Brahms,* 3:138–39 n. 2.

18. Kalbeck refers to Brahms's op. 32, no. 9 (1864), with a text by Georg Friedrich Daumer after the fourteenth-century Persian poet Hafez Shirazi (in German, *Hafis*).

19. Kalbeck's references are to the fourth movement (*Urlicht*) of Mahler's Second (*Resurrection*) Symphony in C Minor. The text of that movement, from Achim von Arnim and Clemens Brentano's *Des Knaben Wunderhorn,* concludes with the lines "Der liebe Gott wird mir ein Lichtchen geben / Wird leuchten mir bis in das ewig selig Leben!" (Loving God will give me a little light, / will show me the way to eternal, divine life!") Hans Koeßler (also Kößler) was a Budapest-based pianist and composer with whom Brahms socialized during his summers in Ischl.

20. Kalbeck refers to Brahms's Two Sonatas for Clarinet and Piano, op. 120 (1894).

21. Kalbeck refers to Arthur Schopenhauer's essay "On the Vanity and Suffering of Life," in vol. 2 (1844) of *The World as Will and Representation,* trans. E. F. J. Payne (New York: Dover, 1966), 573–88.

22. The text of the first of the *Four Serious Songs, Denn es gehet dem Menschen,* is from Ecclesiastes 3:19–22. That of the second, *Ich wandte mich,* is from Ecclesiastes 4:1–3. Kalbeck's German citation is from *Denn es gehet dem Menschen* (Ecclesiastes 3:19). The phrase *vanitas vanitatum omnia vanitas* (vanity of vanities, all is vanity) is from Ecclesiastes 1:2. "Vanitas vanitatum vanitas" is a poem by Goethe reflecting on this theme.

23. A reference to Goethe's *Faust,* Part 2.

24. A reference to Aeschylus's *Prometheus Unbound,* in which the Titan Prometheus sides with Zeus to overthrow Zeus's father, Cronus.

25. See Schopenhauer's "On the Vanity and Suffering of Life": "It is . . . correct to regard work, privation, misery, and suffering, crowned by death, as the aim and object of our life (as is done by Brahmanism and Buddhism, and also by genuine Christianity), since it is these that lead to the denial of the will-to-live." Schopenhauer, *The World as Will and Representation,* 2:584.

26. The text of the third song, *O Tod,* is from Sirach 41:1–2.

27. Kalbeck's reference to Pausanias is obscure; he might be referring to the Greek physician of that name who lived in the fifth century BCE.

28. *Bellum omnium contra omnes:* war of all against all. The Latin phrase is from John Hobbes's *Leviathan* (1651). Kalbeck's discussion, however, once again suggests a reading of Schopenhauer, who cites this phrase in his discussion of human suffering in *The World as Will and Representation,* 1:331–33; and *On the Basis of Morality* (1841), trans. E. F. J. Payne (Indianapolis: Hackett, 1995), 131–38.

29. Kalbeck refers to a Vatican commission of 1513–15, for which Raphael produced cartoons depicting events from the lives of the apostles, which were subsequently woven into tapestries by the Belgian painter and tapestry maker Pieter van Aelst (Gordon Campbell, ed., *The Grove Encyclopedia of the Decorative Arts* [Oxford and New York, 2006], 153).

30. From Wolfgang Menzel, *Christliche Symbolik* (Regensburg, 1854), 2:201. *(Trans.)*

"A Modern of the Moderns": Brahms's First Symphony in New York and Boston

SELECTED AND ANNOTATED
BY GEORGE S. BOZARTH

By far the biggest Brahms event in America during the 1870s was the arrival on these shores of the controversial First Symphony. Expectation had long been building in Europe over whether Schumann's "Messiah" of 1853 could fulfill his mentor's prophecy and write a worthy successor to Beethoven's Ninth—or as Schumann put it after hearing Brahms's expansive early piano sonatas, "when he will lower his magic wand to where the massed forces of chorus and orchestra will lend him their powers, then even more wondrous glimpses into the spirit world will be forthcoming."[1] In one sense Brahms had already fulfilled this prophecy: with the German Requiem *of 1867–69 and the other vocal-orchestral works that followed, he had united chorus and orchestra in a manner that transcended the earthly realm. But none of those compositions was a symphony.*

"I shall never compose a symphony!" Brahms declared out of frustration to his friend Hermann Levi in the early 1870s. "You have no idea how it feels to our kind when one always hears such a giant [as Beethoven] marching along behind."[2] Nevertheless, in the autumn of 1876, after working on it for at least fourteen years, Brahms finally unveiled his First Symphony—in the same year that Wagner mounted his full Ring *cycle. Premiered in Karlsruhe on November 4 with Otto Dessoff conducting, the piece was soon heard in Breslau, Cambridge, Leipzig, London, Mannheim, Munich, and Vienna.*

In New York, two of America's foremost conductors, Theodore Thomas and Leopold Damrosch, vied with each other for the American premiere, with the Damrosch Orchestra winning the race on December 15, 1877, beating its rival, the Thomas Orchestra, by just a week.[3] After hearing both performances, the critic for the New York World *set the tone for the American reception of the work over much of the next half-decade, acknowledging the demands it places on listeners and raising an issue that remains a topic of critical discussion today—the role of quotation and allusion in the piece. (This and all of the reviews that follow originally appeared uncredited; only in this first instance have we been unable to identify the author.)*

New York World
23 December 1877

The real interest of the evening centered upon the Brahms Symphony, which stood at the head of the programme. There is no living musician about whose compositions there is a greater variety of opinions, or these opinions more changeable, than the same Johannes Brahms. People whose patience is limited, and whose ears itch for taking melodies—well or ill elaborated—may find enchantment at a first hearing of such limpid works as Raff's "Leonore" Symphony. But let a Brahms "Requiem," or wonderfully complex and original variations, or symphony, for the first time sound forth, and they will compare the work to muddy water and perhaps sigh for the clearness of a Mozart or a Gluck. But if such a work as the "Leonore" Symphony be performed side by side with a work of like character by Brahms, after a few hearings of both the relations will be reverse. The former work, notwithstanding the almost universal delight it at first arouses, soon becomes comparatively wearisome, while the latter seems to grow more and more beautiful, and adverse judgments of its originality and merits are gradually fused into enthusiastic approval. Almost every one (even of his admirers) is at first disappointed in a new work by Brahms. There is one striking peculiarity about [Brahms's] works—they at first seem filled from beginning to end with resemblances to familiar themes; and, what is for the time more exasperating, these resemblances seem purposely to have been modified into attempted originality by the concealment of slight changes in form, or color or the like. Many hearers express the hasty judgment that the elaboration and harmonization may be remarkably good, but there is not an original theme to be found. But, with few exceptions, the very passages which at first appear least original will by-and-by thrill these rash judges with feeling and power, not only in themselves, but especially as they are served with all their surroundings. The resemblance will for the most part be seen to consist in turns of phrase, and in combinations of these with coloring familiar in connection with them. But when the coloring changes, and Brahms covers them with the syncopated iridescence of which he is such a master, the resemblances vanish and presently new beauties drive them from the memory. A striking instance is to be found in the introduction (*più andante*) to the last movement of the symphony, where, over the rippling surface of the *pianissimo* string orchestra, the ethereal tones of the horns breathe forth with mysterious power. The second and last phrases of the horn passage [mm. 32–33 and 37–38, in C major], in form and color both, irresistibly recall the introduction to Schubert's C Major Symphony [mm. 6–8, the horn solo]; and the shading of the passage recalls that part of Schubert's Andante, in the same symphony [mm. 148–160], so particularly admired by Schumann. But when the flute succeeds the horn with the same notes, the resemblance is gone, and we are constrained to acknowledge that there is no want of originality in essence to complain of. Brahms is not a mere copyist of the old masters whom he studies and admires so much. . . . He thoroughly assimilates what he learns, so that it becomes fused into new truth and beauty, and on reappearing, it is never clumsily managed, and must be acknowledged to be Brahms's own. . . .

As a general opinion of this symphony, it must be acknowledged to be a great work. If Brahms has more talent than genius, then that talent is nearer to genius than anything we have had since Schumann. While listening to [this] symphony, you get glimpses, but they are mere railroad glimpses, of the great masters, from time to time. Should Brahms be blamed for thus occasionally showing what beautiful landscapes surround his own domain? Not when that to which he has a clear title is so extraordinarily beautiful in itself. The work on this symphony is simply wonderful, and by it Brahms shows himself to be an artist of the highest rank in the use of materials at his command. The colors may often seem thickly crowded together, but study and the choice of proper points of observation will bring out the lines and the perspective with beautiful effect.[4]

The following month, Brahms's symphony was played three times in Boston—two well meaning attempts, on January 3 and 31, by the Harvard Musical Association Orchestra under the direction of Carl Zehrahn (a conductor said to have had "a convincing beat with no mannerisms" and to be "a conservative in interpretation");[5] and one performance, on January 16, by the highly trained Theodore Thomas Orchestra, which had taken the piece on tour.[6] Several of Boston's newspapers responded with perceptive reviews. Although the work seemed extremely modern to all ears—William Foster Apthorp later recalled that "Brahms's C minor symphony made us stare . . . ! I doubt if anything in all music ever sounded more positively terrific [i.e., terrifying] than that slow introduction to the first movement did to us then"— most of Boston's critics made a sincere effort to grasp its import.[7]

John Sullivan Dwight (1813–93), the founding father of music criticism in Boston and president of the Harvard Musical Association's board of directors, had been covering the symphony's progress for a year on the pages of his influential

Dwight's Journal of Music. *He now wrote a perceptive review after each of its three Boston performances.*

JOHN SULLIVAN DWIGHT
Dwight's Journal of Music
19 January 1878

FIFTH HARVARD SYMPHONY CONCERT. The experiment in the last concert (Jan. 3) of an essentially "modern" programme, in which new works had the lion's share—in deference for once to the continual complaint of critics and fault finders—afforded small encouragement for following up the "new departure." There was no increase of (paying) audience; indeed the sale of tickets has been larger in several of the preceding concerts, which offered no such stimulus to curiosity. The season tickets of course are a fixed quantity and count alike in every concert. The holders thereof may have turned out more generally than they had done of late, piqued by the same love of novelty which made professional musicians, and all of the numerous class who are wont to expect "complimentary" admission upon such occasions, eager to hear (themselves and wives) a notable new Symphony. This is all there was in the appearance of a "better house" that afternoon. And when the fact is stated that, of those eager crowds, a large proportion coolly left the hall before the Symphony was half over—(unhandsome conduct, surely, if they were among the clamorers for novelty)—it may well be doubted whether it would be politic, or not rather suicidal, for the management, to play much longer on that string. The truth is, the new music is *not* popular, and it is hard to escape the conclusion that the demand for it (we mean as publicly expressed in newspapers) is either frivolous or not sincere.—But our business here is with the *music* of the concert, with the following programme and performance:—

1. Overture to "Euryanthe"...Weber

2. Pianoforte Concerto in A minor, Op. 16...............Edward Grieg

   Allegro molto moderato.—Adagio.—Allegro moderato.

   William H. Sherwood.

3. Allegretto, from Third Symphony, Op. 15........................Gade

~~~

1. Pianoforte Solos:—

    a. Fugue in E minor……………..………..……..................Handel
    b. Nocturne in F sharp, Op. 15, No. 2…….…..…………Chopin
    c. Scherzo, from Suite, Op. 31…..……………..................Bargiel

William H. Sherwood.

2. Symphony, in C minor, Op. 68……………......Johannes Brahms

(First time in Boston.)

    1. Un poco sostenuto; Allegro (C minor).
    2. Andante sostenuto (E major).
    3. Poco Allegretto a grazioso (A-flat major).
    4. Adagio (C minor); più Andante; Allegro con brio (C major).

The programme and the concert have been called "splendid" in some quarters where we have long ceased to look for any praise; and the term is not entirely inappropriate. It was at least a brilliant programme, and for the most part brilliantly performed. If any complained of dullness, it was not until they had listened to the middle of the first movement of the long anticipated new Symphony; and that was partly perhaps the fault of Brahms, but quite as much their own fault, or, rather, owing to their own want of preparation and of more familiarity with a work not luminous upon a single hearing. . . .

And now we come to the main feature of the programme, the Brahms Symphony, about which there has been so much discussion, and such sweeping judgments have been uttered both in praise and condemnation, some wildly shouting: "The Tenth Symphony!" [and] others pronouncing it dry, pedantic, depressing and intolerable, a thing which one can hardly sit through with patience.

We must confess that it has grown upon us as we have become more familiar with it through several rehearsals and some study of the score and the four-hand arrangement. It is at least an *earnest* work. There is matter in it; themes and motives which are pregnant, pertinaciously adhered to and consistently developed. It has a pervading unity of plan and spirit, and grows to a great climax. The musical texture is ingenious, complex and masterly: nothing seems loose or vague. The instrumentation, too, is masterly, although we have not noticed in it any exquisite surprises, any fresh bite of original effect or contrast, such as we get in Gade, or in Liszt, or Raff or Wagner; it is all rather of a uniformly rich, subdued and sombre hue; depth and fulness being the distinctive characteristic, although no extra instruments are employed, with the exception of a Contra-Fagotto, whose place had to be supplied here by the Tuba.

We are sure those who will hear it several times will find the first movement much more interesting than they did on the first hearing, though probably not less depressing. It is difficult to understand at once. The principal theme is hardly like a theme at all, and it is some time before one seizes it and holds it in his mind; the short accessory motives, on the contrary, are positive and pregnant, and continually recur with passionate significance and point. The slow introduction, beginning grandly with chromatic thirds ascending in the strings, descending in the reeds and flutes, while the tympani and basses continually sound the same deep C, in six-eight strong and regular pulsation, foreshadows the coming themes and phrases of the Allegro. It seems indeed as if some august sacrificial ceremony were preparing. This short introduction is, to our mind, one of the finest portions of the Symphony; this and the *Finale* are the best. But the *Allegro* is depressing; like most of the new compositions on a large, ambitious scale, it seems to us *sick* music; it certainly is not music which a sick man may listen to and feel better. It is wearisomely full of chromatics and of restless modulation. Nor do we find in it a positive originality. It is not much akin to Wagner, we were pleased to find; but it suggests older things continually. Schumann's "Manfred" music was in our mind more hauntingly than any other through the whole first movement; but there were also positive resemblances for a few bars now to the *Coriolan* and now the *Leonora* Overture, and frequent floating reminiscences of the Ninth Symphony. And here we may mention, in other parts of the work, a wearisome excess of a certain Schumannish trait: namely those catch-breath rhythms, where the expected accent at the beginning of a measure falls on *nothing*,—accented silence; a fine effect when sparingly used, but exasperating when it occurs too often.

The *Andante* (E major) opens in a clearer mood, much as any old master (Haydn, Mozart) might have written, and gives a short-lived promise of an interval of peace and comfort. Only for a few measures! when the sickness and the restlessness return, and still the heart is full of heaviness. Yet many a beautiful detail will reward a closer study; near the beginning, for instance, a peculiar long melodic passage by the oboe continued by the clarinet.—The *Allegretto*, in its pastoral simplicity,—a quiet Intermezzo in the usual place of the Scherzo—is perhaps the most readily appreciated and most fascinating piece of all. The fond duplication of a measure in each half of the first melodic period, and the blithe answering theme in thirds, have an air of unaffected genuineness. In this simpler music at least you feel that there is heart. But this too grows uneasy ere 'tis done.

It was a pity that so many left the hall before the arrival of the last movement; for it is this that makes the great effect, and leaves the impression that all that went before, however seen as in a glass darkly, was tending steadily to an almost sublime conclusion. The introductory *Adagio* is a stately preparation of the popular "Joy" theme, so palpably and closely imitated from Beethoven, filling the mind with expectation of relief and the dispersion of the clouds before a brilliant sun. There is a passage in it quite Beethoven-like, where the strings, *pizzicato*, seem to be groping as on tiptoe in the dark and feeling for a door of exit. And when the time quickens to the *più Andante* (mark the correct use here of the word *Andante*, which means *going*, and not slow) a fascinating phrase rings out from the horn, amid the rustling *pianissimo* of strings, which is at once echoed by the flute as from the sky above, and thrills one like the sudden omen of a clear day in the East. This is worked out with great power, and then begins the joy theme (*Allegro non troppo*, but *con brio*), which, however, we do not find so joyous, nor of so popular a stamp as that in the Ninth Symphony. The development is exceedingly rich, broad and splendid, the horn phrase heard ever and anon in the midst of it, besides many reminiscences of earlier movements. It is comparatively cheerful and exciting, the master movement of the work; and yet we cannot say it seemed to us inspired, inspiring and uplifting, glorious, transporting in the same sense, or the same degree, as the Finale of the Ninth or of the Fifth Beethoven Symphony. And after all, allowing all praise to this last movement, we cannot escape a total impression of the Symphony as something depressing and unedifying, a work coldly elaborated, artificial; earnest to be sure, in some sense great, and far more satisfactory than any Symphony by Raff, or any others of the day, which we have heard; but not to be mentioned in the same day with any Symphony by Schumann, Mendelssohn, or the great one by Schubert, not to speak of Beethoven.

Such is our impression so far; we shall doubtless find more in the work on further hearing; our interest in it will increase, but we foresee the limit; and certainly it cannot become popular; it will not be *loved*, like the dear masterworks of genius.—A word of hearty praise is certainly due to the Conductor and the Orchestra, for giving us upon the whole so clear and strong a rendering of so wholly new and difficult a work upon such short rehearsal. The musicians took it up with zeal and energy, and generously *gave* an extra rehearsal in their desire to bring it out as well as possible.[8]

JOHN SULLIVAN DWIGHT
Dwight's Journal of Music
2 February 1878

The Fifth Subscription Concert of Theodore Thomas, took place in the Music Hall on Wednesday evening, Jan. 16. The attendance was but middling and, like all concerts of the kind this season, this one also was apparently unremunerative. The admirable orchestra gave us some of its very best work,—mind, we do not say works: these were good, bad and indifferent, to-wit:

1. Selected Movements .... Handel

Hornpipe, Larghetto, Allegro molto.

2. Masonic Funeral Music.......................... Mozart

3. Symphony, C minor, Op. 68.............. Johannes Brahms

4. Serenade, No. 3, (String Orchestra).............. Volkmann

Violoncello Obligato by Mr. Charles Hemman.

5. Overture—"Struensée" .... Meyerbeer

[. . .]

The Brahms symphony was certainly about as finely rendered as it would be possible to have it in this country, perhaps anywhere. It had been most thoroughly and critically studied and rehearsed; every detail, every phrase in the complex contrapuntal web coming out clear and unmistakable, and the sound of all the reeds and brass was beautifully true and musical; the great Contrafagotto, also, gave new depth and grandeur to some passages. With all the praise for faultless playing, we take it the general audience were not much wiser as to the intrinsic merits of the composition than they were before,—those, we mean, who had heard it played for the first time by our own musicians. It is all cant, a fore-gone conclusion to say that it required this orchestra to give us any right conception of the Symphony. Hearing it repeatedly helps the understanding, and the better orchestra will sound the best whatever work it plays; but no appreciative, intelligently musical person need wait for a perfect orchestra to tell him what the work is in itself, and whether he ought to go into ecstacies about it. We did not find that we admired it any more or any less upon this second public hearing. Interest us it did surely, but uplift and inspire us it did not, not even the last movement. It was still depressing, over-labored, unspontaneous, with more of will than genius in it, more of enterprise and calculation than of the creative spark.

JOHN SULLIVAN DWIGHT
Dwight's Journal of Music
16 February 1878

HARVARD MUSICAL ASSOCIATION. The sixth Symphony Concert, after the double pause in the middle of the series of ten, drew a somewhat larger audience than usual. Whether it indicated the beginning of a revival of the concert appetite here generally, or whether it was the curiosity to hear the Brahms Symphony again, we cannot undertake to say. We think, however, that the whole programme proved enjoyable. It was as follows:

Overture to "The Water-Carrier" . . . . Cherubini

Aria:—"Il mio tesoro" from "Don Giovanni" . . . . Mozart

Alfred Wilkie.

Overture—"The Naiads" . . . . Sterndale Bennett

Songs, with Piano-forte:—

    a. The Garland . . . . .Mendelssohn
    b. The Hidalgo . . . . .Schumann

Alfred Wilkie.

Symphony, in C minor, Op. 68 . . . . .Johannes Brahms

(Second time.)

After a third hearing, the Brahms Symphony left essentially the same impression on us as before. We do not think we need to go into any further criticism or description of the work. That we found more in detail to interest the mind we freely grant; and we may even say that in a certain sense its power and beauty,—its intensity above all—and the thoughtful ingenuity, the constructive skill shown in it, grow upon us. This has been the case particularly with the first and the last movement,—most of all the expectant prelude to the popular theme, or Joy tune, together with the tune itself, so brilliantly worked up to a final climax. And still the total influence of the work is depressing. It does not seem inspired; it did not spring from the clear heaven of invention; it shows more of painstaking calculation than of the imaginative faculty or quality. Its author was in earnest, and had a good outfit of experience and means to work with; and that is what saves it. But will it save it long? Whether it is to take a place among the immortal Symphonies at all,—not to speak of "the immortal Nine"? We see that Mr. Thomas, after some feeling of the public pulse, has abandoned his intention of giving it here again this week, and has come to the conclusion that Beethoven is better bait.—As for the performance, people seemed surprised at the smoothness, the clearness, the intelligent accent and the spirit with which the whole work was rendered by our orchestra after only one rehearsal since the preceding concert. It was most creditable to the musicians and above all to their Conductor, CARL ZEHRAHN.

The unsigned review of the Thomas Orchestra's performance in Boston's Saturday Evening Gazette *was penned by the conservative and caustic Benjamin Edward Wolff (1836–1901). A professional musician of English-Jewish birth, his father and grandfather had been directors of orchestras and he himself had conducted theater orchestras in Philadelphia, New Orleans, and Boston before becoming editor of the* Gazette, *where he remained until 1894.[9] As Louis C. Elson recalled, Wolff, who was "one of the fiercest opponents of the Wagnerian music," was often "sublimely savage in his reviews"; "his bitter sarcasm and invective made him feared by many who held different opinions."[10] But Elson granted that Wolff was "by education and attainments thoroughly fitted to exercise the critical faculty," and his writing could be "witty, keen, and analytical."[11]*

BENJAMIN EDWARD WOLFF
Saturday Evening Gazette
24 January 1878

The entertainment was especially interesting for the opportunity it afforded for a second hearing of the Brahms Symphony, this time by an orchestra that had given it long and careful study, and had played it several times in public. Upon listening to the work again under these more favorable circumstances, we find nothing to change in the general tenor of the judgment we have pronounced upon it. Certain passages were ordered more clear, and there were broader effects of light and shade produced, but the work, as a whole, seemed to us as hard and as uninspired as upon its former hearing. It is mathematical music evolved with difficulty from an unimaginative brain. How it ever came to be honored with the title of "The Tenth Symphony," is a mystery to us. Can it be that the Boucicaulting system of puffery has crept into German musical art?[12] The Tenth Symphony! This noisy, ungraceful, confusing and unattractive example of dry pedantry before the masterpieces of Schubert, Schumann, Mendelssohn, Gade—or even of the reckless and over-fluent Raff! Absurd! In all that Brahms has written he has shown himself to be a composer without a heart. We cannot call to mind a single work of his that impressed us save for the learning shown in it. All that we have heard and seen from his pen abounds in head-work without a glimmer of soul. In fact, we will even venture so far as to whether Brahms possesses true musical genius in the sense that the recognized masters of the art possessed it. As for this symphony, we believe that it would have fallen flat upon the world had it been left to its way upon its own merits; but it was enthusiastically lauded from the outset, Schumann's praise of the composer was unearthed and noisily shouted as an *avant courier*, and the sensationalism of the day was brought to bear in stimulating curiosity. The warmth was all in the praises of the composer's friends, for there is none in the symphony. The last movement is a brilliant piece undoubtedly, and had the preceding movements been as fine, the composition might have easily taken rank among the great symphonies that have followed the Choral [Symphony of Beethoven], but even then it would scarcely have deserved the overwhelming praises bestowed upon it. A symphony that demands in its hearer a profound technical knowledge to understand, that appeals only to the wonder of the student, may show the composer's industry and his learning, but this is artistic egotism and not genius, save of that kind shown in the manufacture of the intricate Chinese carvings in ivory. But even in these the workmen are skilled in the art of concealing art, while Brahms, on the other hand, delights only in obtruding his art. It is possible that as we grow more familiar with this symphony it may become clearer to us, but we might pore over a difficult problem in mathematics until the same result was reached without arriving at the conclusion that it is a poetic inspiration. While there is much that is lovely and inspired in art that will better repay the study, and while life is too short to exhaust the beautiful, we feel that it is a wanton waste of time to devote it to long contemplation in order to discover whether or not this Brahms symphony is the most stupendous musical triumph of our day.

Another unsigned review of the symphony's Boston performances was published in the Boston Daily Advertiser, *one of that city's premier newspapers. Its author was Henry Austin Clapp (1841–1904), a Shakespeare scholar and student of drama history who was educated at Harvard and joined the staff of the* Advertiser *in 1868 in the dual role of drama and music critic. As a theater critic, Clapp was viewed as "erudite, incorruptible, and fair";*[13] *his writing style has been characterized as reflecting "the leisurely, elongated construction of his era, but . . . marked by genuine erudition, peppery wit, and a determined fairness."*[14] *After hearing the first two performances of Brahms's symphony, he could write the following:*

HENRY AUSTIN CLAPP
Boston Daily Advertiser
17 January 1878

The work certainly grows upon the listener, and one is so conscious of the progress made in enjoyment and comprehension of the symphony after a second hearing that he hesitates to predict what favor the work might win from him after many repetitions. We venture, however, at this stage of our acquaintance with the symphony to express a doubt—amounting with ourselves, we think, to a personal conviction of the contrary—that this work demonstrates its author's right to a place beside or near Beethoven, or that it entitles his admirers to disregard the claims of Mendelssohn and Schumann in ranking this composition as the greatest since the Ninth Symphony. Johannes Brahms—though the slow development of his fame indicated in him a late ripening of a sort very usual with musical geniuses, who as a class have been marvelously unconscious—has had the immense advantage of Schumann's trumpet-tongued announcement of his worth. Schumann's reputation as a composer is fortunately much better grounded than his repute as a prophet, but his unquestioned skill as a critic made his statement of the power and promise of Johannes Brahms extremely influential.

Brahms has avoided the dangers which attend upon rapid and careless composition, has written slowly and carefully, and has known how to make prudent use of popular expectation. But may it not be fairly questioned whether this mode of composing, as well as the chief works by which Brahms has added to his reputation, do not indicate the patience and laboriousness of the student rather than the affluence and self-derived fruitfulness of a true musical genius? And are there not hints of such a truth even in this admirable symphony? But despite the saucy doubts and fears which refuse to be dispelled when we try to look at Brahms as the leading composer of the century, we find his new symphony a noble and an imposing work. The closing movement is certainly its most impressive part, but we agree with the accomplished critic of the *Tribune* in profoundly admiring the originality of the sombre opening *allegro*, in which mental and spiritual gloom and conflict are shown with wonderful dramatic and picturesque skill, and in which the forms, both by their number, their novelty and their intrinsic beauty, suggest a depth and richness of resource which would belong only to a composer of the first rank. The two following movements, though pleasing, are so much lighter, and we think we must say thinner, that by contrast they seem a little inadequate, and the themes of the third movement, though graceful,—the first one being especially so,—in their original statement we find to be rather dryly worked out. The last movement may well be designated as magnificent. It shows a strong grasp, great learning, a large mind in the author. Of the last hundred measures Beethoven himself might surely have been proud at any stage of his career. One expression made in a former article upon this symphony we find, however, that we must qualify. The last movement is not, we find, exactly joyful; it is rather very *intense*; it lacks the spontaneous and simple quality, the *outwardness*, we might say, of joy; and in this respect it strongly and interestingly differs from its prototype of the Ninth Symphony. And in this difference we find the keynote of one of Johannes Brahms's chief peculiarities as a composer. He is a modern of the moderns, and this symphony is a remarkable expression of the inner life of this anxious, introverted, over-earnest age, which cannot even be glad in a frank and self-forgetful spirit.

We close with many thanks to Mr. Thomas for his brilliant and wellnigh faultless interpretation of this very difficult work, and for the new and clear light which his orchestral performance has thrown upon it. Such a re-introduction to such a work of art is indeed a true and lofty delight.

After the first performance of the symphony by the Harvard Musical Association Orchestra on January 3, Edward Henry Clement (1843–1920), the progressive music, drama, and art critic for the preeminent Boston Evening Transcript, *found it to contain "a large quantity of mere surplusage, a strenuous iteration and reiteration," and to be lacking "sustained strength . . . unity, and balance, and reserved power," in spite of "passages of great splendor and effectiveness, and beauties and fancies with the stamp of true musical fire upon them."[15] As evidence of how much difference the quality of the interpretation could make, Clement's censure turned to unqualified praise after hearing the Thomas Orchestra's performance some days later.*

EDWARD HENRY CLEMENT
Boston Evening Transcript
17 January 1878

Mr. Theodore Thomas achieved last evening his crowning triumph in Boston, demonstrating that it is for his revealing and illuminating touch that we must wait before worthily comprehending or enjoying even one of the greatest works of art. This acknowledgment was unreservedly made to him in the prolonged and hearty applause with which a grateful public recalled him after the new Brahms Symphony had been unfolded to them,—as all felt, notwithstanding the previous hearing, for the first time. . . . The new symphony lay in the minds of those who heard it at the Harvard symphony concert "a mighty maze but not without a plan." Mr. Thomas last night held it up so that its masterly design and unity as a whole were felt at once, and then passed along through individual beauties and elegances of the tapestry, displaying its lovely figures . . . and arabesques each by itself and in its relations, and even exhibiting the ingenuity and skill of the weaving and needlework. Besides the delight in the new-found beauty of design and proportion in the work, there was an unforgettable lesson received—that intelligent, refined and sensitive conducting toward the adequate interpretation of the wider and deeper significance and connection of musical phrases and sentences is a *sine qua non*, independently of the question of technical drill of the orchestra. The coupling of this symphony with Beethoven's can now be understood. The masterful grasp and repose of the composer, able to conceive in the mightiest strain of musical invention and sustain and express his ideas in musician-like work worthy of the conception, are unquestionable. In whatever phase of the noble creation, whether the bold, original, intense allegro, after the richly chaste and fittingly elegant introduction; the simple, sweet, romance-like melody sustained with all the riches of symphonic writing throughout the slow movement; the lighter charm of the lovely flowing passages of the poco allegretto e grazioso or the grandly Beethovenish finale with the splendors of a thorough symphonic development interwoven with immense and unflagging and unerring strength amid pæans of triumph—all shows the strongly vital, fertile genius, in healthy and manly culture and self-control, and employing with masterful ease and the finest unconscious artistic sense and feeling all the resources of the divine art. To have such a work, after a first bleared view, spread forth with all the brilliant light and clear shadow, delicate, sensitive turns of expression, and modulation of color, force and tempo, which Mr. Thomas brings to the perfecting of his tone-pictures in "values" and perspective, was luxury indeed.[16]

Reviewing the Thomas Orchestra concert for the Boston Courier *was William Foster Apthorp (1848–1913), a graduate of Harvard College, where he had studied piano, harmony, and counterpoint with that institution's first professor of music, the composer John Knowles Paine. As a child, Apthorp had been taken by his parents to study art in Dresden, Berlin, and Rome, and he developed into an accomplished linguist who could speak all the major languages of Europe. Apthorp began his career as a critic writing for the* Atlantic Monthly *(1872–77),* Dwight's Journal of Music, *the* Boston Courier *(1876–80), and the* Daily Evening Traveller *(1878). He went on to help shape Boston's musical tastes as reviewer for the* Boston Evening Transcript *(1881–1903) and program essayist for the Boston Symphony Orchestra.*

WILLIAM FOSTER APTHORP

Boston Courier

20 January 1878

The Brahms symphony was once more the central point of interest. It was indeed superbly played; the orchestra has never given more convincing evidence of that thorough and conscientious rehearsing for which Mr. Thomas has become noted. Every phrase in the whole wonderfully complex work was well-considered and clearly rendered: every smallest detail was made the most of. In how far Mr. Thomas's conception of the composition is in sympathy with the composer's intention it were impossible to say. It certainly seems at first sight as if no composer could have intended such an unbroken chain of slow movements without the faintest hint at anything approaching to a nimbly running phrase, as Mr. Thomas gave us, counting from the end of the first movement up to the entrance of the la[st] Allegro. To be sure there is nothing in the tempo marks in the score to contravene Mr. Thomas's conception, and it is pretty well known that Brahms is somewhat prone to forget that the element of tediousness is worth a moment's consideration from an earnest artist. And yet it is hard to believe that Brahms should have so miscalculated the perviousness to boredom which makes most mortals tire of even the most luscious linked sweetness when it is too long drawn out. The effect of the second and third movements and the first part of the fourth was certainly unfortunate. As Grétry exclaimed after listening for some time to an opera of Méhul's, in which the composer had composed his string-orchestra of violas, 'celli and basses, without violins: "I would give a hundred francs for an E-string!" one feels like crying out long before the last movement of Brahms's symphony: "A hundred francs for an *allegro*." Upon the whole, the symphony is disappointing.

One cannot surely help recognizing it as an exceedingly earnest work throughout. The composer has in no instance allowed himself to substitute mere gorgeousness of orchestral coloring for an idea: he has worked hard and faithfully towards very high ends, but the symphony sounds for the most part morbid, strained and unnatural; much of it even ugly. The composer seems to have been forced to hold his inspiration by the very hair of the head that it should not escape him. He is often involved and obscure, rather than profound. One meets now and then with passages of great beauty, but they are so exceptional as to seem almost out of place; the rays of gracious light are so few and far between that they do little more than to make darkness visible. What of deep feeling, sentiment and passion there is in the music is no doubt as genuine as it is intense. The symphony is no cooked-up sham, but sentiment and passion do not of themselves constitute a work of art; they must be embodied in a perspicuous and artistic form. In the matter of melody some will call Brahms deficient, and others will call him strong. Melody has become, by this time, a pretty vague term. Berlioz once said in reference to his own works: "My melodies are often of very large dimensions, and shortsighted, infantile minds do not clearly distinguish their outlines." Brahms may possibly say the same. Yet we must say that in a composition in which certain melodies are not the be-all and end-all, but the texts which are to be treated musically—in other words, the themes—the rational dimensions of a thematic phrase find their natural limits very soon, and a theme which is too long, or too vague in character to be readily grasped by the ear, and easily remembered, is unfit for clear contrapuntal development. Nothing is more charming than the old and yet ever young effect of different instruments calling to and answering each other across the orchestra, but when it comes to an oboe and a clarinet making absolute speeches at each other (*vide* for instance, a passage in Brahms's *andante*), the listener's mind is at so great trouble to remember what the first has said, that it is impossible to appreciate whether the reply of the second is pertinent or not. If the theme of a movement is too vague to appeal directly and by itself to a listener's imagination as a firmly grasped idea, its further development will be incomprehensible to him. The orchestra may discuss the theme with admirable wisdom and in perfect counterpoint, but the listener will get no satisfaction, simply because he does not know what the talk is all about. But I must not leave this symphony without a word of heartiest admiration for the theme of the last movement. That is really superb. Strong, pithy and concise. It does, to be sure, remind one of the Ninth Symphony. But it only reminds one of it; it is no plagiarism. Pity only that one is so tired out by what has gone before that even this glorious outburst fails to awaken a lasting enthusiasm.

After a third hearing, Apthorp, who had advocated the performance of more modern music to his fellow board members at the Harvard Musical Association, still had strong reservations about Brahms's symphony.

WILLIAM FOSTER APTHORP
Boston Courier
3 February 1878

The Brahms symphony again! One can, by this time, form something approaching a definite notion of the merits of this extraordinary work. Sooth to say, it does not improve upon acquaintance. The best that can be said of it is that it is genuinely intense music. Whether it tears its passion to tatters or not may be a matter of opinion, but the passion is really there. Some persons will undoubtedly call it learned. Well, judged by the standard of musical learning that most contemporary composers can boast of, it may certainly be called so. But to call it learned is to admit that musical science, as such, is at a rather low ebb today. A composer may show considerable ingenuity in working out his themes in an unprecedented way, and in producing striking effects by such working out, but if the general effect is horribly dissonant, if the parts "mutually rub their skins off," as Berlioz says, by grating one against another, it cannot be called good counterpoint, and poor counterpoint is no very good earnest of musical learning. No, Brahms seems to lose sight of the fact that the human ear does not willingly bear more than a certain degree of harsh treatment. The ear that can stand such a violent and sustained assault as this symphony without flinching, must—one would think—have been rendered so callous by ill-usage as to be almost senseless to the less strident appeals of pure musical beauty. Yet the symphony is highly ingenious, at times strangely powerful, and if the power is not well sustained, the ingenuity is beyond all doubt. It is interesting to see how a man can unite so many and heterogeneous elements to form a whole that is not absolutely chaotic. He has rarely succeeded in making that whole harmonious and finely organized, and that is just where his "learning" is at fault. Remember, this is not a question of that preponderance of the brain over the heart, of which we hear so much nowadays. A man may have a very strong brain, and yet have very little learning. In Brahms's symphony there seems to be no lack either of brain or heart, but the brain shows a lack of training: it plunges and struggles to express what the heart dictates, so that the intellectual effort is more prominent than anything else.

It would take a long time, additional performances as taut as Thomas's, and much honest struggling in his public columns before Apthorp would be able to discern the disciplined relationship of heart and mind in Brahms's First Symphony and admit to his readers that the "work is getting interesting. It is the serpent, and we are the poor little fluttering bird that is spellbound by its glance."[17] Only in December 1883 would he acknowledge that "Brahms's great symphony—we now write great without any misgivings—at last produces the impression upon us that we have been waiting for through so many years."[18]

NOTES

1. Robert Schumann, "Neue Bahnen," *Neue Zeitschrift für Musik* 39 (28 October 1853): 186; repr. in Max Kalbeck, *Johannes Brahms*, rev. ed. (Berlin, 1912–21; repr. Tutzing, 1976), 1:127.

2. Quoted, from communication with Levi, in Kalbeck, *Johannes Brahms*, 1:165.

3. On the intense competition between Thomas and Damrosch over this symphony, see Walter Damrosch, *My Musical Life* (New York, 1930), 24–26.

4. This review proceeds to chronicle the interpretative differences between the performances by Damrosch and Thomas.

5. Henry M. Dunham, *The Life of a Musician Woven into a Strand of History of the New England Conservatory of Music* (Boston, 1931), 43.

6. Thomas was scheduled to perform the symphony a second time, on February 13, but instead he programmed Beethoven's Seventh Symphony. John Sullivan Dwight reported that he made this change "after [gaining] some feeling of the public pulse" (*Dwight's Journal of Music*, 16 February 1878).

7. William Foster Apthorp, "Musical Reminiscences of Boston Thirty Years Ago," in *By the Way* (Boston, 1898), 2:80–81.

8. Apthorp reported that there had been three rehearsals (*Boston Courier*, 6 January 1878). The orchestra's second performance of the work was presented after the usual single rehearsal (*Dwight's Journal of Music*, 19 January 1878).

9. William Brooks, "Wolff, Benjamin Edward," in *The New Grove Dictionary of American Music* (London, 1986), 4:561; obituary from the *Boston Herald*, 7 February 1901.

10. Louis C. Elson, *The History of American Music* (New York and London, 1904), 323.

11. Elson, "Musical Boston: Its Orchestras, Clubs and Musical Institutions," supplement to *Music and Drama* (New York), 3 June 1882.

12. A reference to the Irish melodramatic actor Dion Boucicault (ca. 1820–1890).

13. Tice L. Miller and Don B. Wilmeth, eds., *Cambridge Guide to American Theatre* (Cambridge, 1993), 116.

14. Gerald Bordman, in *The Oxford Companion to American Theatre*, 2nd ed. (Oxford and New York, 1992), 147.

15. *Boston Evening Transcript*, 4 January 1878.

16. Clement's second review, also praising the symphony, appeared in the *Boston Evening Transcript*, 1 February 1878.

17. Ibid., 26 December 1882.

18. Ibid., 31 December 1883.

PART III

MEMOIRS

∞

Eduard Hanslick
Johannes Brahms: The Last Days
Memories and Letters

TRANSLATED BY SUSAN GILLESPIE, ANDREW HOMAN,
AND CAROLINE HOMAN

INTRODUCED BY KEVIN C. KARNES

ANNOTATED BY LEON BOTSTEIN AND
KEVIN C. KARNES

These two selections by Eduard Hanslick (1825–1904) were published together in At the End of the Century *(1899), the fifth installment of the illustrious critic's decades-long project to document the unfolding "living history" of his contemporary musical culture.[1] Collectively, they serve as a richly detailed, deeply personal obituary for the recently departed artist. Rather than attempting to assess the impressions left by Brahms's music upon the world of his time, "The Last Days," which Hanslick dated 3 April 1897 (the day of the composer's death), recounts Brahms's final summer, spent among friends in Ischl, his convalescence, and the last concerts he attended in Vienna. It features Hanslick's recollections of discussions he had with Brahms, quotations from Brahms's letters to him, and excerpts from a letter sent to Hanslick by Brahms's doctor in Karlsbad. The second essay, "Memories and Letters," elaborates on the form of "Last Days," providing substantial excerpts from Brahms's correspondence with the critic; a number of letters are cited in full. Spanning more than three decades, from 1863 to 1896, these letters consider, among other topics, Brahms's distaste for written correspondence and his ideas about the value of composers' letters and sketches for music-historical study; his commitment to music pedagogy; his responses to various events in contemporary musical life (including the publication of Hanslick's 1854 aesthetic treatise,* On the Musically Beautiful*); his political views; and his remembrance of his departed friends, Theodor Billroth and Clara and Robert Schumann.*

As discussed elsewhere in this volume, Hanslick and Brahms became acquaint-
ed around the time of Brahms's first concert in Vienna, held at the Gesellschaft der
Musikfreunde on November 29, 1862.[2] A close friendship soon developed, with
Hanslick becoming a member of Brahms's innermost circle and regularly accompany-
ing him to concerts, on holidays, and to intimate gatherings of friends, fellow
musicians, and loved ones. The selections translated below of Hanslick's Am Ende
des Jahrhunderts *(Berlin, 1899) are from pages 365–409. All endnotes are edi-*
torial and all ellipses are given as in the original.

Johannes Brahms: The Last Days (Vienna, April 3, 1897)

Alas, we have lost him, too, the true, great master and loyal friend! He,
who until recently was able to vaunt the fact that he had never been sick
in his entire life, not even for a single day! That had continued to be the
case until the end of the summer, when he suddenly became sick without
realizing it himself. In Ischl, some friends pointed out to him that his face
had acquired a sickly yellow hue. With the explanation that he never looked
at himself in the mirror, he cut the conversation short, since it irritated
him. Brahms, the sixty-four-year-old, never wanted to hear about sickness,
care, or precaution. He felt that his enviable constitution made him immune.
About five years ago, when he told me, with naïve satisfaction, that he had
earned a nice fortune, which Simrock was managing for him in Berlin, I
remarked: "You have written a will, right?"— "A will?" he cried, completely
astonished, "I am still fresh and healthy!"— "Exactly," I explained. "If you
put it off until you are really old and sick, then you will either never get
to it, or you will do something stupid." Brahms was silent and seemed to
be wrestling with the thought as if it were totally foreign to his world. A
few days later, he brought a sealed will to me for safekeeping. I held on to
it for the time being, until Simrock arrived in Vienna to take the document from me at my request. As the youngest of the three of us, he would
most likely outlive us.

   In Ischl, Brahms finally took his friends' advice to get medical attention.
The doctors explained his jaundice as the symptom of the early stages of
liver disease and sent Brahms to Karlsbad. With great reluctance he obeyed
this advice, though his love of Ischl was as great as his dislike of any "serious health resort." At the end of August 1896, he arrived in Karlsbad. I
had contacted two musical friends there (Professor Emil Seling and Music
Director Janetschek) and asked them to meet Brahms at the train station
and to help him find lodging and anything else he needed. When they
helped him get off the train, both were so horrified by his terrible appearance,

Eduard Hanslick

as they later wrote to me, that it was hard for them to keep him from noticing their reaction. After Brahms had overcome the impression of the
unfamiliar, he began to like Karlsbad more than he had anticipated. "How
sorry I am," he wrote to me in early September, "that I won't be able to
be there on the eleventh, and there is not much more that I need to say
to you.* I wanted to write a nice, conversational letter to you, but this morning I was deluged with so many taxing letters that I really cannot begin.
However, I am very thankful for this jaundice, since it finally brought me
to illustrious Karlsbad. I've been greeted by more glorious days here than
we had all summer. Additionally, I have an absolutely charming apartment
("The City of Brussels") in the house of the most gracious people, which
I am really enjoying. Hoping that you are satisfied with these cursory greetings, your J. Br."

The letter from Brahms's excellent physician in Karlsbad, Dr. Grünberger,
on September 24, was not so reassuring. He wrote: "After repeated close
examinations and three weeks of continuous observation of the patient,
my conclusion is that there is a critical swelling of the liver, with complete
blockage of the bile ducts, which has resulted in jaundice, digestive problems, etc. Nevertheless, I could not directly establish that the liver was
regenerating. . . . I cannot help but portray the condition as a really serious one." No doubt, the excellent physicians whom Brahms consulted after
his return here were certain about his incurable sickness, even if they were
not willing to call it by its bleak name. Most important, Brahms himself
could not be allowed to suspect it. I witnessed his lively reaction to psychological impressions when I visited him one morning and found his
voice to be noticeably more powerful and his movement much more unre-
stricted than the day before. "Yes," he said in a more satisfied tone than I
had heard from him in some time, "I am really reassured. A group of
doctors was just here, and after very close examination they found nothing dangerous in me!" In fact, in the first two to three months after his
six-week regimen at Karlsbad, his condition did not seem to worsen; however, it also did not improve. Brahms went on walks quite often, and his
swaying gait and bent posture were apparent. He also became very testy,
especially tempestuous, and disquieted whenever someone asked about
his state of health or claimed that he looked better. If one was brave enough
to ask him, he typically answered: "Every day a little bit worse." That was
also objectively correct. A slow but constant worsening of his state became

---

* We had hoped that Brahms would come on September 11, like last year, to spend my
birthday with friend Victor [von Miller-Aichholz]. He did send a long, witty birthday
telegram from Karlsbad.

clearly noticeable. The yellow, almost orange-colored tint kept getting darker and gave his once lovely blue eyes an uncanny expression. His once powerful, heavyset body shrank down to a horrifying gauntness. Long white hair hung down over his wrinkled, haggard, distressed face. Nevertheless, four weeks before his death he was still attending lunch at friends' houses, and sometimes he even went to the Burgtheater, which he attended as eagerly as he avoided the opera. "I urgently ask you," he wrote to me at that time, "please spare Bösendorfer and Reinecke and use the enclosed ticket to go see Anzengruber's *G'wissenswurm*! It is an excellent piece and will please you greatly—it will be truly refreshing. But you probably know that it is a sad piece." The last opera performance that Brahms attended was *Heimchen* by Goldmark, whom he personally loved and admired.[3] In the theater and at the dinner table, Brahms nodded off more frequently than ever. He was already quite weak when Strauss's new operetta *The Goddess of Reason* came out; still, he repeatedly asked me to reserve a seat for him in my box. He had the warmest regard for Johann Strauss, and he had really enjoyed his last piece, *Waldmeister*. On a fan owned by Mrs. Adele Strauss, under the opening measures of *The Blue Danube*, he wrote, "J. Brahms, who would have liked to have composed this." On March 13 he appeared punctually at the Theater an der Wien for the premiere of *The Goddess of Reason*, but he felt too unwell to stay until the end. After the second act, he left the theater, protesting, as usual, against offers to get a carriage for him or to accompany him home, which seemed prudent. By means of a cunning pretense, we were able to convince him to be accompanied by my brother-in-law. It was the last time Brahms entered a theater. He had already stopped going to concerts. He would have liked to have gone to Marcella Sembrich's concert, and he paid her a personal visit to excuse himself from attending.[4]

The last concert that Brahms attended was the Philharmonic on March 7, 1897. The memory of this must be deeply etched in the minds of everyone who was there. It began with Brahms's Fourth Symphony in E Minor. Immediately after the first movement there was a round of applause so vigorous that Brahms eventually had to emerge from the back of the director's box and bow in gratitude. This ovation was repeated after each of the four movements, and at the finale, it seemed as if it would never end. A shudder of awe and painful sympathy ran through the entire audience; clearly, many had the inkling that this was their last opportunity to greet the pained figure of the beloved, sick master. This extraordinary homage was all the more powerful, since his E-Minor Symphony had never been popular. His friends, who were able to measure this glowing success against the cold reception of the work in 1886, were inexpressibly happy for Brahms about this triumph. But inner joy could not really set in; the pain of worry and sympathy could not be driven away by music.

Brahms's condition went downhill from there. His feet no longer obeyed him, so his friends took him for carriage rides in the Prater.[5] Even this rare pleasure lasted only for a short time. Eight days ago, Brahms had to be brought to bed. He bristled against this at the time, but never left his bed after that. He was so powerless in those final days that he seemed numb even while he was awake. With indescribably touching care, his friends Victor von Miller-Aichholz, Arthur Faber, Dr. Fellinger, and their wives kept Brahms from feeling abandoned. It seems that Brahms was not conscious of the hopelessness and danger of his condition; his friends and doctors lovingly nurtured this illusion. Even the newspapers, through which he occasionally thumbed, were so courteous as to withhold reports about his serious illness.

Brahms's last compositions (op. 121) were the *Four Serious Songs*, which were set to words from the Bible. They are permeated with a bitter lament about the ephemeral nature of human beings and the dread of death. That winter, when they were sung for the first time, they seemed to us to be a bad omen, and there is no doubt that music history will regard them as a remarkable foreshadowing of Brahms's death. Yet, when Brahms composed the songs, he was still in fair health, and even months later he was still completely untouched by thoughts of death. Still, the *Serious Songs* remained his last—a prelude to his death.

When we jovially celebrated Brahms's sixth-third birthday with our circle of friends in May, no one had any inkling that it was to be his last. We will no longer celebrate the seventh of May.

Memories and Letters

1.

Friends and admirers of our dear master are constantly importuning me not to withhold a collection of his letters from the general public and from the loving interest of those who stood closer to him. Often the collection of Billroth letters is mentioned, whose incalculable significance, not only for his friends, has been demonstrated by the extraordinary success of a third edition.[6] The letters from Billroth to Brahms that are published in this selection could not but increase the demand for the answers of the latter. Unfortunately, the two sides are unequal. United in deeply felt friendship and mutual admiration, the two men were fundamentally different in many things, and specifically in their correspondence. For Billroth's open, communicative spirit, letter-writing was a need; for Brahms it was a burden. When Billroth came home late at night after a productive or socially active day, he lit his lamp and wrote until midnight—confiding, often quite voluminous letters about the impressions that the concert or play he had just seen, the latest book or the newest acquaintance had made on him. In this way he seemed to enjoy his pleasure all over again, and as with his joys, so also with his trials, which he shared willingly with us.

Not so Brahms. Often, when I entered his apartment to find him at his desk, he would point with a heavy sigh or an ill-tempered curse to a stack of letters: "I am supposed to answer all that!" On occasion the accursed pile had grown to alarming proportions: business letters from publishers, concert directors, festival committees, interspersed with invitations from Viennese friends and acquaintances, tributes and autograph requests from out-of-towners. Brahms dealt with all of this as curtly as possible; he had attained virtuosity in the art of the extremely brief response. Where it was not a complete breach of etiquette, he used postcards, whose format considerably cut off any possibility of more extensive description. He wrote very fast and always used goose quills, in order not to be held up in his rush by a hard steel nib. The place and date are lacking on almost all of his letters; for a signature he made do with the abbreviation *J. Br.* His distaste for signing his full name grew stronger, along with his worry that his letters might be snapped up and sold by autograph collectors.

Brahms had had an unfortunate experience. In a Berlin auction catalogue, among other autographs that were offered for sale, stood a "detailed letter from Johannes Brahms to his father." Horrified to see his most intimate family relationships and childish outpourings exposed to the curiosity of strangers, he wrote immediately to the bookseller in question; but a friend had gotten there before him, had already acquired the letter for Brahms and sent it to him. After that, Brahms was even more cautious and taciturn in his letters. He avoided confidences concerning his personal relationships, especially his youth, even in oral, and all the more in written communications. Judgments on modern musical trends or living composers—in a word, those things that would be of greatest interest to us—are only very rarely found in his letters, and then only in bare outlines. That with every passing year he was sought after more annoyingly by autograph hunters can be imagined. Brahms took care of this piece of business *alla breve*, too: five lines for notes tossed off unevenly, a theme of two or at most three bars, and his signature. Period.

Once, however, there was a case of an autograph that went far beyond this easy model, a formal letter that was intended for publication. The music writer La Mara (Fräulein Marie Lipsius in Leipzig), to whom we are indebted for numerous interesting publications, asked Brahms for his permission to reprint in a volume of musicians' letters several missives of his that had found their way into her hands. The courteous request of this lady, with whom he was personally acquainted, seemed to upset him greatly, as the following letter to me of May 1885 shows:

Dearest friend! The enclosed two letters will make the situation clear to you. Impractical as always, I recently did not wait for your card, but gave Dr. Fellinger, who was visiting me, a letter addressed to you and the unsealed one addressed to Lipsius—with my instructions to mail the latter in case he did not have a chance to show it to you in Vienna. But Mrs. Fellinger copied the letter. Thus I can send it to you after the fact and ask you for a favor. Read it and tell me whether it is foolishness or contains any of the same! I consider myself capable of all kinds of things in this regard—but I would be happy to hold my tongue! I can very well write another one in retrospect, or make changes in this one: So, I ask for your opinion!

Give Simrock my best regards, and [tell him] I am writing to him either yesterday or tomorrow! But the devil take it, if one is plagued like this with letters from and to Miss Lipsius, then the already scant desire to write letters is entirely for the birds.

So, you, too, forgive the peevish letter—but this business annoys me. My heartfelt greetings; live as well, contentedly, and happily as you deserve.

Cordially, your J. Brahms.

For further explication I permit myself to append Brahms's letter to Fräulein Lipsius, from the *Musikerbriefe* which she later published:[7]

Vienna, 27 May 1885

Dear Fräulein!

Indeed I have the temerity to ask you to leave the letters in question unpublished. I know and admit that I never write otherwise than reluctantly, hurriedly, and carelessly, but I am ashamed when an example like yours comes to my attention. It takes a kind of courage to write to an unknown, educated, well-intentioned man as carelessly as I did in this case. But even admitting that such letters get printed, to give one's express approval to that—that would be something else than courage! If you will permit me to state expressly here that no one can do me less of a favor than to print letters of mine—nevertheless I will be glad to make an exception for this one. You can include it in your book all the more easily, since your readers will learn from it that it is I, rather than you, who have taken care not to draw from the intended inclusion of my letters any conclusion as to the content and value of the remainder of your book.

There are, as I know not only from Schiller and Goethe but also from the most enjoyable personal experience, plenty of people who write letters gladly and well. But then there are also people like me, and their letters, if the writer otherwise deserves it, should be read and interpreted with indulgence and great care. For example, it pleases me to save a letter from Beethoven as a memento; but I can only be horrified when I imagine all the things such a letter may be taken to mean and explain!

I feel similarly about the posthumous works of a musician. How eagerly I have always tracked down such traces, studied and copied them many times. For example, how dear to me, in the cases of Haydn and Franz Schubert, were these countless, superfluous proofs of their diligence and genius. I have always wished that such valuable and instructive treasures would be copied for larger libraries, so that they would be available for the person who is seriously interested in them. I do not wish to elaborate on the very different sentiments with which I see these beloved treasures in print—or myself work to ensure that this is done, at least, in an orderly fashion! It is unbelievable how, in this case, things get misunderstood and misinterpreted—and whether such publication is necessary, good, or superfluous and even harmful, I don't know!

Taking into account the risk that you will find the beginning of this epistle to be vain hypocrisy, I remain your respectful, devoted

J. Brahms.

How characteristic, how substantive this letter is in all its brevity. It proves that Brahms lacked only the desire, not the talent for writing. Once he saw himself compelled, in place of his precious postcard, to get out a clean sheet of stationery and exercise some care in style and expression, he could write masterfully—clearly, concisely, not at a loss for any sharply descriptive term. Since for him thoughts were there in order to be kept silent or to be expressed in musical tones, he mistrusted his ability to express them in firm literary form. And yet he was compelled to express his written thanks, now for a high honor, now for the election to an academy—for

Brahms nothing could be more unpleasant! In such cases it was his custom to come grumbling to me with his draft. Not only did I not want to
alter a word, but I was forced to admire many a sentence for its precise
expression and sculpted form. Brahms always instinctively found the right
medium between excessively humble modesty and proud self-confidence.
Once he wanted to sweeten the onerous task by at least making a joke. He
walked in with an entirely unaccustomed, mysteriously pleased expression and whispered that he had written something quite new and wanted
to show it to me—not a soul had seen it yet. After he had kept me dan-
gling for some time in the most delighted anticipation, he cautiously pulled
out his draft of an acknowledgment letter (if I am not mistaken, for the
Order of Maximilian) and gloated over my disappointment.

It is regrettable that Brahms was only very rarely and reluctantly induced
to respond by letter to musical questions. His profound musicological
and technical knowledge, combined with such clear, sharp judgment, could
have provided a treasure trove of information, whether he was speaking
about his own projects and compositions or those of others. Brahms was
capable, in private conversation, of commenting on musical matters with
such fluidity and liveliness, especially if they were of current interest—
matters of the Musikverein, programs of our larger concerts, etc. With pen
in hand he became monosyllabic. As for speaking about his own compositions or plans, his own reticence held him back all his life. Just as sensitive
was the response of his modesty to praise from others. His unwillingness
to pass on flattering letters that had been sent to him was very difficult to
overcome. The request by the widow of Hans von Bülow that Brahms
entrust to her, for purposes of publication, several letters of her husband's caused Brahms great uneasiness, for Bülow's letters overflowed
with enthusiasm and devotion. Nevertheless, Brahms could not give Mrs.
Marie von Bülow a negative answer. So he sought out from among his
large correspondence with Bülow five or six insignificant notes, in which
nothing was discussed but concert programs, apartment furnishings, and
other practical matters, and brought them to me. I declared that it was an
injustice to Bülow to attempt to represent this brilliant virtuoso of letter-
writing, as well, in a published collection, by means of such trivial and
uninteresting scraps. Brahms thanked me sincerely for my plainspoken
veto and decided, with a heavy heart, to deliver more extensive and substantive letters of Bülow's to his widow.

On the occasion of his adaptation of German folk songs, Brahms sent
a number of letters with a significant musical content to Professor [Philipp]
Spitta in Berlin. Another extensive and content-rich letter was occasioned
by youthful compositions of Beethoven's, with which he had become

acquainted through me —the Cantata on the Death of Emperor Joseph II and the Cantata on the Accession of Emperor Leopold II.[8] Both works had never been printed and were thought to be lost. A musically educated businessman, Herr Friedman, had purchased the two scores, copied in a clear hand, from a secondhand dealer in Leipzig and sent them to me to examine. I was just about to leave for Karlsbad and sent the cantatas, after leafing through them hurriedly, to Brahms, who wrote me the following letter about them in May 1884:

Dear friend! You departed and left me a treasure, without having looked at it yourself. I must write you a few words of thanks on the subject so that you will have an idea what the treasure signifies. For it is quite beyond doubt that, with this, the two cantatas have been found, which Beethoven wrote in Bonn on the death of Joseph II and the accession to the throne of Leopold II. In other words, two important works for chorus and orchestra from a time to which, until now, we could not ascribe any compositions of significance. If it were not for the historical dates (1790), we would certainly guess at a later period—but only because we would know nothing of this earlier time! But even if there were no name on the title, one could guess no other author—it is all Beethoven through and through! There is the beautiful and noble pathos, the grandeur of the feelings and fantasy, the power, yes even violence of expression. And then there is the voice-leading, declamation, and, in these last two areas, all the peculiarities that we can observe and ponder in his later works.

First, I am naturally interested in the cantata on Joseph II's death. On this subject there can be no "occasional music"! If we were to celebrate today that unforgotten man, who is still not replaced, we would do so as warmly as Beethoven and everyone else did at that time. And for Beethoven it is not occasional music, either, when one considers that the artist never stops developing artistically, nor struggling, and that one is probably more likely to observe this in a younger artist than in a master. The first lament is already entirely [Beethoven] Himself. You would not doubt it at any note or at any word. A recitative follows, extremely lively: "Ein Ungeheuer, sein Name Fanatismus, stieg aus den Tiefen der Hölle . . ." [A monster, his name fanaticism, climbed out of the depths of hell . . .]. (In an aria he is trodden to death by Joseph.) I cannot help myself: At this point it is a particular pleasure for me to think back to that time and—as the strong words indicate—to the way the whole world realized what it had lost in Joseph. But the young Beethoven also knew what great things he had to say, and he said them loudly, as is appropriate, in a powerful prelude. And now, to the words "Da stiegen die Menschen ans Licht" [Then mankind ascended toward the light], comes the magnificent F-major movement from the finale of *Fidelio*.[9] There, as here, the touching, beautiful melody is given to the oboe. (Admittedly, it doesn't agree with the vocal part, or does so only with great difficulty.) We have many examples of the way our master used his ideas a second time in a different place. Here I find it especially pleasing. How deeply Beethoven must have felt the melody in the cantata (in other words, the meaning of the words)—as deeply and beautifully as he did later when he sang the love of a woman—and of liberation—to its end. After more recitative in arias, a repeat of the first chorus closes the work; but I don't want to describe it further; nor, in any case, the second cantata. For here the music itself is more interesting than any particulars concerning Beethoven.

But now, dear friend, in my thoughts I already hear you asking when the cantatas will be performed, and when they will be printed?*And here my joy is at an end. Printing has become so much the fashion, especially the printing of things that have no claim to it. You know my long-standing, fond wish that the so-called complete works of our masters—even in the case of their secondary, but certainly in the case of their most important works—should not be printed all too completely, but—and here *really comprehensively*, should rather be incorporated in good copies into the larger libraries. You know how eagerly I have sought, at all times, to get to know their unpublished works. However, to possess *everything* of many a beloved master *in print* is more than I wish for. I cannot find it right and proper for amateurs and young artists to be seduced into filling their rooms and their brains with all the "complete works," and thus confusing their judgment.

The honor of a complete edition has not yet fallen to our Haydn.[10] And a really complete edition of his works would be as impossible as it would be impractical; but perhaps—and how desirable, in comparison—a *selection copied* from among them, and this in multiple copies, in our public libraries. How little, in comparison, is done regarding new editions of various works whose study and transmission would be desirable. So, for example, older vocal music of all sorts. You will object that they are not needed, either—but they should be and they

---

*On Brahms's initiative, the *Cantata on the Death of Joseph II* had its premiere performance by the Gesellschaft der Musikfreunde in November 1884.

will be more and more, without a doubt. Here sacrifices would be quite in order and would certainly be worthwhile in every respect.

But these are vast themes, and I won't fantasize more variations on them for you; they develop all too exclusively from a minor key, and I know very well that the same are quite possible and necessary in major.

But come soon and share the very special feeling and pleasure of being the only person in the world besides myself to know these deeds of a hero.

Cordially your   Johannes Brahms.

2.

Brahms, whose works were composed in large part (and probably the most beautiful part) in Austria, by no means limited himself to his own musical creation. He also developed a varied practical activity that richly benefited the arts in Austria. An almost negligibly tiny part in all this was played by instruction. This is the activity, even if it is only practiced to a modest extent, that disturbs the musician most sensitively in the sphere of his own musical thought, and therefore it seems to be qualitatively the most unwelcome. As far as I know, the well-regarded concert singer and voice teacher Frau Neuda-Bernstein is the only talent in Vienna who can boast of having enjoyed piano lessons with Brahms.[11] In his capacity as a member of the board of directors of the Gesellschaft der Musikfreunde, which enjoyed an inestimable advantage as a result of having such a great authority in its midst, Brahms worked zealously for the promotion of musical education in its broadest extent. Brahms was able to have a strong influence on the programs of the concerts of the society, and also on the naming of professors at the conservatory, as well as artistic directors. He occupied a position as conductor in Vienna on two occasions, each time only for a short period: with the Singakademie (1863) and the concerts of the Gesellschaft (1872–74).

Another musical office that Brahms occupied, not in the public eye, but influentially and with quiet seriousness, was his membership of more than twenty years on the Commission for the Conferring of Artists' Scholarships.[12] In 1863, the Ministry of Education had given life to this new institution, whose activity consisted in the awarding of annual scholarships to deserving and talented artists who had already emerged as creators of independent works. As a result of this measure, a separate, permanent budget was created for the first time, dedicated by the state to the education and support of individual artists. Three members of the commission were named in each of the three sections (poetry, visual arts, music), and together they evaluated and judged the requests that had been submitted. The section on music was entrusted to me, and thirty-four years later it still rests in my hands. At first, Esser and Herbeck were my colleagues; later Brahms took Esser's place, and Goldmark Herbeck's.[13] Unfortunately, Goldmark, on account of his extended stay in Gmunden, was rarely in a position to participate in the evaluation of the compositions that had been submitted. Therefore, the business at hand was almost always dispatched only by Brahms and myself. In general, I would go over the submissions, which were usually very numerous, alone, discard whatever was not in accordance with the guidelines or was unquestionably bad, and then consult with Brahms about the rest. If there were only a few submissions that invited more serious consideration, I would make myself comfortable on the sofa with a cigar and read the pieces that had been sent in. In this I had frequent occasion to admire Brahms's rapid comprehension and the accuracy of his judgments. When there was a larger quantity of compositions that demanded more exact evaluation and mutual consideration, then I would send them, with my recommendation, to Brahms, from whom I would receive the whole, often very weighty package back complete with his written comments. These were generally kept very short— for his suggestions almost always corresponded to mine—but were usually peppered with satirical remarks about this or that talentless supplicant.

Thus Brahms was untiring in his efforts to serve his adoptive fatherland Austria with word and deed in affairs of music pedagogy. In the summer of 1889, when Brahms received the Austrian Order of Leopold at the request of the Minister of Education Dr. von Gautsch, there was a general feeling of happiness and gratification. When I wrote to congratulate Brahms (with a certain amount of feigned surprise) on receiving this distinction, I received the following answer from him:

Ischl, 1889

Dear friend! A thousand thanks for news of you, which I had been looking forward to quite eagerly. I hope your plans remain as they are, or become even more favorable once you get to Ischl.

What surprised and astonished me was *your* astonishment and surprise about my medal and the fact that the people "in high places had such a clever idea." The latter thought had never crossed my mind at all, when I wondered to whom I might actually owe the medal. There are, after all, very complicated machines at work in the state;

this time I believed you, above all, to be in complicity and one of the instigators. Otherwise I am looking about myself in a futile effort to figure out who might have suggested and promoted it. In general, there is more to it than mere artistic attainment, and as far as all this "more" is concerned—whatever name it may go by—I have precious little to show for myself.

This time, for the first time, I was at least well behaved afterward, as I answered the many telegrams, letters, and cards! I had such a friendly impression that the Austrians *as such* were happy about it that I necessarily had to thank them politely. I would like to ask you, in all earnestness, to tell me how I should comport myself toward those "high places." May I at least be permitted to wait until after the official notification? Should I write to the Ministry of Education, or to His Majesty directly? Or should I request an audience?

You will find me here until—I must finally leave for the music festival in Hamburg! I must, for my Honorary Citizen adventure was entirely too lovely and agreeable, with everything that came along with it.[14] However, I am alarmed to see my telegram to the mayor in print! It sounds altogether foolish, "the greatest beauty, which can only come from human beings"—as if apart from that I had been thinking of eternal salvation! But our dear Lord did not occur to me at all in that connection, I was only thinking in passing about the so-called gods and the fact that when a pretty melody occurs to me, it is far preferable in my mind than an Order of Leopold, and if they should grant me a successful symphony, it is dearer to me than all honorary citizenships. With cordial greetings; come soon!

3.

Before he became a regular summer guest at Ischl, Brahms's custom had been to spend his summer vacation alternately in Baden-Baden, Wiesbaden, Thun (in Switzerland), and a few times in Pörtschach and Mürzzuschlag. From all these places I received greetings from him; letters or notes, which without claim to any significant content still contained one or the other interesting piece of personal information, striking expression, or lovable trait. I have the sense, and submit myself willingly to it, that after any great loss our hearts hold fast to even the most modest tokens of memory. In the case of the following letters from the '60s and '70s, I was thinking first of Brahms's special friends and admirers. But where didn't he have those!

The first letter refers to Brahms's selection as director of the Vienna Singakademie in the year 1863. The invitation reached him in Hamburg and found him not entirely decided to accept it. "It is," he wrote to the head of the association, "a particular kind of decision that entails giving up one's freedom for the first time. However, whatever comes from Vienna sounds twice as beautiful to a musician, and whatever calls him there, tempts twice as strongly."

He wrote to me in the summer of 1863 on that subject:

My dear friend! You will be surprised that the most delighted and grateful reply does not arrive more rapidly than your own and other friendly letters reach me. But I feel like someone who is praised undeservedly and would prefer to hide for a while. I, who after receiving the telegraphed dispatch (from F., who always has to have the upbeat!) firmly desired to be satisfied to have received such an honorific offer and not to tempt the gods further. But now I shall accept it all the more certainly, and come. And since for my part there is no remaining question except whether I have the courage to say "yes," why, it shall come to pass. If I had declined, my reasons would only have seemed strange to the Academy and to you Viennese in general. Here I must also send you my most sincere thanks for your book *On the Musically Beautiful*, to which I owe many hours of enjoyment, of clarification, indeed of literal relief.[15] Every page invites one to build further on what has been said, and since in doing so, as you have said, the motives are the main thing, one always owes you double the pleasure. But for the person who understands his art in this manner, there are things to be done everywhere in our art and science, and I will wish we might soon be blessed with such excellent instruction on other subjects. For today, with cordial greetings and thanks, your

Joh. Br.

The following letter from August 1866 refers to the Waltzes for Four Hands, op. 39, which were dedicated to me.

Just now, writing the title of the four-hand waltzes, which are to appear shortly, your name occurred to me quite of its own volition. I don't know, I was thinking of Vienna, of the pretty girls with whom you play four-hands, of you yourself, the lover of all that, the good friend and whatnot. In short, I feel the necessity of dedicating it to you. If it is agreeable to you that it should remain thus, then I thank you most sincerely; but if for some reason you do not wish it, then express yourself on the subject and the printer will receive the counter-command. It consists of two volumes of innocent little waltzes in Schubertian form. If you don't want them and would rather see your name on a proper piece with four movements, "your wish is my command." In the next few days I am leaving for Switzerland. Shall I complain to you about the fact that I was not in Vienna last winter? My arrival next year can express it better. In considerable haste and old friendship your

Joh. Br.

Hermann Goetz, the composer of the *Taming of the Shrew*, had left behind at his death a great opera, *Francesca di [sic] Rimini*, which was performed for the first time on September 30, 1887, in Mannheim, as completed by Ernst Franck. Concerning the quite widespread belief that Brahms had a hand in this completion, the latter wrote me from Baden-Baden in October 1877:

Dearest friend! In the *N. Fr. Presse* [*Neue freie Presse*] it says that I completed the *Francesca di Rimini*. This is not true; Franck orchestrated the overture and the third act alone, following the sketches; I merely looked his work over and was enormously pleased at its lovely seriousness and diligence, which I would not have thought him capable of. On the occasion of the *Taming of the Shrew*, by the way, he demonstrated the same loving devotion, then as now with the best of results. He can really not be praised enough for what he has done for Goetz (his idol), and if you had known that excellent man and most estimable artist, you would have had the most intense joy over little Franck, to whom alone Goetz owes a peaceful death and his Francesca owes her life.[16]

But the notice to which you refer is found in many papers; I, however, do not like to write. Wouldn't you like to devote a couple of words to this? I can only excuse the fact that I let it go for so long because if the opposite were the case I would most assuredly remain silent. . . . Actually, I had written so small because I wanted to chat with you quite unhurriedly, but since then the pen has lain idle for hours. I have been spoiled for letter-writing. I hope to enjoy a few fine fall days here in Liechtenthal (near Baden-Baden). But it won't last long and then the Karlsgasse and the others will reclaim me. Dessoff comes by often and is very pleased—even when he sees new notes of mine. But now transmit my best greetings to your own and other households! Until our next happy reunion!

A letter from Pörtschach from September 1878 refers to the Hamburg Music Festival with which the anniversary of the Philharmonische Gesellschaft in that city was to be celebrated.[17] I had received an invitation to it, along with the urgent request to give the committee word as to whether Brahms, from whom no answer had been received, could definitely be expected in Hamburg. Brahms responded to my inquiry as follows:

Pörtschach am See, September 1878

You have preached the doctrine of deportment to me in public once before; I do not wish that it should happen again through no fault of my own, and therefore I am telling you that it is the fault of the Hamburgers if I do not appear at their festival. I have no occasion to display good breeding and gratitude; on the contrary, a certain amount of incivility would be appropriate, if I had the time and inclination to ruin my mood with it. But now I won't spoil yours, either, by detailed descriptions and will therefore say only that despite an inquiry there has been no mention of any honorarium or other remuneration. This is a highly questionable valuation of me, poor composer, and I lose every right, for example, to sit next to your wife at the feast table! So I beg this time for consideration toward my already damaged reputation as a well-bred fellow. In the matter of the symphony I ask for no special consideration, but I fear that if the conducting is not entrusted to Joachim, as I wish, there will be a miserable performance. Now, the dinners in Hamburg are good, the symphony has a propitious length—you can dream yourself back to Vienna while all this is going on! I am thinking of going to Vienna quite soon, but I have again been excellently pleased in Pörtschach. With cordial greetings for you and your wife.

Your J. Br.

In spite of this very dubious reply, Brahms came to the festival after all, and it went off brilliantly and enjoyably. Clara Schumann, at that time already sixty years old, played Mozart's Concerto in D Minor with perfect mastery and youthful fire. The following evening [September 28] brought Brahms's Second Symphony, which he directed himself after a welcome that included an orchestral flourish and a laurel wreath. Joachim played the first violin. After the symphony, the ladies from the chorus and the first few rows of seats in the audience threw Brahms their bouquets. He stood there, as it says in his lullaby, "covered with roses, trimmed with carnations." During the outing to Blankenese many interesting and famous artists found themselves on the deck of the steamer in animated conversation: Brahms, Ferdinand Hiller, Niels Gade, Friedrich von Flotow, Theodor Kirchner, J. [*recte*: Karl] Reinthaler, and others.

In May 1880 I had received the newest volume of songs (op. 84) in Karlsbad and written to him, quite captivated by the "Vergebliches Ständchen" (no. 4). He responded from Ischl:

> I am full of pleasure as I thank you for your letter, for it was really a very special one for me, and I am in an extremely good humor as a result of the good-humored correspondence! In my position, one can't write a great N.B. after something just because one thinks one is in a position to do so, but it is the most pleasant form of flattery when someone else does.
>
> And this time you have hit my bull's-eye! For this one song I would give up all the others and the W-album in the bargain.[18] But from you the confirmation is of immensely serious value to me! I have known for a long time that your excellent sniffer doesn't miss any really excellent morsel (this is more annoying when we are eating oysters).
>
> With dedications I am in a bad spot. I owe so many, more or less, that I hesitate to begin paying them back. I must think up a special method of proceeding, perhaps by publishing a thematic catalogue in which a fancy name appears next to every piece?! Talk that over with Simrock some time. —
>
> It would be very nice if you would come to Ischl; it is really splendid here and taking walks extremely pleasurable.
>
> Whether I am actually going to Bayreuth? Bülow, who is going there in August with his bride, is also trying to seduce me, or rather asks me whether I would like to join them.* If you should happen to be about to throw away a Bayreuth brochure in a fit of annoyance, then put a postal wrapper around it instead and send it here; for us such things are exotic and interesting.
>
> Please give my best regards to Simrock, Dvořák, and even better ones to your singer. And you yourself are warmly thanked, again, for your friendly words.

---

* Brahms never visited Bayreuth.

In Karlsbad I had thanked Brahms cordially for the third and fourth volumes of his Hungarian Dances for four hands, which he has played there so often with my wife. In these two volumes, Brahms really works little miracles of harmonization and rhythm, which raise the art of the "arranger" far above that of the anonymous "singer" of these simple folk melodies. One should give the same melodic raw material to another composer, and see what he or she would make of it! By the way, two of these pieces are entirely Brahms's own invention, without his finding that important enough to boast about.[19] Brahms wrote back to me in Ischl:

> I am so pleased about your pleased and nice words that I must let you know immediately. You know, the things give me pleasure myself, for once. How happy I am if others feel the same way and are kind enough not to make a secret of it! With best greetings to your second half and your second pair of hands cordially your J. Brahms.

4.

Brahms's general education was much more comprehensive and deep than one might think on superficial acquaintance with him. The things that had been denied him through the hardships and deprivations of his youth he later made up with persistent energy. An admirably quick gift of comprehension and an equally extraordinary, never-failing memory supported him in his studies. Often one would only discover years later, after some cue gave him the necessary impetus, how well versed he was in literary matters. It never occurred to him to flaunt his wide reading; he preferred to hide it. The absolute opposite of Liszt, who constantly tosses around Dante, Shakespeare, Goethe, Michelangelo, and Albrecht Dürer in his musical essays, along with Plato, Spinoza, Kant, and Hegel, of whom he himself has scarcely read a single chapter. Perfectly obnoxious, in Brahms's eyes, were those newest critics who quote Schopenhauer and Nietzsche the minute they take up a new opera or symphony.

How intimately Brahms knew our classical literature, how deeply he had absorbed the masterworks. Some of his literary sympathies were not entirely comprehensible to me, for example, the fact that he could read Jean Paul over and over again, right into his old age. The same was true of the comic novels of Swift and Fielding, the latter in German translation. He had no talent for foreign languages and never learned enough French for even the most minimal household use. He approached the latest literature with a very hesitant selectivity. The trouble with the new books is undoubtedly that they prevent us from rereading the old ones. The realistic products of our modernists incited Brahms's dislike; but he read the novellas of Gottfried Keller and the poems of his friend J. V. Widmann in Bern with never-failing pleasure.

Brahms even followed politics—that otherwise avoided and despised Cinderella-subject for artists—attentively. In one of his letters I even find passionate involvement with a particularly Austrian incident. In June 1883 he writes to me from Wiesbaden:

> Dearest friend! I must shout out my hurrah to someone, my happy, firm hurrah to the professors in respect of your letter to Rector Maasen.* One must be as much an Austrian as I am, love the Austrians as much as I do, to feel sad every day I read the newspaper, and then suddenly, as now, to feel such a deep pleasure. Unfortunately, I regularly read only the *Fremden-Blatt*, which a princess-friend of mine receives here and sends to me, I am still grateful to Lamezan for the box on the ear he gave the paper this winter. If I could only get the confiscated issues, I would subscribe to the *Neue freie Presse*!
>
> And friend Billroth still doesn't want to become a Wagnerian? What is he waiting so long for; sooner or later he will have to do it.

Brahms had become a good Austrian and at the same time remained a faithful Reichs-German. He read the historical works of Sybel and Treitschke, and finally Oncken's book about Kaiser Wilhelm, with the warmest sympathy and interest.[20] He had a passionate admiration for Bismarck, was pleased to receive presents of each of his portraits, loved his speeches, and was familiar with everything that had been written about the Iron Chancellor. Three weeks before his demise, when the treacherous illness had robbed him of all pleasure in living, he complained to his friend Herr Arthur Faber that he could no longer retain what he read. "I only want to read about Bismarck; send me the book by Busch, *Bismarck and His Men*."[21]

Rodenberg's *Deutsche Rundschau* counted him among its most appreciative readers.

Among modern painters there were two in particular whom Brahms held in high esteem: the old master Adolph Menzel and Max Klinger, who had achieved fame in our days. The affection was returned in both cases.

---

* In the year 1883, in a debate in the Lower Austrian Parliament (in which, as Rector, he represented the university), Professor Maasen had come out in favor of a Czech-language elementary school.

Menzel, who despite his advanced age always remained fresh and agile, visited Brahms repeatedly in Vienna, and celebrated him with exceptional attention in Berlin. Klinger was inspired by Brahms's music to create many of his most notable works. After receiving Klinger's most recent illustrated book *Fantasies*, Brahms immediately wrote to me:[22]

> Dear friend! Just to look at the newest *Brahms-Fantasy* is more pleasure than to listen to the previous ten!* But since I cannot very well bring them to you, I would like to ask you to pay a call on me—and to bring some time, for it takes at least as long as the above-cited ten or other earlier ones.

As much as the brilliant boldness of Klinger's illustrations impressed me, I was not able to share Brahms's rapture in every case, least of all at the cover illustrations of the songs that were published by Simrock.[23] Quite incompetent to give an expert opinion, I was nevertheless unable to conceal my feeling that here the one-sidedly realistic and violently characterizing manner pushed beauty too much into the background, even damaged it without compelling necessity. I could not comprehend why, for example, Homer had to be portrayed as a repellently ugly old man with tufts of white hair all over his stark naked, miserable body—or why the charming melody of one of Brahms's songs is reflected in Klinger's work not as the figure of a lovely girl, but rather as a coarse and ordinary one. "You are not wrong," Brahms replied," but all that does not bother me—it is a work of genius." I had to think of Eitelberger, who in a mood of wild opposition once cried, "That damned thing beauty—it is responsible for all the problems of painting!"[24]

Brahms expressed his gratitude and admiration for Max Klinger by dedicating to him the *Four Serious Songs*, op. 121. From Brahms, who was always remarkably sparing with his dedications, and in recent years almost entirely avoided them, this dedication meant more than a little. It became all the more significant since the *Four Serious Songs* remained his very last work.[25] Yes, these not merely serious but inconsolable strains of death and decay were a prelude to Brahms's departure from this life, although he did not suspect it. Since then Herr Sistermans has performed them as a kind of requiem for the master himself in almost all German cities, one after the other, which added a memorial meeting for Brahms to their concerts or music festivals. Certainly these *Four Serious Songs* had always

---

* Brahms, Fantasies for Pianoforte, op. 116. To these seven fantasies Brahms clearly also reckons the three *Intermezzos*, op. 117.

been perceived and interpreted as a certain premonition of his own death, although Brahms was still in good health when he wrote them. I thought in my own mind that they had an immediate connection to the death of Clara Schumann, which left him deeply shaken. But today I must declare this supposition to be erroneous. Brahms's intimate friend Herr Alwin V. Beckerath, one of the most well-informed supporters of music in the Rhineland, writes to me from Krefeld on this subject:

> Brahms came (in May 1896) directly from Bonn, from Frau Schumann's funeral, to the country home of my brother-in-law Weyermann in Honef, where we were celebrating a small private chamber music festival together with Barth from Hamburg and a few musicians from Meiningen. On the first day Brahms was very agitated, but the beautiful, still country and the comfort of the household soon began to do him good, and instead of one day, as he had originally planned, he stayed five. On the second day he told Barth that he had something new, and would like to show it to us some time in a quiet moment. We accompanied him with pounding hearts to a remote room, where there stood an upright piano, and there he performed the *Four Serious Songs* for us, from the manuscript. "I wrote these for myself for my birthday," he said. From this you see that these compositions do not stand in any causal relationship to Clara Schumann's death. Besides the *Four Songs*, he also brought new organ pieces [op. 122]. We were all deeply moved and a sorrowful premonition filled my heart—unfortunately it proved to be right.[26]

Toward the end of his life Brahms had to overcome two painful losses in quick succession: in February 1894 Billroth died, in May 1896, Clara Schumann. It was in perfect accord with his strong, solid, and taciturn nature that he wanted to speak and hear as little as possible about it. As soon as he learned of Billroth's death, he came to me full of sympathy, but admitted that he felt something like a "feeling of liberation" on account that he no longer had to witness the sad withering away of our friend, that giant of intellect and physical strength. He expresses this later, too (from Ischl), in a few lines to me that refer to my *Billroth Recollections*, which were published in the *Neue freie Presse*:

> Let me thank you very cordially for the sincere joy that your Billroth essays have given me. This is a sacrificial offering of rare beauty and a sign of friendship of the sort that can only be given by a good man.

Even people who were not so close to him will read your words with delight; doubly so everyone to whom Billroth was dear.

As for me, let me confess why they did me particular good: They have freed me from the memory of the sick Billroth; not until now have I been freed from the painful feeling and memory of the last years and think and love the man as I knew him earlier and as you have sketched him so lovingly.*

Billroth and Brahms were joined in the most intimate personal friendship; Billroth, in addition, felt an enthusiastic admiration for Brahms's compositions. Just as he never tired of playing these through with me in four-hand

---

* Every time I attend a performance of *Wallenstein's Lager*, I take pleasure in the lines: "Ein Hauptmann, den ein Anderer erstach, Ließ mir ein paar falsche Würfel nach" (A captain, who had stabbed another, left me a pair of loaded dice). These two lines, a small eloquent memorial to the collaboration of two great poets, are by Goethe. He had inserted them into Schiller's manuscript to motivate the peasant's acquisition of the false dice. A similarly improving addition, insignificant but interesting, may be found in Schumann's opera *Genoveva*; but with the difference that here it was not the older, more experienced poet who was helping the younger, as in *Wallenstein's Lager*, but the much younger one helping the elder, the student helping the master. Fourteen bars in *Genoveva* are by Brahms. We only learn this now, forty years after Schumann's death, and only—how strange!—from the latest (fourth) edition of Billroth's letters. In response to a remark of Billroth's that he did not believe Brahms would compose an opera, the editor of Billroth's letters (4th ed., 1897), Dr. Georg Fischer, makes the following note: "Brahms did not compose an opera. But it has been unknown until now that he participated in an opera, even if it was only with fourteen bars, by writing the conclusion of Siegfried's song in the third act of Schumann's *Genoveva*." This occured in the year 1874, as the opera was about to be rehearsed at the Royal Theatre in Hannover. Frau Clara Schumann sent the singer Max Stägemann, who had been cast in the role of the Palatine Count, the Brahms addition, with the explanation that she was not only completely in agreement with it but thought this conclusion to be very desirable from the point of view of its effect. The addition is not found in the score as Schumann had edited it after the premiere in Leipzig (1850), or as it was copied later for Munich, Vienna, and Wiesbaden, or in the printed piano reduction prepared by Clara Schumann [1851]. For Hannover, the fourteen bars were stitched into the score as an addendum. When I compare this addition (which I have before me in the form of a copy) with Schumann's original, in which it is lacking, I can't help admiring the correctness of Brahms's perception. He felt that in Schumann's version the song has no satisfying conclusion, but that instead there is a questioning half-cadence on the dominant chord; further, that this half-cadence "Mich trennt keine Macht mehr von dir!" (No longer will any power separate me from you!) is followed much too quickly and abruptly by Siegfried's words, "Wer sprengt so eilig ins Thor herein?" (Who gallops so hurriedly through the gate?). Thus it was as much in the interest of the drama as of the music alone that Brahms separated the two so heterogeneous halves of this scene by means of the insertion of his fourteen helping bars. Today this has little practical relevance; *Genoveva*, musically so noble and deeply felt, but dramatically hesitant and anemic, finds all doors closed to it—with or without the Brahmsian insert. But for the history of the opera and for admirers of Brahms and Schumann it is a particularly appealing item.

versions, so also he never failed, after the premiere performance of any new Brahms piece, to write to me about the impression he had received. I had spoken to Brahms once about these so detailed, beautiful musical letters of Billroth's, and Brahms, otherwise so uncurious and even less eager for praise, expressed the wish to see something of these unpublished critiques written in the spirit of friendship. I quickly gathered up three or four of Billroth's letters and sent them to Brahms. Just a moment too late, I was dismayed to remember vaguely that in one of these letters there was a cutting remark about Brahms. Billroth, namely, comparing Brahms with Beethoven, made the observation that our friend, along with the great advantages of his model, also shared some of the latter's personal weaknesses; that like Beethoven he was often inconsiderate and painfully harsh toward his friends, and that he could no more rid himself completely of the effects of his neglected upbringing than Beethoven could. I was not only perfectly miserable that I had acted so carelessly toward my two best friends, but had to fear, in the balance, that Brahms, in one of his sarcastic moods, might tease and embarrass Billroth about his remark. Brahms rescued me promptly from my distressing state. His answer to my letter of apology is as remarkable and straightforward as it is revealing about his character:

> Dear friend! You need not worry yourself in the slightest. I barely read the letter from Billroth, stuck it back in its envelope, and only shook my head quietly. I shouldn't mention anything to him about it—oh, dear friend, unfortunately that is quite automatically how these things go with me! The fact that even old acquaintances and friends think one to be something quite different than what one is (or, in their eyes, pretends to be) is an old experience of mine. I know that earlier I would have kept silent in such a case, dismayed and taken aback—nowadays I am long since calm and take it as a matter of course. To you, good and kindhearted man, that will seem hard or bitter—but I hope that I have not strayed too far from Goethe's dictum: "Blessed is the man who can shut himself off from the world without hatred."[27]

> Very cordially your
>
> > J. Brahms

The two last letters of Brahms that I possess have a long history. They concern several letters of Robert Schumann (from Endenich sanatorium, near

Bonn) to his wife and to Brahms. The latter, who knew of my enthusiastic veneration for Schumann, the musician and the man, had sent me the letters to make copies of them more than twenty years earlier. I would have liked very much to see them printed, these touching communications, which show us the ailing Schumann in a kind of mild and transfiguring light. He therefore asked Clara for her permission. She gave it, by letter, after some hesitation. But later, with the anxiousness that was peculiar to her, took it back again. Since neither Brahms nor I had the slightest wish to oppose the sentiments of the venerated woman, we did not speak further about this matter. Not until after Clara's death did our conversation turn to it again; in a letter to Brahms I expressed the wish that these last utterances of Schumann's might not be lost to his faithful congregation. Brahms initially responded to my presentation with the following note (July 1896 from Ischl):

> With my whole heart in agreement with you, I am sending this on ahead only because it will probably become a longish letter that reiterates my yes, and I am also occupied with the thought of writing to Marie Schumann.— So: until then!
> Very cordially your J.B.[28]

And in fact the "longish letter" (it reached me at the end of July in Heringsdorf) did not keep me waiting for long. It reads:

> Dearest friend! Everything that you write is accurate and true and of concern to both of us. So I shall only say briefly that a portrait of Robert Schumann in Endenich from your pen was always my fervent wish. Like you, I had Clara's consent. Then came N. N.'s involvement and her change of heart. It affected me more severely than it did you—but for your sake, which I tried, like other things of this sort, to get over in silence.
> Confidential dealings with women are difficult—the more difficult, the more serious and confidential the matters at hand. In this case one must take into account as a mitigating factor that Frau Schumann did not see her husband at that time and it is understandable that she did not like to hear mention made of the sick man. Now Maria is in possession of the entire written estate and may dispose of it. Again I ask you to consider how difficult her situation or that of the three sisters is—toward such a possession!
> I do not believe that they will do anything without asking me for advice; but whether they will *do* anything on my advice, I do not

know. In any case, I would like to present our case to Maria and ask her to entrust us with the remaining material (relating to Endenich), or initially to give her friendly assent for you to use whatever is now in your hands.

Now it is my urgent wish that you should not hurry with the *publication* of your work. For it is possible that we may receive everything relating to this question, and then: I am the only one who came together often with Schumann during that time, and you are the only one to whom, rather than to my own pen, I should like to entrust my memories. Nothing remarkable will come of them, but still—shouldn't we spend a few quiet hours on it?

In earnest friendship your

J. Brahms

One can see that the matter weighed on his mind. He reports to me on the same matter in early September 1896 from Karlsbad with the following lines:

I would have sent the enclosed letter from Marie Schumann to you long ago, if I had been certain of your address. I had sent your letter to Marie at that time and asked her to entrust us with additional material having to do with Endenich. I referred in a precautionary way to the passage about "us children" by saying: They would probably overlook a certain sensitivity in this matter on your and my part. Women, etc.

Perhaps we may yet find other suitable material in Vienna—if not, we have done our best.

In the letter that Brahms mentions at the outset, Fräulein Marie Schumann answers him in the affirmative (Frankfurt, 17 August): "Do what you feel is right, in my mother's memory, and that will suffice for me." However, she responds to the wish to receive yet other letters of Schumann's with the words: "I must first have read the material through in tranquility myself and gained an overview before I give anything out of my hands. But for that *several years* will be required."

So it then remained, with only those few letters published that Brahms had communicated to me so many years ago and to which Joachim made a very valuable addition.

One had to have known Brahms for a long time to get through to the golden underlayer of his taciturn being.[29] He was as indefatigable in generous deeds as he was inexhaustible in the art of keeping them a secret. How many young musicians he voluntarily helped with a loan, "payable at some undetermined future time," that he never intended to remember of his own accord! He spared no pains to give moral support, encouragement, or recommendation to aspiring talents. Very different from certain world-famous artists, who are more likely to help out with money than with their patronage, but preferably with neither. Brahms took pleasure at every deserved success of others. It is known how energetically he expedited the general recognition of Dvořák. As honorary president of the Wiener Tonkünstlerverein (Viennese Society of Composers), whose evening receptions he attended regularly and with pleasure, he was a zealous promoter of competitions, especially chamber music competitions, to bring young talents to the fore. When it came to the examination of the anonymous manuscripts that had been submitted, he showed astonishing acuity in guessing, from the overall impression and technical details, who the author was, or at least his school or teacher. Last year Brahms was very interested in an anonymous quartet whose author he was quite unable to identify. Impatiently he waited for the opening of the sealed notice. On it was written the heretofore entirely unknown name: Walter Rabl. He was awarded the prize at Brahms's recommendation; the piece was performed publicly and recommended to Simrock, who immediately published it.[30]

Not always courteous in his manners, Brahms nevertheless possessed a pleasing courteousness of the heart. How much he enjoyed it when he could give pleasure to others, especially if it could be a surprise! Thus one Sunday morning I found him busily packing several bottles of champagne into a basket. "They are for . . . , whose new orchestra piece is being performed today. When he sits down with his family to dine after the concert, he shall have a pleasant surprise!"

Shortly before his last illness, the wife of an excellent composer who lived in Bohemia visited him. Brahms encouraged her, telling her how advantageous it would be for her husband's career to move to Vienna. "Yes," the woman said, "if only life in Vienna were not so expensive for a large family!"—"If that's all it depends on," replied Brahms, "then take as much of my wealth as you need, without further ado; I myself need very little." The good woman broke out in such intense tears of emotion that she could not respond.

In Brahms there lived a powerfully developed sense of justice that to strict jurists might perhaps have seemed all too sensitive. A characteristic story, at whose beginning I was present, but whose conclusion I did not learn about until Brahms's very last days, may serve to confirm this. Once at Brahms's apartment I met a pale, interesting-looking woman of about forty, the divorced wife of a retired officer (if I am not mistaken, he lived in Bavaria). This woman, whose nervous loneliness was kindled to flickering life only in the presence of ardent music playing, was an enthusiastic admirer of Brahms's music and no less of the composer himself. The latter visited her occasionally in her nearby apartment Auf der Wieden, moved more by humane compassion than by personal sympathy.

One day, it may have been twenty-five years ago, Brahms told me that Frau Amalie M. had died and left him some music, attractively bound volumes of Brahms's piano compositions from his first period. Every title page showed, in a delicate hand, the name of the deceased. Brahms offered me these volumes, which I accepted gratefully and still possess. Then he never again spoke of this female admirer. Not until three weeks before his death did the critically ill Brahms tell his friend Simrock that at that time he had been named by Frau Amalie as the sole heir to her quite considerable fortune. He had felt this disposition to be a severe injustice toward her former husband, had hurried without delay to the notary and renounced the estate in favor of the husband. The latter was informed at once, came to Vienna, visited Brahms, and, with thanks, took possession of the estate that had been ceded to him.

Anyone who has become lovingly accustomed to living with Brahms now feels as if our music has lost its backbone. But these insignificant pages are devoted not to his great significance as a musician. They are only intended to contribute to the understanding of the character of the noble, rare man in whom his circle of close friends has lost no less than the musical world has lost in the artist.

NOTES

1. On Hanslick's "living history" project, see Kevin C. Karnes, *Music, Criticism, and the Challenge of History: Shaping Modern Musical Thought in Late Nineteenth-Century Vienna* (Oxford and New York, 2008), chap. 2.

2. See the introduction to Hanslick, "Discovering Brahms," in this volume.

3. *Das Heimchen am Herd,* opera by Karoly (Karl) Goldmark, premiered in Vienna on March 21, 1896.

4. Marcella Sembrich, a Polish-born soprano who made her Metropolitan Opera debut in 1883.

5. The Prater was Brahms's favorite park in Vienna. It was by far the largest park in the city and possessed racing facilities and an amusement park. It had been given over to public use in the eighteenth century by Joseph II, and was the site of many annual festivities and celebrations.

6. Georg Fischer, ed., *Briefe von Theodor Billroth* (Hanover and Leipzig, 1895; 3rd ed. 1896).

7. La Mara [Ida Maria Lipsius], ed., *Musikerbriefe aus fünf Jahrhunderten* (Leipzig, 1886), 2:348–50.

8. WoO 87 and WoO 88.

9. The *sostenuto assai*, where Leonora unlocks Florestan's chains and exclaims, "O Gott, o Gott, welch ein Augenblick!"

10. A complete Haydn edition was begun by Breitkopf & Härtel in 1907 under the editorship of Brahms's friend Eusebius Mandyczewski, but only reached ten volumes. A new edition from the Haydn-Institut in Cologne began publication in 1958.

11. Probably the same Rosa Bernstein mentioned in Max Kalbeck, *Johannes Brahms*, rev. ed. (Berlin, 1912–21; repr. Tutzing, 1976), 2:135.

12. Kommission für Erteilung von Künstler-Stipendien.

13. Heinrich Esser (1818–72) was one of the principal conductors at the Imperial Opera. In 1860–61 he served as artistic director. Esser also conducted at the opening of the new opera house in 1869, directing, among other things, an overture he had written for the occasion. Johann Herbeck (1831–71) took over the directorship of the opera between 1870 and 1875 and was concert director of the Gesellschaft der Musikfreunde. Karl Goldmark (1830–1915) was a prominent composer who settled in Vienna after 1860 and is best known for his *Rustic Wedding* Symphony and several operas.

14. In the spring of 1889, Brahms had been awarded the Honorary Freedom of Hamburg; the formal ceremony took place on September 14. Five days earlier, Brahms's *Fest- und Gedenksprüche*, op. 109, had their premiere by the Cecilia Society; that must be the "festival" to which Brahms refers in this letter.

15. Hanslick's influential aesthetic treatise *On the Musically Beautiful* (*Vom Musikalisch-Schönen*) was first published in 1854 and reprinted repeatedly thereafter.

16. Hanslick uses a play on words—the German *Götze* (idol) is almost identical with Goetz's name. (*Trans.*)

17. The festival took place on September 25–28.

18. Perhaps a reference to the Waltzes, op. 39.

19. Based on remarks by Joachim, Kalbeck identifies three dances, nos. 11, 14, and 16, as "ureigenster [most authentic] Brahms." See Kalbeck, *Johannes Brahms*, 1:66.

20. Brahms had, in his library, works by both Heinrich von Sybel and Heinrich von Treitschke. See Kurt Hofmann, *Die Bibliothek von Johannes Brahms* (Hamburg, 1974). The Oncken book is Wilhelm Oncken, *Das Zeitalter des Kaisers Wilhelm* (Berlin, 1888–92).

21. Moritz Busch, *Bismarck und seine Leute während des Krieges mit Frankreich* (Leipzig, 1878).

22. Max Klinger, *Brahms-Phantasie: Einundvierzig Stiche, Radierungen und Steinzeichnungen zu Compositionen von Johannes Brahms* (Leipzig, 1894).

23. The song collections, opp. 96 and 97, whose title pages are reproduced in Kurt Hofmann, *Die Erstdrucke der Werke von Johannes Brahms* (Tutzing, 1975), 204 and 206.

24. Rudolf Eitelberger (1817–85) was the most significant and influential art historian of his day in Vienna. A medievalist, he was the founder of the Viennese School of Art History. He was also instrumental in reorganizing the Academy of Fine Arts and the city's museums.

25. The Eleven Chorale Preludes for Organ, composed in June 1896, were published posthumously as op. 122 in April 1902.

26. Further material on Brahms's activities in Krefeld and relationship with the Beckerath family is provided in Heinz von Beckerath, "Remembering Johannes Brahms: Brahms and His Krefeld Friends," trans. Josef Eisinger, in this volume.

27. "Selig, wer sich vor der Welt / Ohne Haß verschließt." The quote is from Goethe's poem "An den Mond," written between 1776 and 1778. (*Trans.*) For further discussion of this incident and an alternate translation of Brahms's letter to Hanslick, see Styra Avins, ed., *Johannes Brahms: Life and Letters*, trans. Styra Avins and Josef Eisinger (Oxford and New York, 1997), 700–701.

28. Marie Schumann, one of the surviving daughters of Clara and Robert Schumann, later collaborated with Berthold Litzmann on the publication of her mother's correspondence with Brahms.

29. The "underlayer" reference is to the practice of painting over a gold sizing. (*Trans.*)

30. This was the Piano Quartet (with clarinet), op. 1, published with a dedication to Brahms. Brahms had mentioned the Rabl work in a letter to Simrock of 17 December 1896. See Brahms, *Briefwechsel*, rev. eds. (Berlin, 1912–22; repr. Tutzing, 1974), 12:208.

Richard Heuberger

My Early Acquaintance with Brahms

TRANSLATED, INTRODUCED, AND ANNOTATED
BY STYRA AVINS

Richard Heuberger (1850–1914) was not only the choral conductor and composer he allows us to meet in this memoir: he was also an engineer and a journalist. In 1881 he secured a post as music critic for the Wiener Tagblatt, *and then in 1896 for the* Neue freie Presse, *Vienna's newspaper of record. He wrote many operas and, above all, operettas, the first of which became quite famous (*Der Opernball*). He must have had a good memory and a good ear for the spoken word, for in his two memoirs of Brahms one has the impression of hearing the voice of the composer.*

Heuberger's most extensive memoir of Brahms records his diary jottings from 1875 to 1897, during which time (especially after 1880) he regularly lunched with the composer. Heuberger apparently went directly home and set down the contents of their conversation. When Brahms discovered Heuberger's intent to publish his diary he was, in Heuberger's words, entrüstet *(enraged), and he compelled the rueful journalist to forswear the project. Heuberger promised, and kept his word. The conversations were not published until 1971.[1] A few biographers knew of his work, however, and were apparently granted some degree of access to it; the works of both Florence May and Max Kalbeck include information that could have come only from the diary.*

The little memoir presented here falls outside the circumstances of Heuberger's diary jottings, which must be the reason he felt free to contribute it to the Berlin journal Die Musik. *It provides a personal and revealing glimpse of Brahms as a human being. It was published as "Aus der ersten Zeit meiner Bekanntschaft mit Brahms," in* Die Musik 5 (1902): 223–29. *All punctuation marks, including the frequent ellipsis-style dots and the dashes (familiar to Germans as the* Gedankenstrich) *are Heuberger's. All endnotes are editorial.*

I saw Brahms for the first time in November 1867. He came to my home town of Graz, where on November 11 and 14 he gave concerts with Joachim (at the Saale der Ressource).[2] I remember precisely the deep impression that the performance of Beethoven's Sonata for Piano and Violin in C Minor, op. 30, no. 2, made on me. The two Brahms compositions played by the Master—at that time a blond, lean, markedly professorial type— appeared to me as decidedly perplexing stuff . . . and yet, they were the E-flat-minor Scherzo (op. 4) and the *Handel* Variations [op. 24]! That is not remarkable! At that time Brahms was known almost exclusively as the arranger of *In stiller Nacht*.[3] Apart from that only very few of his works were known to very few people. Here and there the B-flat Sextet [op. 18] and the B-Major Trio [op. 8, first version] were attempted with timid curiosity. Only a small circle felt a close connection with the new genius.

A few years later, at the end of April 1873, Brahms came again to Graz. He was looking for a summer place—in Gratwein, I think—and took the opportunity to spend a few days in the friendly town on the Mur.[4] On April 27, 1873, he was also present at a concert of the Graz Singverein in the Evangelical Church as well as at the final rehearsal on the day before. If the concert found him in the nave of the church, he had, so to speak, also taken part in the rehearsal, albeit not in a musical capacity. The rehearsal took place in the choir, rather late in the afternoon. At the time I sang tenor in the Singverein and played the piano at rehearsals. L. Wegschaider, the conductor, had just begun Bach's *Trauerode* when Brahms suddenly emerged, unnoticed by any of us singers, and placed himself to the left of the organist.[5] He read along in the organ part, occasionally turning pages. Gradually it became dark . . . the organist, situated in the least favorable location, could barely see. Without a word, Brahms pulled the stub of a candle from the pocket of his overcoat, lit it, and for the rest of the rehearsal provided light for the organist, who was dumbfounded by this rare distinction. . . . In this way, as I recall, was I introduced to Brahms. But my timidity in the presence of famous people caused me to content myself with the fewest possible words. The possibility of personal contact during the summer fell by the wayside, because after a few days Brahms suddenly left Gratwein. As he told me many years later, "a couple of aesthetic females" had driven him away. He absolutely could not bear anyone making a cult of his person.[6]

After I had moved to Vienna in the mid-1870s as chorus master of the Wiener Academischer Gesangverein, to which Brahms had close connections, I soon came into contact with the Master.[7] Before this happened he had had a powerful influence on me without knowing it. I had attended the sensational performance of the *German Requiem* in the Large Hall of the Musikverein (March 1875), which finally secured Brahms's fame.[8] It was all

Richard Heuberger

the more meaningful as a few days earlier, in the same place, Wagner had performed excerpts from the *Ring des Nibelungen* and was the center of musical interest. Brahms surely had not had in mind a counter demonstration against Wagner. The colossal success of <u>his</u> work was probably foreseen least of all by himself. On that day, however, Brahms had thoroughly converted me as well as so many others for whom there was nothing worth talking about besides Wagner. Now I knew that <u>two</u> great men existed.

The first personal contact was arranged by Dr. H. Staniek, then President of the Wiener Akademischen Gesangverein. He persuaded me to accompany him to invite Brahms to a performance of the "Akademische." When we called on him (in 1876), Brahms was already living at Carlsgasse 4 and received us very kindly. The visit was short, I do not recall details. Soon, though, an opportunity came for closer acquaintance. On January 5, 1877, Prof. Billroth organized at his home a grand musical evening at which choral works by Brahms and Goldmark were to be performed under the direction of both composers. At Brahms's suggestion, I directed the preparations. The rehearsals took place in the private home of the Oser family.[9] The day before the performance, Brahms and Goldmark came to the final rehearsal. Brahms, with a reputation for being testy, now conducted his *Marienlieder*, op. 22, *Abendständchen*, op. 42, and *Von alten Liebesliedern*, op. 62, with few changes to the nuances I had rehearsed. Goldmark, so thoroughly charming in private life but so generally feared at rehearsals, indefatigably practiced the same places over and over— . . .

The performances went splendidly—Brahms and Billroth thanked me warmly for my efforts; a mighty drinking party closed the evening.[10] In the same year I was once more brought together with Brahms by an affair having to do with Billroth. On December 13, the "Akademische" gave a "Billroth Evening" to celebrate its famous honorary member. Brahms could not miss that! I invited him to participate in the festivities, which were thoroughly geared to students. Without a second thought he agreed to conduct a few choruses, namely *Ich schell mein Horn* [op. 43, no. 3] and *Das Lied vom Herrn von Falkenstein* [op. 43, no. 4], which I had arranged for male chorus.[11] Brahms came to the last rehearsal on December 12 and was tumultuously greeted by the all-student chorus I had rehearsed. He immediately took over conducting and then asked if we would sing something else that we had prepared for performance. Engelberg's merry "Dr. Heine" had been studied down to the last detail; we harbored no doubts about performing it for the Master. He appeared all the more delighted and surprised that not a single sheet of music was used. I had no score, the accompanist no piano part, and none of the well over 200 singers had a page of music in hand. Brahms gave the performance uncommon praise. — After the rehearsal he went with us to Zur schönen Laterne, the pub much beloved at the time by Viennese students. He had been a longtime regular there and was well known, probably initiated by Dr. Eyrich, my predecessor as director of the Wiener Akademische.[12] That evening, the first lengthy talk between Brahms and myself took place. For the entire evening we sat next to each other, and I remember—I no longer know how we came to it—that Brahms spoke in detail about Mozart's *Marriage of Figaro*. He emphasized the exemplary way in which Mozart handled the enormous difficulties of the libretto. "Mozart composed no conventional libretto, but a complete, well organized comedy."

He was untiring in his admiration of the brilliance and technical mastery.—
The party broke up very late. The next day I picked Brahms up at his
apartment to accompany him to the celebration. I entered just as he was trying to fasten the sash from the "Akademische." He hadn't put it on properly,
I fixed it, and then we went together to the Sophiensaal.[13] Billroth came
soon after our arrival and the festivities began. Since his youth, Brahms had
known and loved the student songs down to the last detail, and he sang along
as powerfully as his totally broken and raw voice allowed. He told me that as
a boy he had a very fine soprano voice but sang too much when his voice was
changing, so that his vocal apparatus was virtually stunted.

After that I met Brahms repeatedly at Professor Gänsbacher's, his longtime friend.[14] Gänsbacher often invited him to the open rehearsals that
regularly took place at the famous voice teacher's home on Sundays at
noon. When well disposed, Brahms accompanied one or another female
student, but above all he spiced the conversation with his caustic wit.

Thin-skinned one must not be, for he gave his suggestions wrapped in
the form of a razor-sharp joke. That he knew very well.—When I once
sought to show him some of my own compositions—it was on May 10,
1879, at one of Gänsbacher's matinees—he said, "Would interest me very
much—but you mustn't be sensitive!"

I had always labored under the delusion that I was <u>not</u> sensitive, that I
tolerated and <u>loved</u> good advice . . . when I looked up the Master in his
apartment two days later and played a number of my newest things for
him—when Brahms then gave me his opinion about them—I noticed
that I was vain, childish, and very thin-skinned. I left the well-meaning
Master almost in tears. But here I would like to sketch what he said to me.

Brahms had great pedagogical talent; that has become ever clearer to
me in the course of time. Certainly not for teaching in the ordinary sense.
In this respect he resembled his friend Billroth, who only shone his light
as a marvelous teacher on those who were already skilled practitioners.
Brahms could have achieved great things with talented young people who
had already finished their studies. As far as I know, he would have been
ready to hold a kind of master class at the Vienna Conservatory—even
casually—something that had long existed at the Academy of Fine Arts.
"The couple of notes I write in winter don't matter," he once said as I questioned him on this point, remarking that he would hardly want to sacrifice
his time for that kind of work.*

---

* Brahms loved to find related occupations that apparently interfered with his work. He
always told me "You should find work that is congenial to you, so to speak, that benefits
your own work. I have always noticed that those who only 'live for art' accomplish little."

Hellmesberger, director at the time, probably had no understanding of the good fortune it would have been for the institution and for many aspiring artists to receive instruction from someone like a Brahms, to be permitted to profit from his experience gained from on high.[15]

As I armed myself for the visit to Brahms mentioned above, I packed up the manuscripts of a number of finished songs and choral things. Brahms began reading the little volume, leaning at first on the piano; then he sat down at the piano and started again from the beginning. To avoid bursting out with his very justifiable view that the pieces were hardly mature, he praised the choice of texts, saying repeatedly, "Gebildeter junger Mann—" (Well-educated young man—). He meant, however, that I, like many youngsters, eagerly went after such exotic things that I fell into difficulties I was not yet equipped to handle. He turned immediately to a very metrically complicated place in a song and showed me that the musical material did not correctly respond to the rhythm of the poem. He dealt so firmly with the construction because earlier, with a few friendly words, he had said that the mood had been captured pretty well. He dwelt particularly on a juncture of meter and rhythm that had run askew. He said, "One can certainly produce such irregularities, but they must be well grounded in the material and stand on sure footing. If you compose a phrase of three or five measures you have to watch how you return to the right place in the duple rhythm [wiederum an richtiger Stelle in den geraden Rhythmus kommen]! And that sort of construction must always be fully clarified by the bass. The bass must be a kind of mirror image of the upper voice." Then he took a blank sheet of music paper, and in the empty measures delineated only by vertical strokes, he began to write out the text I had composed so that each word stood there rhythmically correct. He thought that was a very good system for a beginner. One must always keep an exact account so that the rhythm of the word and music coincide. Then he improvised the entire song—at times quite wonderfully. That these were all merely technical things that had nothing in common with the actual <u>poetic</u> nature of musical creation was something he stressed repeatedly along the way.—Returning once more to the songs, he went into the construction of my melody in the greatest detail, honed and refined it until it had a different, fundamentally better aspect and in addition had acquired a markedly sounder harmonic underpinning. As I exclaimed, oddly enough, that it had occurred to me that way, he opined, "It <u>shouldn't</u> occur to you that way! . . . Do you think that any one of my 'few decent songs' occurred to me ready-made? I went to a lot of trouble over them . . . you know, with a song—don't take this literally—one must be able to <u>whistle</u> it . . . <u>then</u> it's good."—

Brahms also had much to criticize regarding the accompaniment. I had changed the figuration at a rhythmically unsuitable place . . . he stopped himself and showed me how, without damaging the character, indeed enhancing it, I could have moved the change of figuration to a rhythmically significant place. I'll add here that at Brahms's urging, I undertook a fundamental reworking of my Orchestral Variations on a Theme by Schubert after it had already been performed in a concert of the Vienna Philharmonic. The reworking had nothing to do with the orchestration—which Brahms had praised—but rather with a more satisfactory method of introducing new motives. He had given me hints from variation to variation as to the manner and methods I could use to change and improve them.

Continuing to correct the songs, Brahms did not keep only to the artistic, but also considered it worthwhile to discuss the mechanics of writing. He found that I had not written quarter note under quarter note, and I had thereby hampered legibility. He advised me to take care to write the slurs over groups of notes with precision; to draw the stems of notes above the middle line of the staff downward and below the middle line upward; to set the accidentals ♯ and ♭ precisely on the lines and spaces they were destined for—in short, to take more care over the outward appearance of the musical script. "Take a look at this," he said. He brought from the next room the autograph score of Wagner's *Tannhäuser* and opened the long B-major section of the second act: "On every line, on every page, Wagner has set five ♯s in their places with painful exactness, quickly and fluently written in spite of all that precision. If someone like that can write so nicely, you too must learn how!"[16] He leafed through the entire movement and almost reproachfully pointed out just about every sharp. The more Brahms talked himself into a sort of didactic wrath, the more subdued I became. I fell utterly silent, however, when Brahms reacted as though stung by my remark "that Wagner above all should be held responsible for the confusion that reigns among us young people" . . . "Nonsense—<u>misunderstood</u> Wagner has done it to you all; those of you who may become confused by him understand <u>nothing</u> about the real Wagner. Wagner is one of the clearest heads that ever was in this world!"

In the course of the interview, which certainly lasted close to two hours and by the end of which scarcely a single good shred remained of my wretched songs, I had finally fallen into an appropriately guilty mood. Brahms seemed finally to have noticed it as well, and after his fashion said a few words of encouragement. Above all, he advised me to write <u>a great deal</u>, to write fluently, and not to go looking for highbrow curiosities [*geistreichen Wunderlichkeiten*]. I have never published the songs dissected by him. According to Brahms, there was no prospect of success in reworking them. I soon understood that he was right.

In the fall of 1880—I'm skipping over several similar visits, even if they were not of such depressing content—Brahms said to me once that he had seen manuscripts of a number of my pretty songs at the home of the singer Fräulein Pauline Knee, an outstanding dilettante (at present married to Werthner in Vienna), and that he had accompanied the lady. "I suppose you will excuse me after the fact, that while playing, I changed a number of things." . . . He was of the opinion that with a few strokes all sorts of things could be presented in a more concise, more pithy, and more witty form. After a few days I appeared at Carlsgasse 4 with the volume of songs. (The volume was later published by Kistner in Leipzig as my op. 13.) Brahms first took up the song "Bitt ihn, o Mutter." He found the tone of it quite excellent but took exception to the passage "Ich sah zwei Augen am letzten Sonntag" (I saw two eyes last Sunday). At that time this phrase was about twice as drawn out as it is now. "Those must have been some eyes! —" said Brahms, grinning, "but for everyone else they are perhaps not interesting enough." — He improvised a condensed version of the spot, almost exactly as it now appears in the printed edition. I wrote it down from memory after I reached home, and kept it. — In the song *Sagt, seid Ihr es, feiner Herr,* he insisted that several "piquant intervals" in the voice part would give more emphasis to the humor of the narrator. Going on to the ballad *Die Wolke,* Brahms found the ending eminently unsuccessful. At the time I had ended the piece almost rabidly. At the words beginning with "da schlug der Donner" (the thunder struck) Brahms was in favor of a mild, conciliatory ending which he immediately improvised and which I—with very few deviations—preserved. For many a harsh word—for which, by the way, I am today still infinitely thankful—he richly compensated me on other occasions.

There can scarcely be anyone who could censure more sharply than he, but also scarcely anyone who could praise more warmly. The one arose from his tremendous seriousness, the other from his equally great goodness. Most people have paid more attention to his seriousness than to his goodness. He was a diffident person, who hid from the world, almost apprehensively, every soft emotion. Those who knew him from his mild side, however, had to love him that much more dearly.

NOTES

For the elucidation of several obscure identifications I am indebted to the very kind efforts of Mag. Thomas Maisel and Archivist Dr. Egon Bruckmann of the Archive of the University of Vienna, to Dr. Markus Urbanz, also at the University of Vienna, to Dr. Mag. Andrea Strutz at the University of Graz, and to Dr. Michael Lorenz, Vienna, all of whom went to some trouble on my behalf. My thanks to Josef Eisinger and Siegmund Levarie for reading and improving my translation, and to Prof. Levarie for his insights into Brahms's musical comments.

1. Richard Heuberger, *Erinnerungen an Johannes Brahms: Tagebuchnotizen aus den Jahren 1875 bis 1897*, ed. Kurt Hofmann (Tutzing, 1971; rev. ed., 1976). To date, copyright issues have prevented its translation.

2. Die Ressource was Graz's leading social club. It possessed a large room suitable for a variety of occasions including cultural events.

3. Presumably in the version dedicated to the Wiener Singakademie in 1863, WoO 34, no. 8. Heuberger's comment is a striking example of his provincialism, of which more later. As a choral conductor in Graz, he apparently knew nothing of the already popular waltzes, op 39.

4. That is, Graz, which lies on both sides of the river Mur. Gratwein is a small town about ten miles northwest of Graz.

5. Leopold Wegschaider (1838–1916) was active as a choral director in Graz into the twentieth century and held a number of important posts in Styria. The Trauer-Ode for the funeral of Christiane Eberhardine, Queen of Poland and Electress of Saxony, *Laß Fürstin, laß noch einen Strahl* (BWV 198), is one of Bach's grandest choral works.

6. "Ein paar ästhetische Frauenzimmer." *Frauenzimmer* is a slightly derogatory word.

7. The choral society of the University of Vienna was founded in 1858 and is still in existence as the Universitäts-Sängerschaft Barden zu Wien. In 1869 Brahms was made an honorary member after conducting the chorus in the premiere of his *Rinaldo*, op. 50, on February 28 of that year. Among other famous honorary members were Richard Wagner and Dr. Theodor Billroth, both named in 1872.

8. Recte: February 28, 1875. Heuberger's comment is another, more striking example of his curious provincialism. The fame of the *German Requiem* spread rapidly after the war of 1871, when it was played all over Germany. Moreover, by 1875 Brahms had already published the Hungarian Dances, the op. 39 waltzes, the first book of *Liebeslieder* Waltzes, and the Lullaby—music that made his name and fortune even at the time. He had been awarded the Maximilian Medal in 1872, concurrently with Wagner. But it is an interesting sidelight on the reception history of Brahms that an Austrian as much involved with music as Heuberger knew so little at that date about his music or career.

9. Josefine Wittgenstein Oser and her husband, Nepomuk Oser. Brahms was on very friendly terms with two generations of many Viennese Wittgensteins.

10. For "drinking party," Heuberger writes "Symposion," an archaic usage harking back to the original meaning of the word.

11. Solo songs from his own high-spirited days in Detmold, Göttingen, and Hamburg. No. 4 dates from 1858 at the latest, no. 3 from 1859 or earlier. Published in 1867 as op. 41, no. 1, and with a slight change of title to *Ich schwing mein Horn*, Brahms himself had arranged *Ich schell mein Horn* for four-part male chorus. A version of it for four-part women's voices was in the repertory of the Hamburg Frauenchor by 1859. Brahms must

have liked Heuberger's arrangement, which was published for men's chorus and orchestra in 1879, since a copy of it was in his possession when he died.

12. Franz Eyrich (1839–73), Doctor of Law, was the conductor of the Wiener Akademischer Gesangverein from 1866 to 1870, then honorary conductor from 1872 until his untimely death in 1873.

13. A famous gathering place and dance hall-cum-concert hall, where Strauss conducted his ballroom orchestra. In more recent times, many great recordings were made in its spacious room before the building burned down in 2001.

14. Josef Gänsbacher (1829–1911), one of the first to befriend Brahms when he arrived in Vienna. Brahms owed his appointment as director of the Vienna Singakademie in 1863 in large part to him, and they remained in amicable contact for life. A jurist by training, Gänsbacher became a member of the voice faculty at the Vienna Conservatory.

15. The violinist Joseph Hellmesberger Sr. (1828–93) was director of the Vienna Conservatory from 1851 to 1893 as well as the leader of the Hellmesberger Quartet, which he founded. For decades, he played a decisive role in Vienna's musical life.

16. It is not clear what autograph this could be. For a time, Brahms did possess Wagner's autograph of the Paris version of the *Venusberg* music from *Tannhäuser*, which is the *first* scene of the *first* act. It was given to him as a gift by Karl Tausig. It is also true that Act 2 scene 4 is in five sharps, but Brahms did not own this portion of the manuscript. Further deepening the puzzle, by the date Heuberger gives for his visit to Brahms (May 10, 1879), Brahms no longer had the manuscript. At Wagner's insistence it had been returned to him in June 1875 (for his trouble, Brahms received in exchange a gold-stamped first edition of *Das Rheingold*). The only way Heuberger could have seen a *Tannhäuser* manuscript in Brahms's flat was by visiting him before the latter's departure from Vienna at the end of April 1875—an impossibility, given that Heuberger says his first personal contact was in 1876. We are left to ponder the vagaries of the human memory, and to wonder just what it was Brahms did show him.

Heinz von Beckerath
Remembering Johannes Brahms
Brahms and His Krefeld Friends

TRANSLATED BY JOSEF EISINGER
INTRODUCED AND ANNOTATED BY STYRA AVINS

Heinz von Beckerath's memoir of Brahms is really a double one, since most of it is in the words of his father, Alwin von Beckerath (1849–1930). Heinz (1876–1940) was nine years old when Brahms first arrived as a guest in his parents' house; Alwin was a fine amateur violinist and violist devoted to Brahms's music. The friendship with Alwin flourished over the course of many years, during which Heinz grew up and made his own observations. Alwin must have had the intention to publish something about his long connection to Brahms, but never did so. Eventually it was his son who put the notes in order and contributed some of his own memories and commentary. Heinz's writing was largely unsophisticated, and he was certainly no scholar. The memoir was written with little attempt to distinguish between the remembrances of the author or his father, and we have retained its style virtually intact, adding only a few emendations in square brackets. We have made minimal modifications in the listings of the various concert programs. All endnotes are editorial.

Brahms's involvement with the von Beckerath family dates from 1874, when he struck up a friendship with a music-loving vintner and violinist, Rudolf von Beckerath (1833–88), and joined him and Fritz Simrock for a weeklong hiking expedition in the high Alps. The friendship soon extended to others in Beckerath's musical and well-to-do family: his nephew and brother-in-law, Alwin von Beckerath; his nephew by marriage, the pianist Rudolf von der Leyen (1851–1910), also a vintner; and their wives and children. Willy von Beckerath (1868–1938), one of the sons of Rudolf, sketched what is arguably the most famous portrait in all Brahms iconography— Brahms seated at the piano, cigar in mouth, arms stretched to the keyboard, feet stretched to the pedals.

The family seat was Krefeld, a Rhineland town just north of Düsseldorf. By the time of this memoir, family members were also settled in Wiesbaden and Rüdesheim.

A portion of the memoir describes a private music festival during Whitsun (Pentecost) weekend of 1896, held on the Hagerhof estate that belonged to yet another Beckerath relative, Walter Weyermann (Heinz's uncle).[1] *By chance, Clara Schumann was buried on that weekend in nearby Bonn. Brahms was in attendance at the funeral service, of course, along with several other people who appear in the narrative. After the funeral, Brahms took refuge with his friends for the next four days, traveling to Hagerhof in the company of Richard Barth (1850–1925) and Rudolf von der Leyen.*

The memoir is uniquely informative about two issues that are frequently discussed in the literature without taking into account Brahms's comments as they are related here: Brahms's wish to hear his symphonies with a "really big orchestra," and his life-long regret over his behavior toward Agathe von Siebold. Specific musical comments also find a place, with respect to tempi in the first movement of the String Quintet in F Major, op. 88, and the dynamics and effect of the opening of the fourth movement of the Piano Quartet in C Minor, op. 60. This memoir provides the clearest exposition of Brahms's intent when arranging his songs in a given opus, his view of the complete opus as a "bouquet."

The memoir appeared originally as "Erinnerungen an Johannes Brahms: Brahms und seine Krefelder Freunde," in Die Heimat (Krefeld) 29/1–4 (1958): 81–93. *It appears here in translation by kind permission of Dr. Reinhard Feinendegen, the present publisher of* Die Heimat.

On the morning of a lovely, sunny day in the early spring of the year 1885, an animated, chatty group of people wandered through the countryside of the Lower Rhine. The high-spirited company had traveled by train from Krefeld to the village of Grefrath, which is situated on the main train line to Holland. In those days Grefrath was one of many settlements in the vicinity of Krefeld in whose houses chattered the looms of the Krefeld silk manufacturers. The villages were all spotlessly clean and friendly. To the west of Grefrath the view is limited by the range of hills left by an Ice Age moraine, and from its heights one looks toward Holland; to the east, the distant view is limited by the mountain ranges beyond the Rhine. Grefrath lies at the edge of broad meadowlands through which the little river Niers winds its way. On its banks lies the small weavers' village of Mülhausen, which houses several substantial farmsteads and one of the many water mills of the region. A tree-lined country road leads there from Grefrath.

This is the road along which the high-spirited group was walking, Johannes Brahms among those leading the way, chatting vivaciously, bareheaded, hands behind his back. He was accompanied by the artists who had taken part in the previous day's concert: the soprano Frl. Maria Fillunger, the alto Frl. Auguste Hohenschild, the tenor Herr H. van der Meden, the bass Herr E. Hungar, the music director August Grüters and his wife, the concertmaster Richard Barth and his wife, as well as Brahms's close musical friends from Krefeld—altogether some twenty persons. Once they reached the little village they crossed the little river on a bridge. In the village street that follows the river's course, children were playing and Brahms delighted them with candies that he magically produced out of his coat pocket. At the lower end of the village, on the banks of the Niers, stood a large, Frankish farmhouse that had been converted into a pleasant inn. Here the party made a stop. As was the custom in that region, the farmstead was surrounded by water-filled ditches, and passing through a covered gate one entered into the area between the buildings that soon opened toward the little river. Several boats were tied up in the clear water along its banks. There the party amused itself for a while before sitting down at the flower-bedecked table where fish, fowl, and other local produce were served to them. Brahms was in the best of spirits. The concert had been very successful and the lovely sun-drenched countryside delighted these lovers of nature.

Following the midday meal, it was customary at parties to remain seated at the table for a cup of coffee, and afterward, a glass of punch, during which time Brahms closed his eyes for a while. As might be expected among a population dedicated to singing, there was no shortage of songbooks, and the small circle sang a variety of quartets in high spirits and finally, Mendelssohn's four-part chorus *Entflieh mit mir und sei mein Weib* (Come flee with me and be my wife) from *The Trilogy of Passions*.[2] My father, in those days called Uncle Alwin by Brahms, conducted and made great demands on the singers involving tempo changes and dynamics, which they followed with ease. Brahms sang along with his rough voice and amused himself royally. In the evening, the party was back in town.

I was then nine years of age. I will now continue my report, always following essentially an account written at that time by my father, for the most part in his own words, also drawing on my memory of stories told to me by my parents, as well as my own experiences. How was it that in the 1880s Brahms was so fond of coming to Krefeld, and did so often?

Krefeld was, at that time, a friendly, spotlessly clean, and wealthy town, whose only industry was manufacturing silk and velvet. The manual looms gradually disappeared and the weavers went to work in the large mechanized textile mills. The town's rural surroundings with pleasant forests had the appeal of a Lower Rhenish countryside and a climate strongly influenced by the sea. In the town of Krefeld the prominent citizenry were much devoted to sociability, the arts, and, above all, to music. Herr Musikdirektor August Grüters was the conductor of the Singverein and of the orchestral and symphonic concerts. Working together with him in the Concert Society was my father, Alwin von Beckerath, and the brother of my mother, Rudolf von der Leyen, who wrote the lovely book *Brahms als Mensch und Freund*.[3] They worked together in planning the programs.

In the year 1880, the plan was to perform Brahms's 2nd Symphony, op. 73, and the *Triumphlied*, op. 55. In the summer of 1879, my father wrote to his uncle, Rudolf von Beckerath, owner of a vineyard in Rüdesheim and a good friend of Brahms, to commission him to invite Brahms on behalf of the Concert Society to conduct the two works on January 20, 1880. A short time later, the joyful affirmative acceptance arrived by way of Rudolf von Beckerath, after which Direktor Grüters took the matter in hand. Brahms was very fond of playing with Rudolf von Beckerath, who owned a beautiful Stradivarius violin.

My father now continues his story. Brahms arrived several days before January 20 in order to conduct several rehearsals of the orchestra and the chorus. I played in the orchestra along with Rudolf von Beckerath at the second desk of the first violins. It was astonishing how Brahms contrived to transform the orchestra, for whom this music was still utterly unknown territory, so that at the performance it far outdid itself. Such pianos and crescendos the audience had never before heard, and the same applied to the chorus. That is also why the effect was so tremendous. The jubilation of the audience was indescribable. The program of the January 20, 1880, concert was as follows:[4]

Under the direction and with the participation of Johannes Brahms
Performance of the following compositions by Joh. Brahms.
1. II. Symphony in D Major op. 73,
2. Rhapsody op. 53. Fragment from Goethe's "Harzreise im Winter" for Alto Voice, Male Chorus and Orchestra. The alto solo sung by Frl. Adele Assmann from Berlin,
3. Piano pieces, performed by the composer,
4. Lieder, performed by Frl. Assmann,
5. *Triumphlied* (Revelation, Chap. 19) for Eight-Part Chorus and Orchestra op. 55.

At the society's social evening in Rudolf von der Leyen's home, I asked Brahms, with the agreement of Direktor Grüters, whether it would suit him if the concert committee also invited Joachim for the Violin Concerto next year, when Brahms would be back. To which Brahms answered: "Well, Barth in Münster plays it excellently." I then asked Grüters to put the same question to Brahms, and he received the same reply. That settled it: concertmaster Richard Barth from Münster would come next year.[5]

For the concert that took place on January 25, 1881, Brahms again arrived several days early. The program was as follows:

1) Academic Festival Overture op. 80 by Joh. Brahms,
2) Aria from *Enzio* (Caro padre) by Handel, performed by Jenny Hahn, Frankfurt a. M.,
3) *Schicksalslied* (Hölderlin) for Chorus and Orchestra op. 54 by Joh. Brahms, conducted by Joh. Brahms,
4) Violin Concerto by Joh. Brahms op. 77, performed by Konzertmeister Richard Barth, Münster, conducted by Joh. Brahms,
5) *Egmont* Overture op. 84 by Ludwig v. Beethoven,
6) Lieder,
7) Hungarian Dances by Joh. Brahms, arranged for Piano and Violin by Joseph Joachim, performed by Richard Barth, at the piano Joh. Brahms,
8) Sanctus from the B-Minor Mass by Johann Sebastian Bach for six-part chorus.

As always, Brahms stayed at Rudolf von der Leyen's, while Barth stayed with us. Both of them were manifestly very comfortable in their quarters. Barth played the concerto quite exquisitely. There was also chamber music.

Chamber Music Soirée 26.1.1881,
1) Sextet in B-flat Major op. 18 by Johannes Brahms,
2) Fantasy op. 17 for piano by Robert Schumann,
3) Lieder,
4) Quintet op. 34 by Johannes Brahms for Piano and String Quartet,
Performers: Dr. Johannes Brahms,
Fräulein Jenny Hahn from Frankfurt am Main
1. Violin, Konzertmeister Richard Barth from Münster,
2. Violin, probably Rudolf von Beckerath, Rüdesheim,
1. Viola, Kammermusikus C. Knotte, Wiesbaden,
2. Viola, Herr Hermann Friese, Krefeld,
1. Cello, Kammermusikus Hertel, Wiesbaden,
2. Cello, Musikdirektor Aug. Grüters.

Barth then decided to come to Krefeld as concertmaster with a fixed salary of 600 marks, and married. The remainder of his income would have to come from teaching and from chamber music evenings with

Direktor Grüters. I played 2nd violin in the quartet, later viola. It was the beginning of a time filled with the most serious and noblest of delights. Barth understood how to demonstrate that the best possible artistic results can only be attained through the greatest exertion of all powers and the most severe self-criticism.

With Richard Barth playing violin, me viola, concertmaster Schwormstedt cello, and Rudolf von der Leyen piano, we played the Brahms piano quartets. By the time Brahms came for the third time, in January 1883, the quartet already played well together. We had studied the A-Major Piano Quartet in particular. Brahms came six days before the concert in order to conduct the rehearsals for his B-flat Major Concerto and the *Parzenlied*. The concert took place on January 23, 1883, with the following program:

1. *Leonore* Overture by Beethoven,
2. Part V from the *German Requiem*, op. 45, for Soprano Solo and Chorus by Johannes Brahms, Soprano Solo Frl. Antonie Kufferath,
3. Concerto No. 2, B-flat Major, op. 83, for Piano and Orchestra by Johannes Brahms, performed by the composer,
4. *Gesang der Parzen* from Goethe's *Iphigenie*, for six-part Chorus and Orchestra op. 89 by Johannes Brahms, under the direction of the composer,
5. Lieder, performed by Frl. Antonie Kufferath,
6. "Hallelujah" for Chorus, Orchestra, and Organ by Handel.

Brahms was in the best of spirits because he found the orchestra to be dramatically improved and he was very satisfied with the chorus.

The concert came off gloriously. Musicians had come from far and near, and after the beautiful performance of the *Parzenlied* there was boundless enthusiasm, with shouts of *da capo* and *bis* ringing out one after the other until Brahms again raised the baton. The ladies of the chorus had brought along flowers, which they now threw at Brahms amid great jubilation. This was not as harmless as intended, for the flowers were tied into flat bouquets with wire, as was then the custom, and Rudolf von Beckerath, who sat at the first desk, had to hold his arms over the head of Brahms to shield him. The repetition of the *Parzenlied* succeeded perhaps even more wonderfully than its first rendition.

The soprano Antonie Kufferath, who was friends with us and the von der Leyens, had told Brahms that we had studied the A-Major Piano Quartet. Thereupon Brahms remarked, at the dinner table, that he had a burning desire to play his A-Major Quartet. This did take place later, in the von der Leyens' house. After the first movement Brahms said: "*Donnerwetter,* this really calls for paying attention and playing well!" There was great joy, and the difficult piece was finished quite splendidly. When Brahms made his comment, he might have been thinking back to 1880, when he was in Krefeld for the first time. Rudolf von Beckerath had then played first violin, Grüters cello, and the ancient musician Friese, viola. They played the C-Minor Quartet, op. 60, without a rehearsal, and Friese admitted to me afterward that he had gotten lost in the first movement after 20 measures and had not found his place again until the last measure. This time, Brahms was well satisfied, and as he got up from the piano, he patted my cheek lightly as he passed, the way he probably did with our children.

I would like to add to the words of my father that as children my younger brother and I were a little afraid of this, because Brahms, or Onkel Brahms as we called him, patted our cheeks quite vigorously. But this did not prevent him from always being our good friend. He liked talking with us, used to sit between us at the table in our playroom, and looked at picture books with us. My father writes: He was delightful with the children. Always stimulating and cheerful and teasing incessantly, he sat between them in the children's room for hours, or he would lie down with them on the floor where they played. Brahms called my parents Onkel Alwin and Frau Mariechen. My mother played piano very well, as did her brother, Rudolf von der Leyen.

My father now continues. Occasionally Brahms would also dine with us by himself. On such days there was a big, freshly baked ham with thick beans for the midday dinner. When the ham was being served he would exclaim happily, "And what might that be?" and ate with enormous enjoyment. The theme of the conversation changed frequently; Brahms was astonishingly well read. "Goethe read a great deal more than I," he said. Once, at a sizable dinner party, the cook inadvertently salted a large pike twice and my wife was fairly desperate. Brahms was well aware of it and helped himself twice to a large serving. And a glass of good wine was never lacking on such occasions.

For his morning pint, Brahms joined friends and visiting artists in a pleasant inn that had good Kitzinger beer. It was served to him in a jug that had belonged to old Papa Friese, and on its lid were engraved the opening measures of the Brahms Piano Quintet. It amused Brahms to push the jug suddenly toward the visiting musicians and pose the unexpected question, "What is this from?" which was often followed by rollicking laughter.

The Krefeld String Quartet—Richard Barth first violin, I second violin, Direktor Grüters viola, and M. Schrempel (cello soloist) cello, with Papa

Friese playing second viola—had studied the Quintet, op. 88, that appeared in 1882, and had performed it with great success at a chamber music evening in the winter of 1882. When Brahms arrived at the beginning of 1883, we asked him if we might play it for him. Brahms agreed immediately, and on Sunday morning the musicians assembled in our house. Brahms, very interested, wandered around the music room while we played, humming happily, his hands at his back. When Grüters played the lovely triplet theme in the first movement somewhat dryly, he interrupted with a loud "Ah, das müssen Sie etwas unverheirateter spielen!" (Ah, that you have to play a bit more like bachelor!) That aside, everything went well up to the coda of the finale, Presto $\frac{3}{8}$, which we had practiced very diligently. There we got a surprise. Brahms merely said, "Na, das ging aber flott" (Na, that was mighty speedy), and then we had to repeat the coda in an accelerated allegro tempo. (Joachim had written to Brahms that he had initially taken the whole last movement too fast.) This made it much clearer for the listener, and it was probably what Brahms wanted. He always took moderate tempi; utter clarity and a warm feeling were always what mattered most to him. (To this one might add no inappropriate rubatos, the natural flow of the melody, no accelerandos in the crescendos.)

Brahms complained to me that most singers, men and women, arranged his songs for themselves in a way that was quite arbitrary, according to however they suited their voices, disregarding the trouble he always took to assemble his lieder like a bouquet of flowers. His complaint was, indeed, quite justified. Where do you find a singer who performs entire lieder works by him, apart, perhaps, from the *Magelonenlieder*?[6] With what fine sensitivity and poetic feeling had he tied together the lieder bouquets! This is also why it is regrettable that Ophüls had so cruelly pulled these bouquets apart to have them printed in the order of their lyricists. This was without a doubt the reason that Ophüls had to wait so long for Brahms's thanks for his onerous labors.[7]

My father had to remind Brahms of this occasionally. Brahms replied that he would have found great pleasure in reading through the texts as he had arranged them, while recalling the music. He talked of flower bouquets that had been picked apart by Ophüls, who, he added, "was pleased when he finds worms [in them]." The individual songs gain quite exceptionally by their particular sequence. The famous singer von Zur-Mühlen probably sang the songs mostly as they had been arranged. At a party one evening he told my parents that he had studied the songs when they first appeared, but had then let them lie for about a year before taking them up again to sing them in public. During a dinner party he once told my parents, jokingly: "I am not an artist, I am a conjurer." I still remember his moving performance. He also told my parents that he had once sung Schubert's *Winterreise* for Bismarck, with Herr von Keudell at the piano. The next day Bismarck told him: "Mühlen, I cannot afford to have that happen to me again. The whole night through, I was coming and going" (Ich bin die ganze Nacht ein- und aus-gezogen).[8]

My father's account now continues. During an evening gathering at the home of Herr X, the president of the Concert Society, Brahms was first seated next to the wife of the then Lord Mayor, who was unfortunately not musical. After a while he winked to Frau Direktor Grüters, and on some pretext he asked her to sit next to him for he needed to speak to her. Soon afterward, Richard Barth broke a wine glass out of nervousness, whereupon Brahms called to him across the table: "Barth, just put the shards into the bookcase—gold-stamped books—and not a soul will notice them."

When Brahms came to Krefeld again in 1885, we (Barth violin, I viola, and Schwormstädt cello) played the wonderful Piano Quartet in C Minor, op. 60, with him, after we had prepared it meticulously. When he sat down at the piano, he said with a serious mien: "These are my Sorrows of Werther." We then began rehearsing the piece painstakingly. Brahms played superbly and with the deepest emotion, and the three of us did our best to follow him in that. It was noteworthy that in the first part of the last movement, he could not get the choral motive of the strings soft enough; even when we were already playing pp, he continued to shush us. It was supposed to sound like a mere breath from far away. Then the effect is indeed heartrending.

I experienced my greatest musical pleasure as a result of the Horn Trio [op. 40]. Professor Leonhardt Wolff, who had kindly left me his lovely viola, advised me to have the horn part of the trio transcribed for viola. The experiment was surprisingly successful. Barth and I studied the piece diligently with my brother-in-law, Rudolf von der Leyen, and when Brahms heard about the trio he was immediately very interested. He had again come several days before the concert, and he insisted on playing it with us. We played it first in our house, and it succeeded quite splendidly. Brahms was pleasantly surprised by the beautiful, novel sound. We had to repeat it immediately and, at his request, played it twice more at the von der Leyens'. It evidently gave him great pleasure and he shouted, "Darauf müssen wir reisen" (This we must take on tour). He immediately wrote to Simrock to have the viola part engraved.

My mother later played the Horn Trio with concertmaster Ofterdinger and the horn player Nauber, professor at the conservatory in Cologne. Herr Nauber remarked that he was particularly grateful for the beautiful piano playing and the moderate tempi, which allowed him to bring out properly the gorgeous horn passages, something that was not always as agreeably possible.

My father's account now continues. Once, after a substantial noonday meal in our home, Brahms played the piano as evening approached. In those days, his playing was in good shape. He played organ pieces by Bach that he himself had arranged for piano, and, later, Viennese waltzes.[9] The infinitely graceful appeal that he wrung from this music is quite unimaginable. The music room was on the second floor and the guests were already below in the vestibule. It was already late and some lights had already been extinguished when Brahms said to my mother, "Shall I fetch them all back up?" He then sat down at the grand piano and began to play the waltzes. Silently, they all returned to listen to the beautiful music. On another occasion in our house he played Beethoven's Sonata, op. 111, quite wonderfully, and much else.

The programs for the two concerts, on January 27 and 28, 1885, were as follows:

27.1.
1. III. Symphony op. 90 by Johannes Brahms, conducted by the composer,
2. Pogner's Address from the *Meistersinger* by Richard Wagner,
3. *Anakreon* Overture by Cherubini,[10]
4. Lieder by Johannes Brahms [op. 71, no. 5; op. 33, no. 5; op. 72, no. 5]
5. First chorus from the *Triumphlied* for eight-part Chorus, Baritone, Orchestra and Organ, op. 55 by Johannes Brahms, conducted by the composer.
   Soloist Georg Henschel, Berlin, Organ L. Brünsing, Krefeld.

28.1. Fifty-Year Anniversary Festival of the Singverein
1. "Am Himmelfahrtstage," eight-part Chorus, op. 79, no. 3, by Felix Mendelssohn,
2. Romances for four-part Chorus, op. 93a nos. 1 and 4, and no. 2 as added pieces, by Johannes Brahms, conducted by the composer,
3. Quartets for four solo voices, op. 64 no. 1, op. 92 no. 1, op. 31 no. 1 by Johannes Brahms,
4. Lieder "Memnon" and "Rastlose Liebe" by F. Schubert, "Sängers Trost" by R. Schumann and "Meine Liebe ist grün" by J. Brahms,
5. Piano Pieces: Capriccio by Robert Schumann and March by Franz Schubert,

6. *Liebeslieder*, Waltzes for Piano for Four Hands and Singers, op.
   52, by Johannes Brahms,
   Soloists: Dr. Johannes Brahms from Vienna,
           Frl. M[arie] Fillunger from Frankfurt a. M.,
           Frl. Auguste Hohenschild from Berlin,
           Herr H[ermann] von der Meden from Berlin,
           Herr E[rnst] Hungar from Cologne.

It was on the following day that the excursion which I described at the
beginning took place.

In the evening of the same day, my father continues, the whole company dined at the home of Alfred Molenaar, one of the Friends of Music.
Brahms sat next to my wife and was very animated. Following a humorous toast to the ladies by Herr Molenaar, Brahms now prodded my wife
to offer a toast to the gentlemen, saying that he would prompt her. He
tapped a glass on her behalf. My wife rose and spoke very merrily and
brightly of the "gentlemen of Creation." Brahms hissed, "That's the way,
that's the way," "better and better," and was pleased as punch with the orator, whose speech was received with great applause.

In the chamber music recitals that followed the Singverein Festival on
January 30, I had the honor and the pleasure of playing viola in the first
performance of the Two Songs for Alto and Viola with Piano Accompaniment, op. 91. Auguste Hohenschild sang and Brahms sat at the piano.
Fräulein Hohenschild sang beautifully, but in the first song before the
repeat she skipped one measure of rest. "Ah, she still owes us that measure of rest!" Brahms said to me as he left the stage. He was much amused
to hear how assiduously Frl. Hohenschild had studied the songs, for she
had mentioned to him that she was practically sight-reading them. But
Brahms will rightly have perceived this as modesty.

A younger sister of my wife was visiting while Brahms stayed with us in
those days, and in her lively way she asked Brahms for a few notes in his
hand to give to her girlfriend. Brahms quickly agreed and wrote out the
first measures of *Singe Mädchen, hell und klar.*[11] When my wife then alluded
to this unknown girl now being wealthier than we, he said in a kind voice,
"Oh, just write me a postcard when I am back in Vienna, and you two will
get something." And he kept his word, for upon sending the card to remind
him, we received by return mail the manuscript of the *Tafellied*, op. 93b,
with the dedication, "Affectionately dedicated to Alwin and Mariechen and
a few others, J. Brahms." On the lower left side, after the ending, Brahms
had written the beginning of the viola part of the first song of op. 91, and
the words "it was lovely on January 29, 1885" (the date was January 30).

Brahms could not have given us any greater joy. But we would not have had the great joy of playing with the great musician if Barth had not been in Krefeld. Owing to his enchantingly beautiful violin playing, his wonderful phrasing, his big and noble tone (he played on a Stradivarius that had been rebuilt for him; he bowed from the left, since his left hand had been injured by a glass shard when he was a child), he also ennobled the playing of his fellow players so that in our ensemble playing he actually lifted us beyond our ability. Brahms played his chamber music works with us with genuine contentment and enjoyment.

He commented to Rudolf von der Leyen that no other town offered him such pleasant music making. That judgment had not a little to do with our having thoroughly studied the music ahead of time.

Barth had the same ennobling influence on the orchestra as well. He furnished the string parts with bowings and fingerings and established separate rehearsals for strings and winds. By the time Brahms arrived, the difficult things were already surprisingly good, so that once, during a rehearsal, he loudly acknowledged the excellent preparation by the concertmaster. That was too much for Direktor Grüter's self-esteem, although it was justified. From that time on, there were regrettable differences between the two musicians, which gradually destroyed their friendship. In performances, Grüters may well have relied too much on good luck. Barth resigned his post as concertmaster in the winter 1886–87. He was still here to play the Beethoven Violin Concerto and the Adagio from Spohr's 7th Concerto in the concert of December 14, 1886. Richard Barth then became music director at the University of Marburg and, in 1894, general music director in Hamburg.[12]

That brought to an end the glorious, unforgettable time of constant music making with this outstanding violinist and musician, as well as the Brahms concerts in Krefeld.

The Krefeld string quartet had also studied Brahms's A-Minor Quartet, op. 51, no. 2, in which my father (viola) and Richard Barth (violin) had somewhat different views concerning the tempo of the last movement. In my father's opinion, Barth's tempo was somewhat too fast. My father thereupon wrote to Brahms to ask for his opinion. In response, he received the letter reproduced below. Brahms had written it on the blank page of a letter from the concertmaster in Winterthur, who had a difference of opinion with his music director regarding the tempo of the "Gaudeamus" in the Academic Festival Overture.

I also reproduce the concertmaster's letter:

Winterthur, the 10th of December 1885

Highly esteemed Master!

Revered Doctor!

Trusting in your kind benevolence, I take the liberty of taking up a few moments of your precious time by asking you to read these lines and to be kind enough to answer them.

In last night's subscription concert of the Musik-Kollegium, your Academic Festival Overture was played for the first time and, I might add, received with enthusiasm.

The undersigned concertmaster and the 2nd Conductor of the Collegium (a former student of the Leipzig Conservatory and a compatriot of your distinguished self) differed with Direktor M. with regard to the tempi of the wonderful above-mentioned overture, and this disagreement gave rise to a quarrel in which not only the two quarrelers but the Music Collegium were participants. The question regarding who is right needs to be resolved authoritatively and with great urgency.

My request to you, with which I dare to trouble you, esteemed Master, amounts to checking the enclosed tempo indications (according to MU) and kindly stating, in a few words whether you agree with them or not, and possibly providing the correct tempo markings next to them.[13] (The tempi indicated in the attachment are those employed by the director here. The quarrel revolves around the *L'istesso tempo un poco maestoso*, which, in my view, ought to be played not with a quarter note = 124, but with a half note = 80.)

Because the decision reached in this matter is of great significance for me—it is a question of going or staying for me—I had the courage to appeal to your benevolent kindness, and I hope for a kind and early answer.

> In expectation of the same, I remain
> with highest esteem and reverence,
> Your
> Hans Winderstein

P.S. The affair has already had consequences, in that the Musik-Kollegium has just informed me in writing that, until further notice, I am prohibited from exercising my duties! You can see, therefore, that clarification is urgently needed!

Now for the letter from Brahms to my father:

Dear Uncle Alwin,

You can see, I get this quite often!

But in your case, where your neck is not on the block, I can quite easily start you on a subscription for metronome markings. You pay me a tidy sum and each week I will deliver to you—different numbers, for with normal people they cannot remain valid for more than a week.

Incidentally, *you* are right, and the first violin as well!

In a decent quartet, the viola must be the retarding element—But you don't need my wisdom and I don't have any numbers.

So, please pass my very cordial greetings all around, and here and there my tender ones. I'm coming to Cologne for the 9th of February and I hope I can then swing myself up into your arms!

All the best, your J. Brahms

My father goes on:

In 1885, Brahms came to Krefeld once again with the Meiningen Kapelle under von Bülow, and on that occasion Brahms himself conducted his 4th Symphony. He stayed again with von der Leyen and told me one day that while the Meiningen Kapelle played his symphony splendidly, he had the desire to hear it also performed by a really large orchestra one day, e.g. the Frankfurt orchestra. But he had qualms because of Bülow. I told him that, in my view, this ought not to be the crucial issue. Then Brahms did indeed do it, and Bülow resented it, as he had predicted.[14]

Brahms told us also that the last time he was in Frankfurt, he had been assigned the place of honor between two elderly ladies at a festive dinner following a concert. At which he told the committee member in charge, "Couldn't we dine at a separate small table? Because, you see, Fräulein Spies and I are engaged." And in that way he spent the evening very pleasantly. Pranks like that may have contributed to the myth that there were tender feelings and even love between the two—myths that were circulated by Kalbeck and the sister of the singer Spies.[15] Anyone who knew Brahms well had to know that he would never have played such a prank if such sentiments had actually been in his heart.

On another occasion, Brahms talked about how Steinbach had once told him in Meiningen, before a rehearsal, that the Hofkapelle had studied the Orchestral Variations, op. 56a, very meticulously. Brahms was very pleased to hear this difficult piece played by such a splendid orchestra, and he was about to step on the podium and reach for the baton when Steinbach swiftly beat him to it in order to conduct it himself. "That's the way they all are," Brahms said.[16]

We met Brahms again in 1890 in Cologne, where Franz Wüllner had invited him to hear (for the first time) his 3 Motets, op. 110, just published, and sung by the superb first graduating class in choral singing. The *Fest- und Gedenksprüche*, op. 109, were also performed. The accomplishments of the chorus were overwhelmingly beautiful in both sound and expressivity.[17]

My wife asked Brahms to come to Krefeld in order to get to know our new house and our new grand piano, and Brahms did travel with us to Krefeld at that time. Again he stayed with the von der Leyens and was gracious to everyone as always, but how he did miss Barth! And so he played piano tirelessly, mostly for four hands with Rudolf von der Leyen, and mainly Schubert. Brahms also paid a visit to Musikdirektor Grüters, but, not finding him at home, he merely left his card.

In the years that followed, during the Easter and Whitsun holidays small chamber-music festivals took place in the homes of my parents and Rudolf von der Leyen, in which artists friendly with them took part. One postcard from those days has been preserved; it is from the famous pianist, Frau Professor Engelmann, née Emma Brandes, who was then living in Utrecht and later in Berlin.[18] The postcard is to Frau Luise Bezold, a woman friend of hers in Leipzig, and on it are recorded the programs of four days in Krefeld. The concerts took place in the homes of the two families, and their musical friends in Krefeld were also invited.

The participants were:
Piano, Frau Emma Engelmann, Rudolf von der Leyen, Miss Wild, England,
Violin, Prof. Richard Barth, Marburg,
Viola, Prof. Leonhard Wolff, Bonn,
Viola, Alwin von Beckerath,
Cello, Professor Robert Hausmann, Berlin,
Voice, Frau Antonie Kufferath-Speyer, London.

Saturday, 16.4.92, in the evening at Beckerath's.
Schumann, Fantasy op. 17—Canon in A-flat Major, Frau Engelmann,
Brahms, Cello Sonata F Major, op. 99, Frau Engelmann and Prof. Hausmann,
Brahms, Violin Sonata G Major, op. 78, Frau E. and Prof. R. Barth,
Brahms, Quartet in G Minor, op. 25, Rudolf von der Leyen, Barth, von Beckerath, Hausmann.

Sunday, 14.7. Matinee at von Beckerath's.
Brahms, Cello Sonata, F Major op. 99, Frau E. and Prof. Hausmann,

Schumann lieder, "Nußbaum," "Ihre Stimme," "Lehn deine Wang an
meine Wang," Rud. v. d. L. and Frau Speyer,
Brahms, Violin Sonata in G Major op. 78, Frau E. and Prof. R. Barth,
Schumann, Canon in A-flat Major, Frau Prof. Engelmann,
Scarlatti, Pastorale and Presto, Frau Prof. Engelmann,
Brahms Lieder, Three "Regenlieder" (Groth), "Botschaft,"
"Sehnsucht," "Die Kränze," "Frühlingstrost," Frau E. and Frau Sp.,
Brahms, G-Minor Quartet op. 25, Rud. v. d. L., Barth, Beckerath,
Hausmann.

17.4., in the evening at von der Leyen's
Bach, G-Minor Fantasy and Fugue
Bach, A-Minor Prelude and Fugue
Bach, D-Minor Toccata
Frau Engelmann on the Steinway concert grand instead of the organ,
Brahms Lieder, "Feldeinsamkeit," 3 Heimwehlieder (Groth),
"Nachtwandler," "Alte Liebe," Frau E. and Fr. Sp.

Monday, 18.4., Matinee at von der Leyen's
Brahms, Cello Sonata in E Minor, op. 38, Frau E. and Prof. H.,
Schumann, 4 *Mignonlieder,* Fr. E. and Miss Wild,
Brahms, Violin Sonata in A Major, op. 100, Frau E. and Prof. B.,
Bach, Fantasy and Fugue in G Major for Organ, Frau E.,
Beethoven, Serenade op. 8, for String Instruments, Barth, Wolff,
Hausmann,
Brahms, Lieder, "Serenade," "Minnelied," "Verzagen," "An die
Nachtigall," "Am Meeresstrande," "Nachtigallen schwingen,"
"Blinde Kuh," "Mainacht," Frau E. and Frau Sp.

18.4., in the evening at Beckerath's.
Brahms, A-Major Quartet, op. 26, Frau E., Prof. B., von B., Prof. H.,
Beethoven, Variations on "Bei Männern welche Liebe fühlen," Frau
E. and Prof. H.,
Brahms, Adagio from the Violin Concerto, op. 77, Rud. v. d. L. and
Prof. B.,
Schumann, Fantasy op. 17, Frau E.

Tuesday, 19.4., in the morning at von Beckerath's.
Brahms, Clarinet Trio, A Minor, op. 114 (with viola),
Brahms, Variations in D Major, op. 21, no. 1, Frau E.,
Brahms, Violin Sonata in D Minor, Frau E. and Prof. B.,

Mozart, Violin Sonata in G Major, Frau E. and Prof. B.

Besides that, Frau Prof. Engelmann also played two piano pieces by von Herzogenberg; Brahms, Study after Bach; Bach, Fantasy in G Major for Organ.[19]

What a glorious time it was, when private musical offerings like these were possible! The artists concerned were close friends of my parents and von der Leyen. Starting in 1893, these small music festivals took place partly at the estate of my uncle, Walther Weyermann, in Hagerhof near Honnef on the Rhine. Frau Weyermann, my mother's sister, was also an outstanding pianist. My father, who organized these get-togethers, had also invited Johannes Brahms and received the responses that follow.

My father had already written to Brahms in 1891 to express my parents' grateful joy over the beautiful new compositions. Brahms answered: "My warmest thanks for your kind greeting. This is something one really likes to hear, and it takes one back with all one's senses to the dear circle! With my heartfelt greetings, your devoted J. Br."

From Brahms, regarding the 1892 invitation: "You can make your Easter even merrier and invite the prettiest pianist for the Trio—what won't I do in order to please you! As a result, I now have to write the letters to Simrock, leaving me only enough time to inform you by means of this measly post-card! When you enjoy your festive meal in Uerdingen, do greet the entire company from me—I wish I were there—particularly, of course, for the Trio and the Quintet;

Most affectionately, your J. Brahms."

(Today Uerdingen is a part of Krefeld-on-the-Rhine).

Reply to the invitation to Hagerhof 1894, when my father had asked Brahms for a picture for my mother's birthday:

"Dear friend. For Frau Mariechen? That calls for haste, and so I will save my thanks for your report about the festival until later. The only things of interest, I suppose, are the ladies and the walks in the Siebengebirge. You will understand why I am not so interested in your programs when I tell you that I am just about to publish the first sensible thing.

"'A bit late,' I hear you say. But that does not matter as long as you will say yes to it later on. And so, until the next time, I am, with warm greetings to all my friends." Instead of a signature there was a small photograph which shows him walking in the Fellingers' garden.

"The first sensible thing" were the folk songs.[20] A large picture of Brahms was enclosed with the letter, showing him in the Fellingers' library, with the words "for Frau Mariechen, with affectionate greetings. J. Br."[21]

Then another letter from Brahms arrived, written on a form for telegrams: "Uncle Alwin, Jungfernstraße. (Our house was on the Jungfernweg.) Genoa.

"So that's settled, March 25, Genoa, Weyermanns, masses of accommodations and masses of pianos on the familiar flat roof. Honnef writing slipup noticed right away, bring canned sardines, very popular in Italy. Affectionate greetings all over the place.   J. Br."[22]

The Weyermanns had previously lived in Genoa.

In April 1894, Professor Richard Barth, who had taken part in the family music festival in 1894, wrote from Marburg to my father, among other matters: "Our time together was magnificent from A to Z; we did make such wonderful music together, as never before, and over it all hovered such an especially brilliant star in the heavens that we are still quite filled with it and will remain so until days as splendid as that return!

"And, dear friends, you all played so magnificently that I cannot express what heartfelt pleasure it gave me!

"Greetings also to dear Herr Piening (soon afterward chamber musician in Meiningen, later professor, cellist, and a student of Prof. Hausmann) who performed really outstandingly well, do tell him that, too."[23]

In the year 1892, my father's account continues, we saw Brahms once again in Berlin. Three concerts had been arranged for the dedication of the Beethoven House—on October 4, 5, and 6—one each for Bülow, Brahms, and Rubinstein.[24] In the Brahms concert, the B-flat Major Sextet, op. 18, the D-Minor Violin Sonata, op. 108, and the Clarinet Quintet, op. 115, were performed by the Joachim Quartet, Brahms and Mühlfeld (clarinet). Brahms and Joachim had not rehearsed the sonata ahead of time and the performance suffered as a result, but the sextet and quintet were all the more beautiful for it.

It was lovely to be staying together with Brahms in the old Hotel Askanischer Hof in the Königgrätzer Street. When on the first day I went to see him in his living room with alcoves, he greeted me with: "Sollte das nicht ein Bratschiste sein!" (Ah, is that not a violist!) and introduced me with the words "*Mein Leibbratschist*" (my *personal* violist) to the conductor Radecke, who was present.[25] He was in shirtsleeves, and when my wife entered he quickly put on his coat. He was charming to us, like an old good friend. Richard Barth and his wife were also staying in the same hotel. One morning I caught up with Brahms when he was about to come into our room to inform us that he would be playing piano pieces at Simrock's at 11 a.m. That was a happy surprise.

A considerable number of musical friends had assembled at Simrock's. Brahms played all the piano pieces that were published as opp. 116 and 117, with the exception of the first D-minor piece, which he did not have securely in memory. Upon my request he repeated the *Lullaby*, op. 117, no. 1, and upon the request of Dr. Krieger, a nephew of Menzel's, he repeated the E-major piece, op. 116, no. 6. In the evening, after the concerts, we got together for a glass of beer in a pub on Potsdamer Street. Old Menzel was also there and the two great artists sat quietly and contentedly next to each other.[26] On Brahms's other side sat Mühlfeld, who at first did not know how to respond to Brahms, who had presented him with a figurine of a clarinet-playing piglet. We had to make it clear to the dear man that he had played so very beautifully and that he should recognize the joke for what it was. That made him very happy and he accepted the piglet gladly as a memento.

In September 1894, my father received the following postcard from Mühlfeld in Munich (a pretty picture of a Bavarian holding a lute and a glass of beer, and of a Bavarian girl, both in Tyrolean costume): "Esteemed Herr von Beckerath. Master Brahms has commissioned me to inform you that he has composed two sonatas for viola and piano (op. 120), which for the past few days I have played for the time being—lacking a viola—on the clarinet (with the Master himself in Berchtesgarden, at the Duke of Meiningen's). Devoted greetings, Richard Mühlfeld. Friendly greetings, Fritz Steinbach."

My father's report continues. I must recall another lovely, unforgettable encounter with Brahms in Frankfurt, with Mühlfeld also present. It was in February, during the cold winter of 1895, that we traveled in crisp frosty weather up the Rhine, through the snowy countryside. It was a glorious trip in bright sunshine. Upriver from St. Goar, the Rhine was frozen solid. Sappers attempted to keep a channel open near the Lorelei by blasting, but the mass of ice was too overwhelming. It was delightful to observe how, in many communities, traffic had developed over the ice, from shore to shore, on foot or in carriages. The path through the ice labyrinth was marked with small spruce trees, and at the start and finish there were high masts with billowing flags. In Bingen a lot of shacks and tents stood on the ice. We, Rudolf von der Leyen, and the Weyermanns arrived in Frankfurt around noon, and before long Brahms, who knew of our arrival, came to the Swan Hotel to greet us. He was in the best of spirits and told us that Aunt Laura von Beckerath had invited him and Mühlfeld to Rüdesheim for the following day and that we should all come along. There we would hear the clarinet sonatas in a small circle, which was really delightful beyond all expectations. In Frankfurt there was a Museum concert in the evening, in which Mühlfeld played a Weber concerto and, at the end, the Academic Festival Overture was supposed to be played, but the remaining program escapes me (the Second Symphony by Brahms was played at the beginning, in which a *da capo* of the third movement was demanded).[27] At the concert we had five seats in the first row, next to Frau Schumann. Only one seat, next to her, remained empty in case Brahms should still come. Frau Schumann greeted us like old acquaintances with her distinctive, enchanting graciousness. The concert had long since begun, when, following the first movement, a side door opened near us to the left, and Brahms, stooped over and with quick steps, sneaked in front of us to his seat next to Frau Schumann, waving friendly greetings to us as he passed. (The audience had noticed him, however, and had applauded.) Mühlfeld played the concerto very beautifully. When the Academic Festival Overture was about to be played at the end, Kogel, the conductor, came down from the podium to ask Brahms to conduct the piece himself.[28] Brahms declined quite resolutely and pointed to his attire. But Frau Schumann lent a hand and beseeched him so lovingly with: "Ach, Johannes, tu es doch!" (Oh Johannes, please do it!). At which he relented and climbed up on the podium. When the audience saw his figure appear, jubilation swept through the hall. Brahms opened the score, letting his pince-nez drop at the same time, so that in view of his shortsightedness he actually conducted from memory. Sustained by such enthusiasm, the overture came off gloriously. I have never heard it better, and never-ending applause thanked him when it was finished. Prof. Willy von Beckerath immortalized the occasion in his five sketches.

At around noon on the next day, the whole company traveled to Rüdesheim with Brahms and Mühlfeld. Brahms sat the whole time hatless at an open window, gazing at the sparkling icy river. At the railway station in Rüdesheim some primitive sleds were waiting. Brahms immediately swung himself like a young man onto the box and sat next to the coachman, while Aunt Laura and Mühlfeld sat in the sled. After lunch everyone went for a walk over the ice to Bingen and back. It was wonderful to stroll in the calm and clear cold over the seemingly infinite expanse of ice. Following afternoon tea, there was music making, first the two sonatas, op. 120, and after a pause the three *Fantasiestücke* by Schumann.[29] I was allowed to turn pages for Brahms in the two sonatas, but must admit that I gained only a general impression of something beautiful. I recognized the full importance of these splendid pieces only after studying them closely. Mühlfeld played beautifully, and in the second sonata Brahms asked Mühlfeld, before each movement, "Können Sie noch?" (Can you still go on?) and then they played on. The Schumann pieces were delightful. After the music it was time for dinner, and kitchen and cellar rose to the occasion. In the morning, unfortunately, it was time to say farewell, and we parted with heartfelt thanks to our dear hostess and hopes for getting together again soon.

My father writes that he heard the two clarinet sonatas played by Brahms and Mühlfeld once more, in Berlin.

In the autumn of 1895 there was a music festival in Meiningen, with Brahms in attendance. On July 11, 1895, Herr Direktor Fritz Steinbach wrote about it as follows to my father:

The music festival will definitely take place this year from September 27 to 29, inclusive. The final rehearsal for the Passion will be on the 26th.

Program
Bach—Beethoven—Brahms

September 27 at 11:00 a.m.: First Chamber Music Concert
        Beethoven—Quartet op. 18,
        Brahms—Sextet, B-flat Major, op. 18
        Beethoven—Quartet C♯ Minor
        Joachim—Quartet with Eldering and Piening.

At 7 p.m.: Passion According to St. Matthew (in the church)
    Soloists: Johanna Nathan, Frau Walter Choinanus,
        Kammersänger Anthes, Kammersänger Perron,
        Opernsänger Fenten.
    400-member choir, 40-member choir for the Chorale,
    100-member boys' choir, 75-member orchestra (8 flutes, 8 oboes).

September 28 at 7 p.m.:   Concert (in the theater)

I.

Bach,	Brandenburg Concerto no. 6,
Brahms,	Double Concerto (Joachim, Hausmann),
Brahms,	Solo Quartets with Piano,
Brahms,	Variations on a Theme by J. Haydn,

II.

Beethoven,	E-flat-Major Piano Concerto,
Brahms,	First Symphony.

September 29 at 11:30 a.m.:   Second Chamber Music Concert (in the theater)

Brahms,	Clarinet Sonata,
Beethoven,	Quartet in F Minor or the Harp Quartet,

Brahms,　　　Clarinet Quintet,
(Joachim Quartet with Mühlfeld).

At 5 p.m.:　Concert (in the church)
　　　　　Bach, Cantata (50) for Double Chorus,[30]
　　　　　Beethoven, Missa Solemnis,
　　　　　Brahms, Triumphlied.

Kalbeck reports that the program was altered slightly (unfortunately I do not have the program).

First Chamber Music Concert:
　　　　　Beethoven, Quartet, op. 131 [recte: op. 130 in
　　　　　　B-flat Major]
　　　　　Brahms, Clarinet Sonata F Minor,
　　　　　Beethoven, Quartet op. 59, no. 3;

Second Chamber Music Concert:
　　　　　Brahms, Clarinet Quintet,
　　　　　Beethoven, Quartet, C♯ Minor,
　　　　　Brahms, Quintet G Major, op. 111.[31]

In the concert of September 28, the Handel Variations were played instead of the Haydn Variations for piano, according to Kalbeck.

Steinbach's letter then continues: "I hope that additional words of invitation are superfluous. But I would be delighted if I could welcome Krefeld's faithful Brahmsians here at the festival. Would you be kind enough to inform Herr von der Leyen of the program? In the middle of August I am traveling to Brahms in Ischl so as to recuperate a bit. Today I conducted the 54th choir rehearsal since the middle of April, here and in the other participating towns of the land. Accordingly, I can promise you a worthy festival.

"The chamber music programs are not yet in final form.
　　　　　　　　　　　　　　"With best greetings
　　　　　　　　　　　　　　Your Fritz Steinbach."

Unfortunately, my parents and the von der Leyens were unable to come to Meiningen.

After I passed my *Abitur* in the spring of 1895, I [HvB] was allowed to undertake an extensive voyage that took me first to Schachen, to see relatives and friends on the Bodensee, then to Munich, and finally to the music festival in Meiningen. Next to his living room, Herr Kammermusikus Piening, who had been my cello teacher when he was still in Krefeld, had another small sleeping chamber with a bed. That is where I was put up. Consequently I lived almost together with the orchestra musicians and spent splendid days in Meiningen. The lovely warm autumn weather contributed to the festive mood. The little town, the surrounding wooded heights, the large park and the venerable ducal castle, the beautiful theater, the bright and friendly church—it was all enchanting and created a small universe of its own, in which the participants of the festival moved about in an elevated mood. Besides the concerts, I was able to listen to the rehearsals. I chiefly recall the rehearsal of the Double Concerto in the theater on the morning of the 28th. Only the stage was illuminated and I could make out only a few listeners in the theater. Then began the Double Concerto. The beauty and power of Joachim and Hausmann's playing were overwhelming, and the orchestra under Steinbach played to perfection. In this way was created a rendition of this wonderful work, which, in its spontaneity, may not quite have been attained at the evening's concert. I still recall that I was moved most deeply, and that I felt heartily grateful for having experienced this performance. The enthusiasm at the evening concert was overpowering. At the end, following the First Symphony, the excited audience would not rest until Brahms stepped—a little awkwardly— onto the stage to express his gratitude for the ovation. Kalbeck reports how Brahms spent those glorious days in high spirits. He mentions that Herr Eduard Speyer reported to him that Brahms had expressed his regrets at the absence of his Krefeld friends with the words: "Was soll ich nun von den Schlafmützen am nahen Rhein halten?" (What am I supposed to make of those sleepyheads on the nearby Rhine?)[32] It was surely not spoken as it reads. *C'est le ton qui fait la musique* applies here as well.

At the final church concert I was sitting in the church where the right transept begins, quietly awaiting the wonderful sounds from the choir stall that would delight the listeners below. Next to me (on the aisle), a seat had remained empty. Shortly before the start of the concert, Brahms came into the church through an entrance behind me and sat down on that chair. I started and said softly, "Good day, Herr Doktor." Brahms answered: "Ah, somebody from Krefeld is here after all." He listened quietly. I was so impressed by all this that I can no longer recount the details today. I don't know if Brahms asked me why my parents had not come. Soon the music began.

And now came the last unforgettable reunion with Brahms at Hagerhof, near Honnef-on-the-Rhine, during Whitsuntide 1896. Alexander von

Humboldt has described the view from Rolandseck across the Rhine, with the islands Nonnenwerth and Grafenwerth, looking toward the Siebengebirge, as one of the loveliest he knew. In 1896 there was no significant traffic in today's sense. Nature was still in the thrall of the Romantic era, and one could picture how the young Brahms, together with the sons of Deichmann, had wandered upriver on the way to the Mosel, knapsack on his back. Afterward he had visited the Schumanns for the first time, in Düsseldorf.[33]

Standing on the Rolandseck, if one looks out over the broad flat Honnef basin on the other side of the Rhine, one discerns a small valley at the foot of the mountains. On some of its slopes, vineyards flourished, protected from the raw north and east winds, while the little valley itself was almost entirely taken up by the large park of the Hagerhof estate's manor house, built in English Gothic style. Meadows and lovely groves of trees alternated in the park, in its ponds the frogs croaked, and at night fireflies flew through the silent, damp forest and flowers bloomed very near to the house.

My uncle Walter Weyermann, owner of Hagerhof along with his musical wife, had commissioned my father to invite artists of his acquaintance to Hagerhof for a small music festival at Whitsuntide. They all accepted the invitation gladly: Professors Richard Barth, Hamburg (violin), and Leonhard Wolff, Bonn (viola), with their wives; Bram Eldering, Meiningen (violin); Karl Piening, Meiningen (cello); and along with them a few friends of music, such as Frau Laura von Beckerath, Rüdesheim, and her son, the painter Prof. Willi von Beckerath, and Dr. Gustav Ophüls. Of course, the von der Leyens and my parents were part of the inner circle. This is what was going to be played: three string quartets, Brahms A-Minor, Beethoven F-Minor, Schumann A-Major; then the Sonata for Piano and Two Violins by Handel; furthermore, three sonatas for piano and violin, Kreutzer Sonata, Brahms G-Major and A-Major; furthermore, two trios, Beethoven B-flat Major ["Archduke"] and Schubert B-flat Major; and finally, the Piano Quintet by Schumann. In addition, Brahms then played his Piano Quintet.

Dr. Gustav Ophüls has written about these days in considerable detail in his book *Erinnerungen an Johannes Brahms*, but here I will report what my father tells of those lovely days.[34]

As early as Friday morning, the string quartet had begun rehearsing the three quartets. In the afternoon, my wife played the B-flat Major Trio by Beethoven with Barth and Piening. On Saturday, Frau Weyermann played Schubert's B-flat Major Trio with Barth and Piening, and [Brahms's] A-Major Sonata with Eldering. In the afternoon, Rudolf von der Leyen and Barth played the Kreutzer Sonata and the G-Major Sonata by Brahms.

The funeral of Frau Schumann took place on Whitsunday and caused an interruption of the musical offerings, since several of the participants attended the memorial service in Bonn. Those who remained were in a quiet holiday mood until suddenly, at about 11 a.m., the telegram arrived: "Bitte um ein Bett und ein Kouvert Brahms" (Request a bed and place-setting Brahms). Everyone started to scurry about in preparation for the reception of the beloved Master. A second wire asked that dinner be delayed until 6 p.m. In the forest, birch saplings were cut for decorating the main entrance and the young girls spelled out the letters "J. B." with flowers in front of the stairway. But the banners stretched over the stone walls from some windows were removed by order of the host, so that only the greenery and flowers remained. Later on, when Brahms strolled through the park with me, he looked back toward the house and said, "But I saw just one banner on the outside of the building." Brahms arrived at around four o'clock with Rudolf von der Leyen and Leonhard Wolff. He stepped carefully over the flowers and greeted everyone warmly. After a cup of

Brahms and the Hagerhof Circle in 1896. From left to right: Gustav Ophüls, Brahms, Bram Eldering, Alwin von Beckerath.

coffee, the company strolled in groups around the park. The heavens granted us the loveliest spring weather throughout these days. Brahms was quiet in the beginning, but evidently in a contented mood. When Professor Wolff asked whether the string quartet could play his A-Minor Quartet for him, Brahms cheerfully agreed. Although they played well, a desire to make more music did not rightly develop. Brahms himself suggested that we postpone it until morning. He was not about to leave right away, then! During dinner, when, in response to the host's halting invitation, Brahms wanted to ask those present to remember his departed friend, his voice failed him and tears ran down his beard. After that, the mood was more relaxed. After the meal, everyone went walking in the woods again. Brahms was tired after his very strenuous and anxious journey and the day's excitement, and he went to sleep early. The others soon followed his example.

Following a sound sleep, Brahms's healthy constitution permitted him to go rambling in the park as early as six o'clock. Elise, the kind cook, had prepared a cup of coffee for him and had to tie his shoes for him. There developed a kind of friendship between her and Brahms in the early mornings, which the good Elise thought back on with pride for many years. After a communal breakfast and a short walk, the music making began. At first Brahms played his Piano Quintet with the string quartet; then followed the A-Major Quartet of Schumann. While it was being played, Brahms sat thoughtfully next to the window and gazed out over the flower garden into the park. Afterward he played his C-Minor Trio with Barth and Piening. After the music everyone went for a little walk, and the Weyermanns' young daughter, in the riding ring, showed off her two small dressage ponies. On the way back to the house, Brahms asked me if another piano might be available. I told him right away that there was a pianino in the daughter's room, which my sister-in-law would certainly be glad to put at his disposal. That pleased him and he said that after the second breakfast[35] he wished to perform a new composition for us and requested that, to begin with, only Richard Barth, Rudolf von der Leyen, Leonhard Wolff, Ophüls, and I with my wife and her sister, Frau Weyermann, be present. We assembled in complete silence while most of the others were having a siesta. As Brahms sat down at the piano, he said: "For my birthday, I wrote something for myself. It is the most godless stuff that was ever composed." With that he began the introduction to the first of the Four Serious Songs. The vocal part he indicated in his rough voice. Leonhard Wolff wanted to help him out, but he would have none of it and sang with the deepest emotion. An anxious feeling gripped my heart, as though I apprehended the looming, sad end of the passionately loved and revered Master. Then

Brahms had someone fetch another manuscript from his suitcase, the eleven Chorale Preludes, and he played those as well. (The following morning, Brahms again gathered a group of festival participants around him and played the new things for them as well.)

At six o'clock, everyone gathered for a festive meal at the lovely flower-bedecked table. The ladies wore light-colored dresses and only happy faces could be seen. There were several speeches, and Brahms was in the most animated and happy mood. He sat between Frau Laura von Beckerath and the hostess, and across the table from my wife and Richard Barth. After the meal, everyone went strolling for a while in the mild spring evening, and spent the rest of the evening in jovial companionship, to the great delight of Brahms as well. At the end, Eldering performed an excellent musical recitation at the piano in the mystical glow of two wax candles. It was the story of the very exuberant little girl, Lenchen, and her grandmother.[36] The hour was very late when the evening had run its untroubled course.

On Tuesday morning, Rudolf von der Leyen played the Schumann Piano Quintet with the string quartet, while Brahms was upstairs inspecting the library. After the Quintet, Handel's Sonata for Two Violins was played, and when Brahms heard these sounds, he immediately came downstairs and asked me, with keen interest, what this was. He did not know the piece and was so delighted with it that he had it played for him twice more in the course of the day, with Frau Weyermann playing the piano part. Brahms then played his B-Major Trio and the morning music came to a close with Beethoven's F-Minor String Quartet.

In the afternoon, several of the participants left. Brahms bade them farewell with deep emotion, particularly Rudolf von der Leyen. He ran after the carriage a little way, waving his handkerchief. The next morning, he played the Schubert B-flat Major Trio with Barth and Piening and, in the afternoon, he traveled up the Rhine together with Frau Laura von Beckerath.[37]

In those days Brahms also used to go on small outings with my parents, and he told them during a conversation that "it had been so difficult for him to forgive people, that they had prevented him from marrying. That it would have been impossible for him to come back to his wife and have to tell her that it had again come to nothing." In his gentle manner, known only to his close friends, he added: "I dealt like a cad with Agathe." So it seems that the poor man tortured himself with his love throughout his life's struggle, while bestowing such marvelous works of art on humanity. Agathe von Siebold hovered over his life like an angel.

It was my good fortune to take several photographs in those days, and they are appended to these lines. Brahms thanked me for them in a friendly letter, in which he expressed the hope to be able to thank me again next year.[38]

And to conclude, I present the lines that my parents wrote to Eugenie Schumann in the year 1926.

"Brahms did not often speak of your parents, and then [he did so] only in the narrowest circle. He probably did not want even those close to him to catch a glimpse into his heart, which beat so passionately and constantly for these two great and singularly beloved persons. On only a single occasion did he speak to us of your father's illness and the Endenich period. Your father had expressed a desire for reading matter and had included the Bible in the list of books he wanted. At the time, that had been interpreted as an indication that his condition was deteriorating. 'The people did not know that in darkness, we North Germans are accustomed to finding our Bible.' Of your mother he spoke only with eyes glistening and in greatest reverence and love for the splendid woman. On another occasion, when Brahms was again our only dinner guest and was feeling at his ease, he suddenly blurted out that it could happen to him that he would say unpleasant things to people whom he otherwise dearly loved and treasured. It was almost as if a malevolent spirit forced him to do so, that he could not suppress it, he just had to say it. Afterward he would regret it sincerely. It was touching how the great man made this modest self-confession.

"In the afternoon of that sad Whitsunday 1896 we walked with Brahms alone in the quiet park of the Hagerhof and then continued on through the beautiful spruce forest to an observation point. Stepping out of the forest, one beholds a wonderful panorama of the Siebengebirge, the Rhine valley, Godesberg and Bonn, and, after gazing at the view quietly for some time, Brahms said, 'Now I have nothing more to lose.'

"He was not satisfied with the funeral oration, because the speaker had mostly celebrated the great artist and had failed sufficiently to memorialize the outstandingly splendid woman and mother. Later, at the large dinner table, he was noticeably at pains to show that he felt at ease in the company. But on the inside, he was still deeply moved, and when he tried to respond to the sensitive speech of the host, his voice failed him in the midst of his pain and mourning. It was devastating for all of us. The next morning, while Schumann's A-Major Quartet was being played, Brahms sat at the window and looked out constantly into the lovely flower garden with his head propped in his hand, and large tears rolled in his beard."[39]

On June 5, Brahms wrote to Frau Fellinger from Ischl: "I spent a few days in the Siebengebirge, where every year a sizable number of particularly dear friends get together at a large estate owned by a mutual friend. This year, I thought less than usual of joining them. Fortunately, I allowed myself to be taken along.—How empty and gloomy I would have felt on my journey home and here, and how delightfully the solemn memorial service now faded away amid the splendid scenery, the exceptional company, and the most beautiful music."

Whenever I look back to those days of my youth, a song by Brahms in his op. 97 comes to mind: "Ein Vögelein fliegt über den Rhein, und wiegt die Flügel im Sonnenschein . . ." (A little bird flies over the Rhine, wafting its wings in the sunshine . . .).

NOTES

We would like to thank William Melton (Hauset, Belgium) for indispensable aid in obtaining Heinz von Beckerath's memoir, and William Horne (New Orleans) for specialist assistance.

1. The holiday known as Pfingsten in German-speaking countries, while based on the religious feast of Pentecost, is celebrated largely as a secular welcoming of spring in Europe, during which schools and businesses are closed for several days. We have chosen to translate Pfingsten as Whitsun or Whitsuntide (and Pfingstsonntag as Whitsunday), a term perhaps more familiar to British and Canadians than to Americans, since the alternative Pentecost carries a more religious connotation, which was hardly in the minds of the celebrants at the Hagerhof.

2. From the set of six choral songs, *Im Freien zu Singen*, op. 41. Beckerath's reference to *The Trilogy of Passions*, which is not Mendelssohn's title, is obscure. He may be referring to Goethe's *Trilogie der Leidenschaft* (Trilogy of Passion).

3. Leipzig, 1905.

4. For full details of this and following concerts, see Renate and Kurt Hofmann, *Johannes Brahms als Pianist und Dirigent* (Tutzing, 2006), 184, 196–97, and 246–48.

5. During the years when Brahms and Joachim were not on speaking terms, Richard Barth was Brahms's preferred violinist.

6. Ironically, this is one set of songs that Brahms claimed *not* to want sung as a cycle. "Only German thoroughness would prompt anyone to sing the whole thing," he once exclaimed. But despite the complaint so clearly expressed in this memoir, Brahms himself repeatedly accompanied performances by singers who took apart his bouquets, including all those mentioned in the memoir. The practice of singing entire opuses of his songs was virtually unheard of, as Brahms knew perfectly well.

7. At issue is Gustav Ophül's now classic work, *Brahms Texte: Vollständige Sammlung der von Johannes Brahms componierten und musikalisch bearbeiteten Dichtungen* (Berlin, 1923). What originated as the project of a musical young man eager to please Brahms became instead something that irritated him. Rather than present the poems Brahms set to music in order of their composition, which is what Brahms would have liked, Ophüls organized them in various categories and by alphabetical order. He identified sources, and gave variant versions. Brahms seems to have taken offense. The time line as given in Beckerath's memoir is confusing: by the time Ophüls was immersed in his project, Brahms was mortally ill, and Brahms's complaints must have been passed on by mail rather than in conversation.

Ophüls wrote his own account of the text project in his *Erinnerungen*. Not surprisingly, his own account of Brahms's disappointment is more muted than appears here.

8. A reference to the opening two lines of *Gute Nacht*, the first song of *Winterreise*. "Fremd bin ich eingezogen/Fremd zieh' ich wieder aus" translates roughly as: "As a stranger I came/As a stranger I go." Raimond von zur-Mühlen (1854–1918) was a prominent singer and student of Julius Stockhausen. Von Keudell was a diplomat serving Bismarck, and a good pianist.

9. Brahms made the piano arrangements of Bach's Toccata in F Major, BWV 540, and Fantasy in G Major, BWV 572, while still in his twenties. These transcriptions remained among his favorite show pieces throughout his playing career. Long considered lost, Brahms's notations for the piano transcriptions, marked on a nineteeth-century edition of Bach organ scores once owned by Robert and Clara Schumann, have now been located. See *American Brahms Society Newsletter* 25/2 (2007): 4.

10. Overture to the opera *Anakréon ou L'amour fugitif*, 1803.

11. Op. 84, no. 3.

12. Barth's rehearsal technique mirrored the practices inaugurated by Hans von Bülow in bringing the Meiningen Court Orchestra to its high level of performance. Barth had other organizational abilities as well. As the eventual conductor of the Hamburg Philharmonic, he used his executive talents to organize it, for the first time, as a modern professional orchestra with a fixed roster of players under contract.

13. MU refers almost certainly to the conductor of the Winterthur orchestra, Edgar Munzinger (1847–1905), who taught and directed the Musik-Kollegium and was a composer. It is noteworthy that his antagonist, Hans Wilhelm Gustav Winderstein (1856–1925), also taught at the Musik-Kollegium and was a composer as well.

14. In outraged anger, Bülow tendered his resignation as conductor of the Meiningen Hofkapelle abruptly, leaving his patron Duke George II utterly at a loss. Bülow would not answer Brahms's letters. That the Frankfurt "Museum" Orchestra numbered more than seventy players in contrast to Meiningen's forty-nine was to him irrelevant. Bülow had been counting on conducting the Brahms's Fourth Symphony *himself* in Frankfurt (albeit with the *Meiningen* Orchestra), and he saw Brahms's wish to conduct the work in that city—with Frankfurt's own orchestra—as a betrayal. Brahms made the concert arrangements at this time, but the actual performance did not take place until the following spring (March 5, 1886).

For correspondence between Brahms and Georg on the matter, see Herta Müller and Renate Hofmann, eds., *Johannes-Brahms im Briefwechsel mit Herzog Georg II. von Sachsen-Meiningen und Helene Freifrau von Heldburg* (Tutzing,1991), 58–64 (letters 24–26). As Beckerath's memoir makes clear, however, Brahms left out some of the story in his explanation to Georg II. It was Brahms himself who initiated his performance with the Frankfurt Museum Orchestra, contrary to what he wrote to the Duke. There is no doubt that he regretted offending Bülow, and he worked for over a year to restore their friendship.

15. Mina Spies, author of *Hermine Spies: Ein Gedenkbuch für ihre Freunde von ihrer Schwester* (Leipzig, 1905).

16. Variations for Orchestra on a Theme by Haydn, op. 56a. Fritz Steinbach (1855–1916) was for many years Bülow's successor in Meiningen, highly regarded by Brahms as a conductor of his music. According to R. and K. Hofmann (*Brahms als Pianist und Dirigent*), all performances of this work in Meiningen in his presence were conducted by Brahms himself.

17. March 13, 1890. Brahms first heard his op. 109 in Hamburg several months earlier, but the event described here was the first complete performance of op. 110.

18. Emma Brandes Engelmann (1855–?), one of Clara Schumann's most promising students, was wife of Brahms's good friend Theodor Engelmann and mother of their four children. After her marriage, she continued her career in home concerts such as the one described here.

19. See note 9. As the Fantasy in G Major was not published, one has to wonder how Frau Engelmann had acquired the music.

20. *Forty-nine German Folksongs,* WoO 33, published in June 1894. Brahms made similar comments to Joachim and Philipp Spitta.

21. Despite Beckerath's account, the photograph was most likely taken in the library of Viktor von Miller zu Eichholz. The widely distributed photo is often misattributed.

22. A puzzling communication; one wonders what the Beckeraths made of it.

23. Karl Theodor Piening (1867–1942). In 1894 he was appointed to the position of Solo Cellist to the Meiningen Court Orchestra, and later became its last Kapellmeister (1915–1920).

24. The occasion was actually the inauguration of the Saal Bechstein, with Bülow scheduled to give the opening program. Illness forced Bülow to cancel. He and Brahms never saw each other again.

25. Rudolf Radecke (1829–93) or his brother Robert (1830–1911), both of whom were choral conductors from North Germany.

26. Adolf Menzel (1815–1905), one of Germany's most distinguished artists. Although he and Brahms met rather late in their lives, they became good friends.

27. The other pieces on the program were an aria from Bruch's *Odysseus,* Handel's Concerto Grosso in D Minor, no. 10, and four songs by Brahms. Further details in Hofmann, *Brahms als Pianist und Dirigent,* 302.

28. Gustav Friedrich Kogel (1849–1921), conductor of the Museum Concerts in Frankfurt from 1891 to 1903.

29. Presumably op. 73.

30. "Nun ist das Heil und die Kraft," BWV 50. The powerful cantata fragment was one of Brahms's favorite works, which he twice performed in Vienna during his tenure as music director of the Gesellschaft der Musik.

31. As indicated by Beckerath, Max Kalbeck provides a different account of the programs for the two chamber music concerts. According to Kalbeck, the first program included Brahms's F-Minor Clarinet Sonata and Beethoven's String Quartets in C Major, op. 59, no. 3, and B-flat, op. 130; the second included Brahms's String Quintet in G, op. 111, and Clarinet Quintet, op. 115, and Beethoven's String Quartet in C-sharp Minor, op. 131. (Kalbeck has an apparent misprint, giving the opus number of Beethoven's B-flat Quartet as op. 131, but it is unlikely that the real op. 131 was played on both programs.) See Max Kalbeck, *Johannes Brahms,* rev. ed. (Berlin, 1904–14; repr. Tutzing, 1974), 4:408.

32. The Rhine is almost two hundred miles away from Meiningen. Even today, there is no direct route from the river to that city. For Edward Speyer's description of the festival, see his *My Life and Friends* (London, 1937), 100–102. The account is partially included in Kalbeck, *Johannes Brahms,* 4:406ff.

33. Brahms's letter to Joseph Joachim of 21 September, 1853, decribes the trip. See *Johannes Brahms, Briefwechsel,* rev. eds. (Berlin, 1912–22; repr. Tutzing, 1974), 5:8–10.

34. That year Whitsunday fell on May 24. The Hagerhof house concerts took place from May 23 through Wednesday, May 27. Although the musicians gathered at Hagerhof learned of Clara Schumann's death only one day before her burial, their proximity to Bonn allowed several of them to be present at the service. For accounts of the weekend, see the memoir of Richard Barth, in Kurt Hofmann, *Johannes Brahms in den Erinnerungen von Richard Barth* (Hamburg, 1979), 62–63; and Gustav Ophüls, *Erinnerungen an Johannes Brahms: Ein Beitrag aus dem Kreis seiner rheinischen Freunde* (Berlin, 1921; repr. Munich, 1983). See also Styra Avins and Joseph Eisinger, "Brahms's Last Whitsuntide: A Memoir by Karl Theodor Piening with a Modern Appreciation," *American Brahms Society Newsletter* 26/2 (2008), 1–4.

35. *Gabelfrühstück,* the breakfast of cold cuts eaten with a fork, as opposed to the early morning coffee and roll.

36. The performance may have been a melodrama based on the popular storybook *Die fromme Helene* (Pious Helen), by Wilhelm Busch (1832–1908), best known for *Max und Moritz*. Helen is given to playing pranks and comes to a bad end.

37. The concerts of this weekend mark the last time Brahms is known to have participated in any kind of performance.

38. A number of them are reproduced in Ophüls, *Erinnerungen an Johannes Brahms*.

39. Note the difference between this account of the first hours at Hagerhof and the one that appears earlier in the memoir, where Brahms is dexcribed as being "in the most animated and happy mood" (pp. 374–75).

Gustav Jenner
Johannes Brahms as Man, Teacher, and Artist

TRANSLATED BY SUSAN GILLESPIE AND
ELISABETH KAESTNER
INTRODUCED BY KEVIN C. KARNES
ANNOTATED BY LEON BOTSTEIN AND
KEVIN C. KARNES

Though there were many aspiring musicians in Brahms's Vienna—including Richard Heuberger and Heinrich Schenker—who sought his counsel on their compositions, Gustav Jenner (1865–1920) was Brahms's only long-term, regular student.[1] Jenner's introduction to Brahms came through Klaus Groth, a respected poet and friend of Brahms who had been uncommonly moved by Jenner's early lieder. In the autumn of 1887, Groth began what amounted to an intensive lobbying effort with Brahms on behalf of the young artist from Kiel. He wrote to Brahms directly on the matter and enlisted the help of the singer Hermine Spies, a close friend of the elder composer.[2] His interest piqued (and after a meeting in Leipzig and a heartfelt appeal from the would-be student), Brahms invited Jenner to Vienna at the beginning of 1888, promising, as Jenner recalls below, that "whatever you might wish to have from me is at your service in full measure."

Jenner departed for Brahms's adopted hometown on February 13, 1888, and spent the rest of that winter and spring studying counterpoint with Eusebius Mandyczewski, music historian and archivist at the Gesellschaft der Musikfreunde, and "free composition" with Brahms. He remained in Vienna for the next seven years, continuing his work with Mandyczewski, meeting with Brahms during summers at Ischl, and building a modest catalog of mostly vocal works, which were programmed and generally well received by members of Brahms's circle. Appointed to the faculty of the University of Marburg in 1895, he resided and taught in the latter city until his death a quarter-century later.

Jenner's memoir of his studies with Brahms is one of the most valuable sources for Brahms's ideas on compositional technique, about which he spoke rarely. In its author's detailed discussions of sonata and variation forms and the music of J. S. Bach, Mozart, Haydn, and Beethoven, it also provides a glimpse of the effects of Brahms's teachings upon the mind of the pupil. What follows here is the complete text of Jenner's memoir, published as Johannes Brahms als Mensch, Lehrer und Künstler *(Marburg, 1905). All endnotes are editorial.*

It was in Leipzig in late December of the year 1887 that I first met Brahms. He had traveled there to oversee the performance of two of his newest works, the Double Concerto and the Piano Trio in C Minor, and he knew that I was coming from Kiel to visit him, to ask him to give his opinion of my musical abilities based on a selection of my compositions. This is how it came about.[3]

On the advice of one of my teachers I had sent several of my songs to Simrock in Berlin to inquire whether he might be inclined to publish them.[4] But Simrock wrote back that he was just on the point of leaving for his summer vacation and therefore would not be able to give me an answer until nearly fall. Then one day I got a call from Klaus Groth, who was very fond of me and a loyal advisor in every respect. I can still see him standing at the gate of his garden waving his arms as I came into sight: "Come quickly," he called, "I have good news for you!" And, beaming with pleasure, he handed me a letter from which I learned that on his summer vacation in Thun, Simrock had paid a visit to Brahms and shown him my song manuscripts. It seemed that these had piqued his interest, but he had advised Simrock not to print them. Now he wished to learn more about me and to meet me whenever the opportunity should arise.

With this, far more was accomplished than the publication of the songs, which didn't matter much to me in the first place. My long-cherished secret wish to become personally acquainted with Brahms was about to come true, and in what a splendid fashion! It may be safely assumed that I would gladly have departed at once; however, since my means did not permit such a long journey on short notice, I had to console myself for the time being with the prospect of the favorable opportunity Brahms had mentioned. This finally arrived, as mentioned above, at the end of the year. Groth wrote to Brahms to ask whether he would like to see me in Leipzig and received the reply that I would be welcome.

Gustav Jenner

In Hamburg, as had been arranged, my friend Julius Spengel joined me, and then we went on to Berlin to see Joachim. There, for the first time, I experienced one of the Joachim Quartet evenings. Immediately after the concert we set off with the quartet for Leipzig and arrived late at night at the Hotel Hauffe. I will never forget the feeling that came over me as I saw on the guest list the name "Johannes Brahms, Vienna." He had already gone to bed. Through an odd coincidence I was given a room directly adjacent to his, and, as I entered, the sound of hearty snoring announced the presence of the great man. I undressed quietly and lay down with a strange feeling of mingled awe, pride, and anxiety.

When I descended the following morning, Brahms had already breakfasted. He was smoking with evident relish and reading the newspaper. I was almost taken aback when I saw him, for I had pictured him—I don't know why; perhaps I was thinking of our German types—as being tall, and so at first I could hardly grasp the fact that this short, plump gentleman was Brahms. But the sight of his head banished all doubts.

Brahms received me with a pleasant and direct friendliness, indicated that he understood why I had come, and was able, with just a few brief questions, which he posed quite casually, to help me over the first awkwardness and shyness, so that in no time I was convinced of the kindness of his nature and placed my unqualified trust in him. He also made sure that I could thoroughly enjoy the wealth of beautiful new experiences that there were for me to enjoy during those unforgettable days. Once during a walk he put his arm in mine familiarly, remarking that he didn't see well, which was quite true, and said: "If you have brought along something nice to show me, then you may just leave it in my room." On New Year's Eve a large number of us were gathered around Brahms, and as the bells announced the New Year, someone stood up and spoke the simple lines: "We waited for the New Year, now it comes; and with it a good spirit, Johannes Brahms." I felt that these words had a special meaning for me; I knew that for me it really was the beginning of a new year, a new time, a new epoch in my life, even though I could not yet imagine, at that time, to what an extent this would be true.

After the chamber music concert, in which Brahms himself played the piano part of the C-Minor Trio, the reception at the inn with the Leipzig musicians and patrons lasted an inordinately long time. The holidays had come and gone. Joachim, Hausmann, and Spengel had already departed, and I, too, would soon have to think about leaving. But Brahms had not yet said anything about my work, and that was the reason I had come. True, he had said quite often, in the presence of others, that I had talent, as a kind of social legitimation, but I was still hoping for an hour of private conversation.

It was after three in the morning when we arrived at the Hotel Hauffe that night. How overjoyed—and at the same time amazed—I was, when, at that hour, as he was saying good night, he announced that he would be waiting for me at seven in the morning in his room, to talk with me about my compositions. I arrived punctually at the appointed time and found him fresh and rosy, the soul of geniality, at his breakfast. The busy days, which, in addition to the concerts, had placed unusual social demands on him, seemed not to have affected him in the slightest. From a very large case he extracted two equally large cigars and lighted one of them. Every puff betrayed the enjoyment of the connoisseur. In the presence of such strength I didn't want to betray any weakness, and so I bravely lit up the proffered cigar, although I was not comfortable smoking so early after having been up all night—and then the genuine article! I also could not prevent my cigar from going out now and again; Brahms, undeterred, helped me to relight it. At the same time he was examining my work.

I had brought with me a trio for piano, violin, and cello, a choral piece with orchestral accompaniment, women's choruses *a cappella*, as well as some songs, and I found that he was minutely prepared, down to the tiniest detail; just as later, without exception, he never went over pieces with me that he had not thoroughly scrutinized ahead of time. After some preliminary remarks to the effect that he had received a generally positive impression of my compositions, he first handed back the choral work with orchestral accompaniment, which had turned out rather long, with the words, "Too bad about the pretty little poem." It was Klaus Groth's "Wenn ein milder Leib begraben." The women's choruses suffered the same fate; I got them back with the equally uncomforting assurance: "This kind of thing is very hard to do."

But then he went over the trio and the songs with me all the more exhaustively.

At the first movement of the trio there was much turning of pages back and forth. With devastating precision Brahms demonstrated to me the lack of logic in the structure; it was as if the whole thing dissolved into its component parts in his hands. With growing horror I saw how loosely and weakly the parts were joined together. I realized that the bond that was supposed to hold them together was less an internal than an external one; it was nothing more than the device of the sonata form. The essence of form began to reveal itself to me, and I suddenly realized that it is not enough to have a good idea here and there; that one has not written a sonata when one has merely combined several such ideas through the outward form of the sonata, but that, on the contrary, the sonata form must emerge of necessity from the idea. I was already making the discovery that precisely those passages from which I had promised myself the most did not seem to interest Brahms at all. At such enthusiastic passages, where my heart beat faster and my eyes focused expectantly and anxiously on his, he calmly and coolly criticized "sleepy, lazy" basses, pointed out weak harmonies, suggested replacing a few notes with others that were more logical and, at the same time, allowed the idea, which had gotten stuck in my harmonies—had lost its ability to develop, so to speak—to emerge clearly and powerfully.

It was a painful disappointment for me to realize that often, when I thought I had done the best work, this was just when my imagination faltered. The whole, moreover, was lacking that broad and deep undercurrent of feeling that produces the unity of effect in a work of art, by finding the same lively expression throughout the work and giving all the separate parts, however disparate and far removed from one another they may be, their distinctive stamp. Sentences such as "That could just as well have been something else" gave me, even then, much food for thought. After only a few moments I had come to the depressing conclusion that my entire composing career betrayed the tendency to succumb weakly to whatever inspiration happened to strike me, that it indulged in childish pleasure over "beautiful" details, that it was nothing but purposeless groping: in other words, dilettantism. Brahms showed me how my eye had fastened with truly touching tenderness on unessential things, while overlooking the essential ones that made all the difference. Naturally, these weaknesses showed up most glaringly in the slow movement; but it is understandable that I must confess that precisely this movement, with its youthful enthusiasm, was my favorite. And thus, to my bitter disappointment, the entire glory of this beloved Adagio melted away before my watching eyes into empty nothingness. For my suffering, which Brahms probably sensed, he offered only the dubious consolation that "such a long adagio is the most difficult of all."

In the Scherzo I had attempted to be "original." Following a public performance, my friends in Kiel and, if I remember correctly, even the newspapers had loudly praised the originality of this section. Unfortunately, it did not hold up either; its originality was slowly but surely transformed into pure nonsense. We came to the end of this movement remarkably quickly, and Brahms said, in a well-meaning way, "Of course, you *will* promise me not to write anything like this again."

The finale was a rondo. Here I did relatively well. I was amazed when Brahms stopped at a phrase that did not seem to me to deserve any particular attention, with the words: "You see, that is a good sign." I remembered clearly that when I worked on this passage it had flowed from my hand without particular effort; but since no further explanation was forthcoming, it remained completely unclear to me what agreeable characteristics this passage actually contained. Only one fact seemed to be beyond doubt, that there must be things in musical creation of which I knew absolutely nothing. And so Brahms turned my attention from dreamy sentiments down toward the depths, where I could only guess that in addition to feeling there must be another factor at work, which, in my case, for lack of ability and knowledge, was operating only very imperfectly: understanding. I saw not only that I had to learn but also, at the same time, where I had to learn. At present I was lacking a solid foundation of knowledge. I began to comprehend why Brahms, when I answered his question as to what I was doing by telling him that I was learning instrumentation, had laughed out loud and asked disparagingly whether I didn't know that it "had to be learned, even when one's five senses were in good working order." The feeling that I was on the wrong path grew more and more distinct.

I think it not useless to consider the meaning of this expression by Brahms more closely, and grant myself a small digression for this purpose.

As obvious as it is that a composer needs to become familiar with and thoroughly study the technique of the various instruments for which his compositions are written, so is it certain that he can achieve an idea of their intrinsic character and essence of sound only through the study of scores combined with practical experience, neither of which poses especially exquisite difficulties for anyone who has his or her "five senses in good working order." However, the ultimate reason for the unique, indescribable magic of Mozart's works, Beethoven's grandiose power, Weber's marvelous brilliance, and the Wagnerian orchestra's blinding splendor lies in the unique sensibility of these individually so different artists; otherwise one need ask from whom Titian, Rubens, or Rembrandt learned to mix colors so peculiar to each.

These colors and sounds are not like interchangeable garments loosely draped around figures or ideas, but rather part of the very essence, experienced as such; whereas the copied or virtuosically enhanced sounds of the masters must seem more or less like senseless and soul-less caricatures. People in earlier years so often reproached Brahms as unable to orchestrate, without noting the absurd contradiction of this statement; as if to orchestrate was an art in its own right and could be learned by all and any empty-head in no time, yet his whole life remained beyond the grasp of a master such as Brahms. Now that one has learned to better understand and love his idiosyncrasies, one also suddenly discovers how marvelously beautiful his orchestra sounds and so totally unlike the orchestras of other masters. It is a cheap thrill, given the high technical perfection of our instruments today, to mix sounds together this way and that, and by such experimentation "to find new unimagined sounds"; however, to convey the magical quality of a single instrument is far more difficult, for here one must prove melodic creativity; however, to be able utterly to preserve the magic of separate instruments playing with, as well as against one another, in the midst of the commingled sounds of the orchestra, thereby "finding" new sounds—for that one must be born a symphonist. How can it be that of the many modern Wagner imitators, almost none has shown lasting success in the area of dramatic music? And how can it be that in the area of the so-called symphonic poem, where ideas are popping up like weeds, a chase after new sound effects has arisen, the effect of which, after a few applications, fails to impress?

I return to the subject. With the songs I got off a bit more easily. It is true that here, too, to my great discomfiture, several were immediately laid aside without even being considered: these were the great, powerfully expressive ones, for which I had such high expectations. But then, on the other hand, some of the small ones were looked at closely. Now a few words of recognition were spoken, for example: "That is something you don't forget, once you have seen it"; or: "That could have turned into a good song."

After all that, I felt like someone who after a long journey on the wrong road believes that he is nearing his destination, only to become suddenly aware of his error and see the goal recede behind the faraway horizon, unreachable for his failing powers. The friendly and confiding manner with which Brahms had received me in the previous days had given me a certain security and self-confidence that now, to tell the truth, began to wobble perilously. But in spite of the unmercifully hard criticism that my compositions had experienced at his hands, not an ironic, much less a mean word was ever spoken, and everything seemed to be softened by a goodwill that won my confidence: he showed me, without leniency or any possibility of objection, that I didn't know how to do anything. But the high vantage point from which he made his judgments, which I could only intuit but not comprehend, actually gave me courage. For before my eyes a new world was dawning. I saw the correct road to the land of true art, clear and palpable in front of me, even if that realm itself was still lost in fog.

I had come to Brahms for the purpose of asking his advice; this had also been Klaus Groth's understanding. Neither he nor I would ever have conceived the bold idea of asking Brahms to take me on as his student; for we both knew perfectly well that Brahms lived as a private gentleman in Vienna and did not teach. I was merely to get from him confirmation that I was not without talent, along with a few pointers for the immediate future. I did, of course, notice that, in his comments on my work, he repeatedly used the phrase, "Yes, I might be able to be of use to you"; whereby he expelled the first syllable quickly and energetically in a manner peculiar to him. But I didn't rightly know what to make of these words; at least in my timid state I didn't dare to interpret them to mean that he might be prepared to instruct me, and so I asked him modestly for his advice. After a strict examination of what I had done up until that time, Brahms said: "You see, you haven't yet learned anything proper about music; for everything you are telling me about theory of harmony, attempts at composition, instrumentation, and the like, is in my opinion worthless." Then he asked me how old I was, and when he heard that I had just completed my twenty-second year, he made no secret of his qualms that it might already be too late, and then he continued: "First find a teacher who will instruct you in strict counterpoint; the best ones are among the cantors in the villages; he doesn't need to be so famous as Mr. X" (here he gave a well-known name). "It is absolutely essential that one see the world through this glass for a good long time. You will have plenty to do there for several years. But write to me."

On the same day, I traveled back to Hamburg, where I remained for some time. A concert of the Cäcilien-Verein conducted by Spengler offered the performance of those works for women's choir that Brahms had put to the side with the remark that this kind of thing was very hard to do.[5] That's how it seemed also to me at this point, at any rate I had lost all confidence in my compositions, despite the applause of the public. I was in an uncomfortable mood, as I could no longer see clearly what I ought to be doing.

At this point, I would like to briefly recall an experience that I am fond of remembering because under different circumstances, it could have changed the course of my whole life and may not have been without influence on my decisions: not long thereafter, in Hamburg, I came to know Tchaikovsky.

In those days he was also in Leipzig, and I had seen him there in the director's box of the Gewandhaus during the New Year's Concert. At the time, he was beginning his travels through the capitals of Germany to promote the performance of his compositions. This is what also brought him to Hamburg, and I was introduced to him at a big party in his honor that Herr von Bernuth had given after his concert. His appearance was elegant and charming; he combined fine worldly manners with an enchanting gracefulness, so that one felt an immediate attraction to him. Tchaikovsky invited me in a friendly manner to visit him the following morning to show him some of my compositions, and that's how I brought him the same works I had just finished showing Brahms in Leipzig. Tchaikovsky appeared interested in them, but it was very instructive to see how in the matter of judgment different things were of concern to him than to Brahms. He talked much more than Brahms, but in expressions that were far vaguer. There was much talk about pleasant moods and more general things, all of them addressing more the character of the piece of music at hand. Brahms, by comparison, attacked the structure of the piece, and with a confident glance, exposed the weaknesses in musical structure. The whole piece had to be tightly built not to appear devoid of footing and substance before this unmerciful glance, and all wonderful dreams disperse into nothing, along with all "pleasant moods" and enthusiasm.

Tchaikovsky invited me somewhat abruptly to come with him to Petersburg. The kindly noblesse of his charming and extremely sensitive nature attracted me; except the calm and thoughtful assurance and definiteness of Brahms's nature were too much on my mind, I had felt too distinct a glimpse of the clarity of his spirit to be capable to even consider this thought seriously, although then, as already mentioned, it was far from certain what the near future would have in store for me. Brahms had hardly spoken a word from which I could not derive immediate benefits; he had done me a nearly invaluable service by strengthening inevitably my own conviction of the worthlessness of my work. Tchaikovsky did everything to make this conviction waver, but I felt clearly that his judgment demanded nothing from me and was, in this regard, completely unfruitful and useless; I could not learn anything from it.

I spent nearly a whole day alone with Tchaikovsky. Understandably, I had the inclination from time to time to talk with him about Brahms, but I realized that he felt uneasy about Brahms, apparently he felt repelled by his personality.

I also met Hans von Bülow at that time in Hamburg; I sat behind him and his charming wife during the Tchaikovsky concert. He was in good spirits and delighted in the play of the young Sapellnikoff whose performance of the Tchaikovsky Piano Concerto in B-flat Minor, dedicated to von Bülow, was exquisite. Finally, as if intoxicated, I traveled back to Kiel.

Immediately upon my arrival, as if something might otherwise interfere, I acted upon a resolve that had grown out of everything I had considered during my travel: I wrote a letter to Brahms in which I poured my heart out confidingly and finally asked him to make an exception and take me on as his student. Then I went to Klaus Groth to tell him about it. We did not remain in uncertainty for long: Brahms answered immediately from Vienna with the following words:

Honored and dear sir:

I must overcome a certain shyness—but finally I have no other advice for you than to come here and study with Mr. Eusebius Mandyczewski.[6] Mr. M. is a young, very able man who will certainly be agreeable to you in every way. Whatever you might wish to have from me is at your service in full measure. I would hope that you might be able to come to a decision quickly so that you could make use of the rest of the winter! The summer will probably mean a long pause.

In great haste and with warm greetings for you and Klaus Groth,

Your devoted

Joh. Brahms

The decisive turning point in my life had arrived. Thanks to the sacrifices of high-minded friends in Kiel, whose names have been withheld from me to this day, I was able soon afterward to depart for Vienna, where, on February 13, 1888, in the morning, coming straight from the station, I walked into Brahms's room.

Again it was early in the morning; again he offered me one of the big cigars from the familiar bulky case; and again I was unable to prevent it from going out repeatedly as I talked. But already at the second match Brahms said: "You don't seem to deserve a good cigar," and never again until the day he died did I receive one of the "genuine ones," but was always, unlike others, made to settle for an Austrian imitation.[7] At the same time I was soon to experience what he meant by his words in the letter "Whatever you might wish to have from me is at your service in full measure." First he introduced me, at the archive of the Gesellschaft der Musikfreunde, to Mr. Mandyczewski, who was to be my counterpoint teacher; then, for the first time, I ate lunch with him at the Red Hedgehog, and after lunch he took me to look for an apartment, whereby he exhibited a weakness for the older buildings.[8] On these strolls through the city he immediately drew my attention to what holy ground we were treading on. In front of one house he would say, "This is the 'Eye of God,'" and in front of another "Hats off, this is where *Figaro* was written."[9] We were in the Rauhensteingasse, too.

Finally, in the so-called Freihaus auf der Weiden, near his own apartment, we found a room that suited my needs. "The young man is fond of music," Brahms said to the landlady. "Will he hear here a little piano playing, singing or such, from time to time?" She was afraid she couldn't oblige. "Well, then it is not so important." Then he gave me one of his coffee-makers, plate, spoon, knife, and fork, so that I was comfortably installed right on the first day. His library was open for my use, and his purse likewise. I could have as much money from him as I needed, but I never found it necessary to take any and never did borrow anything. In the evening he took me with him to the Vienna Tonkünstler-Verein (the composers' association), of which he was the Honorary President, and advised me to become acquainted with a Dr. Rottenberg, who was about my age and whose friendship has become infinitely dear to me.[10]

It was agreed that my counterpoint work with Mandyczewski should begin at once. With him I limited my work to strict counterpoint, bringing my free compositions to Brahms, not necessarily at any agreed-upon time; rather, whenever I had finished a piece, I gave it to him, and a few days later it would be discussed in the morning between ten and twelve. In regard to the counterpoint studies, he merely inquired now and again how far I had gotten—for example, when he visited me in my room and happened to find me working on such a project.

In the beginning I would pick him up every day at half past twelve to go with him to lunch at the Red Hedgehog. Then, as was his custom, he would take his coffee either there, or, if the weather was fine, in the Stadtpark, and afterward he would take a longish walk, often in the Prater.[11] As a rule I could not afford this luxury, namely the time. But in the evenings, generally after a concert or after the opera, we would meet again in the Hedgehog as agreed, usually with Rottenberg, often, too, in a small group with the Kalbecks, Doors, Brülls, and other Viennese musicians.[12] Sometimes he would also bring strangers, to whom he would graciously demonstrate the superior qualities of the Hedgehog. When there were a lot of people present he had a tendency to be reticent, or else he would bubble over with good-humored jokes and high-spirited witticisms that spared no one. With deep nostalgia, however, I think back to those splendid evenings on which Rottenberg and I sat alone with him in the low-ceilinged back room, where his portrait now hangs, and the taciturn Brahms warmed up and allowed us a glimpse of his deep and strong human soul. But he never, on such evenings, spoke of his work, and extremely seldom of himself and his life. It is true that during our lessons I often had the good fortune to hear him speak of himself; it was nearly always in a state of excitement. The occasions when he spoke calmly about himself were more infrequent; this occurred on long walks—for example, when he had made a few children happy with candy in the Prater, or when I walked home with him in the evening. Then I could make bold to ask him about this or that aspect of his life or his works without being immediately rebuffed. Unfortunately, in the second winter I already had to deny myself the pleasure of eating lunch together with Brahms every day, since the Hedgehog grew too expensive for me. Brahms, it is true, always maintained that the Hedgehog was the cheapest restaurant in Vienna, and in fact he understood how to manage in such a way that he always paid less than I did and yet ate better. He was quite extraordinarily frugal in his daily life: seventy to eighty kreuzer were the most that he required for his midday meal, including a small glass of Pilsner beer or a quarter-liter of red wine.[13] In the evening he scarcely drank any more than that. It is only because the opposite has been asserted so often that I feel it is my duty to describe this in such detail, in accordance with the truth.

The first two weeks in Vienna were rounded out with a task that I had taken on in order to raise money. Under the circumstances to which I have alluded, which alone had made it possible for me to stay in Vienna, I felt that I should apply for a scholarship that was offered at that time, and I told Brahms about it. He tried to talk me out of it: "I have never wanted to apply for anything like that." But finally he accepted my rationale and asked me to show him the pieces I had done for the application. I remember giving them to him with some hesitation and asking him whether I should send them in at all. But Brahms said: "Anyone who knows the slightest thing about it can recognize talent, and no one is going to expect you to turn out masterpieces." So I gamely sent them off.

In March my real studies with Brahms began. The first lesson is one that I will never forget: It was bitter. On the same day on which he had encouraged me so nicely to send off my creations, he asked me whether I wouldn't bring him back the songs I had shown him in Leipzig, so that he could talk about them with me in more detail. During our lessons he always sat at the piano, my work lay on the music stand and I sat next to him. But no note was ever played on the piano, the only exception being when he wanted to give a concrete example of wrong notes or other bad parts of a composition by demonstrating their ugly effects. With a sole exception, namely once in Ischl when Rottenberg and I were called on to demonstrate some of my variations for four hands, I was never permitted to play anything of mine on the piano for him.

Since Brahms had judged the songs relatively leniently in Leipzig, I hoped to hear good things. But now he suddenly changed his tune. He took up one song after the other, demonstrated mercilessly, expressing himself forcefully, but always appealing only to my faculty of understanding, how poor these songs were. He criticized my poor, pampered dears so roundly that there wasn't a good beat left in them and the tears leapt to my eyes. And yet that was only the introduction; I was about to feel his pedagogical rod even more sharply. He stood up and fetched a few loose, yellowed sheets. It was the manuscript of those songs by Robert Schumann that Brahms would later publish himself in the supplemental volume of Schumann's works.[14] Then he sat down again at the piano, played and sang them for me, especially that touching song "An Anna," whose melody Schumann used in the F-sharp-Minor Sonata, op. 11, with such enthusiastic sentiment that he could not forbear to weep tears of emotion, which came easily to him. "Yes," he said, standing up, "Schumann wrote that when he was eighteen; talent is what you need, nothing else will get you anywhere." Then, as if the cup of humiliation were not full, he handed me back the badly rumpled and wilted bouquet of my songs and dismissed me with the ironic words: "So, young man, continue to amuse yourself in this way," an expression to which Brahms was very partial and which I would have to swallow many times more.

I stood as if thunderstruck. The situation could not have been made more bitterly or heartwrenchingly clear to me. Only recently he had called my work talented and done everything to bolster my self-confidence. Why, then, had he called me to Vienna to see him—not, finally, to tell me that I was without talent? In the days that followed it was necessary for me to keep this constantly before my eyes, in order not to despair completely. For I might as well say right away that Brahms never again spoke an encouraging word, much less a word of praise, about my work. In addition to this, his entire manner toward me changed from that day forward. True, when we were alone, he remained the same familiar, dear, paternal friend, but in any larger group I soon learned to remain completely silent, since I could be certain that he would respond to even the most harmless remark by cutting me off with an infinitely condescending "Well, you are still quite young," or "That is not so critical," or some similarly blunt remark. I will not deny that I fell prey to periods of complete despondency, even despair, to which I feared I would succumb. Of not inconsiderable influence, moreover, was that my studies in counterpoint with Mr. Mandyczewski were only advancing with difficulty. The fruit of long hours of the most arduous labor was often only a few bars, and for a very long time I could not feel their positive effect on my work, so that however bravely I might resist, I could not but begin to doubt my abilities. My tranquility of mind threatened to desert me at work and to be replaced by a nervous haste by means of which I wanted to force more significant results more quickly.

Things went on like this for a considerable period, before I really learned how to work. Not until a whole year later did Brahms remark on some occasion: "You will never hear a word of praise from me; if you can't stand that, then whatever is inside you only deserves to go to waste." This sentence was my salvation. Why Brahms applied this strict and austere method of pedagogy toward me, whether perhaps he found something frivolous, immodest, or even arrogant in my demeanor, I do not know. But it is certain that he acted according to his dictum, which he repeated countless times: "One mustn't spoil the young." Perhaps, too, he was thinking of his own youth, of how many difficult battles he had fought through to their fortunate conclusion. "It is not easy to find someone who has had as hard a time of it as I have," he said to me once as I sat alone in the Hedgehog with him on his birthday; and then he recounted sad events that were, in part, already known to me from Klaus Groth's stories. "If my father were still alive," Brahms said, "and I were sitting in the orchestra in the first chair of the second violins, then at least I could say to him that I had accomplished something." He could speak with justifiable pride, for everything he was, he had become through his own efforts.

But sometimes he played a softer tune. Thus, later, he might have expressed his satisfaction by showing me, after my lesson, the most beautiful treasures from his collection, or playing for me works I did not know by Ph. E. Bach, Scarlatti, and others. Or he would read me foolish letters that had just arrived, like the one from a stranger in Kapstadt who, being so satisfied with the piano that had just been delivered, wanted another—this turned out to be the clumsy ruse of an autograph hound, a breed to whom Brahms was not exactly obliging. Or he would show me gifts from equally unknown admirers and tell me to keep them. Sometimes, on a beautiful spring morning, he would be prepared to give away everything that was lying around his apartment. His books he was very particular about. But on one occasion, as he was returning a cycle of Rückert's songs I had composed, he made me a gift of Rückert's poems, which he loved very much.[15] The book contained a dedication and his signature. He scratched out the former with a knife, but let Rückert's name stand and only said: "Now, with just a little bit more depth." I also soon noticed that when certain passages were passed over without comment or individual pieces were not commented on at all, these were the ones in which there was the least to criticize. True, I learned nothing about their value, and it was therefore not at all out of the question that they might be of precious little significance. It was only in a roundabout way that I occasionally heard, for example from Rottenberg, whether the content of my work had been of interest to him. In his dealings with me, he was occupied solely with the measure of perfection.

Brahms lived in the Karlsgasse No. 4 on the upper floor, No. 8, in three rooms. One entered through his bedroom—a common inconvenience in Vienna. I have often lived in circumstances in which I had to pass through the bedroom of my landlord in order to get to my own: "If it doesn't bother the gentleman, then it doesn't bother us," was the usual comment. Over his bed there hung an engraving of J. S. Bach. Through a glass door one then passed into the simply furnished living room, in which stood the grand piano and the desk; above the latter hung the well-known medallion portrait of Robert and Clara Schumann, with a lovely dedication to Brahms in Schumann's own hand. Toward one side was the library, in which a lectern could also be found. The windows of the living room and the library, which faced toward the front of the building, were always closed, while the windows of the bedroom, which looked out on the courtyard of the Technical University, were open day and night.[16] During lessons Brahms was always dressed in slippers, trousers, and a wool shirt. Since he was nearsighted, he wore a pair of glasses, which he exchanged for a pince-nez when he went out.

Since it was common knowledge that Brahms could almost certainly be found at home in the morning, we were often interrupted by visitors. As soon as we caught sight of such a visitor from our seat at the grand piano by looking through the curtain of the glass door, Brahms would flee with great bounds into the library, where I gave a signal by means of prearranged signs as to whether or not he should put on a jacket. He always did when a lady came by. It would be untrue if I were to maintain that Brahms was always polite to his visitors. On the contrary, I was often witness to embarrassing scenes, particularly in the case of visits by unknown artists in whom he had no interest. If he felt someone had come out of curiosity, or wanted something from him that he was not inclined to give, or perhaps even wanted something unreasonable, then he knew how to dispatch such a visitor in an amazingly short time. It is not entirely without cause that Brahms developed a reputation as a boor, although few individuals could be as charming as he. Not long ago a famous artist told me that he only went to visit Brahms when he could be sure he would not be at home.

As far as my actual instruction was concerned, Brahms didn't give me any definite assignments. In general I could work on whatever I wanted. But in the beginning he recommended that I write songs with short stanzas and practice the form of the variation. "Writing variations is the smartest thing you can do for the time being." Later he asked for sonata movements and sonatas.

If I now attempt to share, from these lessons, some things that I believe are of general interest and may perhaps be of use here and there, it is not that I am deluding myself about the great difficulties I will face in this endeavor. The danger of saying things that are misleading or even false is in fact very great, since I am continually forced to generalize from a specific example. In this short study, it would not have been possible to apply the method of quoting each example along with Brahms's corrections and observations. But anyone with any insight knows that generalizations drawn from individual statements, even when these are undoubtedly correct, are always risky in matters of art and often turn things that are correct in themselves into utter falsehoods. For this reason I would like to state that I have been very careful, both in my selections and in my presentation, and that every sentence is based on my personal experiences in the lessons. I would rather say too little than too much. Furthermore, I would like to state explicitly that I have always made Brahms's own words clearly identifiable through the use of quotation marks. Otherwise it is not he who is speaking; rather, I am describing my own convictions, as they have been formed, admittedly, on the basis of my Brahmsian instruction. However, I am not so presumptuous as to suggest that it would be appropriate for me to identify myself or my opinions with his, based on this instruction.

Brahms's way of speaking had something abrupt, fragmentary about it. He was not one to discourse expansively on a subject. In contrast to so-called eloquent people who, when they speak, evince pleasure at their own words, he gave the impression that he spoke only reluctantly and only as much as was absolutely necessary. His sentences were uttered precisely and pointedly, and here he always hit the nail on the head; but he concealed far more, in fact often the main thing, without which his words could not be properly understood. This became all the more pronounced if he was in a situation in which he was forced to speak about himself. Everyone who was close to Brahms knows how abruptly and almost dismissively he could speak of his own works; on this subject in particular it was harder than ever to understand him correctly. He was quite conscious of the value of his works, but his nature, with its manly modesty, made it endlessly difficult for him to talk about himself. Often he tried to extricate himself with a joke, but naturally it is impossible that this should always have been recognized, so an awkward atmosphere could easily develop. Usually, when he spoke seriously about himself, he was in a state of embarrassment, which was often mingled with anger if someone pressed him whom he did not think had the right to do so. If, as was the rule, he did not feel confident from the outset that he would be understood, then he was capable, unless restrained by a sense of general regard for the person with whom he was speaking, of pulling the wool over that person's eyes in the most outrageous fashion, and with perfect equanimity. The saying "Since truth is a pearl, cast it not before swine," as Theodor Storm has it, was sacred to him; and there were in effect very few individuals who were not sometimes reckoned among the swine.[17] But he took it well, as I often had occasion to remark in my own case, if one protested and struggled valiantly to escape from this rather unpleasant circumstance. And if one succeeded in winning his confidence in this way, then he was also capable of finding that person worthy of the truth.

I have always retained the impression that, of all song forms, Brahms valued strophic songs the most. This sentence can easily lead to misunderstandings, as Brahms indeed never expressed anything so definitive about the subject to me, but he did once say something similar to me about his own songs. Once, during a walk, Brahms began a conversation with the words, "There must be among my songs one that is called *Feldeinsamkeit*." I remarked, as disinterestedly as possible, that I was familiar with it. Now he told me how upset he had been that Klaus Groth had also expressed objections to the famous *gestorben bin* and had even gone so far as to suggest changes in the text by Allmers.[18] He defended Allmers's text in the warmest of terms and added: "There is nobody about whom one can be certain that the Philistine won't come out in him someday." From the text we moved on to the subject of the music, and then, thinking of the wonderful effect of that particular piece and the genius expressed in its strophic form, I steered the conversation to the subject of the mysterious effects that are inherent in that form. Brahms picked up this theme, and in the course of our conversation uttered the following phrase: "My little songs are more appealing to me than my big ones," which, as an illustration of what has been said, could only mean that a successful strophic song was what he preferred. During my lessons, too, I always had this impression.

When he discussed a song with me, the first thing to be examined was whether the musical form fully corresponded to the text. Mistakes along these lines he criticized especially sharply, as a lack of artistic sense or the consequence of inadequate comprehension of the text. In general, he demanded that if the text allowed a treatment in strophes, this was what should be utilized. In order to become clear as to which texts were to be treated in strophes and which were not, he recommended a close study of the complete songs of Franz Schubert, whose acute artistic sense he said was evident even in his most unassuming songs. "There is no song by Schubert from which one cannot learn something."

It is very difficult to bring forth anything generally valid about this point.

It is in no way exhaustive to say, for example, that when the text of a lied is constructed in stanzas in which the basic mood is captured in every single detail or in quite varied images, the strophic compositional approach is the only appropriate one. For as much as the strophic form seems the musically most fitting expression for the stanza text, even for texts in which the above does not apply, it is not uncommon that particularities, seeming trifles, even superficialities impede strophic treatment, or stand insurmountably in its way, not to mention the case in which the whole conception of a poem, in form and content, absolutely demands to be musically disassociated from the metric stanza. It is also certain that the composer's vast, inexhaustible world of musical rhythms takes the place of the poet's stanza, with immeasurably richer means: but applied at the right moment, drawn from sufficient depth and executed with artistic maturity, the strophic composition of a lied will have a superior effect over any freer treatment of the same text. If one calls to mind Brahms lieder in light of these general contemplations, the meaning of the Brahmsian saying quoted earlier: "My little songs are more appealing to me than my big ones," becomes clear.

The most rigorous form of the strophic song in music is the one in which the same melody repeats for each stanza, with unchanged accompaniment, as seen innumerable times with Schubert, Schumann, Brahms, among others. One of the most magnificent examples that takes but a single freedom, an introduction appearing in the beginning, is "Nähe des Geliebten," one of the most beautiful German songs by Goethe and Schubert, a song born of longing in word and tone. Considering this song it is unpleasant to imagine how one of those unthinking composers of so-called lieder, seduced by the abundance of imagery in the text, might render this poem in music. What a scene would we endure, particularly here! Schubert wrote a simple melody for this text, encompassing a few measures. But what a mistake to think this melody was composed for the first stanza of the Goethe poem, after which the following stanzas could be simply rattled off! Oh no, this melody welled up from the same deep-seated, uniform feeling from which poured the poet's images, saying but one thing in ever so many new ways.

The melody is the musical expression of the impact of the entire poem's effect upon the composer, and so, as always with Schubert, it happens that in every new verse, the melody glows more richly and appears to say something new, as with the new text the expression of the basic sensation becomes ever more explicit and intense. Of course partly it is the melody which, through the artistic talents of the composer, yields in a supple manner to the specific words of each verse, so that no dissonances are created that severely disturb the whole.

When my teacher Eusebius Mandyczewski worked on the critical edition of the complete Schubert lieder, he showed me how Schubert had modified a melody that he had written to the words of the first stanza to benefit a part in the text of a later verse, and how he had chosen this modified melody for the first stanza as well, even though the earlier version was decidedly more suitable.[19] He could have kept both parts of the melody, after all. Apparently he cared more to keep a strict strophic song and his artistic sense suggested that effects rather should intensify in their details than diminish. By the way, I believe that this is an utterly important condition in the emergence of genuine folk songs.

However, the strophic song does not always have this strict form. At times, the composer changes the accompaniment in subsequent verses while strictly keeping the same melody, as Brahms has done in his folk songs; or he changes the tempo, or maybe introduces a freer ending, or offers variants or even variations of the first strophe, as Brahms did in "O versenk, o versenk," in *Feldeinsamkeit* or in *Wie Melodien zieht es*; or only the beginning of the strophic melody returns but is developed further in totally new ways; one could call such form a transitory form to the freely through-composed lied in which the stanza of the text is completely dissolved. A composer may also blend a poet's two stanzas of the same meter into one melodic unit, or treat several stanzas in the same way with only a few treated differently, as in Brahms's *Falkenstein Lied*.[20] A thorough study of Brahms's lieder according to these aspects is extraordinarily instructive and shows him at a height of artistic sensibility that is at least not surpassed by Schubert.

Although in the beginning Brahms recommended to me that for the time being I should write short songs, irrespective of whether they be strophic or not, he allowed me full freedom. Naturally I chose my texts myself, except that at my request he would lend me collections of poems. In his bedroom there was an armoire that was stuffed full from top to bottom with "lyrics." He knew and read just about everything there was; but he once told me that he had almost never bought a book himself. Into that armoire also disappeared those volumes that were sent to him by the modern poets of the day, always without success. But I often held in my hands the proof that he had read even the most miserable, pitiful scribblings. Once, in one of these volumes, I found a poem that Brahms had marked with signs of his most extreme displeasure: in it, Rückert was arrogantly and contemptuously dismissed. I mentioned this to Brahms, and he said, "I know, a fellow like that abuses Rückert!"

Brahms demanded from a composer, first of all, that he should know his text precisely. He also meant by this, of course, that the construction and meter of the poem should be thoroughly clear to him. Next, he recommended to me that before composing I should carry the poem around with me in my head for a long time and frequently recite it out loud to myself, paying close attention to everything, especially the declamation. I should also mark the pauses especially and follow those later when I was working. "Just imagine to yourself Lewinsky reciting this song," he said once as we were discussing a song with almost no pauses, "here he would certainly stop for a moment."[21]

It is particularly pleasurable to observe the way that Brahms knew how to treat these pauses in his songs, how they are often an echo of what precedes them, often a preparation for what follows (*Von ewiger Liebe*); how here, at times, the rhythm undergoes an artistic development and the accompaniment is raised to a factor that has its own independent influence. He placed great importance on these pauses and their treatment, and they are often, in fact, an unmistakable sign that the composer is an artist who creates with freedom and assurance, not a dilettante groping in the dark, influenced by every chance occurrence.

Once the song's structure had been examined from all these angles, there followed a consideration of its individual parts. At those points where language inserts punctuation, the musical phrase has cadences; and just as the poet, in his purposeful construction, ties his sentences more or less closely together using commas, semicolons, periods, etc., as his external signs, so the musician, similarly, has at his disposal perfect and imperfect cadences in a variety of forms to indicate the greater or lesser degree of coherence of his musical phrases. The importance of the cadences is immediately evident, for it is through them that both the construction and the proportion of the various parts are determined. Thus Brahms, too, focused my particular attention on them.

Here the main thing was to understand the combination and opposition of the three great factors in music—rhythm, melody, and harmony; to understand, for example, that a cadence that is harmonically and melodically perfect will have a weaker effect if it does not occur simultaneously with the rhythmic cadence; that such an occurrence may, in one instance, be a grievous error, in another an effective means of joining the phrases together; that the weaker cadence must precede the stronger; and finally that the proportion of the various parts must correspond to the text. Sometimes Brahms showed me passages where the cadence was not well motivated rhythmically, and from this circumstance he proved irrefutably that the cadence had been inserted at that point because the imaginative energy had flagged. Often, in such cases, a six-four chord appears, more or less like a rescuing, comfortable armchair into which the exhausted fantasy can collapse prematurely. "Draw a line under every six-four chord and examine closely whether it is in the right place," said Brahms, and, from my experience with my own and others' compositions, I can say that this rule is truly a fruitful, even a golden one. As excellent as the effect of this chord can be—naturally I am referring only to cadential six-four chords—it is often nothing but the symptom and, in its flabbiness, the true reflection of a completely lame and exhausted imagination.

The location and form of the cadences is linked, in the closest possible manner, to the course of the modulation. Here Brahms called for the tightest possible reins and the most extreme consistency. Even in the case of a very long song whose subsidiary phrases were extended and internally consistent, the principal key always had to be clearly articulated and its dominance over the secondary keys maintained by means of clear relationships, so that, so to speak, the sum of all the keys utilized in the piece combined to create an image of the tonic key in its activity. That precisely the lack of clear identification of a key, even the tonic, can serve as an excellent means of expression is in the nature of the matter. The splendid freedom we sense in Brahms's creative power is rooted in part in his instinctively sure sense of the unified character of the modulation; and the saying that it is only by subordinating himself that man can be truly free finds in him a beautiful confirmation.

How often, when listening to songs, particularly modern songs, must one wonder why a certain song has to end in A-flat major and find no answer except that it began in A-flat major? Here the composer, who appears to move so freely in his modulations, has actually become the slave of an idea whose true meaning he does not seem to grasp. He would be much more consistent in his arbitrariness if he ended in some other key into which he had been led just as his text was coming to its conclusion. For a unified modulation does not in any way preclude the use of even the most distant keys. Quite the contrary, these keys become distant only by virtue of the fact that another key governs; this is what gives them their expressive power. They say something different; they are like the colors of a painting that contrast with the background color and are simultaneously contained and intensified by it.

Among other things, it was to help me acquire a reliable sense of the unified character of the modulation that Brahms had me imitate in my own compositions the modulations from *adagio* movements of Mozart or Beethoven. "If Beethoven goes from C major to E major, you do the same; that is how I used to do it myself," he told me. With regard to the overall course of the modulation, with the exception of individual divergences, the guiding principle was: The straight path is the best path. In specific instances, too, as he corrected me, I often thought of the saying: "Do you want to wander farther and farther away? Look, the good things are so near." And precisely these nearby, good things—how often they are overlooked because our vision has been obscured by the force of a hastily conceived idea and we have neglected the essential things in favor of inessential ones, so that we can't see the forest for the trees!

After what I have just said, it should be clear that Brahms was not one to be impressed by a few "interesting" phrases or by complicated and "atmospheric" accompanimental figures. His eye remained keen. Sometimes he used a drastic but unusually simple means to open my eyes and make me sense quite clearly that under that sumptuous and glittering cloak lay hidden a pitiful, shabby, and undernourished being, which could not possibly show itself naked. Brahms would cover up the upper system of the piano accompaniment with his hand, and, pointing to the vocal line and the bass, he would say, with an expressive smile: "I read only this." Through such a procedure the unnaturalness of the invention was often demonstrated to me *ad ocolos,* as it were; I no longer understood how I could have arrived at such a dreary melody and such boring basses, unless I were to assume that I had actually been captivated by the accompaniment figures. In other words, that I had been unfree. The determining role of the melody and of clearly perceived basses created in good counterpoint was an absolute requirement for him, one that remained in force even when the overall design of the song was at its most artful. Brahms, as I have mentioned, loved to elevate the accompaniment to a fully equal, even independent, element and sometimes to move it canonically in relation to the voice. But one never has the impression that the melody has been invented under the coercion of the canon. The canonic form never develops into the controlling element, but serves, on the contrary, only as a means of increasing the charm of the vocal melody. And the melody will always and unhesitatingly break the form whenever its powerful and sublime flow so dictates. But if only a few poor crumbs from the piano accompaniment are allotted every once in a while to the vocal part: for such a concoction Brahms could never permit the dignified appellation of "song."

On the other hand, Brahms could never be satisfied, of course, by a pretty, well-accompanied melody and nothing more. In one case, when my melody did not seem to him to do justice to the text, he said, "Write yourself another text underneath that." Brahms believed strongly in something that can be briefly characterized as *Wortausdruck* (word-expression). Often one will find in his songs remarkable melodic turns of phrase that have evidently been brought about by certain individual words in the text. But far from disturbing the melodic flow, these phrases seem to be essential components of the melody, imparting a particular physiognomy to it. Indeed, they often resemble the kernels of motives from which the whole melody seems to grow. It is instructive, in this context, to study which passages of text Brahms handles this way in his songs, while he passes over others that seem to offer the composer an equal opportunity to indulge in such characteristic turns of phrase. One will then find that here, too, his keen eye always separated the essential from the inessential. Nor did he ever compose any so-called mood poems consisting of nothing but an accumulation of this kind of word-painting. When the melodic line followed a particular verbal expression too closely, he would criticize it with the words: "Think more of the larger picture!" And with that, he hit the nail on the head.

Although Brahms's awesome talent and enormous experience made it self-explanatory, I nevertheless often found it amazing to observe how the creative process of my compositions seemed, from the first moment, completely transparent to him. The occasions when I learned the most from him were when he would not only point out the mistakes themselves, but also reveal how they had come about. At the same time, he was not always pleased if I showed him the same pieces, especially songs, in reworked form. He preferred to have me bring him new songs in which the errors he had inveighed against were avoided. He spoke from his own experience when he said: "It is rare that a piece, once it has been completed, becomes better through revision; usually, it gets worse." Then he advised me never to begin the working-out of a song before the whole thing had taken definite form as an outline, either in my head or on paper. "When ideas come to you, go for a walk; then you will discover that the thing you thought was a complete thought was actually only the beginning of one."

Again and again he would impress upon me that I should mistrust my own ideas. I have often had the experience that precisely those ideas that become rooted in the mind, like an *idée fixe*, are the natural obstacle to free creation, because one falls in love with them and, instead of being their master, becomes their slave. "The pen is not only for writing, but also for deleting," Brahms would say. "But take care. Once something has been written down, it is hard to get rid of it. But if you have come to the conclusion that it will not do—even if it is good in itself—then don't think about it for long: simply strike it out." How often one attempts to save such a passage, and thus ruins the entire thing! Sometimes passages like this also serve to conceal the troublemaking elements, whose presence I might have intuited but would not have looked for there at all. When Brahms then subjected these very passages to his candid critique, I was hurt and surprised at first because these passages were my favorites, until I came to see that I hadn't found the troublemaker because I had inadvertently assumed that this particular spot must be allowed to stand under any circumstances. I have had the opportunity to feel the truth of those Brahmsian judgments myself; they are the result of long suffering and unrelenting self-criticism.

What I have just said may seem to be contradicted by the fact that a Brahms manuscript often bears a great many corrections. For example, the Clarinet Trio, op. 114, is very heavily "patched" and pasted over. But these corrections have to do with particular details of the composition. Even a composer as technically secure as Mendelssohn was constantly making changes in his works, sometimes while they were bring printed.

Another obstacle that often stands in the way of the young composer cannot be overcome early enough: learning how to "write" in the first place, that is, to master the technique that is necessary before the composer can even begin to form his ideas freely and put them down on paper. This problem is related to the superficial, thoughtless, and completely wrong-headed method of musical education in which our young people are wont to be instructed, whereby a composer finds himself in the position of having to free himself with great effort from an instrument that he has, up until that point, used only as an expedient for his composing. With an education like the one Mozart, for example, enjoyed, such a method is precluded from the first. Natural talent obviously makes a great difference here, but in this matter even the greatest talent cannot escape the necessity of an appropriate and reasonable education. Even Mozart had to begin by mastering the technique of writing; that he was able to do this while still so young is due not least to his excellent father.

In not a few cases a composer who has already emerged from childhood without having acquired this technique may be held back by a kind of false pride that is fundamentally nothing but vanity, and which Brahms sought to discredit in my eyes by saying: "You must learn how to work. You must write a lot, day after day, and not think that what you are writing always has to be something significant. It is the writing itself that matters in the first place. I don't always want to see it. That's what the stove is there for. You must make many songs before a usable one emerges!" I can state most definitively that Brahms understood the last sentence in the most literal sense, and I can cite a large number of texts that, according to the evidence of his own words, he may have composed but never published; instead, he destroyed them. Perhaps it may be of more general interest if I remark here that Brahms's first violin sonata is the fourth. Three previous ones were suppressed because they did not pass his criticism.

"Writing variations is the smartest thing you can do for the time being," Brahms had told me at the very beginning of my instruction, and so one of the first assignments I brought him was a theme with variations for piano. I had preceded these variations with a poem whose four stanzas had exercised a determining influence on the same number of groups of variations, in the sense that each individual stanza preceded each group as a motto. Brahms was delighted with this notion and told me that he had once carried out the same idea, but nothing had come of it. Then he criticized the excessively large number of variations, which must necessarily detract from the idea. "The fewer variations, the better; but then they must say everything that is to be said." The variations themselves were much too free for him; for he was very exact when it came to this form. Beginning with the choice of a theme, he recommended the greatest caution. "For only a few themes are suitable." Even though I had succeeded in inventing one that he considered suitable, he advised me that next time it would be better to look for one in Schubert or somewhere else. As a model, he named Beethoven's variations, which he said I could not study too closely. Everyone knows nowadays that Brahms himself has scarcely any rivals in this area. Not once did Brahms, in the whole time he was teaching me, refer to one of his own compositions for purposes of instruction. It was as if they did not exist. The anecdote is well known about the time when Beethoven, confronted by someone who showed him a composition and complained that he himself had committed the criticized error in his own works, said with annoyance, "*I* am permitted to do that; you are *not*." I am aware that once, in a similar situation, Brahms told someone—not me, for in such things I was always very circumspect—"Have I ever offered you my compositions as a model?"

Whatever one may think about the variation as a form in its own right, its value must be seen in the fact that it was truly born of the spirit of instrumental music. Through the variation, instrumental music first cut free from its ties to vocal music and forms; by means of the variation, it acquired its own independent instrumental style. There is no instrumental form where variations did not play a role; no great master of instrumental music who did not cultivate them intensely. Their importance is, however, more far-reaching: for their essence is most intimately connected to the essence of all things in art and nature. What else is the abundance of forms in the manifest world but a variation on the single, great mysterious theme: life? Wasn't it Goethe's wonderful dream to find that one primordial plant from which all others developed?[22] For to vary means to develop, and what else does the artist ultimately do but develop? Nowhere in the arts is the spirit of nature expressed in a purer and more concentrated way, free of any form from the world appearances, than in music, especially instrumental music. Its realm begins only beyond the manifest world, where the realm of the other arts that adhere more closely to the physical ceases to exist. For just as the spirit of nature becomes apparent through the emergence of forever new forms, all based however on a single underlying original *ur*thought, so we see at work in the most manifold forms of instrumental music a spirit that is its loyal image. The form in which this spirit finds the most musical expression, however, in which the essence of instrumental music, I would say, finds its most characteristic form, is the variation: that form in which new creations are developed from seeds, that, dormant in the musical theme, loyally reflect the *ur*form of that theme on the one hand, while on the other being filled with their own, independent life.

What Brahms thought about the variation I do not know; it seems to me, however, that something along these lines could be gathered from his compositions. When I speculate about what he might have said to the sentences above, something I do constantly as I write this, it seems to me very likely that he would skip over them with a mumbled "oh well, and so on." For he did not think much of tirades about art, especially not if they came flavored with a taste of philosophy. He believed nothing much would come of it. To me, though, it was important to point out the educational value of the variation form, which should be convincing enough without further ado after what I've said above.

No form is as well suited for teaching the beginner to differentiate the essential from the inessential, for developing artistic and strictly logical thinking, for protecting the imagination from arbitrary flights of fancy, and for clearing the mind to appreciate pure form. Obviously, to embellish the melody with some ornamentation is not enough; instead, one must penetrate deep to the core of the theme and generate something new from it without touching its form. Brahms at first guided my attention to the bass of the theme. "The bass is more important than the melody," he said. Not that the bass had to be kept under all circumstances. The bass, complementing and explaining the melody, gives the melody of the upper voices its specific physiognomy, and varying the bass can modify the whole character of a melody to a greater extent than varying the melody itself. Therefore Brahms insisted that variations of the bass—despite new turns— should not arbitrarily destroy the meaning and character of the original course of a modulation, not even if the course and final point of the modulation are changed, as is often the case in Brahms's music. The variation, though, does not cover only the melody but the rhythm and harmony of the theme as well; here again, one has to vary and develop from what is given if the whole is not to acquire the stamp of capriciousness. Brahms urged: "You have to keep your eyes fixed on your goal and that's only possible if the bass is firmly anchored, otherwise you'll be in a sort of limbo; and now straight on to the goal without wandering further afield."

This general rule, so important to follow when working on variations, made me think spontaneously of my work in counterpoint on a given *cantus firmus*. Here, too, the freely working imagination stays firmly grounded, is protected from capriciousness by the will, which is focused on a clear, consciously recognized goal. Only a keen, incessantly practiced artistic sense can build such a firm foundation, however, only with a formidable energy of the will is one able not to lose sight of that goal, but to reach it on a straight path: and these two factors determine, to a large extent, whether the work of art is shaped into the inevitable form that assures its deeply enthralling effect. In the variation genre the essential element is presented by the theme; by preserving this essence within the form, one exercises and sharpens reason, fortifies the will, and deepens the imagination as it becomes accustomed to exhausting a single idea.

Brahms did not criticize my changing keys in specific variations. The theme and kind of variation is likely to influence this question. But it is certain that Brahms himself, as well as Beethoven, made limited use of the change of keys, and that he regarded the chaconne of Bach as the most rigorous, most elevated form of the variation.

Brahms's Opus 9 proves how deeply the young Brahms had already penetrated the nature of theme and variations. Nevertheless, it seems as if here Brahms only played with the form, as he did later on only on one occasion: in Opus 23. It is certainly no coincidence that the themes of both works were written by Robert Schumann. Much of a personal nature has found expression here. How curiously far they seem from the variations Op. 21 and Op. 24, which in their rigor of form show Brahms already at the peak of his mastery![23] Whoever wants to become acquainted with the splendid power and idiosyncrasy of Brahms's creative strength should study his variations, as they are scattered throughout his works; nowhere else will one gain such deep insight into the workings of this master.

During the early part of my stay in Vienna, I lived only for my work, nothing disturbed me, the whole day was at my free disposal. Later on, however, various obligations came up that no longer permitted such concentrated efforts. In time, I succeeded in getting some students, and even though they were few in the beginning, I was able in this way to contribute at least something to my cost of living. I cannot say that Brahms helped me in any way in this endeavor, but nevertheless he was happy about every single student I could announce. Once, he expressed his views on this in a short and concise manner: "You also have to teach; I too had to do it and I found the experience to be as dreadful as anyone would." On the other hand, I owe Brahms the full extent of my social standing in Vienna: he introduced me to almost every circle he frequented, and his recommendation always provided mighty support. Thus many a door I would hardly have dared knock on opened as if by itself. This also brought me to the Fellingers, where I found a second home.[24] What I owe to this family has no place in the context of this paper; may I only mention here that my life will not suffice to make up for it. Later on, many an advantage grew from my becoming secretary of the Wiener Tonkünstlerverein, the Viennese

Society of Musicians. Brahms, as Honorary President, was hardly ever absent from committee meetings. Furthermore, opportunities were soon offered to work as conductor; at first in Baden near Vienna, where I, a Protestant, directed Catholic Church music; later on, women's choirs in Vienna were added. Because of all this, I also managed to acquire a some-what firm footing as a musician in Vienna, something Brahms saw with pleasure. From the very beginning, he urged me not to miss anything that might help me to gain a solid and respectable livelihood. One morn-ing after a lesson he had a serious talk with me and said, among other things: "One cannot feel like a complete person unless one stands on solid ground as a citizen of the State, fulfilling one's obligations. Don't you want to marry?" I answered that this was my firm intent. "Well, now," he continued, "just don't have any fantasies about the low life. When I con-sider how much I hate the people who deprived me of marrying." There was something distressing in the way these words burst out of him, in utmost agitation. I sensed that he was touching upon a sorrow in his life. Not long thereafter, he suddenly offered me a position as Municipal Director of Music, a position that would have provided for me well. At that time, I not only intended to marry, I even wished to marry as soon as possible, and I have to confess, the temptation, presented totally by surprise, was quite big. However, my studies in counterpoint were still in the beginning stages, so I refused his offer steadfastly, after careful consideration. He said nothing but: "Oh well, on we go."

A huge interruption of my studies was also imminent. Foolishly, I had again and again postponed fulfilling my military duty as a one-year volunteer. Of course, my friends in Kiel, including Klaus Groth, hoped that I could be completely exempted if Brahms put in a word for me. Only, I myself opposed this position because I neither could nor wanted to expe-rience this duty as a burden, no matter how inopportune it was. Brahms's similar views became apparent when he bade me farewell in Hamburg on my trip to my mother in Schleswig, where I joined my regiment of choice. "I cannot express how much I envy you. If only I were still as young as you, I would join you in an instant. I missed out on that, too."

Immediately after completing my course of duty, I returned to Vienna to resume my studies. However, as Brahms had already implied in his first letter to me, presented above, summer also brought a break every year. For, whoever possibly can leaves Vienna during the hot summer months, and since both Brahms and Mandyczewski, as well as all the families I was friends with, were absent from Vienna during the summer months, I had no other choice but to leave as well, whether to go home or to such a place as presented itself. Brahms had the habit of leaving early for the country, most often toward end of May; at times he first went on a trip, however, in those days until the end he went to Ischl for most of the summer. Every year before I started my summer travel, I visited him there to show him the completed work of mine he had not yet seen and to receive further suggestions. For Brahms himself, the summer months were the real work time—at least during the last ten years of his life. It goes without saying that he also worked on his compositions in Vienna during the winter, although I can only say this with any certainty about one work, since I saw it. In Ischl during the summer, however, he would develop the work, here it would mature to completion. Here, too, the early morning hours were the most important to him. He rose with the sun, even earlier: often by 5 a.m. he had already started his "run" through the woods around Ischl, working without pause, and the yield would be entrusted to paper during the early morning hours; as a rule, the main work of the day was completed by 10 or 11 a.m. He lived in one of the last houses, which lay somewhat elevated above the street, in the direction of Strobl.[25] Since it was built on a slope, one could exit from Brahms's rooms, on the upper level in the back of the house, directly to the outdoors; a few steps farther stood a bench, and in a few minutes one could reach the woods, which came down toward the house from the mountain. Of course, the idyllic quiet and seclusion of the location was somewhat disturbed by the children of the landlords, decent and simple folk who lived in the lower part of the house and had been generously blessed with offspring. This unfortunate circumstance, combined with the exaggerated simplicity of the home that could sometimes be embarrassing to Brahms when he had visitors, compelled him once to look for a different summer lodging in Ischl, while he was still in Vienna. He traveled there, exclusively for this purpose, and returned in quite a cheerful mood. Asked how he made out, he told me that after some searching, he had found a lodging that met his expectations in every regard. Since he had some time on his hands before his return trip, however, he decided out of a feeling of fondness for his old home to make a pilgrimage there; now his landlords welcomed him in such a friendly manner and especially the children were so happy about his visit, that he did not have the heart to tell them he had taken up other lodging; so instead he let it seem self-evident he would return come summer. And that's what happened. Brahms settled with the new landlord and moved into his old place for the summer, which he loyally kept until the end of his life.

My annual visits to Brahms in Ischl were always events I anticipated with special pleasure: for here I usually presented him with larger works that took longer to create. I always stayed with him for some time and here passed glorious days with him in wondrous nature. It seems to me that here he was always in an especially happy mood, equally ready to joke or be serious. Frequently we roamed about the environs of Ischl, where he was intimately familiar with the most beautiful paths through the woods. For Brahms loved nature passionately. Even during wintertime, on every second or third Sunday, if nothing else interfered, he would hike across the countryside with some of his friends. We would meet at 8 or 9 in the morning in front of the Opera House and return home only when it was dark. A sprightly walker with staying power, his pace was quite fast as long as we stayed on the plains. In later years, his corpulence made climbing more arduous. Once in Ischl, on an extremely hot day, he and I hiked up to a mountain lookout. Under the influence of the heat and the ascent, his appearance slowly turned so alarming that I was often tempted to urge him to turn back, and I was very happy when we finally reached the top. A severely cold evening followed the hot day. However, when we arrived, tired and late, at his home, Brahms sat down with me on the bench next to his house, took his jacket off and, drenched as he was, enjoyed contentedly the cold night breeze blowing about him. Though accustomed to similar situations, I dared express my concern that he might catch cold. If I felt too cold, he answered simply, I should speak up, and we could go inside.

The following day after lunch he suddenly had the idea that we might pay a visit to every famous female pianist who was vacationing in Ischl—each summer, there were quite a few. So we wandered from house to house and whoever was home welcomed us, happy and astonished. He introduced me as a young composer who, in every regard, gave high respects to the ladies.

After Ischl, I brought to Brahms the first sonata I wrote in Vienna. Already pretty much in the beginning of my studies Brahms had recommended, as mentioned before, that I take movements of Mozart, and particularly Beethoven sonatas, and subject them to a most exacting study—I should analyze their structure to the finest detail, account for every note in no uncertain terms, and attempt to emulate them with my own themes. He certainly did not mean to say that, following this procedure, something worthwhile in its own right would see the light of day; rather he wished that through this exercise of re-creation, my reasoning would be sharpened, my musical sensibilities refined, my sense for form purified: in short, I was supposed to learn how to think with musical logic.

Possibly at first every beginner re-creates more or less unconsciously whatever has made the strongest impression on him. But it is precisely through such conscious doing that he learns. All great masters, without exception, have followed this obvious path. Bach literally wrote himself into the manners and styles of his great predecessors, although they were as different as Pachelbel, Buxtehude, and Frescobaldi. "As you know, I can pretty much assume and imitate any kind of style and composer," says one Mozart letter. What Beethoven did was no different. This is the normal course of development, for a great man initially inspires the one who follows to imitate him rather than do things differently. In any case I am concerned that people will be only too ready to discard the educational approach that Brahms pursued with me as something of no practical value.

How on earth should a young musician, to whom nature offers no model whatsoever, acquire effective tools of his trade? How should he become acquainted with the means of his art? How many times I heard Brahms exclaim ironically, in anger: "Everything has to be learned, people know that. Music is the only thing you don't need to learn: either you know it or you don't!" That an artist above all has to learn to understand his world and its art is obvious. For we only call a person a great man when, infused by the spirit of his time, he has the energy and the skill to be able to apply the lever in the right place, and move it. Woe to the man, however, who is strong but whose tools are not in good order: the lever will fail. Brahms in no way believed that a person who had barely passed the requirements for theory of harmony and could write counterpoint for 36-voice orchestra, or set a brilliant piano part, had learned everything there was to learn. Musicians who believe they have achieved the essence of technique that way are just as far removed from the sacred nature of the art as a poet who has assembled a pile of mood-filled words and thinks he has written a poem, or a painter who is not able to draw. It would seem obvious that a young musician be trained in musical thinking and feeling so he learns to understand from the ground up what is unique to his art, but such thinking is in no way applied in practice. For example, a musician has to learn that throwing together themes is no more the mastery of counterpoint than whirling about key signatures can be called freedom of modulation; that declamation of words may not be confused with melody, and that one cannot have laws for the creation of instrumental forms that have nothing whatsoever in common with the nature of music. Rather, it is necessary to penetrate to the innermost core of this nature and not cling to the external aspects, nor to confuse schematic aspects of form with its essence. In this way, from skin to core, in Brahms's view, every musician has to create his tools and only then would they be reliable: "That's how I did it, too," he would say. Whoever fails to advance beyond the clever handling of the means acquired through imitation, who does not bring his own self to bear or successfully hold his own even within the truest imitation but simply empathizes with what his model created, that person cannot be helped: for he is lacking the most important ingredient, creative talent.

Brahms called the first sonata movement I brought to him an experiment that was doomed to fail because the main theme was in no way suited to the sonata. He advised me to be diligent in studying the themes of Beethoven's sonatas and to observe their influence on the construction of the movement, as well as to consult Schubert sonatas for comparison's sake. It would lead me too far afield to illustrate how instructive such a comparison is, how it teaches indeed more than could be learned in theoretical deliberations. But exactly this goes to the heart of the matter. That Brahms was not simply concerned with the purity of form, on an external level, needs no special comment. If something needed to be criticized in this regard, he simply said: "That's poorly done"; or by contrast, once when I had successfully applied a complicated canon in a trio of the Scherzo of a violin sonata, one in which it was easy to glimpse the joy of achieved technique, he simply skipped over it and dryly remarked: "Yes, it is a canon." For the meaning expressed in the form to matter, the form had to have a unique correspondence with the idea. Music in the form of a sonata and a sonata itself are two very different things, after all.

Imitating sonata movements, as mentioned above, was, above all, supposed to give me a concept of the essential character of the sonata form—I was supposed to learn that it is something completely different to re-create a form and to create music that is conceptualized and executed in the spirit of a form, and to recognize that form and idea exert an essential determining influence on one another. Only he who creates within the spirit of a form creates freely, only his forms come alive; in the other case form becomes a shackle and degrades into a fixed pattern.

Now, what is a sonata?

I have created an embarrassing situation by posing this question, since I have no illusions at all about being able to answer it. An artistic form, in a way similar to phenomena in nature, cannot be explained, at best it can be described; its essence is revealed only through metaphor and artistic creation. It cannot possibly be my intention here to discuss musical-technical aspects in further detail; they can only be understood through practical studies. Rather, I turn to other questions which, while closely connected to the one above, have a certain topical interest.

Is it not pointless these days even to get involved with the sonata form? Is it not a thing of the past? Hasn't Beethoven written the last symphony, as Richard Wagner has put it? Isn't it an anachronism to write sonatas today?

Anyone who has adopted Wagner's ideas about art, who places himself in the position of the one "all-encompassing" art, and recognizes the musical drama as the only true living form of art—for that person everything mentioned above having to do with art is over and done with. In Wagner's terms, absolute music is not "art." Beethoven becomes the artist who "errs out of necessity," since music itself is not capable of creating living forms. She is a female organism that must first be fertilized by poetry for a living creation to emerge. All its forms are borrowed, or arbitrary. The fugue and the sonata are examples of arbitrary products that have no inherent artistic necessity: music lacks moral intentionality, and so forth. All this can be recognized—from the point of view of the *Gesamtkunstwerk*. Such a position in some ways allows Wagner to declare that music should no longer continue to exist as independent, "egoistic" art. "Who now will be to Beethoven what *he* was to Mozart and Haydn, in the realm of absolute music?" Wagner asks, and goes on: "The greatest genius would not here avail, precisely because the genie of absolute music no longer needs him."[26] Such sentences only prove that we are dealing here with a Fanatic of the Idea whose perception of basic historical facts is largely clouded. You can believe this the way you believe dogma. The historian must protest. He cannot allow such arbitrary questions as the one posed above. After all, the history of art demonstrates that development does not always proceed in one and the same direction, but that high points are achieved and then, with different perspectives, new goals are strived for, usually at first with rather meager results. The further development of instrumental music was in no way dependent on someone coming along who was to Beethoven what he was to Haydn and Mozart. When Bach died in 1750, many an insightful person believed that music had reached the highest completion imaginable; and in one sense they were right, given their perspective: nobody has yet climbed past Bach. Haydn, however, was already born, and not long after he wrote his first immature symphonies. What matters is not the oft-repeated notion of "reaching beyond," but rather the original and healthy power of creation.

Without going so far as to question whether absolute music has a right to exist and be further developed, there remains the open question about the sonata form. No doubt the sonata occupies a central position in the complete instrumental oeuvre of Brahms. Brahms's very arrival is a living protest against Wagner's statements, and his compositions prove that their creator considered false the tenet that since Beethoven the sonata has had no intrinsic value. But what is there to say about this question of legitimacy of the sonata since Beethoven? Here, I'd like to try to make a small contribution toward an answer, one that will evolve by itself as I follow

Brahms the teacher and, as far as possible in a short space, consider the nature of the sonata form more closely. Even though Brahms's personal influence recedes in this presentation, it will still be experienced strongly by those who keep their sights on his works, which will sound into the new century like an urgent call for serious German art.

These days one often hears the notion that Beethoven with his powerful works somehow smashed or blasted or otherwise destroyed the form of the sonata, a tale often recounted with more fantasy than insight. I have no idea what fantastic ideas these statements are based on. One can't help but think of the wild man; one sees how he literally swings his club so that parts of the sonata form fly off like shards of clay. Yet it remains a curious fact that Beethoven himself wrote sonatas and symphonies, works that, it must be acknowledged, possess marvelous strength of form up through the late quartets. Even if he thus destroyed the existing form of the sonata, he nonetheless gave it a new form. But the argument continues: since Beethoven was such a giant, sonatas after him have no more right to exist. Correctly stated, this sentence should read something like: Beethoven has so exhausted the form of the sonata that no artist after him can possibly say anything different or new that would have any meaning. I do not know how anybody would want to defend such a sentence today, and would like to raise the question whether any artist can exhaust a form of art. No doubt some art forms have outlived themselves and slowly died. One would have to examine why this happened. The most interesting question should be whether these forms were derived as purely as drama from poetry or the sonata from music, or whether these were hybrid forms that were constructed artificially, out of nothing more than the perceptions of an era. He for whom the sonata form means nothing but a kind of scheme or set pattern may have no second thoughts in exclaiming: "Away with these pathetic petty dead forms!" I believe, however, that such a person underestimates the importance of the sonata. He blames the form rather than the spiritually bereft artist for compositions stillborn through mindless formalism. It should also be kept in mind that the entire development of instrumental music from Bach to Beethoven took place nearly exclusively within the form of the sonata.

The principles of the sonata do not provide a rigid scheme, but rather an idea that originated in the dualism of thematic content. It is therefore a dramatic idea. From this, a form develops which, rejecting everything extraneous to music and created purely from the very nature of music, is the result of thinking and perceiving in a musically logical manner; a form that changes as often as the idea it is based on, being utterly dependent on the content of the theme and the conflicts that arise therefrom, and which can therefore be as different as Mozart's little C-Major Sonata is from Beethoven's Ninth Symphony without ceasing to be a sonata; a form as diverse as the poetic drama and its musical counterpart.[27] Conceived in the broadest sense as a cyclical form, the sonata is without doubt comparable to the drama in poetics: the richest form of instrumental music, because on the one hand, it can incorporate all other instrumental forms, and on the other it has given expression to every glory that distinguishes our modern art, the result of a marvelous and rapid development, from the art of Bach.

There is a musical form that evolved purely from the essence of music, just as the sonata did, and has a lot in common with it yet is entirely different: the fugue. The fugue is also based on an idea, indeed, on an eminently dramatic idea. Here, too, we have a dualism of themes; here, too, the form changes with the thematic content. The fugue, however, is more one-dimensional than the sonata. Since the primary elements of music are movement, music can be expressed according to two principles—one, juxtaposition, and the other, succession: thus there is polyphonic and homophonic music. Though within a fugue the latter principle is given ample space to unfold its inexhaustible richness, the core of the dramatic idea that determines its form lies in the simultaneity of contrasting theme and counterpoint: the principle of counterpoint. By comparison, the Haydn sonata initially emphasized the homophonic principle; the dramatic main focus was anchored in the succession of contrasting themes. Only in the course of time did the sonata prove superior to the fugue because it was able not only to incorporate both principles but to merge them so that the dramatic character could find equal expression with either one of the two principles. Thus the sonata achieved a style more fitting for the expressive possibilities of music. The history of the sonata, then, is the history of this process of amalgamation.

Mozart already experienced the dramatic possibilities of the sonata in greater depth than Haydn. His glorious and rich character equipped him to dive more deeply into the true primary essence of music, contrapuntal polyphony, which has, we know, been described as the faithful portrayal of the interplay of metaphysical forces in the universe. Herein is the source of the power of Mozart's melodies to touch infinity itself, herein the unique, refined, and spiritual character of his instrumental music! His melodies are grounded naturally in the universal, the elemental, the eternal; from here they spring forth, as do Nature's tree and flower. This melodicity of highest potency developed out of polyphony and gives Mozart's sonatas their unique imprint; through it Mozart searches for and finds his unique solution to the inherent conflict.

There are people naïve enough to call Haydn and Mozart *Schablonen-Komponisten* or "stencil" composers, people who even claim that Beethoven initially composed in stereotypes à la Haydn or Mozart—the Beethoven of the famous early period—that only later did he find his own voice. I admit he was busy learning from them. How rarely, though, has a composer distinguished himself as Beethoven did with his Opus 1. Admittedly, he was already twenty-five years old then. But what was it that made Opus 1 so famous? First of all, nothing more than the striking originality of his genius, immediately recognized by his peers and which almost shocked the aging Haydn. It is ridiculous to want to accuse Beethoven of working with stencils, but petty to search for signs of greatness in apparent deviations from traditional form. Beethoven's greatness obviously lies first in his genuine capacity for feeling; this is expressed primarily, in my view, through the unusual depth of his understanding of the sonata idea; therein is rooted the immense, all-encompassing power of his thought, no less than in the high perfection of form which is the result of a tremendous will focused on a relentlessly strict musical logic. One must say it in all firmness: no composer ever used musical form more stringently than Beethoven. His stringent use of form is as far removed from formalism as an idea is from a stencil; it is tantamount to a strictly logical development of the musical thought process. Following the laws of musical reasoning was always Beethoven's highest principle, even when composing the *Pastoral* Symphony. That such a man, with his dramatic fighter-nature, was able to achieve such beautiful clarity and perfection of form makes him one of the greatest personalities in all of world history.

From the outset, all of his struggles aimed at achieving this perfection, as his sketchbooks prove, all of his creative acts offer the picture of a man who, working hard while investing enormous willpower, wrestled incessantly toward this perfect completion. This is what captures and jolts so unspeakably in his works; we experience them as a manifestation of our own longing for completion. Whoever claims that Beethoven destroyed the sonata form deprives him of his crowning accomplishment.

Beethoven would not have been who he was if he had not felt in Mozart's art its high accomplishment; to heighten it in Mozart's style must have seemed impossible. If then Mozart was inspired to his ultimate and highest achievements by the works of Bach, as previously suggested in different words, so did Beethoven prove that all of this was part of a progression that was in no way complete, but could ultimately be concluded only when the essence of music was exhausted.

He was the right man to apply the lever where it was needed, and his tools were in good order. He was also meant to penetrate deep into the primary essence of music, where he could test his equipment. The amalgamation from which our modern style of instrumentation came into being could only be achieved in this way. Beethoven has created it, and given it its characteristic dramatic shape. This style, however, is generated from the sonata idea; together, they developed and grew to become that force, inherent in a Beethoven symphony, through which all contrasting elements infuse one another and dissolve into a higher unity. What in Mozart's music develops harmoniously one from the other, one melody apparently releasing the next, now stands in brusque confrontation; the battle erupts with more intensity, the dramatic power of the style is incomparably more forceful. The theme, in accordance with the idea, starts to play a more important role, becomes more significant, more meaningful for the entire movement. Often it is a complicated creation in its own right and contains sharp contrasts that become the crucial point of the whole movement. Despite utmost unity, it can nearly always be broken into motives, in a few cases it is nothing but motive, though the motive then becomes the lever for the movement. Beethoven found all of this prefigured in Bach's music, if in a different form. Now the core of the idea is neither polyphony nor homophony alone but a balance of both: the style becomes truly free. The way Beethoven offered it, all was completely new; it resulted from work incessantly focused on this crucial point by a man whose nature provided all the necessary prerequisites for such a monumental task. As a result, his struggles were not fruitless, or forced or artificial. One senses this path was inevitable given the evolution of things; thus also the miraculous perfection that contemporaries could comprehend as little as they had Mozart's.

In the above description of the development of the sonata, I have tried to refer briefly to all aspects Brahms inspired me to consider when looking at a sonata while I studied his as well as classical works, although with me Brahms never engaged in historical reflections. Of course, I am totally aware of how little I have said about the nature of the sonata; nevertheless, it still appears to be more than if I had allowed myself to be seduced into presenting this detail or that, which in this context would have inevitably remained incomprehensible. I shall try to be consistent with this approach and proceed to a conclusion.

By developing from existing seeds a unique dramatic style, Beethoven transformed the sonata into that which it could and should have become, given its natural form and idea: through him, the sonata achieved the highest form of pure instrumental music, serving as it did the spirit of music in the most perfect and all-encompassing fashion. He died lonely, misunderstood and unapproachable. Nobody was able to gage the tremendous heights to which his energetic flight had carried him. Time, however, unleashed new capacities and turned away from him and his art. And yet he witnessed the arrival of the new art: he experienced *Der Freischütz*; he saw lieder by Schubert; he kissed the young Liszt for his marvelous playing; only his art, the art of the sonata, died with him.[28] For in the hands of the post-classic epigones, the so-called Wiener Tonschule, the sonata form froze into a stereotype; in the hands of their adversaries, meanwhile, it degenerated into virtuosity; otherwise the great Romantics alas developed it, in a spirit of lyricism, thus contradicting its innermost dramatic nature. One can even sense this contradiction in Schumann, and it seems as if he himself became aware of it. In any case, he sensed that new things were in the making and that his art did not embrace all that his time was ripe for. When Brahms came to him and presented him with his first sonatas, it seemed to him as if the one had arrived who had to arrive—the one "called to give expression to his times in ideal fashion."[29] Once again, youthful works expressed an extraordinary originality, and Schumann was astounded: here is yet another! That this could be overlooked in those days is all the more remarkable, since it was the main point of Schumann's famous essay, "Neue Bahnen." A unique style was being developed here, one in which modern sensibilities were fused with old art into an exquisite new unity. The spirit in which the sonata was reborn, however, was Beethoven's. In their conception of the sonata idea, Brahms and Beethoven stand unequivocally side by side. For his sonatas are not modern music fitted into a dated form, but music conceived and executed from the spirit of the sonata, and the form is a necessary conclusion of the idea. Thus the tremendous diversity and freedom of the creative work, the same freedom we admire in Bach or Beethoven, just as splendidly alive in the smaller lyrical forms of the romantics but denied in their larger works, their sonatas and fugues. Compare the motet or fugue of Brahms with that of Bach, a variation or sonata of Brahms with that of Beethoven to become aware of both, their great affinities and their great differences. This recourse to Bach and Beethoven is a recourse to the spirit of music, a kind of kinship that will always be clearly recognizable among great artists who live within a span of not quite two centuries, since the fundamental philosophy and inner experiences of mankind do not change that quickly, whereas everything that is of more secondary importance in art is subject to ever changing taste and even the fashion of the day. The differences reside in the inherent powers of the great creators. "Durable music" was Brahms's favorite expression. He was referring to music rooted in the depths of the spirit of music that never runs counter to it, in contrast to the music that, lacking any inner hold, clings to the superficial and accidental and is quickly swept away by the flow of time, no matter how genuine the experience and attractive the sound, because it cannot satisfy mankind's deep desire for art.

Brahms brought the sonata back to life. Unconcerned about external glory and fame, undeterred by laments and diatribes that mocked and maligned him and his strivings, he pursued his path, working ceaselessly, initially from failure to failure; however, proudly and modestly aware of the purity of his strivings and the value of his work, he was certain his time must come. And he was not mistaken. Even if many to this day still loudly proclaim in word and sound that music cannot by itself generate formal laws and is valuable only as an expression of poetic thought, I doubt whether any one of the individual arts would give up their "egoistic" strivings as a result of the idea of *Gesamtkunstwerk*. A *Gesamtkunstwerk* can exist only through compromise in which each of the contributing arts renounces a good part of its own character in favor of the overall effect. I believe instead that the time will come when people learn to differentiate more clearly the goals of the *Gesamtkunstwerk* from the goals of the individual art forms. And just as one recognizes that the image remains the main task of the art of painting where nature as model and the natural laws of the materials are formally decisive, so will it be realized that the spirit of music can come to fruition completely and perfectly only wherever the natural laws of the material tones have a decisive influence on the formal structure. In either case, a poetic idea can be the foundation of the artwork; yet neither painting nor music can follow the lead of a poetic idea that contradicts the nature of its means without damaging its essence and effectiveness. A Beethoven sonata does not permit any poetic train of thought; in this way Beethoven secured total freedom for his musical creations. One who, like Richard Wagner, declares Beethoven's holding on to this traditional form even in the majestic *Leonore* Overture a weakness, that he should rather have thrown it overboard in favor of a tangible poetic idea misjudges, in my view, the purely musical nature of Beethoven's work and, by forming rash opinions, prevents himself from understanding the superb conception of his works.

Brahms also held on to these forms, or rather, as everything was new with Beethoven, so, too, is everything different here, on the large scale as much as in the smallest ornamental detail. Talk of imitation is as misplaced here as the notion of stencil-based creativity. Brahms's forms grew with the logic of natural organisms. Just as in nature it is always the healthy life force that creates the thousand-fold appearances; so in art a living form cannot be created through technique alone, no matter how perfected, unless it is an expression of genuine human feeling. Brahms's work is alive, and the day cannot be far when the magnificent expression of modern experience found in his works is generally acknowledged. He proved that the sonata is a living form that, rather than having been invented by Haydn or someone else, emerged and slowly grew, as has become more and more apparent in the middle of the eighteenth century and is so well-suited to pure music that it is capable of further developing according to the ever increasing capacity of musical expression. Therein today lies its legitimacy as well, and in nothing else. Who is to say whether sonatas will still be written at the end of our century, and whether posterity will continue to develop these forms further along the path taken. Perhaps completely new and different kinds of forms will emerge from today's efforts, the result of an as yet undeveloped kind of musical expression that may prove superior to the sonata. Who would want to dispute such possibilities? However, for these forms to have "durability," that is, genuine inherent life, they cannot contradict the laws of pure music; they must emerge from the essence of music as purely as the sonata or fugue. Whoever believes music needs extramusical factors to generate its forms sins against the divine art.

Surely, a rich inheritance was passed down to Brahms, but, as Goethe said, only those who inherit great things are able to create great things.

May the twentieth century make good use of its inheritance!

NOTES

1. For Heuberger's recollection of his studies with Brahms, see his "My Early Acquaintance with Brahms," trans. Styra Avins, in this volume. Schenker recalled his own occasional meetings with Brahms in "Erinnerungen an Brahms," *Deutsche Zeitschrift* 46/8 (1933): 475–82.

2. Brahms composed twelve songs to poems of Groth (1819–99), including the famous *Regenlied,* op. 59, no. 3. On Groth's efforts on behalf of Jenner, see Horst Heussner, "Der Brahmsschüler Gustav Jenner," in *Brahms-Kongress Wien 1983,* ed. Susanne Antonicek und Otto Biba (Tutzing, 1988), 249–50. One of Groth's letters to Brahms concerning Jenner is translated in Styra Avins, ed., *Johannes Brahms: Life and Letters,* trans. Styra Avins and Josef Eisinger (Oxford and New York, 1997), 651–52.

3. The concerto was performed on January 1, 1888, with Brahms conducting and Joseph Joachim and Robert Hausmann as soloists. The trio, with Brahms as pianist, was played the following day.

4. Fritz August Simrock (1838–1901) was Brahms's publisher, friend, and advisor. He inherited one of Germany's most distinguished music publishing firms, founded in 1790.

5. Allgemeiner Deutsche Cäcilien-Verein (The All-German Cecilia Society) was a broad-based organization dedicated, first and foremost, to reforming the Catholic Church service in southern Germany and Austria by reviving the music of Palestrina and his contemporaries. Julius Spengel (1853–1936) was a teacher, composer, and pianist active in Hamburg.

6. Eusebius Mandyczewski (1857–1929) was a prominent figure in the musical life of Vienna. He was a choral conductor, teacher of counterpoint and composition, and

holder of significant official appointments in the areas of music education, scholarship, and concert life. But he is best remembered as archivist of the Gesellschaft der Musikfreunde and as a distinguished musicologist—he edited the first complete edition of the works of Franz Schubert—and scholar. He was a close friend of Brahms and mentor for several generations of musicologists.

7. Jenner refers to an Austrian Regie-Trabuco, an inferior, imitation cigar produced by the state tobacco monopoly. (*Trans.*)

8. Zum roten Igel (The Red Hedgehog) was a legendary eating and gathering place in the center of Vienna. It was already well known in the 1830s and 1840s. Until 1870, the Gesellschaft der Musikfreunde was located directly adjacent to it.

9. The "Eye of God": Brahms was referring to the inn and coffeehouse on the Petersplatz where Mozart lived from May to December 1781 with Madam Weber, whose daughter Constanze he later married. It was during these months that Mozart wrote the *Abduction from the Seraglio*. The building was demolished in 1896 and replaced by a new one in 1897.

10. Ludwig Rottenberg (1864–1932), composer, conductor, and pianist, was a student of Robert Fuchs and Eusebius Mandyczewski in Vienna. He was the conductor of the amateur orchestra of the Gesellschaft der Musikfreunde from 1888 to 1892. In 1893, at the recommendation of Brahms, he became director of the Frankfurt Opera. He is best known as an accompanist of singers, among them three with whom Brahms was closely associated: Gustav Walter, Hermine Spies, and Alice Barbi.

11. The Stadtpark is a park in Vienna adjacent to the Ringstrasse, designed along English garden lines and opened in 1862. The park today contains several monuments to composers, the most significant of which, the Schubert monument, was erected in 1872. The Prater was Brahms's favorite park in Vienna. It was by far the largest park in the city and possessed racing facilities and an amusement park. The Prater was given over to public use in the eighteenth century by Joseph II. It was the site of many annual festivities and celebrations.

12. Kalbeck, Door, Brüll: Max Kalbeck (1850–1921), writer, librettist, poet, and music journalist, was Brahms's biographer. Immensely prolific, Kalbeck was a major figure in the world of Viennese letters, particularly with respect to issues of theater and music. He also edited and wrote the biography of the great Viennese satirist Daniel Spitzer. It is for this and his immensely detailed, multi-volume Brahms biography that he is best remembered; a selection from the latter is translated in this volume. Anton Door (1833–1919) was a Viennese pianist and piano teacher. A student of Czerny, Door taught at the conservatory in Vienna from 1869 until 1901. Ignaz Brüll (1846–1907), a Viennese pianist and composer, was, unlike Door, self-consciously a virtuoso. He was a close friend of Brahms and a student of Julius Epstein, who was instrumental in Brahms's initial success in Vienna in 1862. Brüll was also a composer of piano music, operas, and orchestral music. Brahms had little good to say about Brüll's music, however.

13. There were 100 kreuzer to one florin or gulden. Since in 1889 one florin equalled about 40 cents (US), Brahms's typical meal would have cost between 28 and 33 cents. In comparison, the Hotel Sacher charged between one and three florins, 40 cents to $1.20, for its prix fixe menu in 1889.

14. *Robert Schumann's Werke*, series 14, supplement, ed. Johannes Brahms (Leipzig, 1893).

15. Friederich Rückert (1788–1866) was a significant German poet of the first half of the nineteenth century. His poems were set by Schubert, Schumann, Brahms, and Mahler, among others.

16. Brahms's apartment looked out on and was a short distance from two of nineteenth-century Vienna's most important architectural monuments: Fischer von Erlach's

eighteenth-century masterpiece, the Karlskirche, and the Technical University, built in 1815. The latter building was a fine example of Late Classical architecture. It was enlarged in 1838 and 1866. Shortly after Brahms's death in 1897, an extra floor was added.

17. Theodor Storm (1817–88), German poet and prose writer, was one of Brahms's particular favorites—he possessed Storm's complete writings.

18. Hermann Allmers (1821–1902), Frisian essayist and novelist, is best known for two books, *Marschenbuch* (1858) and *Römische Schlendertage* (1859).

19. *Franz Schubert's Werke. Kritisch durchgesehene Gesammtausgabe*, series 20, *Lieder und Gesänge*, ed. Eusebius Mandyczewski (Leipzig, 1884–97).

20. Op. 43, no. 2.

21. Josef Lewinsky (1835–1907) was the most famous and respected tragic actor in Vienna during Brahms's lifetime. He was also known for his impressiveness as an orator. He commissioned the five Ophelia songs (WoO 22) from Brahms for his wife, who was to play the part in the Schlegel translation of *Hamlet* at the Deutsches Landtheater in Prague.

22. A reference to Johann Wolfgang von Goethe's *Metamorphosis of Plants* (1790).

23. Jenner cites Brahms's *Schumann* Variations, op. 9 (1854); Variations on an Original Theme, op. 21, no. 1, and on a Hungarian Theme, op. 21, no. 2 (pub. 1865); Variations for Piano Four-Hands on a Theme by Robert Schumann, op. 23 (1861); and *Handel* Variations, op. 24 (1861).

24. The Fellingers, Richard (1848–1903) and Maria (1849–1925), were among Brahms's closest friends in Vienna.

25. Strobl am Wolfgangsee is a resort town situated, like Brahms's summer vacation spot of Ischl, in Austria's Salzkammergut region.

26. The references in this and the preceding paragraph are primarily to Richard Wagner, *The Artwork of the Future* (1849); see *Richard Wagner's Prose Works*, trans. William Ashton Ellis (London, 1895; repr. Lincoln and London, 1993), 1:130–31.

27. C-Major Sonata, K. 545.

28. Jenner refers to the so-called *Weihekuss*, which Beethoven purportedly bestowed upon the head of the young Liszt after hearing him play in Vienna. This event, now typically regarded as imagined, was widely reported in the literature on Liszt of the nineteenth and early twentieth centuries.

29. Jenner quotes from Robert Schumann's "New Paths" essay, with which the latter composer introduced the twenty-year-old Brahms to the musical world. See Schumann, "Neue Bahnen," *Neue Zeitschrift für Musik* 39 (28 October 1853): 185–86 (at 185); English translation in Schumann, *On Music and Musicians*, ed. Konrad Wolff, trans. Paul Rosenfeld (New York, 1969), 253.

Brahms and the Newer Generation

Personal Reminiscences by

Alexander von Zemlinsky and Karl Weigl

TRANSLATED, INTRODUCED, AND ANNOTATED
BY WALTER FRISCH

Alexander von Zemlinsky (1872–1942) was one of the most talented and promising young Viennese composers of the turn of the century. After an auspicious study period at the Vienna Conservatory, he went on to have a distinguished career as a teacher, conductor, and opera composer. Among his pupils were Alma Schindler (later to become Mahler's wife) and Karl Weigl. Zemlinsky was the first and only teacher of Arnold Schoenberg; the two friends also became brothers-in-law when Schoenberg married Zemlinsky's sister Mathilde in 1901. Weigl (1881–1949) was a prominent conservative Viennese composer and teacher, who served as Professor of Theory and Composition at the Vienna Conservatory after World War I. Zemlinsky and Weigl were among the many Jewish artists who fled to the United States with the advent of the Nazis. Neither found here the kind of respect and acclaim they had experienced in Europe in the years before World War II. These reminiscences appeared in the Viennese journal Musikblätter des Anbruch *4 (1922): 69–70. All endnotes are editorial.*

When I think of the time during which I had the fortune to know Brahms personally—it was during the last two years of his life—I can recall immediately how his music affected me and my colleagues in composition, including Schoenberg. It was fascinating, its influence inescapable, its effect intoxicating. I was still a pupil at the Vienna Conservatory and knew most of Brahms's works thoroughly. I was obsessed by this music. My goal at the time was nothing less than the appropriation and mastery of this wonderful, singular compositional technique.

I was introduced to Brahms at the occasion of a performance of a symphony of mine, which I had composed as a student.[1] Brahms had been invited by my teacher Fuchs.[2] Soon thereafter, the Hellmesberger Quartet performed a string quintet of mine, which Brahms also heard.[3] He asked for the score and then invited me to call on him; he did so with a brief and somewhat ironic remark, casually tossed off: "Of course, come if it might interest you to talk to me about it." This cost me a hard struggle: the idea that Brahms would speak to me about my attempts at composition elevated my already powerful respect to the level of anxiety. To talk with Brahms was no easy matter. The question-and-answer was short, gruff, seemingly cold, and often very ironic.

He went through my quintet at the piano with me. At first he would offer corrections gently, looking carefully at this or that spot. He never really offered praise, but would grow more animated, and ever more passionate. And when I timidly sought to justify a passage in the development

Alexander von Zemlinsky

section that seemed to me to be really successful in a Brahmsian spirit, he opened up the string quintet by Mozart and explained the consummate qualities of this "still unsurpassed mastery of form."[4] And it sounded self-evident when he said, "That's how it's done from Bach up to myself." Brahms's ruthless criticism had put me in an extremely despondent mood, but he soon cheered me up again. He asked about my financial situation and offered me a monthly stipend so that I could work fewer hours and devote myself more to composition. Finally he recommended me to his publisher Simrock, who also agreed to issue my first compositions.[5]

From then on my works fell even more than before under the influence of Brahms. I remember how even among my colleagues it was considered particularly praiseworthy to compose in as "Brahmsian" a manner as possible. We were soon notorious in Vienna as the dangerous "Brahmins."

Then came a reaction, of course. With the struggle to find oneself, there was also an emphatic repudiation of Brahms. And there were periods when the reverence and admiration for Brahms metamorphosed into the very opposite. Then this phase of undervaluation gave way to a quiet reassessment and enduring love of Brahms's work. And when today I conduct a symphony by him or play one of his splendid chamber works, then I fall once again under the spell of the memory of that time: each measure becomes a personal experience.

—Alexander von Zemlinsky

When in my earliest student years I saw Brahms in person for the first time, I knew very little of his music. But the powerful head, surrounded by snow-white hair and a beard, and at that time not yet drawn by the hand of death, left an indelible impression on me. I experienced for the first time the thrill aroused by being in proximity to an immortal.

It took much time and labor before I could make his work my own. I was accustomed to the sensuous power of Mozart and Schubert and the forcefully blazing rhythms of Beethoven. The language of Brahms seemed to me strange and cold. When I finally succeeded—chiefly through his splendid lieder and his chamber works—in gaining entry to this world that had previously been closed, he became one of my great teachers.

It is not my task here to say how and how much my works were influenced by him. This much I must say, however: that I owe to him purity of

Karl Weigl

compositional technique and seriousness of thematic work, and, not last, a new insight into the masters with whom he himself had studied—Haydn, Mozart, Handel, Bach, and the older vocal composers.

Today, direction and desire lead far away from the paths that Brahms trod with manly seriousness. Yet now as then I remain in awe of the spiritual and ethical loftiness of this great master, for whom his art truly meant more than "a play with sounding forms,"[6] who was like few others relentlessly self-critical and was at once a believer and a savior.

—Karl Weigl

NOTES

1. The occasion of the meeting was actually the premiere of Zemlinsky's Orchestral Suite at a concert at the Gesellschaft der Musikfreunde on March 18, 1895. Brahms led his own Academic Festival Overture on the same program. The event is described vividly in Max Kalbeck, *Johannes Brahms*, rev. ed. (Berlin, 1912–21: repr. Tutzing, 1976), 4:400–401.

2. Johann Nepomuk Fuchs (1842–99), Austrian composer, conductor, and from 1888 Professor of Composition at the Vienna Conservatory.

3. The String Quintet in D Minor (unpublished), performed on March 5, 1896.

4. Zemlinsky does not specify which Mozart quintet Brahms was examining: most likely the C Major (K. 515) or G Minor (K. 516).

5. In a letter to Simrock, Brahms recommended Zemlinsky as "both a person and a talent." See Johannes Brahms, *Briefwechsel,* rev. eds. (Berlin, 1912–22; repr. Tutzing, 1974), 4:212. The work that stimulated Brahms's letter was the Clarinet Trio in D Minor, op. 3, which had received a third prize at a composition contest at the Wiener Tonkünstlerverein. Simrock published the work in 1897.

6. A reference to the "tönend bewegte Formen" (forms moved in sounding) that lay at the heart of the aesthetic position on music espoused by Eduard Hanslick in his *Vom Musikalisch Schönen* of 1854.

PART IV

"DEDICATED TO
JOHANNES BRAHMS"

☙

"Dedicated to Johannes Brahms"

PREPARED BY WALTER FRISCH

Something of the esteem in which Brahms was held can be seen by the large number of works dedicated to him by other composers. In a small notebook now at the Wienbibliothek im Rathaus, Brahms himself kept an ongoing handwritten list of dedications (headed "Widmungen") of these titles; the list runs to seventy-eight musical entries, plus four books and one collection of prints. In his own extensive library, Brahms had copies of most of these works, no doubt sent to him by the authors (see Kurt Hofmann, Die Bibliothek von Johannes Brahms *[Hamburg, 1974], esp. the segment "Johannes Brahms' Musikbibliothek," compiled by Alfred Orel, 139–66, which transcribes Brahms's own catalogue of his music collection). The following list presents the titles of musical works and other books bearing printed dedications to Brahms. It has been compiled primarily from Brahms's own hand-written list and catalogue, supplemented by further research (which has also turned up several works written in his memory soon after his death). Where possible, each title has been verified independently in printed bibliographic sources. Full names, dates of publication, keys, performing forces, and opus numbers have been supplied when locatable (Brahms's own list has few such details). The sequence of musical titles follows principally that of Brahms's own "Widmungen" inventory, which was compiled in the order in which he received the items and thus is essentially chrono-logical. One can reasonably assume that a work for which no date is available was published at a time very close to that of a dated work near it on the list. Some works by the same composer have, however, been grouped together; and some works for which a date of publication was found have been placed nearer other works of that date. Where titles are specific or unique, I have tended to leave them in the origi-nal language. Generic titles like "Clavierstücke" or "Quintett" (or even "Romanze") have normally been translated.*

The title page of WoldemarBargiel, *Fantasy* no. 3 for piano (1860), dedicated to Brahms.

Art

Max Klinger, *Amor und Psyche* [46 prints] (Munich, 1880)

Books

Gustav Wendt [trans.], *Sophocles's Tragödien* (Stuttgart, 1884)

Adalbert Kupferschmied, *Linguistisch-kulturhistorische Skizzen und Bilder aus der deutschen Steiermark* (Karlsruhe, 1888)

Eduard Hanslick, *Musikalisches Skizzenbuch: Neue Kritiken und Schilderungen.* Die Moderne Oper, part 4 (Berlin, 1888)

Hugo Riemann, *Katechismus der Kompositionslehre: Musikalische Formenlehre* (Leipzig, 1889)

Hedwig Kiesenkamp [pseud. L. Rafael], *Ebbe und Fluth: Gedichte* (Leipzig, 1896)

Music

Robert Schumann, *Concert-Allegro mit Introduction,* piano and orchestra, D Minor-Major, op. 134 (1855)

Clara Schumann, Three Romances, piano, op. 21 (1855)

Robert Schumann, *Des Sängers Fluch* (Uhland), Ballade for soloists, chorus, and orchestra, op. 139 (1858)

Woldemar Bargiel, *Fantasie* no. 3, piano, C Minor, op. 19 (1860)

Joseph Joachim, Hungarian Concerto, violin, D Minor, op. 11 (1861)

Carl G. P. Gradener, Piano Trio no. 2, E-flat Major, op. 35

Adolf Jensen, *Fantasiestücke*, piano, op. 7

Adolf Jensen, Piano Sonata, F-sharp Minor, op. 25

Johann Peter Gotthardt, *Ave Maria*, tenor, men's chorus, organ, op. 39

Johann Peter Gotthardt, 10 Pieces in Dance Form, piano four hands, op. 58

Ferdinand Thierot, Trio, F Minor, op. 14

Georg Heinrich Witte, Waltzes, piano four hands, op. 7

Ernst Rudorff, *Fantasie*, piano, G Minor, op. 14 (1869)

Max Bruch, Symphony, E-flat Major, op. 28 (1870)

R. Schweida, 7 Piano Pieces, op. 7

Karl Reinthaler, *In der Wüste* (Psalm 63), chorus and orchestra, op. 26

Albert Dietrich, Symphony, D Minor, op. 20 (1870)

Anna von Dobjansky, Nocturnes, piano, op. 2 (1870)

Hermann Goetz, Piano Quartet, E Major, op. 6 (1870)

Louis Bödecker, Variations on a Theme by Schubert, piano, op. 3 (1871)

Julius Otto Grimm, Suite no. 2 in Canonic Form, orchestra, op. 16 (1871)

Josef Rheinberger, 2 *Claviervorträge*, op. 45 (1871)

Franz Wüllner, *Miserere*, double choir and soloists, op. 26

Karl Tausig, arr., Chorale Preludes by Bach (1873)

Julius Stockhausen, Four Songs (1873)

Heinrich Hoffmann, Hungarian Suite, orchestra, op. 16 (1877)

Stefanie Gräfin Wurmbrand, Three Piano Pieces

Karl Goldmark, *Frühlingshymne*, alto, chorus, and orchestra, op. 23 (1875)

Xaver Scharwenka, *Romanzero*, piano, op. 33 (1876)

Theodor Kirchner, Waltzes, piano, op. 23 (1876)

Bernhard Scholz, String Quintet, op. 47 (1878)

J. Carl Eschmann, *Licht und Schatten*, 6 piano pieces, op. 62

Hans Huber, Waltzes, piano four hands, violin, cello, op. 27 (1878)

Otto Dessoff, String Quartet, F Major, op. 7 (1878)

Ferdinand Hummel, Suite, piano four hands, op. 17

Vincenz Lachner, 12 Ländler (1879 or 1880)

Georg Henschel, *Serbisches Liederspiel*, op. 32 (1879)

Robert Fuchs, Piano Trio, C Major, op. 22 (1879)

Adolf Wallnöfer, *Grenzen der Menschheit* (Goethe), alto or baritone solo, mixed chorus, and orchestra, op. 10 (1879)

Constantin Bürgel, Variations on an Original Theme, piano four hands, op. 30 (1879)

J. Gustav Eduard Stehle, 5 Motets, op. 44

Antonín Dvořák, String Quartet, D Minor, op. 34 (1877)

J. C. Gegenbauer, *Transcription de mélodies hongroises*, op. 10

Fran Serafin Vilhar, *Albumblätter*

Karl Nawratil, Piano Trio, E-flat Major, op. 9 (1881)

Leander Schlegel, Ballades, piano, op. 2

Philipp Wolfrum, Organ Sonata no. 3, F Minor (1883)

Rudolf Bibl, *Klavierstücke in Romanzenton*, op. 45

Algernon B. L. Ashton, *Englische Tänze*, piano four hands, op. 10 (1883)

Eduard Marxsen, 100 Variations on a Folk Song, piano (1883)

Charles Villiers Stanford, *Songs of Old Ireland* (1884)

Heinrich von Herzogenberg, Three String Quartets, op. 42 (1884)

Jean Louis Nicodé, Symphonic Variations, orchestra, C Minor, op. 27

Ernst Seyffardt, *Schicksalsgesang* (Geibel), alto solo, mixed chorus, and orchestra, op. 13

Ferruccio Busoni, Six Etudes, piano, op. 16 (1883)

Ferruccio Busoni, *Etude: Tema e Variazioni*, piano, op. 17 (1884)

Richard von Perger, String Quartet, G Minor, op. 8 (1886)

Samuel de Lange, Organ Sonata no. 5, C Minor, op. 50 (1887)

Fritz Kauffmann, String Quartet, G Major, op. 14

Anton Urspruch, *Ave maris stella*, chorus and orchestra, op. 24

Emil Kreuz, Lieder, opp. 1 & 2

Giulio E. A. Alary, String Sextet, op. 35

Anton Rückauf, Piano Quintet, F Major, op. 13

Niccolò van Westerhout, Piano Sonata

Richard Barth, Partita, solo violin, op. 10

Johann Strauss, Jr., Waltzes, *Seid umschlungen Millionen*, op. 443 (1892)

Elie-Miriam Delaborde, *Morceau romantique* (Quintet)

Eugen d'Albert, String Quartet, E-flat Major, op. 11 (1893)

Josef Suk, Piano Quintet, G Minor, op. 8 (1893)

Reinhold Stockhardt, Three Piano Pieces, op. 10

Walter Rabl, Piano Quartet (with clarinet), E-flat Major, op. 1

Vitězslav Novák, *Eclogen*, Four Piano Pieces, op. 11

Julius Röntgen, Ballade on a Norwegian Folk Melody, orchestra, op. 36
 (1896)

Karel Bendl, *Rosenlieder,* three-part women's chorus and piano, op. 121

Arthur Hinton, *Weisse Rosen* (Josef Huggenberger), 6 Lieder

Otto Barblan, Passacaglia, organ, op. 6

Hans Schmitt, Brilliant Piano Etudes, op. 65

Eugen Philips, Piano Trio no. 2, D Major, op. 28

Heinrich von Herzogenberg, Piano Quartet no. 2, B-flat Major, op. 95
 (1897)

Marco Anzoletti, Variations on a Theme of Brahms, violin and piano

Carl Reinecke, Sonata no. 3, cello and piano, G Major, op. 238. "To the
 memory of Johannes Brahms" (1898)

Max Reger, Rhapsody, piano, E Minor, op. 24, no. 6. "To the memory of
 Johannes Brahms" (1899)

Max Reger, "Resignation," piano, op. 26, no. 5. "3. April 1897—
 J. Brahms†" (1899)

INDEX

❦

Index

Subject and Name Index

Page numbers followed by n indicate
notes; italicized page numbers indicate
material in tables, figures, or musical
examples. Also see separate Index to
List of Works.

Notes on the Contributors

Styra Avins is currently a Visiting Scholar at Drew University, where she was Adjunct Professor of Music History in the Casperson Graduate School for twelve years. She is a professional cellist freelancing in the New York area as well as a musicologist. Her publications include *Johannes Brahms: Life and Letters* (Oxford and New York, 1997); a chapter in *Performing Brahms: Early Evidence of Performance Style*, ed. Michael Musgrave and Bernard D. Sherman (Cambridge, 2003); and the biographical article about Brahms in *The Oxford Companion to Music* (Oxford and New York, 2002).

Leon Botstein is president and Leon Levy Professor in the Arts of Bard College. He is the author of *Judentum und Modernität* (Vienna, 1991) and *Jefferson's Children: Education and the Promise of American Culture* (New York, 1997). He is the editor of *The Compleat Brahms* (New York, 1999) and *The Musical Quarterly*, as well as the co-editor, with Werner Hanak, of *Vienna: Jews and the City of Music, 1870–1938* (Annandale-on-Hudson, 2004). The music director of the American and the Jerusalem symphony orchestras, he has recorded works by, among others, Szymanowski, Hartmann, Bruch, Toch, Dohnányi, Bruckner, Chausson, Richard Strauss, Mendelssohn, Popov, Shostakovich, and Liszt for Telarc, CRI, Koch, Arabesque, and New World Records.

George S. Bozarth is Professor of Music History at the University of Washington, Seattle, and the founding Executive Director of the American Brahms Society. The co-author (with Walter Frisch) of the article on Brahms for the second edition of *The New Grove Dictionary of Music and Musicians*, he is the editor of *Brahms Studies: Analytical and Historical Perspectives* (Oxford and New York, 1990); *The Brahms-Keller Correspondence* (Lincoln and London, 1996); *On Brahms and His Circle: Essays and Documentary Studies by Karl Geiringer* (Sterling Heights, Mich., 2006); *Johannes Brahms and George Henschel: An Enduring Friendship* (forthcoming); and the complete organ works of Brahms for G. Henle Verlag and the *Neue Brahms-Ausgabe*. He owns and performs on a collection of period pianos.

Stephen H. Brady, for twenty-five years the head piano technician and curator of early keyboard instruments at the University of Washington in Seattle, has served as editor of the *Piano Technicians Journal* and is the author of *A Piano Technician's Guide to Field Repairs* (Washington, D.C., 1999) and the forthcoming *Under the Lid: The World of the Concert Piano Technician*.

David Brodbeck is Chair and Professor of Music at the University of California, Irvine. His work has focused on nineteenth-century German music and musical life, with a special emphasis on Brahms. In recent years, he has turned his attention to the multiple ways in which political ideology and constructions of social identity figured in the reception of new concert and operatic works in late Habsburg Vienna. Recent and forthcoming publications include essays on Dvořák's reception in Liberal Vienna, the Smetana reception of Eduard Hanslick, the early Viennese reception of Smetana's *Bartered Bride*, and issues of essentialism and Orientalism in Carl Goldmark's *Queen of Sheba*.

Josef Eisinger is Professor Emeritus in the Department of Structural and Chemical Biology, Mount Sinai School of Medicine, New York. A physicist whose research has ranged from nuclear physics and molecular biology to the history of medicine, his latest contribution dealt with Beethoven's final illness. He is a native of Vienna and has published translations of a number of scientific and musicological works, including several in collaboration with his spouse, Styra Avins.

Walter Frisch is H. Harold Gumm/Harry and Albert von Tilzer Professor of Music at Columbia University. He is the author of *German Modernism: Music and the Arts* (Berkeley and Los Angeles, 2005); *Brahms: The Four Symphonies* (New Haven and London, 2003); *The Early Works of Arnold Schoenberg, 1893–1908* (Berkeley and Los Angeles, 1993); and *Brahms and the Principle of Developing Variation* (Berkeley and Los Angeles, 1984).

Susan Gillespie is Vice President for Special Global Initiatives at Bard College and Founding Director of Bard's Institute for International Liberal Education. Her published translations include novels, nonfiction works, poems, and works on musicology and philosophy, including numerous essays by the German philosopher Theodor Adorno.

Andrew Homan teaches German and Humanities at the Lake Champlain Waldorf School. He earned a BA in German and Humanities from the Johns Hopkins University and an MA and MPhil in German Literature from Columbia University. **Caroline Homan** studied ethnomusicology at William and Mary College and earned an MA in anthropology from New York University.

Elisabeth Kaestner, a psychologist and amateur musician born and raised in Germany, has lived in the United States since 1968. She is the translator, with Paul De Angelis, of *Inside 9-11: What Really Happened* (compiled from *Der Spiegel*) (New York, 2001); and translator of portions of *The Nobel Book of Answers*, ed. Bettina Stiekel (New York, 2003).

Kevin C. Karnes is Assistant Professor of Music History at Emory University. He is the author of *Music, Criticism, and the Challenge of History: Shaping Modern Musical Thought in Late Nineteenth-Century Vienna* (Oxford and New York, 2008); and co-editor, with Joachim Braun, of *Baltic Musics/Baltic Musicologies: The Landscape since 1991* (London, 2009). He is presently writing a new book on aspects of Wagnerism after Wagner.

William Miller is a graduate of Bard College and New York University. He has contributed translations to *Adolf Loos: Works and Projects*, ed. Ralf Bock (New York, 2007); *Arcimboldo: 1526–1593*, ed. Sylvia Ferino Pagden (New York, 2008); and *Painting Light: The Hidden Techniques of the Impressionists*, ed. Iris Schaefer, Caroline von Saint-George, and Katja Lewerentz (New York, 2009).

Roger Moseley is currently a postdoctoral research fellow in the Department of Music at the University of Chicago. In addition to the music of Brahms, his research focuses on theories and practices of musical performance and transcription in contexts ranging from Mozart's Vienna to rhythm-based video games. He is also a collaborative pianist and improvises in various eighteenth- and nineteenth-century idioms; recordings of his playing can be heard at his website, www.rogermoseley.com.

Peter Ostwald (1928–96) was founding director of the Health Program for Performing Artists and Professor of Psychiatry at the University of California, San Francisco. His publications include *Schumann: The Inner Voices of a Musical Genius* (Boston, 1985); *Vaslav Nijinsky: A Leap into Madness* (New York, 1991), and *Glenn Gould: The Ecstasy and Tragedy of Genius* (New York, 1997).

Nancy B. Reich has taught at New York University and Manhattanville College and has been a Visiting Professor at Bard College and Williams College. Her biography, *Clara Schumann: The Artist and the Woman* (1st ed., Ithaca, N.Y., 1985; rev. and enlarged ed., 2001), has been translated into several languages and has won a number of awards, including the Schumann Prize, awarded in 1996 by the city of Zwickau, the birthplace of Robert Schumann.

OTHER PRINCETON UNIVERSITY PRESS VOLUMES PUBLISHED
IN CONJUNCTION WITH THE BARD MUSIC FESTIVAL

Brahms and His World
edited by Walter Frisch (1990)

Mendelssohn and His World
edited by R. Larry Todd (1991)

Richard Strauss and His World
edited by Bryan Gilliam (1992)

Dvořák and His World
edited by Michael Beckerman (1993)

Schumann and His World
edited by R. Larry Todd (1994)

Bartók and His World
edited by Peter Laki (1995)

Charles Ives and His World
edited by J. Peter Burkholder (1996)

Haydn and His World
edited by Elaine R. Sisman (1997)

Tchaikovsky and His World
edited by Leslie Kearney (1998)

Schoenberg and His World
edited by Walter Frisch (1999)

Beethoven and His World
edited by Scott Burnham and Michael P. Steinberg (2000)

Debussy and His World
edited by Jane F. Fulcher (2001)

Mahler and His World
edited by Karen Painter (2002)

Janáček and His World
edited by Michael Beckerman (2003)

Shostakovich and His World
edited by Laurel E. Fay (2004)